# THE COLOR-CODED ALLERGY COOKBOOK

**The key to good eating for the food-sensitive**

**GLORIA DIENER AUTRY &**
**T. DIENER ALLEN**

The Bobbs Merrill Company, Inc.
Indianapolis/New York

Published by The Bobbs-Merrill Co., Inc.
Indianapolis/New York

Manufactured in the United States of America

FIRST PRINTING

Designed by Sheila Lynch

**Library of Congress Cataloging in Publication Data**
Autry, Gloria Diener
The color-coded allergy cookbook.

Includes index.
1. Food Allergy—Diet therapy—Recipes.
I. Allen, Terry D. II. Title.
RC588.D53A38 1983 641.5'631 82-17826
ISBN 0-672-52746-4

*For Beverly Gail,*
*Without her I needn't have tried.*
*Without her spirit I might've despaired.*
*From Her Mother, fiddler,*
*and Her cousin, scribbler*

# Contents

# Help is at Hand

## Wheat, Milk, and Eggs will undoubtedly feel left out

Thousands of babies arrive in this world each year with a ready-made set of nutritional no-no's. Some cannot physically tolerate what we rely on as the universal baby food—milk—and sadly, milk may be only one member of a discordant trio. Wheat and eggs are also enemies for many milk-sensitive babies and adults.

I, Gloria, was blessed with a milk-wheat-egg sensitive baby in 1956. It was a difficult start for both of us—rashes and wheezes dominated our lives for years. Finally, after carefully studying our doctors' list of forbidden foods, learning to *really* read labels, and meticulously testing by trial and error, I devised my own ways to feed my baby as well as the entire family. Our doctors applauded my successes and smacked their lips over the sample foods I brought to the clinic. They asked for culinary advice for patients with all types of food sensitivities, advice that, ideally, would be given in book form. I, as a professional violinist, had little expertise as a writer. However, the carefully kept records of my experiments were outgrowing my loose leaf notebook—and my daughter, Beverly, was thriving. Terry, a professional writer and, incidentally, my cousin and friend, came to the rescue to get the material organized and into print.

Bev has now grown up and married. She and her husband are cooking for themselves and their friends, using a copy of that loose leaf book that I began developing with her first itchy reaction to milk. I have continued to feed my family and guests from what has finally grown into this, *The Color-Coded Allergy Cookbook.*

We know all about panic time. If you have a food-sensitive baby or adult to feed, you may still be fighting that helpless feeling that first came over you as you left your doctor's office, clutching a long list of foods to avoid. This book is not based on a take-away system—it is an add-to book. It provides a three-meal-a-day guide to the art of selecting and combining a wide range of delicious, nutritious foods that are compatible with the personal sensitivities of whatever body you inhabit or must feed.

Those who are born with or develop reactions triggered by foods and environmental irritants are faced with problems that must be solved. Doctors use various diagnostic methods and trial-and-error testing that help greatly in isolating enemy foods or elements. Our add-to plan, our color coding of grains, and our coded labeling of each recipe provide clearly marked detours around physical temper tantrums.

At no time do we use wheat, cow milk, or eggs in our recipes. These three comprise a prevalent allergy syndrome—the first reason for this book. If any of these are trouble-free for you, simply use our recipes but replace water or milk substitute with milk. If eggs are not your personal enemy and you would like to support hens and the egg industry, experiment with our egg-free recipes by enriching them with an egg or two. If wheat gives you no problems, replace our alternative flours with wheat flour, adjusting amounts as batter textures or thickenings require.

## Follow your doctor's plan, but he can't move in with you. We can.

The method of this book is the one followed by most of the medical profession during the initial testing and reintroduction of withdrawn foods. We begin with those foods known to produce no adverse reactions in most sensitive eaters. We call these Basic Building-Block foods or **BBB**, see p. 8. Many of our delicious family-favorite dishes use **BBB** ingredients alone. These will maintain weight and health while others are tested and added according to your doctor's plan and our coded directions.

Read "How the Basic Building-Block Plan Works," following, before using the recipes. You should have no difficulty recognizing our color keys or in reading the labeling that codes each recipe. It is as simple as **BBB + Corn + Fruit and + and + and +.** At a glance, hundreds of recipes are matched to your special needs.

## Read labels before you buy. Ingredients lists keep changing.

Learn which four-letter words such as milk and eggs appear in disguise as whey, casein, or albumen. Watch for additives. Salt and vitamin C are generally acceptable, even in the beginning stages of a doctor-prescribed regimen. Sugar, however, must be suspect until you know its source. Corn, barley, and milk are famous for hiding in foods such as breakfast cereals, ham and bacon, or in carbonated beverages and chewing gum. Fortunately, more and more foods are becoming available without additives, but health and comfort may hang by a thread unless you know precisely what ingredients make up the foods you buy.

For example, peanut butter from the market shelf may well contain corn syrup, preservatives, and additives that you have not tested, and any or all of these can cause an unhappy reaction. Don't immediately blame the flareup on peanuts—they may be innocent. And how sad to give up peanut butter for years simply because the first brand tested had sneaked in a no-no behind your back! So, read lists of ingredients. Market aisles are a well-lighted comfortable place to read. Don't miss the opportunity.

## Reorganize your kitchen for battle and stop fearing an attack

Equip your handiest kitchen shelves with BBB staples only (at least at the beginning of your new life). Let the only flour and whole grain within easy reach be rice, soy, or tapioca. Keep safflower or soy oil for sautéing or frying. Push spices and flavorings out of the way, and season with salt, cane or beet sugar, and synthetic vanilla for the initial BBB period. If some members of the family wish pepper or cinnamon, let them reach to the back of the shelf for a last minute shake. See p. 8 for complete lists of BBB foods—stock up on only those until other foods have proven safe.

Is it your habit to thicken gravy with wheat flour? The same reach-and-stir motions result in delicious gravy when the container you dip from is filled with rice flour. Is it your habit to pour cow's milk into all children's glasses? They can just as easily be filled with a tasty milk substitute or fruit juice when those are cold and ready in the refrigerator. Roast beef for Sunday dinner? A lamb roast will give the whole family a nice change and provide sandwiches for trouble-free lunches during the week.

In a half day you can enjoy an orgy of marketing that need not be repeated for a week. Buy BBB staples for your cannister set, allowed basic fruits and vegetables (fresh, canned, or frozen), and supplies of lamb or, if you like, rabbit. Provide at-hand ingredients for cooking main-dish items that cause no spasms or eruptions in your household. If all the food available at family meals is acceptable to all members of the family, food discriminations are not likely to dominate the conversation. You can all get on with the business of living without physical or emotional outbursts. Those family members with no food restrictions who eat lunches at work or school may indulge their urges and appetites at outside meals.

Cook for a full day but certainly not every day. Cook and freeze. Can or store lunch-size or dinner-size containers of homemade soup or stew. Freeze casserole main courses. Space out the serving of frozen meatloaf. Yes, make two or three at a time. While clearing up after dinner, arrange leftovers in TV dinner trays, label, and freeze. Repeat menus only after a nice forgetting period and at times that are convenient for you, the food preparer. Grind lamb or rabbit and freeze into patties. Make up a supply of tasty snack foods from our Between Meal Treats, pp. 349. If freezer space permits, a day of food preparation can supply many meals that require heating time only. Shred up a salad while the entree heats and dinner can be ready in fifteen minutes.

This book provides the means for normal living and tasty eating for every member of your family. It is a guide, not to foods to avoid, but to foods to enjoy, whether or not you may be wheat-milk-egg or almost any other kind of sensitive.

Celiac patients who must avoid gluten will find our color coding and labeling precise guides. All recipes marked **BBB** and all coded white are gluten-free. Those coded blue (corn) and purple (millet) are also gluten-free. However, we occasionally combine grains. Any no-no's for celiacs are easy to spot among the +'s at the top of each recipe. Skip those listing **+ rye, + oats, + barley, or + buckwheat.**

Our simple but detailed coding is a reliable guide for anyone who must avoid specific foods for any reason. For the hyperactive, additives are all labeled **TE&A.** For the vast numbers sensitive to corn, look for blue markings. We have been meticulous in this because corn is a known sneak. For those sensitive to mold, we can't clear the air of spores but we do label recipes **+ Mold.**

We hope you become so familiar with the whole book that the appropriate colors and symbols will pop out at you each time you start to prepare a meal. We promise that, through this book, we will be at your side to help you prepare savory, imaginative meals for the whole family—food-sensitive or not.

## ORDER OF ADDITIONS AND COLOR-CODED GUIDE TO RECIPES

### The Basic Building-Block Plan:

Foods beginning each recipe section use no ingredients except those allowed on the Basic Building-Block program. These are marked **BBB.** They wear no color indicators. Use these foods and recipes during initial testing periods.

### Additions to BBB:

Recipes that include anything other than **BBB** foods are coded white. The white box reminds the food preparer to test the clearly marked additions before presuming them innocent. White says merely, "This recipe contains BBB foods + something." If the added "something" is a food that is troublesome for you, the white box can be marked with your own personalized warning symbol.

## Categories Added under BBB and under each Grain and Meat as they are added:

1. Fruits **(Fruit)**
2. Vegetables **(Veg.)**
3. Nuts and Seeds **(N&S)**
4. Taste Enhancers and Additives—spices, herbs, flavorings, colorings, and chemical additions **(TE&A)**
5. Mold **(Mold)**

## Meats to Test and Add:

1. Beef **(Beef)**
2. Poultry **(Poultry)**
3. Pork **(Pork)**
4. Fish **(Fish)**

## Grains to Test and Add:

1. Rye (coded light blue) ■
2. Oats (coded pink) ■
3. Barley—malt (coded red) ■
4. Corn (coded blue) ■
5. Millet (coded purple) ■
6. Buckwheat (coded lavender) ■

*Note:* Recipes requiring more than one grain are coded in one color only—the color assigned to the grain added last on our ladder of additions. For example, Rye-Cornmeal Muffins, p. 219, is coded blue even though the recipe calls for both rye flour and cornmeal. Mixed Grain Cereal II, p. 261, is coded lavender, the last grain added on our plan, even though it contains rye lt. blue, oats pink, barley, red, corn blue, millet purple, and buckwheat lavender. Check written codes on each recipe until you come to visualize the total rainbow of grains leading up to the code color.

# How the Basic Building-Block Plan Works

Most doctors use a BBB plan that is similar, but not necessarily identical, to ours. Your doctor may ask you to adjust our basic list, but his changes will probably be minor and adjustments in recipes will be easy to make.

We start with known allergy-free foods for an initial two-week period. Then, block-by-block, we add other food groups for individual testing. A fixed date—two weeks or whatever your doctor recommends—can provide strong motivation for staying within the bounds of the BBB list until the red-letter day for adding new taste and texture thrills.

Nutritional balance can be maintained during the first testing period by striving for a daily intake of:

1 or 2 servings of a milk substitute
2 or more servings chosen from the allowed meats
4 or more servings from the allowed fruits and vegetables
4 or more servings of allowed breads, cereals, and starches

If any major food source of vitamins or minerals is omitted for any length of time, your doctor may recommend supplements.

Purchase foods in as pure form as possible. This eliminates some, but not all, prepackaged foods. See, in most of our sections, coded foods "available in markets."

Most doctors agree that foods may be tested in whatever order suits the sensitive eater's taste buds or longings. The order may also be adjusted to suit the food preparer's convenience or good fortune in shopping. However, if order is shifted from that given, either stay with simple, pure foods or be sure to check all the ingredients in a complex or processed food to be tried. Your doctor will tell you if the order of additions to BBB foods he suggests is of significance.

In order to prove each added food friendly, it is to be taken in a large serving for breakfast on the first test day and continued in large amounts at each meal for four days. If an added food produces anything other than happy tasting and digesting, discontinue immediately and wait two days before adding the next food on the test list. The troublesome food or one that leaves suspicions or questions can wait until a later date for retesting. Once a food has been proven compatible, it may be added to the basic list. From then on, use any of our recipes as far along as that particular food in the chain of additions.

For purposes of testing, it is best to assume that generalizations are never true. A food label indicating that sugar has been added to frozen, canned, or bottled fruit juice is not definite enough for our purposes. We need to know whether it is cane sugar, beet sugar, or sugar from corn or barley. Potato bread may or may not tell you in the fine print that it contains wheat flour. You may need to telephone the bakery. Cereals that contain malt flavoring (Rice Krispies, for example) are made of the right grain but the wrong flavoring (a product of barley). Of course, once you have tested corn and barley and found them friendly, you may be able to turn from labels to novels for your reading.

Know your check list and then, reading labels, shop at your own market in both the regular and dietetic sections. If necessary, shop for rice, soy, rye, and lima bean breads and buns in your health food store. Ask your doctor or dietician for a list of recommended shops in your area. See our suggestions on pp. 226–230 for breads to purchase.

During your testing period, avoid all non-prescription drugs—aspirin, decongestants, vitamin supplements, sleeping pills, laxatives, cough syrups, and such. Do inform your doctor if you are taking any prescription drugs for any reason.

Throughout the recipes we use the word "allowed"—allowed oil, allowed milk substitute, allowed margarine—and sometimes we perk up a recipe with a goodie but add "if allowed." In these instances, use allowed foods containing BBB ingredients or ingredients proven acceptable by your personal testing.

A list of this kind was developed, tested, and published by Dr. Albert H. Rowe, clinical allergist. His experience has been further tested and adapted at the Santa Barbara Medical Foundation Clinic by allergists, Jay A. Keystone, M.D., and M. I. Liebhaber, M.D., with Zeb Dyer, allergy physician's assistant, and nutritionist Elaine Ellis, R.D. We have made further additions and adaptations prompted by our experience. You may come to add notes of your own.

In the following pages we give specific guidance as to what is allowed at the BBB stage and why.

Ours is one appendix (p. 369) that is not expendable. You may want to keep a bookmark in it for frequent reference. Here you will find:

1. Fats, Oils, Solid Shortening, and Margarines, p. 369

2. Wheat Substitutes for Baking, Thickenings, Additions to Ground Meats, p. 371
3. Cereal-Free Baking Powder, including recipes for making your own, pp. 372
4. Milk Substitutes for drinking, pouring on cereals or desserts, or for whipping, pp. 376
5. Eggs, either cooking without or restoring (if they are allowable for you) to our recipes, p. 374

Start by checking through the charted BASIC BUILDING-BLOCK FOODS.

## BASIC BUILDING-BLOCK FOODS

| Food Group | Foods Allowed | NO-NO'S for Now |
|---|---|---|
| **MILK PRODUCTS** | Neo-Mull-Soy, an infant formula (no corn syrup)<br>i-Soyalac, an infant formula (no corn syrup)<br>Tofu soybean curd (must not contain added citrus)<br>Ener-G Pure SoyQuik (a powder)<br>Fearn Soya Powder<br>Golden Harvest Soya Bean Powder<br>(See directions for mixing powders, for making soy milk from scratch, and allowed added flavorings, p. 376.) | Milk, cream, butter, all cheese (including cottage and ricotta), ice cream, sherbet, chocolate drinks, malteds, Ovaltine, Cocomalt, and all margarines and other products containing milk, whey, lactal bumin, casein, and caseinate. |
| **BREAD CEREAL STARCH** | Rice (white, brown, or wild), rice flour, arrowroot powder, soy (flakes, grits, or granules), soy powder or flour, potato flour, tapioca or tapioca starch, Cream of Rice, puffed rice (no additives), Rice Wafers (Hol-Grain brand), rice flakes (no additives), Rice Stix (Dynasty and Lee Cheung Woo brands), New Vita Toasted Rice, rice cakes (plain). | All other breads, cereals, pasta, and flours or starches. |
| **MEATS** | Lamb, mutton, and rabbit | All other meats, all poultry, and all fish. |
| **FRUITS** | Apples, apricots, cranberries, grapes, peaches, pears, pineapple, and purple plums. (Fresh, frozen, or canned—packed in water, white grape juice, or in their own juice.) Fresh or frozen fruits are to be cooked. Salt and vitamin C are the only allowed additions to frozen fruits. | All other fruits. |

| | | |
|---|---|---|
| **FRUIT JUICES** | Pure juices of allowed fruits: Apple (natural bottled or frozen). Pear-Grape (natural bottled or frozen). Pineapple (canned without sugar). Homemade or canned with nothing added other than salt, vitamin C, and cane or beet sugar. | All cider and all canned or frozen juices if labels list anything other than the allowed fruit, water, salt, and vitamin C. |
| **VEGETABLES** | Artichokes, asparagus, beets, carrots, chard, lettuce, okra, peas, soybeans, spinach, sweet and white potatoes, yams. Cook all fresh or frozen vegetables except lettuce. Water-pack canned vegetables are allowed if nothing but salt and vitamin C are added. | All other vegetables. |
| **FATS** | Pure safflower oil, rice bran oil, and soy oil. Milk-free margarines made from soy or safflower oils. (Shedd's Willow Run Soybean Margarine and Hains Safflower Oil Margarine are available. Read labels carefully.) Gravies with lamb or rabbit meat juices thickened with allowed flours. | All other fats and oils, even allowed oils if they contain preservatives. All other margarines and gravies. |
| **VINEGAR** | White distilled vinegar. | All other vinegars. |
| **SWEETS** | Cane or beet sugar (brown, raw or white), turbinado or yellow D sugars. Homemade jams, jellies, and marmalades if made with allowed sugars and fruits. Our homemade BBB Powdered Sugar, p. 269 | Corn syrup. All other jams and jellies. Commercial confectioners powdered sugar. |
| **DESSERTS** | Cookies, candies, cakes, frosting, pie crusts and fillings, cobblers, ice creams and sherbets, puddings, desserts with crispy toppings, congealed and fruit desserts. (See our **BBB** recipes.) | All commercially made desserts, candy bars, ice creams, etc. |
| **BEVERAGES** | Fruit juices as described above, water, and milk substitutes as allowed. | Soy milks with corn syrup. All soft drinks, sodas, tea, coffee, etc. |
| **MISCELLANEOUS** | Salt, baking soda, cream of tartar, unflavored gelatin, cereal-free baking powder (Ener-G, Bray's, and Featherweight brands, or our Homemade, p. 373), and synthetic vanilla flavoring. | Chewing gum, herbs and spices, all baking powder containing cornstarch. All other extracts. |
| **COMBINATIONS** | Any mix of allowed foods that tastes good. See suggested menus, pp. 382. See all recipes coded **BBB**. | No restriction, provided nothing is added to allowed foods. |

# Appetizers, Dips, and Spreads

**BBB**

## APPETIZER PICK-UPS

No one need be denied appetizers until some advanced stage of testing and food additions. Try any or all of these Basic Building-Block goodies as appetizers or snacks. All (except artichokes) can be steamed or quickly scalded in salted water without losing their appetizer crispness. They will still meet the cooking requirement of your early testing periods. When cooking is no longer required, they are even tastier and crisper served raw.

| | |
|---|---|
| Asparagus tips 2–3 inches long | Carrot sticks |
| Artichokes | Raw peas |
| Beet sticks, canned or cooked | White potato sticks |

To cook artichokes, a pressure cooker is ideal. Wash and trim plump artichokes. Place on rack in pressure cooker with recommended water under rack. Pour 1 tablespoon white distilled vinegar and ½ teaspoon salt into center of each artichoke. If artichokes are large, steam under 15 pounds pressure 12 minutes. Reduce time to 8 or 10 minutes if artichokes are small or medium. Leaves from these artichokes are attractive and delicious on an appetizer plate, requiring no dip and no other seasoning.

**BBB**

## DEBUT SOYBEAN DIP OR SPREAD

- **1 can (15 ounces ) Hain Soy Beans, drained**
- **1 tablespoon white distilled vinegar**
- **2 tablespoons allowed oil**
- **¼ teaspoon salt**

Mash beans with fork and blend in other ingredients. Spread on rice cakes and broil until hot through. Use carrot sticks as dippers later, when raw vegetables are allowed. *Makes 1 cup*

## BRAISED LAMB HEART SPREAD

**BBB**

See Variations on Braised Lamb Heart, p. 75

*Note:* Tofu, in suggested Tofu Dressing I, may contain minute amount of lemon or lime. Do not use this recipe if highly sensitive to citrus.

## TOFU AVOCADO DIP

**BBB + Fruit + Veg.**

- **1 cup tofu**
- **2 tablespoons lemon juice or white distilled vinegar**
- **1 teaspoon instant chopped onion**
- **1 teaspoon dried parsley**
- **¼ teaspoon garlic powder**
- **¾ teaspoon salt**
- **2 medium avocados, mashed**
- **Hot pepper sauce to taste**

Place tofu and lemon juice in blender. Process, adding 1 tablespoon water at a time until mixture is thick and creamy. Add to other ingredients. Use allowed crackers, chips, or vegetable sticks as dippers. This can be used as pseudo Green Goddess Salad Dressing, if desired. *Makes 2 cups*

## FIESTA GUACAMOLE

**BBB + Fruit + Veg.**

- **2 ripe avocados, mashed**
- **1 tablespoon lemon or lime juice**
- **1 tomato, peeled and chopped**
- **1 teaspoon instant minced onion**
- **¼ teaspoon garlic powder**
- **½ teaspoon salt**
- **Hot pepper sauce to taste**

Combine and serve as a dip with zucchini rounds as dippers. Spread on rice cakes or dip with natural style potato chips. When allowed, dip with RyKrisp (+ **Rye**) or corn tortilla chips (+ **Corn**). *Makes 2 cups*

**Variations:**

1. Add ¼ cup canned diced green chilies.
2. Add ½ cup chopped watercress.
3. Omit tomato and hot pepper. Replace with ¼ to ½ cup green chili salsa. **(+ TE&A)**

## BEAN DIP OR SPREAD

**BBB + Fruit + Veg.**

- **1 can (16 ounces) garbanzo beans or kidney beans, drained, or 1½ cups home-cooked beans**
- **2 tablespoons lemon juice**
- **2 tablespoons allowed oil**
- **1 clove garlic, crushed**
- **½ teaspoon salt**
- **2 tablespoons minced parsley**

Mash beans with a fork and stir in other ingredients. Refrigerate several hours for flavors to blend. *Makes 1 cup*

**Variations:**

1. Add ¼ cup toasted sesame seeds. **(+ N&S)**
2. Add 2 tablespoons millet seeds. **(+ Millet + N&S)**

☐ **BBB + Veg.**

## GARLIC SPREAD

**½ cup allowed margarine (1 cube), softened**
**1 clove garlic, mashed or pushed through garlic press**

Blend garlic into margarine with back of spoon. Spread on toasted allowed bread or crackers. This makes excellent garlic toast when spread on 100% Wheat-Free Rye Bread, when allowed (**+ Rye**). Place under broiler to heat. *Makes ½ cup*

☐ **BBB + Veg.**

## SANTA BARBARA SALSA

**1 can (1 pound 12 ounces) whole tomatoes**
**1 can (4 ounces) diced green chilies**
**1 large clove garlic, crushed**
**1 cup scallions, finely chopped**
**½ teaspoon salt**
**Hot pepper sauce to taste**

Pour tomatoes, juice and all, into large bowl and dice any large pieces. Add remaining ingredients. Cover bowl tightly and refrigerate several hours to allow flavors to blend. For 2 cups salsa, use 1 (16 ounce) can tomatoes and reduce other ingredients by half. This keeps well for several days, and is fantastic as taco sauce, dip, on salad, or with meats. For best results, use a good grade of tomatoes. *Makes 4 cups or 2 cups*

☐ **BBB + Fruit + Veg.**

## AVOCADO SALSA

**1 can (16 ounces) whole tomatoes**
**1 can (4 ounces) diced green chilies**
**¾ cup scallions, finely chopped**
**½ medium green pepper, chopped**
**½ teaspoon salt**
**1 tablespoon lemon or lime juice**
**Hot pepper sauce to taste**
**2 firm, ripe avocados, peeled and diced**

Pour tomatoes, juice and all, into large bowl and dice large pieces. Add remaining ingredients and mix well. Serve as a dip, or as meat accompaniment. This salsa is superb! *Makes 4 cups*

☐ **BBB + N&S**

## Spreads available in markets

Westbrae Roasted Cashew Butter (no sugar or salt)
Westbrae Peanut Butter—Smooth or Crunchy (roasted Spanish and Valencia peanuts—no sugar or salt)
Westbrae Toasted Sesame Tahini (hulled sesame seeds, nothing added)
Sahadi Sesame Tahini (ground hulled sesame seeds, nothing added)
Bread Spread Sunflower Butter (roasted sunflower seeds, nothing added)

## NUT SPREADS

Place oil in blender or food processor and add ¾ cup nuts. Process until creamy. Add remaining nuts and process to chunky or creamy blend, as desired. Refrigerate. *Makes 1 cup*

*Note:* Almonds are somewhat dry and will require more oil. Cashews are especially tasty raw and unsalted. You know all about peanuts.

**BBB + N&S** ☐

3  tablespoons allowed oil or more as needed to process
1½  cups nuts (almonds, cashews, peanuts, other), roasted or raw, salted or unsalted

## ALFALFA SPROUTS DIP OR DRESSING

Purée nuts, sprouts, and salt in blender until smooth. Add oil in fine stream while blender is running at fast speed. Stop and scrape lid and sides once or twice during oil addition if necessary to push liquids back down to blades. Beat until all oil has been added, then a little longer to help thicken. Add vinegar and whiz very briefly. Mixture will not be as thick as mayonnaise. Refrigerate for 24 hours to blend flavors and thicken further. Good as a dip with vegetable dippers, or as a spread on rice or rye (+ **Rye**) crackers. *Makes 1 cup*

**BBB + Veg. + N&S** ☐

⅓  cup raw cashews
½  cup alfalfa sprouts, tightly packed
¼  teaspoon salt
½  cup allowed oil
1½  tablespoons white distilled vinegar

## ZESTY SOYBEAN DIP OR SPREAD

Mash beans with fork and blend in all other ingredients. Refrigerate several hours to allow flavors to blend. *Makes 1¼ cups*

**BBB + Fruit + Veg. + TE&A** ☐

1  can (15 ounces) Hain Soy Beans, drained
1  tablespoon lemon juice
2  tablespoons allowed oil
1  tablespoon instant chopped onion
¼  cup diced green chilies
¼  teaspoon chili powder
¼  teaspoon salt

## HONIED NUT AND SEED SPREAD

Place oil in blender, add sunflower and sesame seeds and process until as smooth as possible. Use rubber spatula to push mixture into blades. Add honey and nuts and process until nuts are chopped fine. Salt, if desired. Refrigerate. If oil separates, stir before using. Spread this on hot toasted rice cakes for a real treat. *Makes 1 cup*

**BBB + N&S + TE&A** ☐

½  cup allowed oil
½  cup raw sunflower seeds
¼  cup toasted sesame seeds
¾  cup combination of nuts— almond, cashew, walnut, or pecan
2  tablespoons honey
Salt to taste (optional)

☐ **BBB + Fruit + Veg. + TE&A**

- 1 recipe Tofu Dressing I, p. 63
- 1 tablespoon lemon or lime juice
- 2 tablespoons allowed oil
- 1 tablespoon minced parsley
- ½ teaspoon Italian seasoning
- 1 tablespoon water
- Dash of cayenne pepper
- 1 teaspoon soy sauce, if allowed (+ Corn)

## TOFU SAUCE OR DIP

Blend Tofu Dressing I with all ingredients and use as dip for artichokes, or for raw vegetables when allowed, or serve on salads. *Makes 1¾ cups*

☐ **BBB + Fruit + Veg. + N&S + TE&A**

- 2 boxes cherry tomatoes
- 1 large ripe avocado
- 1 tablespoon lemon juice
- 2 tablespoons scallions, finely chopped
- 2 canned green chilies, finely chopped
- ¼ teaspoon ground coriander, or 2 teaspoons chopped fresh or oven-dried cilantro
- 2 tablespoons finely chopped, toasted almonds
- 1 teaspoon salt

## STUFFED CHERRY TOMATOES

Wash tomatoes, remove stems, and cut out centers with sharp knife. Drain upside down. Mash avocado and add all other ingredients. Whip until smooth. Spoon filling into tomatoes and arrange on lettuce-lined serving plate. *Serves 8–12*

☐ **BBB + Fruit + Veg. + TE&A**

## Dips available in markets

Hain Natural Onion Bean Dip (water, soybeans, cold pressed soybean oil, tomato paste, toasted onion, chopped onion, sea salt, natural spices, lemon juice concentrate, garlic powder, arrowroot)

☐ **BBB + Poultry + N&S**

- 1 cup finely chopped cooked chicken
- ⅓ cup finely diced celery
- ⅛ teaspoon salt
- ⅓ cup Tofu Dressing I, p. 63
- 2 tablespoons chopped cashews

## CHICKEN-CASHEW SPREAD

Mix first 4 ingredients until well blended. Stir in chopped cashews. Use as spread on allowed crackers, or rice cakes, or allowed bread (in toast triangles, perhaps). This also makes a luscious salad when placed on a bed of lettuce and garnished with pineapple chunks. *Makes 1 cup*

**BBB + Veg. + TE&A + Mold**

Hain Natural Jalapeño Bean Dip (water, soybeans, green bell peppers, jalapeños, cold pressed soybean oil, sea salt, cider vinegar, onion powder, granulated garlic, arrowroot, paprika)

**Spreads available in markets** **BBB+ N&S + Mold**

Westbrae Cashew-Peanut-Date Butter (roasted cashews, roasted peanuts, date pieces coated with almond meal, no sugar or salt)

Westbrae Peanut-Hazelnut-Date Butter (roasted Spanish and Valencia peanuts, roasted hazelnuts, date pieces coated with almond meal, no sugar or salt)

Westbrae Peanut-Pecan-Date Butter (roasted Spanish and Valencia peanuts, roasted pecans, date pieces with almond meal, no sugar or salt)

## SMOKY BEAN DIP

**BBB + Pork + Veg. + TE&A**

- **1 can (17 ounces) Rosarita Refried Beans or Rosarita Vegetarian Refried Beans (−Pork) or Refried Beans, p. 173**
- **1 tablespoon instant chopped onion**
- **1 teaspoon dried parsley**
- **¼ teaspoon garlic powder**
- **¼ cup green chili salsa**
- **1 tablespoon imitation bacon bits**
- **½ teaspoon Wright's Liquid Smoke**

Stir together and refrigerate at least 1 hour to blend flavors. *Makes 2½ cups*

## WATER CHESTNUT AND PINEAPPLE ROLL UPS

**BBB + Pork + Veg. + Mold**

- **1 can (8 ounces) water chestnuts, drained, sliced**
- **1 can (8 ounces) pineapple chunks, unsweetened, drained and towel dried**
- **¼ pound sliced bacon**

Cut bacon slices in thirds. Wrap bacon around chunk of pineapple and slice of water chestnut. Secure each roll with wooden toothpick. Place on rack 5 inches from broiler flame or on rack in 400° oven. Broil or bake until bacon is crispy. Serve hot. *Makes 16–20*

## AVOCADO DIP OR SANDWICH SPREAD

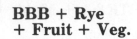

**BBB + Rye + Fruit + Veg.**

- 1 ripe avocado, peeled
- 2 teaspoons lemon juice
- Salt to taste
- RyKrisp or Finn Crisp wafers

Mash avocado with lemon juice and salt. Use broken wafers to dip or spread wafers with dip and add, for open-face sandwiches, whatever colorful foods are allowed. *For example:* cooked shrimp **(+ Fish)**, radish slices, cherry tomato halves, onion slices, or thin slices of leftover meatloaf. **(+ Beef)** *Makes ½ cup*

## TOFU ONION DIP

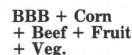

**BBB + Corn + Beef + Fruit + Veg. + TE&A**

- 1 cup tofu, washed and towel dried
- 2 tablespoons lemon juice
- ½ recipe Gloria's Onion Soup Mix, p. 39

Blend tofu and lemon juice in blender, adding 1 to 6 tablespoons water one at a time. When smooth and creamy, blend in soup mix. Refrigerate 2 to 4 hours for flavors to blend before serving. Use allowed crackers, chips, or vegetable sticks as dippers. *Makes 1 cup*

## CRANBERRY MEATBALLS

**BBB + Corn + Beef + Veg. + TE&A**

- 2 recipes Basic Meatballs, p. 87
- ½ teaspoon onion powder
- 4 tablespoons allowed oil
- 1 can (16 ounces) jellied cranberry sauce
- 2 cans (8 ounces each) tomato sauce

Mix meatball ingredients with onion powder and shape into 30 to 40 very small balls. Brown in oil and drain. Heat sauces together, breaking up cranberry sauce as it heats. Pour into 3-quart casserole and add browned meatballs. Cover and bake in 325° oven 1½ to 2 hours. Serve on buffet table with fancy toothpicks nearby. *Serves 4–6*

## BARBECUED SPARERIB APPETIZERS

**BBB + Corn + Pork + Veg.**

- 3 pounds pork spareribs
- ⅔ cup allowed soy sauce (wheat-free)
- 2 tablespoons sugar
- 1 small clove garlic, crushed

Have butcher saw ribs crosswise into 1-inch lengths. At home, cut meat into single ribs and place in large bowl. Combine ⅓ cup water with remaining ingredients and pour over ribs. Cover, refrigerate and marinate for at least 1 hour. Remove from marinade, place in shallow baking pan and bake in 350° oven 1 to 1½ hours. Baste several times with marinade and turn once or twice during baking. *Serves 8–10*

# Soups

## THOUGHTS ON PREPARING SOUPS

Foods acceptable on our Basic Building-Block plan are ideal for making soups. No chance to feel sorry for ourselves in this area!

Soup, broth, stock, bouillon, consommé, potage, purée, bisque, chowder—all these refer to a more or less fluid food prepared by boiling and seasoning fruits, vegetables, meat, poultry, fish, or a combination of these. Variety is almost endless. Soups are highly adaptable for all meals and snacks. For our purposes in this book, soups are a godsend.

Lamb or mutton can provide delicious meat stocks to which we may add their meat and any or all of the following vegetables: artichokes, asparagus, beets, carrots, chard, okra, peas, spinach, soybean sprouts, sweet potatoes or yams, and white potatoes. While lettuce may be eaten uncooked, it, too, provides a tasty flavor and texture when shredded and added to a soup during the last minute of cooking.

Rabbit gives us soup stock very similar in flavor to that of chicken. What better soup starter could we desire?

Vegetables alone are capable of providing a flavorful and nutritious soup stock. To this we may add rice or soy grits, or we may choose to top bowls of soup with soy flakes or soya granules. Even the taste and texture delight, imitation bacon bits, is made of soy flour and soybean oil. Once you have tested and found their artificial flavoring and color friendly, imitation bacon bits are basically BBB food and great for topping bowls of almost any kind of soup.

See Appendix for flours, starches, and cereals that can be used as thickeners for Gravies, Sauces, or Soups.

*Note:* Put on your glasses (if you wear them) to read the ingredients list on soups and soup makings found on market shelves. Most of these contain monosodium glutamate. This must be avoided on a wheat-free food program. Monosodium glutamate is made from glutamic acid, a by-product of wheat.

## VEGETABLE STOCK

**BBB**

- **6 cups any combination of BBB vegetables, chopped or shredded**
- **1 teaspoon salt**

Combine vegetables with salt and 8 cups water. Bring to boil and reduce heat. Simmer, covered, 2 hours. Strain. *Makes 8–10 cups*

**Variations:**

1. Sauté vegetables in allowed oil before adding water.
2. Purée vegetables in blender or force through sieve or colander after cooking and return to stock.
3. Flavor of some soups is picked up by adding 1 tablespoon white distilled vinegar.

## BBB MEAT STOCK I

**BBB**

- **3 pounds raw meat and bones: lamb or mutton shanks, neck, ribs, or rabbit, whole or cut into parts**
- **Salt, to taste**
- **3–4 carrots, sliced**
- **Chard, spinach, beet tops, shredded lettuce, or other allowed greens in amount desired**

Cut meat from bone or not, as you wish, and brown meat and bones in 2 tablespoons allowed oil. Sprinkle with salt and let stand 1 hour. Add 3 quarts water and bring to boil. Skim off foam. Reduce heat and simmer, covered, 3 to 4 hours. Add vegetables for last 30 minutes of cooking time. Lift meat, bones, and vegetables from broth. Refrigerate broth; lift off fat when congealed. *Makes 9 cups*

## BBB MEAT STOCK II

**BBB**

- **3½ cups cooked lamb, mutton, or rabbit with bones and fat**
- **1 teaspoon salt**
- **2–3 carrots, chopped**
- **2 cups chopped chard or spinach**
- **1 cup shredded lettuce**

Soak meat in 4 to 5 cups salted water 1 hour. Bring to boil, reduce heat, and simmer, covered, 1½ hours. Add vegetables and cook another 30 minutes. Strain soup and refrigerate until fat congeals and can be lifted off and discarded. Reserve all lean meat and vegetables to return to broth for soup, or freeze stock in measured amounts for other use. *Makes 8 cups*

## THIN WHITE SAUCE FOR SOUP

**BBB**

See White Sauce Chart, p. 183.
Be sure the one you choose is coded **BBB.**
Cream of Rice White Sauce, p. 184, is also a fine thickening medium.

## ASPARAGUS SOUP

BBB

Press asparagus through colander and set aside. Blend and heat oil and flour in soup kettle. Mix milk substitute and liquid from asparagus and, stirring constantly, add gradually to oil and flour. Cook over medium heat until thickened, but keep below boiling. Stir in asparagus and salt, and simmer, stirring frequently, 5 to 8 minutes. *Serves 4*

- **1 can (14½ ounces) cut asparagus, liquid drained and reserved**
- **2½ tablespoons allowed oil**
- **2 tablespoons rice flour**
- **½ cup allowed milk substitute**
- **Salt to taste**

## CARROT SOUP

BBB

Boil carrots in 2 cups salted water or in stock of choice until soft. Force through colander, or purée in blender. Reheat. *Serves 4*

- **4-5 large carrots, sliced**
- **½ teaspoon salt**

**Variation:**

Steam carrots in 1 cup water or stock and purée in blender. Add 1 cup allowed milk substitute. Heat to just below boiling.

## HEARTY HAREY SOUP

BBB

Boil rabbit and bones with 2 carrots in 5 cups water 2 hours. Remove meat from bones. Drain broth through fine sieve. Chill broth and remove fat. Return sliced or diced meat, remaining carrots, rice, and salt to broth. Bring to boil, reduce heat, and simmer, covered, until carrots and rice are cooked, 20 to 30 minutes. Add spinach last ten minutes of cooking. If thicker soup is desired, mix rice flour in small amount of water and stir into boiling soup.

- **1 rabbit, cut into parts**
- **5-6 carrots, sliced**
- **½ cup rice**
- **1 teaspoon salt**
- **1 cup chopped fresh spinach**

**Variation:**

This soup may be made with any cuts of lamb or mutton. *Makes 8 cups*

## CONFETTI SOUP

BBB

Sauté beets and carrots in oil 5 minutes. Add chard and continue cooking and stirring 20 minutes. Add 6 cups water and vinegar and simmer until vegetables are just tender. Season with salt, if desired. *Serves 4–6*

- **2 tablespoons allowed oil**
- **2 medium beets, diced**
- **2 medium carrots, diced**
- **2 cups chopped chard**
- **1 tablespoon white distilled vinegar**

## CREAMY VEGETABLE SOUP

**BBB**

**2 cups cooked BBB vegetables, fresh, frozen, or canned with no addition except salt**
**2 cups thin White Sauce, p. 183, or Cream of Rice White Sauce, p. 184**

Prepare white sauce as directed. Purée vegetables (in a blender is the easy way) and add to sauce. Heat and serve. *Serves 4*

**Variations:**

1. Vegetable Stock, p. 18, BBB Meat Stock I, p. 18 or BBB Meat Stock II, p. 18, may be used in place of White Sauce. If desired, thicken your choice of stock with choice of thickening agents from Thickeners for Soups, p. 375, or White Sauce Chart, p. 183. When using soy grits, tapioca, or rice, cook in stock until tender, then cool and purée. Add puréed vegetables and reheat.

2. When allowed, try broccoli, cauliflower, winter squash, zucchini, celery, onions, leeks, tomatoes, or green beans. If desired, sauté celery or onions in 1 or 2 tablespoons allowed oil. When onion is proven a friend, use just a touch along with other vegetables. **(+ Veg.)**

3. Season soup with your choice of herbs, when allowed. **(+ TE&A)**

4. When allowed, Beef Broth, p. 25, or Chicken Stock, p. 30, may be used as in Variation 1. **(+ Beef or + Poultry)**

5. When allowed, use for quick broths Steero Instant Beef Bouillon Seasoning and Broth or Cubes **(+ Beef + Veg. + TE&A)** or Steero Instant Chicken Flavor Bouillon Seasoning and Broth. **(+ Poultry + Veg. + TE&A)**

## CREAM OF PEA SOUP

**BBB**

**1 can (17 ounces) green peas, undrained**
**2 tablespoons allowed oil**
**2 tablespoons rice flour**
**2 cups allowed milk substitute**
**½ teaspoon sugar**
**½ teaspoon salt**

Place peas with their liquid in blender and process until smooth. Make thin white sauce of oil, rice flour, and milk substitute. Add sugar and salt to puréed peas and mix into white sauce over low heat, stirring until hot enough to serve but not boiling. *Serves 4*

**Variation:**

Instead of white sauce, use 2 cups BBB Meat Stock I or II, p. 18. Thicken, if desired, with 4 tablespoons rice flour for a hearty soup.

## MOCK BORSCHT

**BBB + Fruit + Veg.**

Sauté onion and garlic in allowed oil until soft. Purée beets or stir vigorously enough to cut fine. Heat stock to boil. Blend flour and lemon juice, then mix with beet purée. Add to soup, stirring constantly. Combine all ingredients and simmer 5 to 10 minutes to meld flavors. Serve hot or, if preferred, chill thoroughly and serve cold with dollop of Tofu Dressing II, p. 68. *Serves 4–5*

- **1 cup diced onion**
- **1 clove garlic, minced**
- **2 tablespoons allowed oil**
- **1 can (16 ounces) julienne beets, undrained**
- **1¾ cups Vegetable Stock, p. 18**
- **1 teaspoon potato flour**
- **1 tablespoon lemon juice**
- **½ teaspoon salt**

## GAZPACHO

**BBB + Fruit + Veg.**

Purée all ingredients in food processor or blender and chill. Serve with dollop of Tofu Dressing II, p. 68, or with croutons made from soy buns. *Serves 4*

**Variation:**

When allowed, add ½ cup mixed herbs—freshly chopped parsley, chives, basil, marjoram. (+ **TE&A**)

- **4 large ripe tomatoes, quartered**
- **1 large cucumber, peeled and chunked**
- **1 medium onion, peeled and quartered**
- **1 green pepper, seeded and quartered**
- **1 clove garlic**
- **2 center slices lemon**
- **2 cups tomato juice, water, or Vegetable Stock, p. 18**
- **1 tablespoon allowed oil**
- **½ teaspoon salt**

## QUICK ONION SOUP

**BBB + Veg.**

Sauté onions in allowed oil until transparent. Add stock and heat. *Serves 2*

- **2 large onions, sliced**
- **2 tablespoons allowed oil**
- **3 cups Vegetable Stock, p. 18**

## QUICK POTATO SOUP

**BBB + Veg.**

Mix all ingredients with egg beater or in blender. Heat and serve. *Serves 1*

**Variation:**

For a gourmet touch, add ¼ teaspoon dill weed. (+ **TE&A**)

- **1 cup allowed milk substitute or Vegetable Stock, p. 18**
- **2 tablespoons potato flour**
- **¼ teaspoon salt**
- **¼ teaspoon onion powder**

## SPLIT PEA SOUP

☐ **BBB + Veg.**

- **1 cup split peas**
- **2 medium carrots, diced**
- **1 medium onion, chopped**
- **2 stalks celery, diced**
- **1 teaspoon celery salt**

Combine all ingredients with 3½ cups water and simmer until peas are tender. Sieve or purée in blender, or serve as is. *Serves 4–6*

**Variation: Pink Pea Soup**

After peas are tender, add 1 teaspoon sugar and 1 can (8 ounces) plain or stewed tomatoes.

## SPRING SQUASH SOUP

☐ **BBB + Veg.**

- **¼ cup allowed oil**
- **1 pound yellow summer squash, unpeeled, sliced thin**
- **1 pound zucchini, unpeeled, sliced thin**
- **1 medium onion, chopped coarse**
- **2 stalks celery, chopped**
- **2 cups Vegetable Stock, p. 18, or BBB Meat Stock I or II, p. 18**
- **Salt to taste**

Heat allowed oil in large skillet, stir in vegetables, and simmer, covered, until tender. Purée in food processor or blender, using stock as needed for liquid. Mix puréed vegetables with remaining stock in soup kettle. Salt to taste and heat. *Serves 6*

## HOMEMADE TOMATO SOUP

☐ **BBB + Veg.**

- **1 can (16 ounces) stewed tomatoes**
- **2 tablespoons allowed oil**
- **2 tablespoons rice flour**
- **2 cups allowed milk substitute**
- **½ teaspoon salt**

Purée tomatoes in food processor or blender. Force through fine-mesh strainer to remove seeds. Heat oil in kettle and stir in flour. Gradually add milk substitute and cook, stirring constantly, until thickened. Heat tomatoes separately, add salt, and stir hot tomatoes into white sauce. Blend well over low heat without boiling. *Serves 4*

**Variation:**

Replace stewed tomatoes with 1 can (6 ounces) tomato paste. *Serves 3*

## LIMA BEAN CHOWDER

**BBB + Veg.** ☐

Boil lima beans in 3 cups water 2 minutes. Remove from heat and let soak 4 hours. Add salt and again bring to boil. Reduce heat and simmer 45 minutes. Add celery, carrot, and green pepper and continue cooking 15 to 20 minutes, or until vegetables are tender. Add ½ to 1 cup water if beans seem too dry.

Sautée onion in allowed oil until transparent. Stir in flour and slowly add milk substitute. Continue stirring until thickened. Combine with bean mixture and reheat. *Serves 4*

- **1 cup dried lima beans**
- **½ teaspoon salt**
- **½ cup diced celery**
- **1 large carrot, diced**
- **1 tablespoon chopped green pepper**
- **1 medium onion, minced**
- **3 tablespoons allowed oil**
- **2 tablespoons rice flour**
- **1½ cups milk substitute**

## BABY LIMA BEAN SOUP

**BBB + Veg.** ☐

Add salt to 4 cups water and cook lima beans until soft, about 30 minutes. Purée in blender or force through sieve or colander, discarding skins. Add oil, if desired, and reheat. *Serves 4*

- **½ teaspoon salt**
- **1 package (10 ounces) frozen baby limas**
- **2 tablespoons allowed oil, (optional)**

## LUCY'S LENTIL SOUP

**BBB + Veg. + TE&A** ☐

Wash lentils and place in covered soup kettle with 4 cups water. Soak 5 to 6 hours or overnight.

Heat oil in skillet and sauté onion, garlic, and carrot over low heat 10 minutes, stirring frequently. Add to beans in soaking water in kettle, bring to boil, and add all other ingredients. Simmer until lentils are tender, approximately 20 minutes. *Serves 6*

**Variation:**

When allowed, add Steero Instant Bouillon Seasoning and Broth, using 2 to 3 teaspoonsful or to taste. **(+ Beef)**

- **1 cup dry lentils**
- **2 tablespoons allowed oil**
- **1 large onion, chopped**
- **2 cloves garlic, minced**
- **1 carrot, peeled and grated**
- **1 can (16 ounces) tomatoes**
- **2 pimientos, chopped**
- **½ teaspoon dried basil**
- **⅛ teaspoon dried thyme**
- **⅛ teaspoon dried oregano**
- **1 teaspoon salt**

☐ **BBB + Veg. + TE&A**

**2 cups dry pinto beans or dry red kidney beans**
**1½ teaspoons salt**
**2 teaspoons chili powder**
**1 can (6 ounces) tomato paste**
**2 cloves garlic, crushed**
**2 medium onions, chopped**
**1 small green pepper, chopped, or 1 cooked potato, cubed**
**2 tablespoons allowed oil**

## BEAN SOUP TEXAS STYLE

Boil beans in 6 cups water, covered, until almost soft, about 2½ hours. Add salt, chili powder, and tomato paste. Sauté garlic, onions, and pepper in allowed oil and mix into beans. Simmer 15 minutes to blend flavors. *Serves 6–8*

☐ **BBB + Veg. + TE&A**

**4 leeks, sliced thin**
**1 small potato, sliced thin**
**Sprig of fresh thyme**
**Sprig of fresh parsley**
**1 tablespoon Cream of Rice, uncooked**
**1 cup allowed milk substitute**
**Salt to taste**

## LEEK SOUP

Bring 3¾ cups stock or water to boil and drop in sliced leeks and potato. Add herbs and cover. Reduce heat and simmer 10 to 15 minutes. Cool and force through sieve or liquefy in blender. Return to soup kettle and reheat. Stir Cream of Rice into milk substitute and pour slowly into simmering soup in kettle, stirring constantly. Simmer 5 minutes. Add salt. *Serves 4*

**Variation:**
Purée soup, chill, and serve as vichyssoise.

☐ **BBB + Veg. + TE&A**

**2 cups green split peas (1 pound)**
**1 medium carrot**
**1 stalk celery**
**1 small onion**
**1 teaspoon salt**
**¼ teaspoon dried thyme**
**1 bay leaf**

## EVERYBODY'S FAVORITE SPLIT PEA SOUP

Heat 6 cups water in large soup kettle and add peas. Grind or grate carrot, celery, and onion in food processor or blender (using ½ cup water for liquid). Add vegetables to peas. Add salt and herbs, and bring to boil. Lower heat, cover, and simmer until peas are mushy, about 1 hour. Stir occasionally during cooking. If necessary, thin with additional water to desired consistency. Top each bowl with imitation bacon bits, if desired. *Serves 6–8*

## TOMATO SOUP

**BBB + Veg. + TE&A**

**1 small onion, chopped**
**2 tablespoons allowed oil**
**1 medium potato, chunked**
**1 can (16 ounces) tomatoes**
**⅛ teaspoon dried basil**
**1 teaspoon salt**

Sauté onion lightly in allowed oil until golden. Add potato, tomatoes, and basil and stir over low heat 5 minutes. Add 2½ cups Vegetable Stock, p. 18 *or* tomato juice. Bring to boil, and simmer until potato is tender, approximately 15 minutes. Cool slightly and liquefy in blender or rub through sieve. Add salt and reheat. *Serves 4*

## BEEF BROTH

**BBB + Beef**

**2 pounds shinbone with meat on**
**1 teaspoon salt**

Trim meat and discard as much fat as possible. Cut meat into small pieces and put in soup kettle. Add 4 cups water, salt and bring to boil. Skim off foam. Lower heat and simmer 4 hours. Discard bone. Strain broth and refrigerate until fat can be lifted off. Reserve meat for sandwiches, hot or cold. Reheat broth to serve as is, or chill and serve cold as jelly (with lemon wedge, if allowed—**+ Fruit**). Or refrigerate or freeze broth for use in more complicated recipes that require beef stock or broth. Double recipe to save energy. *Makes 4 cups*

## VEGETABLE BEEF SOUP

**BBB + Beef + Veg.**

**1 meaty soup bone (2 to 3 lbs)**
**1 teaspoon salt**
**4½ cups tomato juice**
**1 cup diced carrots**
**1 cup diced celery**
**1 cup diced potatoes**
**1 medium onion, diced**
**¼ cup rice**

Bring soup bone, 6 cups water, and salt to boil in large soup kettle. Skim off foam. Reduce heat and simmer, covered, 2 to 2½ hours. Add remaining ingredients, bring to boil, reduce heat and simmer 30 minutes. Cut meat from bone and discard fat and bone. Skim off fat or, preferably, refrigerate overnight and lift off congealed fat. Return meat to soup, reheat and serve. *Serves 6–8*

☐ **BBB + Beef + Veg.**

## QUICK VEGETABLE SOUP

**1 medium onion, chopped**
**1 clove garlic, minced**
**3 tablespoons allowed oil**
**4 cups Beef Broth, p. 27**
**2 cups canned tomatoes, chopped**
**⅓ cup rice**
**1 teaspoon salt**
**1 medium zucchini, sliced**

Sauté onion and garlic in allowed oil in soup kettle. Add broth, tomatoes, rice, and salt. Bring to boil, cover, and simmer 20 minutes. Add zucchini and return to boil. Lower heat and simmer another 20 minutes. *Serves 4*

☐ **BBB + Beef + Veg.**

## SPANISH VEGETABLE SOUP

**1 tablespoon minced onion**
**1 clove garlic, minced**
**2 tablespoons allowed oil**
**2 cups peeled and diced potato**
**2 cups shredded cabbage**
**1 cup canned tomatoes**
**1 cup diced leftover beef**
**1 teaspoon salt**
**6 cups Beef Broth, p. 27**
**3 tablespoons white rice**
**2 tablespoons diced green chilies, canned or fresh**
**1 cup fresh or frozen peas**

Sauté onion and garlic in allowed oil in soup kettle. Add potato and cabbage and continue to cook, stirring, until cabbage is wilted. Add remaining ingredients, bring to boil, reduce heat, and simmer 25 minutes. *Serves 8*

☐ **BBB + Beef + Veg.**

## GUMBO WITH RICE

**1 tablespoon allowed oil**
**¾ pound beef stew meat, cut in small pieces**
**½ cup chopped onion**
**1 cup sliced celery**
**¼ cup chopped green pepper**
**1 can (16 ounces) tomatoes**
**2 cups Beef Broth, p. 27**
**½ teaspoon salt**
**1 package (10 ounces) frozen cut okra, thawed**
**1 cup cooked long grain white rice**

Heat oil in two-quart kettle and brown meat and onion. Add celery, green pepper, tomatoes, beef broth, and salt. Cover and simmer until beef is tender, 1 to 2 hours. Add okra, and cook 5 to 10 minutes longer or until okra is barely tender. Serve gumbo in bowls with scoop of rice in center of each bowl. *Serves 5-6*

## Soups available in markets

**BBB + Beef + Veg. + TE&A**

Steero Instant Beef Flavor Bouillon Seasoning and Broth
Steero Instant Beef Flavor Bouillon and Broth Cubes (salt, hydrolyzed vegetable protein, sugar, caramel color, beef fat, onion powder, natural flavor, garlic powder, spices, disodium inosinate, disodium guanylate)

## BEEF SOUP STOCK

**BBB + Beef + Veg. + TE&A**

- **3 tablespoons allowed oil**
- **4 pounds beef shank cut in 1-inch slices or 4 pounds combination: lamb neck, bony rabbit pieces, veal, beef shanks**
- **3 quarts boiling water**
- **2 medium onions, sliced**
- **1 large carrot, diced**
- **2 stalks celery with leaves, chopped**
- **4 sprigs parsley, chopped**
- **1 bay leaf, crushed**
- **Salt and pepper to taste**

Heat oil in soup kettle and brown bones and meat. Add boiling water. Stir in all other ingredients, return to boil and skim off foam. Reduce heat and simmer, covered, 3 hours. Remove meat and bones and strain stock through fine sieve or cheesecloth. Cut meat from bones and reserve. Refrigerate stock until congealed fat can be lifted and discarded. Nutrients may be extracted from vegetables by straining through jelly bag and adding to defatted stock. Save meat for other dishes. *Makes 6–8 cups.*

## CREAMY BEEF SOUP

**BBB + Beef + Veg. + TE&A**

- **2 pounds beef stew meat**
- **1 teaspoon salt**
- **¼ teaspoon pepper**
- **¼ cup rice flour**
- **¼ teaspoon dried thyme**
- **½ teaspoon garlic powder**
- **2 cups allowed milk substitute**
- **1 large onion, sliced thin**
- **2 packages (10 ounces each) frozen green peas**
- **2 tablespoons minced parsley**

Cut meat into 1-inch cubes, removing as much fat as possible. Combine meat, salt, pepper and 2 cups water in soup kettle. Bring to boil. Skim off foam, reduce heat, and simmer 2 hours or until meat is tender. Combine rice flour, thyme, and garlic powder. Blend in milk substitute and, stirring constantly, add slowly to hot soup in kettle. Cook over low heat, still stirring, until soup is thickened. Add onion, cover, and simmer 20 minutes. Add peas and continue cooking 10 minutes. Garnish soup tureen or individual bowls with minced parsley. *Serves 6*

**BBB + Beef + Veg. + TE&A**

## VEGETABLE SOUP ON THE RUN

- 1 can (12 ounces) roast beef, broken in pieces, or 1½ cups cubed leftover roast beef or pot roast
- 2 cups tomato juice or canned tomatoes
- 1 teaspoon salt
- 2 tablespoons instant chopped onion
- 2 Steero Instant Beef Flavor Bouillon and Broth Cubes
- 1 can (16 ounces) cut green beans
- ⅓ cup Minute Rice

Combine beef, 8 cups water, tomato juice, salt, and onion in soup kettle and bring to boil. Stir in bouillon cubes, green beans, and rice. Reduce heat and simmer 15 minutes. *Serves 6–8*

**BBB + Beef + Veg. + TE&A**

## MINESTRONE

- 2 tablespoons allowed oil
- 2 pounds lean beef stew meat, cubed
- 1 large leek, chopped
- 3 Steero Instant Beef Flavor Bouillon and Broth Cubes
- 1 cup chopped carrots
- 1 potato, peeled and diced
- 1 cup shredded cabbage
- 1 cup diced celery
- 2 medium zucchini, sliced thin
- 1 large green pepper, diced
- ¼ teaspoon garlic powder
- 1 can (16 ounces) stewed tomatoes
- 1 teaspoon dried oregano, crumbled
- ½ teaspoon dried basil
- ½ teaspoon dried thyme
- 1 can (16 ounces) red kidney beans with fluid

Heat oil in soup kettle and, stirring over medium heat, brown beef cubes. Add leek and cook until lightly browned. Add 6 cups water and bouillon cubes, bring to boil, reduce heat, and simmer 1 to 1½ hours. Refrigerate until fat can be lifted from top. Reheat and add all other ingredients. Bring again to boil and reduce heat to hold at simmer 30 to 40 minutes. *Serves 6–8*

## ACROSS-THE-BORDER MEATBALL SOUP

**BBB + Beef + Veg. + TE&A**

- 1 pound lean ground beef
- 2 tablespoons rice
- ½ teaspoon salt
- ¼ teaspoon pepper
- 1 teaspoon dried parsley
- 2 tablespoons allowed oil
- 1 clove garlic, minced
- 1 small onion, minced
- 1½ teaspoon chili powder
- 1 can (8 ounces) tomato sauce)
- 3 Steero Instant Beef Flavor Bouillon and Broth Cubes

Combine beef, 2 tablespoons water, rice, salt, pepper, and parsley in mixing bowl and mix well. Shape into ¾-inch balls. Heat oil in soup kettle, add garlic and onion and sauté, stirring, 5 minutes. Add chili powder, tomato sauce, 3 cups water, and bouillon cubes. Bring to boil, add meatballs, cover and simmer 45 minutes. *Serves 8*

**Variation:**

For a main dish hearty soup, add any or all of the following: carrots, zucchini, cabbage, or canned garbanzo beans. Increase water as needed for vegetable additions.

## HAMBURGER SOUP

**BBB + Beef + Veg. + TE&A**

- 1 pound lean ground beef
- 1 cup chopped onions
- 4 Steero Instant Beef Flavor Bouillon and Broth Cubes
- 1 cup chopped carrots
- 1 cup thinly sliced celery
- 1 cup peeled and cubed potatoes
- 1 cup seeded and chopped green peppers
- 1 teaspoon salt
- 1 bay leaf
- 1 can (16 ounces) tomatoes

Stirring constantly, brown meat in soup kettle over medium heat. Drain off fat and discard. Add onions and continue stirring over medium heat until onions are transparent. Stir in 4 cups water and all remaining ingredients except tomatoes. Heat to boiling, reduce heat, cover, and simmer 30 minutes. Add tomatoes, cover, and simmer another 10 minutes. *Serves 6*

**Variation:**

Replace potatoes with 1 can (16 ounce) julienne beets in liquid. Omit bay leaf and add ½ teaspoon dill weed.

## ONION SOUP

**BBB + Beef + Veg. + TE&A**

- ¼ cup allowed oil
- 2 cups thinly sliced onions
- 2 tablespoons Steero Instant Beef Flavor Bouillon Seasoning and Broth
- 4 toasted soy bun slices

Heat allowed oil in soup kettle, add onions, and cook, stirring, until tender and golden brown. Add 4 cups water and instant broth. Bring to boil, reduce heat, and simmer 30 minutes. Serve with soy bun slice topping each bowl. *Serves 4*

**BBB + Beef + Veg. + TE&A**

- 1 cup navy beans
- ½ pound lean ground beef
- 1 cup cooked or canned tomatoes
- ½ cup grated or minced carrots
- 1 small onion, minced
- 1 medium potato, diced
- 1 cup chopped celery
- ¼ cup rice
- 1 teaspoon salt
- ¼ teaspoon pepper
- 1 teaspoon chili powder

## COLD NIGHT SPANISH BEAN SOUP

Wash beans and soak overnight in cold water. Next morning, drain off water, add all other ingredients and 6 cups cold water. Let come to boil, reduce heat, and simmer until beans are tender, 3 to 4 hours. *Serves 4–6*

**BBB + Poultry**

- 1 stewing chicken (5-6 pounds) or 2 broiler-fryer chickens or 5 pounds chicken necks and backs
- 1 teaspoon salt

## CHICKEN STOCK

Bring chicken to boil in 8 cups water. Skim and reduce heat. Add salt, cover and simmer until chicken is tender—about 1 hour. Remove chicken and discard bones and skin. Refrigerate or freeze chicken meat for other use. Refrigerate stock overnight and remove fat. Defatted stock may be frozen until needed. Heat to serve as clear broth, or reduce by boiling, chill, and serve cold as jellied consommé. *Makes 6–8 cups*

**BBB + Poultry**

- 2 tablespoons chicken fat
- ¼ cup rice flour
- 3 cups Chicken Stock
- 1 cup allowed milk substitute
- 1½ cups cooked, diced chicken meat
- Salt to taste

## CREAM OF CHICKEN SOUP

Make smooth paste of chicken fat and rice flour, add ½ cup chicken stock, and warm slowly, adding remainder of stock while still stirring. Increase heat until stock thickens. Heat milk substitute separately and add to thickened stock. Stir in chicken and salt. *Serves 3–4*

**Variation:**

Add 2 more cups of chicken stock and 1 cup cooked rice, or serve soup over hot cooked rice.

## VICHYSSOISE

**BBB + Poultry**

Purée potatoes with broth in food processor or blender. Pour into soup kettle and cook until potato starch no longer tastes raw. Cool and stir in milk substitute and salt. Chill thoroughly before serving. *Serves 4–6*

- **2 cups peeled and cubed potatoes**
- **2 cups Chicken Stock, p. 30**
- **2 cups allowed milk substitute**
- **1 teaspoon salt**

## QUICK CHICKEN SOUP

**BBB + Poultry + Veg.**

Bring stock to boil, add vegetables, rice, and cooked chicken. Simmer 5 minutes. *Serves 4*

- **4 cups Chicken Stock, p. 30**
- **2 teaspoons instant minced onion**
- **1 cup leftover allowed vegetables**
- **2 tablespoons Minute Rice**
- **1 cup cooked diced chicken**

## ZUCCHINI SOUP

**BBB + Poultry + Veg.**

Sauté zucchini in allowed oil, add ½ cup water, cover, and cook until tender. Purée in blender or food processor with 1 cup chicken stock. Heat remaining 2 cups stock, season, and combine with purée. Heat to serving temperature. *Serves 3–4*

- **2 medium zucchini, sliced thin**
- **2 tablespoons allowed oil**
- **3 cups Chicken Stock, p. 30**
- **¼ teaspoon garlic or onion powder**
- **½ teaspoon salt**

## VEGETABLE CHICKEN SOUP

**BBB + Poultry + Veg.**

Heat oil in soup kettle and sauté onion and garlic until transparent but not brown. Add remaining ingredients and bring to boil. Reduce heat, cover, and simmer 25 minutes. *Serves 5*

- **3 tablespoons allowed oil**
- **1 medium onion, diced**
- **1 clove garlic, minced**
- **2 cups Chicken Stock. p. 30**
- **2 cups canned tomatoes**
- **1 can (16 ounces) cut green beans**
- **½ teaspoon salt**
- **1 medium zucchini, sliced**
- **1 medium carrot, sliced thin**

☐ **BBB + Poultry + Veg.**

- 3 cups Chicken Stock. p. 30
- 2 stalks celery, sliced thin
- ½ cup shredded Chinese cabbage or shredded bok choy
- 1 cup shredded fresh spinach, or bean sprouts
- ½ teaspoon salt

## ORIENTAL SOUP

Heat stock to boiling. Add celery and cabbage and boil gently 5 minutes. Add spinach and continue cooking another 5 minutes. Add salt and serve while vegetables are still crisp. *Serves 2*

*Note:* Diced, cooked chicken may be added for a heartier soup.

☐ **BBB + Poultry + Veg. + TE&A**

## Soups available in markets

Steero Instant Chicken Flavor Bouillon Seasonings and Broth or
Steero Instant Chicken Flavor Bouillon and Broth Cubes (salt, hydrolyzed vegetable protein, sugar, chicken fat, BHA and citric acid, dehydrated chicken meat, onion powder, natural and artificial flavor, parsley flakes, garlic powder, spices, disodium guanylate, disodium inosinate)

☐ **BBB + Poultry + Fruit + Veg. + TE&A**

- 4 Steero Instant Chicken Flavor Bouillon and Broth Cubes
- ½ cup shredded carrots
- ½ cup diced celery
- 1 medium potato, peeled and diced
- ½ cup chopped onion
- 2 cups peeled, chopped fresh tomatoes
- 1 teaspoon salt
- 1 bay leaf
- 4 peppercorns
- 3 cups shredded cabbage
- ¼ cup fresh lemon juice
- 1 tablespoon sugar

## RUSSIAN CABBAGE SOUP

Place in soup kettle all ingredients except cabbage, lemon juice and sugar. Add 6 cups water and bring to boil. Reduce heat and simmer, covered, 1 hour. Add cabbage and simmer 10 minutes longer. Stir in lemon juice and sugar. Remove bayleaf and peppercorns and reheat to serving temperature. *Serves 6–8*

## CHILLED AVOCADO SOUP

**BBB + Poultry + Fruit + Veg. + TE&A**

- **2 tablespoons allowed margarine**
- **2 teaspoons finely grated onion**
- **2 tablespoons rice flour**
- **½ teaspoon salt**
- **2 cups Chicken Stock. p. 30**
- **2 cups allowed milk substitute**
- **2 large avocados, mashed**
- **½ teaspoon ginger**
- **1 teaspoon each grated lemon and orange peel**

Melt margarine in soup kettle, stir in onion and sauté until transparent but not browned. Blend in flour and salt and cook, stirring constantly, until bubbling but not brown. Gradually pour in chicken stock and bring to boil over medium heat, stirring until broth is thickened. Set aside to cool. Combine milk substitute, avocados, ginger, and peels. Purée in blender or beat until smooth with rotary beater. Stir all ingredients together and chill thoroughly. Serve, if desired, with dollop of Tofu Dressing II, p. 68, or with thin slice of lemon to top off each bowl. *Serves 4*

## ONION-POTATO SOUP

**BBB + Poultry + Veg. + TE&A**

- **¼ cup allowed oil**
- **3 medium onions, sliced thin**
- **4 cups peeled and thinly sliced potatoes**
- **4 cups Chicken Stock, p. 30**
- **½ teaspoon dried dill weed**
- **¼ teaspoon salt**
- **½ cup chopped parsley**

Heat oil in soup kettle, add onions and potatoes and sauté, stirring, 5 minutes. Add chicken stock, dill weed, and salt. Bring to boil, cover, and reduce heat. Simmer 30 minutes. Beat soup with wire whisk until potatoes are broken and flaked or purée in blender. Add parsley and reheat to serving temperature. *Serves 6-8*

**Variation:**

Replace onions with 3 cups chopped leeks.

## KICKING GOOD CHICKEN SOUP

**BBB + Poultry + Veg. + TE&A**

- **6 chicken drumsticks or thighs**
- **1 large onion, sliced**
- **2 stalks celery, chopped**
- **1 teaspoon salt**
- **¼ teaspoon pepper, (optional)**
- **1 package (16 ounces) frozen broccoli, cauliflower and carrots**
- **1 package (10 ounces) frozen green peas**
- **3 tablespoons white rice flour (optional)**

Brown chicken, skin side down, in large soup kettle over high heat. Turn and brown second side. Add onion, celery, salt, pepper, and 8 cups water. Bring to boil, lower heat, and cover. Simmer 45 minutes. Lift chicken from broth. Cover broth and refrigerate 4 hours or overnight. Remove congealed fat. When ready to complete soup, bring defatted broth to boil and add chicken and frozen vegetables. Cover and cook slowly 7 to 9 minutes. If slightly thickened soup is desired, mix rice flour with ½ cup cold water and stir into hot soup. Cook, stirring constantly, until thickened. Serve in soup plates with a chicken part in each. *Serves 6*

## CHICKEN MINESTRONE

**BBB + Poultry + Veg. + TE&A**

- **4 tablespoons allowed oil or chicken fat**
- **1 clove garlic, crushed**
- **¼ cup chopped onion**
- **½ cup chopped leeks**
- **8 cups Chicken Stock, p. 30**
- **1 can (15 ounces) Boston Style Soybeans or 1 can (16 ounces) garbanzo beans**
- **1 cup diced potatoes**
- **1 cup diced carrots**
- **½ cup thinly sliced celery**
- **2 cups chopped canned tomatoes**
- **½ cup brown rice**
- **1 bay leaf, crumbled**
- **½ teaspoon dried rosemary or ½ teaspoon dried thyme**
- **2 teaspoons dried parsley**
- **1 teaspoon salt**
- **¼ teaspoon pepper**
- **1 cup unpeeled, thinly sliced zucchini**
- **1 cup frozen green peas**
- **3 tablespoons imitation bacon bits, (optional)**

Heat oil or chicken fat in large soup kettle and sauté garlic, onion, and leeks until transparent but not browned. Add all other ingredients except last three. Bring to boil and reduce heat. Simmer, covered, 30 minutes. Add zucchini and cook another 5 minutes. Stir in frozen peas, cooking until barely tender. Garnish with bacon bits. (You might want to use half and freeze half for another day.) *Serves 10–12*

## CHICKEN SOUP WITH A SOUTHERN ACCENT

**BBB + Poultry + Veg. + TE&A**

- **4 Steero Instant Chicken Flavor Bouillon and Broth Cubes**
- **1 can (16 ounces) tomatoes**
- **½ cup diced onion**
- **1 package (10 ounces) frozen whole or cut okra**
- **1 can (7 ounces) carrots undrained or 1 cup cooked fresh carrots**
- **½ cup brown rice**
- **1 teaspoon salt**
- **½ teaspoon paprika**
- **¼ teaspoon hot pepper sauce**
- **3 cups diced cooked chicken**

Combine in soup kettle 6 cups water and all ingredients except cooked chicken. Bring to boil, stirring frequently. Reduce heat, cover, and simmer 40 minutes. Add cooked chicken, stir well, and continue cooking over low heat another 10 minutes. *Serve 6–8*

## FISH CHOWDER

**BBB + Fish + Veg. + TE&A**

**2 tablespoons allowed oil**
**1 medium onion, minced**
**2 tablespoons white rice flour**
**1 cup peeled thinly sliced potatoes**
**1 cup thinly sliced celery**
**1 cup thinly sliced carrots**
**2 cans (6½ ounces) water-packed tuna, broken in chunks or cooked shrimp or leftover fish fillets or 3 cans (8 ounces) oysters (using liquid to replace part of milk substitute) or 2 cans (6½ ounces) minced clams**
**2 cups allowed milk substitute**
**1 teaspoon salt**
**½ teaspoon pepper**
**⅛ teaspoon dried thyme**
**2 tablespoons minced parsley**
**Dash of paprika**

Heat oil in soup kettle and sauté onion 5 minutes. Blend in flour. Slowly stir in 2 cups water and cook until thickened. Add potatoes, celery, and carrots, cover, and simmer 20 minutes. If desired, purée mixture in blender. Add tuna or whatever fish chosen, and milk substitute. While stirring, heat gently to just below boil. Season with salt, pepper, and thyme. Remove from heat and let stand, covered, 3 to 5 minutes. Serve with garnish of minced parsley and paprika. *Serves 4–6*

## MANHATTAN CLAM CHOWDER

**BBB + Fish + Veg. + TE&A**

**3 tablespoons allowed oil**
**1 large onion, chopped fine**
**2 large potatoes, peeled and diced**
**1 teaspoon salt**
**1 bottle (8 ounces) clam juice**
**2 cans (6½ ounces each) minced clams, undrained**
**1 can (16 ounces) tomatoes**
**½ teaspoon dried thyme**
**2 tablespoons imitation bacon bits**

Heat allowed oil in soup kettle and sauté onion until transparent. Add potatoes, salt, and clam juice. Cover and simmer 15 to 20 minutes or until potatoes are tender. Stir in clams with juice, tomatoes, thyme, and bacon bits. Cover and simmer 15 minutes. *Serves 4*

## HAPPY COMBINATION VEGETABLE SOUP

**BBB + Barley + Veg.**

- **7 cups Vegetable Stock, p. 18 or water**
- **1 cup pearl barley**
- **1 cup diced leeks**
- **1½ cups diced celery**
- **1 cup shredded cabbage or sliced zucchini**
- **1 cup diced carrots**
- **½ cups chopped onion**
- **1 clove garlic, minced**
- **1 teaspoon salt, if using water**
- **1 tablespoon white distilled vinegar**
- **Chopped parsley (optional)**

Bring vegetable stock or water to boil and add barley. Reduce heat and simmer, covered, 30 minutes. Add remaining ingredients and continue cooking, stirring frequently, another 20 minutes. Garnish bowls with chopped parsley, if desired. *Serves 6–8*

## BARLEY SOUP

**BBB + Barley + Veg.**

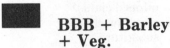

- **6 cups Vegetable Stock, p. 18, or water**
- **¼ cup pearl barley**
- **1 cup sliced carrots**
- **½ cup diced celery**
- **½ cup green beans, fresh or frozen, sliced French style**
- **½ cup chopped onions**
- **1 can (6 ounces) tomato paste**
- **1 cup fresh or frozen peas**
- **1 teaspoon salt**
- **2 tablespoons imitation bacon bits, if allowed (+ TE&A)**

Bring stock or water to boil and add barley. Cook over low heat 1 hour. Add remaining ingredients except bacon bits and simmer, covered, 20 minutes. Serve with sprinkle of bacon bits on each bowl. *Serves 6*

## LAMBURGER VEGETABLE CHOWDER

**BBB + Barley + Veg.**

- ½ pound ground lamb
- 1 can (16 ounces) stewed tomatoes
- ½ cup diced carrot
- ½ cup diced celery
- 1 medium onion, chopped
- 1 clove garlic, minced
- ½ teaspoon salt
- ⅓ cup pearl barley

Brown meat slowly and drain off all fat. Add 6 cups water and all remaining ingredients. Bring to boil, cover, and simmer 1 hour. *Serves 4–6*

## SPLIT PEAS AND BARLEY PEARLS

**BBB + Barley + Veg. + TE&A**

- ¾ cup pearl barley
- ½ cup split peas
- 1 tablespoon instant chopped onion or 1 medium onion, chopped
- 1 tablespoon chopped parsley
- 1 teaspoon salt
- ⅛ teaspoon garlic powder
- ½ teaspoon dried thyme
- 1 carrot, diced
- 1 stalk celery, diced
- 2 tablespoons allowed oil

Bring 8 cups water to boil and add barley and split peas. Return to boil and stir in all other ingredients. Reduce heat, cover, and simmer 45 minutes. *Serves 8*

**Variation:**
Substitute lentils for split peas. Experiment with different herbs, such as basil and rosemary.

## QUICK CORN CHOWDER

**BBB + Corn + Veg.**

- 1 medium onion, sliced
- 2 tablespoons allowed oil
- 3 cups boiling water
- 3 medium potatoes, peeled and cubed
- 1 teaspoon salt
- 1½ cups drained canned corn
- 2 cups allowed milk substitute, heated or when allowed, Chicken Stock, p. 30 (+ Poultry)

Sauté onion in allowed oil until lightly browned. Add boiling water, potatoes, and salt. Cook over medium heat 15 minutes. Add corn and heated milk substitute or stock. Do not boil, but heat to serving temperature. *Serves 4–5*

**Variations:**

1. FRESH CORN SOUP—Scrape kernels from 3 ears of fresh corn. Cook with potatoes until tender. Add hot milk substitute.
2. CREAMY CORN SOUP—Purée potato-corn mixture in blender, add hot milk substitute, and heat.

**BBB + Corn + Veg.**

- 8 cups Vegetable Stock. p. 18, or water
- ½ teaspoon salt
- 8 cups fresh garden vegetables such as: okra, carrots, potatoes, tomatoes, scallion or leek, turnip, parsnip, winter squash, broccoli, lima beans, green peas, eggplant, green beans
- 4 cups quick-cooking vegetables such as: summer squash, crookneck squash, zucchini, leafy greens, corn scraped from cob

## HARVEST TIME SOUP

Bring stock or water and salt to boil in soup kettle. Add first 8 cups of vegetables and simmer 30 minutes. Add quicker cooking vegetables and simmer 15 minutes more or until all are at least tender crisp. Garnish bowls with imitation bacon bits. **(+ TE&A)** *Serves 8*

**Variations:**

1. Vegetables may be served over any cooked allowed grain: rice, soy grits, barley, millet (when allowed), or whatever you like that likes you.

2. This recipe provides a good base for vegetable soups, with or without meats. Replace vegetable stock or water with Beef Broth, p. 27, when allowed. Also add chopped meat. **(+ Beef )** Or use Chicken Stock. p. 30, and chicken. **(+ Poultry)** Add Steero Instant Beef or Chicken Bouillon Seasoning or Broth or Cubes, when allowed. **(+ Beef or Poultry + TE&A)** Part of water may be replaced with tomato juice.

**BBB + Corn + Veg. + TE&A**

- 2 cups leftover cooked vegetables such as: peas, carrots, corn, celery, etc.
- 2 tablespoons rice flour
- 2 cups Vegetable Stock, p. 18, or Beef Broth, p. 27, (+ Beef) or water
- 2 cups tomato juice
- 2 sprigs parsley, chopped
- ⅛ teaspoon pepper
- ⅛ teaspoon dried thyme
- ½ teaspoon salt

## LAST MINUTE SOUP

Purée all vegetables in food processor or blender with flour and the stock, broth, or water. Pour into soup kettle and add remaining ingredients. Stirring constantly, slowly bring to just below boil and continue cooking until thickened. Simmer for about 15 minutes. *Serves 4–5*

## GLORIA'S ONION SOUP MIX

**BBB + Corn + Beef + Veg. + TE&A**

- **4 teaspoons Steero Instant Beef Flavor Bouillon Seasoning and Broth**
- **2 teaspoons sugar**
- **½ teaspoon garlic powder**
- **1 teaspoon onion powder**
- **½ teaspoon paprika**
- **2 teaspoons potato flour**
- **2 teaspoons cornstarch**
- **Dash of pepper**
- **2 teaspoons allowed oil**
- **1½ tablespoons instant chopped onion**

Mix all dry ingredients except onion, then add oil and blend. Add instant onion.

*To make soup:* Bring 4 cups water to boil. Lower heat and stir in soup mix. Cover and simmer 10 minutes. *Serves 4*

*For 1 cup of soup:* Bring 1 cup water to boil. Lower heat and stir in 1½ tablespoons soup mix. Simmer 10 minutes.

Store mix in refrigerator in tightly covered jar. A great mix to keep on hand for recipes of many kinds!

## OLD HOME VEGETABLE SOUP

**BBB + Corn + Beef + Veg. + TE&A**

- **3 pounds beef short ribs or shank**
- **2 cans (1 pound 12 ounces) tomatoes**
- **1 teaspoon salt**
- **2 bay leaves**
- **1 cup chopped onion**
- **2 large carrots, chopped**
- **2 large stalks celery, chopped**
- **½ teaspoon dried oregano**
- **½ teaspoon dried basil**
- **1 can (16 ounces) green beans**
- **1 can (16 ounces) corn or 2 cups cooked wheat-free corn pasta elbows**

On day before serving, place meat, tomatoes, salt, bay leaves, and 4 cups water in large soup kettle and bring to boil. Skim off foam, cover, and keep at simmer 2½ to 3 hours. Discard bones and fat and return meat to kettle. Add onion, carrots, and celery to soup. Stir in oregano and basil and cook, covered, 20 minutes over low heat. Refrigerate overnight to blend flavors and separate fat. When ready to serve, remove and discard fat from surface, add beans and corn, and heat to serving temperature. *Serves 10*

**BBB + Corn + Poultry + Veg. + TE&A**

- ½ cup chopped onions
- 2 medium potatoes, peeled and chopped
- 1 can (16 ounces) whole kernel corn, drained
- 1 package (10 ounces) frozen lima beans
- 3 teaspoons Steero Instant Chicken Flavor Bouillon Seasoning and Broth
- 1 can (26 ounces) tomato juice
- 1 cup diced cooked chicken
- ¼ teaspoon dried dill weed or dried thyme

## HALF-HOUR SOUP

Combine all ingredients plus 3 cups water in soup kettle and bring slowly to boil. Lower heat, cover, and simmer 30 minutes. *Serves 6*

**BBB + Corn + Fish + Veg. + TE&A**

- 2 packages (10 ounces) frozen whole kernel corn, thawed
- 3 tablespoons allowed oil
- ¾ cup chopped onion
- ¾ cup chopped celery
- 3 medium potatoes, peeled and diced
- 3 Steero Instant Chicken Flavor Bouillon and Broth Cubes
- ⅛ teaspoon pepper
- 1 cup allowed milk substitute
- 2 cans (6½ ounces) water-packed tuna, drained
- 2 tablespoons minced parsley
- ¼ cup bacon bits, if desired

## TUNA CORN CHOWDER

Set aside 1 cup corn. Purée in blender or food processor remaining corn, using 2 cups water to facilitate blending. Heat oil in soup kettle and sauté onion and celery until soft but not brown. Add puréed corn, remaining corn kernels, potatoes, bouillon cubes, 1 cup water, and pepper. Bring to boil, reduce heat, cover, and simmer 15 to 20 minutes. Stir in milk substitute, tuna, and parsley. Bring to serving temperature while stirring gently. *Serves 6–8*

**Variation:**

Replace tuna with 2 cans (6½ ounces) minced or chopped clams, undrained. Replace 1 cup water with 1 bottle (10½ ounces) clam juice. Add ¼ teaspoon each dried thyme and basil to season. Garnish with imitation bacon bits, if desired.

## WHATEVER SOUP

**BBB + Millet + Veg.**

- 3 tablespoons allowed oil
- 2 medium onions, chopped
- 2 green peppers, chopped
- 3 cloves garlic, minced
- 1 can (46 ounces) tomato juice
- ¼ cup pearl millet
- 4 cups whatever fresh vegetables are available: corn, squash, celery, cabbage, carrots, green beans, peas, potatoes, leafy greens

Heat allowed oil in soup kettle, add onions, peppers, and garlic and sauté, stirring until soft. Add tomato juice and millet and whatever fresh vegetables are available from your garden, market, or refrigerator—even the dandelions from your lawn. Bring to boil and simmer, covered, 40 to 60 minutes or until flavors blend and vegetables are as tender or as crisp as you like. *Serves 4–8*

## BARGAIN DAY LAMB SOUP

**BBB + Millet + Veg.**

- 1 pound lamb neck bones, shanks or ribs
- ½ medium onion, diced
- ½ large carrot, diced
- 1 clove garlic, minced
- 2 stalks celery, diced
- 2 tablespoons pearl millet
- 1 teaspoon salt

Simmer meat and bones in 8 cups water 2½ hours. Add remaining ingredients and continue to simmer 30 minutes. Chill long enough to congeal fat. Discard fat and bones. Serve soup piping hot. *Serves 6*

# Salads

## ISLAND LETTUCE SALAD

### BBB

- 1 can (8 ounces) unsweetened crushed pineapple, undrained
- Iceberg lettuce, finely torn or shredded

Toss and serve. For a little tartness, add a dash of white distilled vinegar. Or, if extra dressing is desired, use Remarkable Soyannaise, p. 67. *Serves 1 or 2*

## PEACHY PINE-BERRY MOLD

### BBB

- 1 tablespoon unflavored gelatin
- 1 can (8 ounces) unsweetened crushed pineapple, drained, juice reserved
- 1 cup whole cranberries, uncooked
- ¾ cup frozen unsweetened apple juice concentrate
- 1 can (16 ounces) water or juice-pack sliced peaches, drained

Soften gelatin in ¼ cup water. Measure reserved pineapple juice and add water to make 1 cup. Using this liquid, cook cranberries until skins pop. Grind cooked cranberries in blender with small amount of cooking liquid. Dissolve gelatin in remaining hot juice, then stir in apple juice concentrate. Combine all ingredients and chill until firm. *Serves 6–8*

## RING AROUND THE PEAR

### BBB

- 2 tablespoons unflavored gelatin
- 1 can (1 pound 4 ounces) unsweetened pineapple slices, drained, juice reserved
- 1 can (12 ounces) frozen unsweetened apple juice concentrate
- 1 can (16 ounces) water-pack pear halves, drained

Soften gelatin in ½ cup pineapple juice. Measure remaining juice, add water to make 1¾ cups and bring to boil. Add softened gelatin, stirring to dissolve, and blend in concentrate. Arrange pineapple rings in oblong pan that will accommodate 6 to 8 rings. Slowly pour in gelatin to cover. Place 1 pear half, rounded side down, in each pineapple ring. Chill until firm. Unmold on bed of lettuce. If desired, fill pear cups with Tofu Dressing I, p. 63. *Serves 6–8*

## CONGEALED GRAPPLE SALAD

**BBB**

Soften gelatin in ¼ cup water. Dissolve in boiling water. Stir in applesauce and chill until syrupy. Fold in grapes. Chill until firm. *Serves 4*

- **1 tablespoon unflavored gelatin**
- **¾ cup boiling water**
- **1½ cups unsweetened applesauce, homemade or canned**
- **1 cup seedless grapes, halved**

## GRAPE-PEAR SALAD

**BBB**

Soften gelatin in ¼ cup water, then dissolve in boiling water. Add concentrate and stir until thawed. Fold in fruits and chill until firm. *Serves 4*

**Variation:**
Add 1 can (8 ounces) unsweetened chunk pineapple, drained.

- **1 tablespoon unflavored gelatin**
- **1 cup boiling water**
- **1 can (6 ounces) frozen unsweetened pear-grape concentrate**
- **1 can (16 ounces) water-pack pears, drained and diced**
- **1 cup seedless grapes, halved (optional)**

## HARMONIZING FRUIT QUINTET

**BBB**

Soften gelatin in ¼ cup water. Measure pineapple juice and add water to make ½ cup. Combine with apple juice and heat to boiling. Add gelatin to dissolve. Chill until syrupy. Add fruits and chill until firm. *Serves 4–6*

*Note:* Recipe may be doubled for a larger group or to serve again later. Use 1 can (1 pound 4 ounces) crushed pineapple and 1 can each (16 ounces each) peaches, pears, and apricots.

- **1 tablespoon unflavored gelatin**
- **1 can (8 ounces) unsweetened crushed pineapple, drained, juice reserved**
- **1 cup unsweetened apple juice**
- **1 can (8 ounces) water-pack peaches, drained**
- **1 can (8 ounces) water-pack pears, drained**
- **1 can (8 ounces) water-pack apricots, drained**

## APPLECOT MOLD

**BBB**

Soften gelatin in ¼ cup water 5 minutes, then dissolve in boiling water. Stir in concentrate until thawed and chill mixture until syrupy. Fold in apricots. Chill until set. *Serves 4*

- **1 tablespoon unflavored gelatin**
- **¾ cup boiling water**
- **1 cup frozen unsweetened apple juice concentrate**
- **1 can (16 ounces) water-pack apricot halves, drained**

## BBB

## FRUITED CABBAGE SALAD

**3 to 4 cups finely shredded cabbage**
**1 can (8 ounces) unsweetened crushed pineapple, undrained**
**1 unpeeled green apple, diced**
**3 tablespoons white distilled vinegar (optional)**

Combine all ingredients. If tightly covered, this salad keeps well in the refrigerator. *Serves 4–6*

## BBB

## SUNSHINE CARROT MOLD

**1 tablespoon unflavored gelatin**
**1 can (1 pound 4 ounces) unsweetened crushed pineapple, drained, juice reserved**
**2 medium carrots, grated fine**

Soften gelatin in ¼ cup water 5 minutes. Measure pineapple juice and add water to make 1½ cups. Bring to boil, add softened gelatin, and stir to dissolve. Chill until syrupy. Fold in pineapple and carrots. Chill until set. *Serves 4–6*

## BBB

## TOFU RICE SALAD

**1⅓ cups tofu, frozen (or ½ of 16–20 ounce box)**
**1½ cups cooked brown rice**
**1 cup frozen peas, thawed**
**1 can (8 ounces) unsweetened crushed pineapple, undrained**
**1 cup chopped cooked rabbit meat (optional)**
**½ cup frozen unsweetened apple juice concentrate**
**3 tablespoons white distilled vinegar**
**Spinach leaves**

All ingredients should be well chilled. Freeze tofu in water the day or night before making salad. To use, hold under cold running water a few minutes. As tofu softens, dry on paper towels and then squeeze between hands to remove as much moisture as possible. Crumble into bowl with all other ingredients except spinach and mix well. Chill and serve on bed of torn spinach leaves. *Serves 6*

*Note:* Tofu may contain trace of lemon or lime. If highly sensitive to citrus, do not use this recipe.

☐ **BBB + Fruit**

## APPLE-BANANA SALAD

Chop equal amounts of apple and banana. Toss with Remarkable Soyannaise, p. 67, or Tofu Dressing I, p. 63. Garnish with nuts, if allowed, or serve with Nut Dressing, p. 65. (**+ N&S**)

## ALLEGRO CRANBERRY ORANGE SALAD

**BBB + Fruit** ☐

- 1 tablespoon unflavored gelatin
- 1 cup boiling orange juice or water
- 3 tablespoons sugar
- 1 orange, unpeeled
- 2 cups whole fresh or frozen cranberries

Soften gelatin in ¼ cup water 5 minutes. Heat orange juice and stir in gelatin and sugar to dissolve. Grind orange and cranberries with ¼ cup water in blender. Add to gelatin mixture, pour into 4-cup mold, and chill until firm. Unmold on crisp lettuce. *Serves 4–6*

**Variation:**

Omit unflavored gelatin and ¼ cup water. Dissolve 1 box (3 ounces) orange, lemon, or strawberry-flavored gelatin and sugar in 1 cup boiling water. Grind orange and cranberries with ½ cup cold water in blender. Add to gelatin, pour into 4-cup mold, and chill until firm. (+ TE&A)

## SUMMER FRUIT SALAD

**BBB + Fruit** ☐

- 1 cup orange sections
- 1 cup diced unpeeled red apples
- 2 bananas, sliced
- 2 cups peeled, sliced peaches
- 1 cup sliced pears, optional
- ⅓ cup frozen unsweetened apple juice concentrate or 1 can (15 ounces) unsweetened applesauce

Toss all ingredients lightly. Chill and serve. *Serves 6*

**Variation:**

Omit pears and replace with loquat halves.

## BANAPPLE MEDLEY

**BBB + Fruit** ☐

- 1 tablespoon unflavored gelatin
- 1 cup boiling water
- 1 can (6 ounces) frozen unsweetened apple juice concentrate
- 1 unpeeled red apple, chopped or grated
- 1 banana, sliced

Soften gelatin in ¼ cup water 5 minutes. Dissolve in boiling water. Stir in concentrate, then fruits. Chill until firm. *Serves 4–6*

**Variation:**

When allowed, add ½ teaspoon cinnamon. (+ TE&A)

## DUTCH CUCUMBERS

**BBB + Veg.**

- **⅓ cup white distilled vinegar**
- **½ cup ice-cold water**
- **¼ cup sugar**
- **¾ teaspoon salt**
- **2 cups peeled, thinly sliced cucumbers**
- **1 cup thinly sliced onions**

Pour mixture of vinegar, cold water, sugar, and salt over cucumber and onion slices to cover. Chill 24 hours. *Serves 4-6*

## SPROUTS

**BBB + Veg.**

Materials needed: ½-gallon jar, stainless mesh screens (small, medium, and large), and metal or plastic ring. Cheesecloth and tightly fitted rubber band may be used instead.

*Alfalfa sprouts:* Soak 2½ tablespoons seed in ½ jar water overnight. Next day drain, rinse several times in fresh water, and drain well. Place jar in dark place (pantry is great), taking out each morning and evening to rinse and drain seeds. Fourth day, bring out to the light to develop chlorophyll. Rinse and drain as usual. A larger screen should be used from this point on to allow hulls to rinse away. By the 5th or 6th day, sprouts are ready to eat. Rinse off all hulls and drain well. These keep as long as two weeks if refrigerated in airtight bowl with folded paper towel in bottom to absorb extra moisture. Change paper towel occasionally.

*Note:* For sprouts of lentils, garbanzos, mung beans, or soy beans: Soak ½ cup seeds in ½ jar water from 4 to 10 hours or until fully swollen. Rinse and drain 4 times a day. These sprouts are ready to eat on the 3rd or 4th day. Bean sprouts keep well for a shorter time than alfalfa sprouts. Sprouted seeds may be eaten raw, added to soups, or cooked in Chinese or vegetable dishes.

## PINEAPPLE SALAD MOLDS

**BBB + Veg.**

- **2 cups unsweetened pineapple juice**
- **1 tablespoon unflavored gelatin**
- **¼ teaspoon salt**
- **½ cup thinly sliced celery**

Soften gelatin in ¼ cup pineapple juice. Heat ¾ cup juice to boil. Stir in gelatin to dissolve, add remaining juice and salt, and chill until syrupy. Fold in celery and spoon into individual molds. Chill until firm. Unmold on lettuce leaves. *Serves 5*

## TOSSED SALAD

**BBB + Veg.** ☐

- 3 cups torn spinach and lettuce
- ½ cup grated carrots
- 1 cup chopped celery
- ¼ cup scallions, chopped
- 1 cup bean sprouts
- ½ medium cucumber, sliced
- 1 tomato, cut in wedges

Toss with Basic Oil and Vinegar Dressing, p. 64. Garnish with imitation bacon bits and dry roasted soy nuts. *Serves 4–6*

## RED SALAD TRIO

**BBB + Veg.** ☐

- 1 can (16 ounces) julienne beets, drained, juice reserved
- 4 cups shredded red cabbage
- 1 medium-size sweet red onion, chopped fine
- ⅓ cup white distilled vinegar
- ½ cup beet juice
- ¼ teaspoon salt

Combine all ingredients. *Serves 4–6*

## SNAPPY CABBAGE SALAD

**BBB + Veg.** ☐

- 3 cups finely chopped cabbage
- 2 cups grated carrots
- 1 medium cucumber, chopped
- ¼ cup chopped green pepper
- ¼ cup chopped celery

Combine ingredients and toss with Tofu Avocado Dip, p. 11. *Serves 4–6*

## POTATO SALAD

**BBB + Veg.** ☐

- 5 cups diced cooked potatoes (3 medium-large)
- ¼ cup chopped onion
- ½ cup chopped celery
- ½ cup chopped cucumber
- 2 tomatoes, cut in wedges
- ½ teaspoon salt

Combine all ingredients and toss lightly with Tofu Dressing I, p. 63. *Serves 4*

☐ **BBB + Veg.**

Lettuce, shredded
Red cabbage, shredded
Scallions, chopped
Cucumber, sliced
Radishes, sliced
Tomato, cut in wedges

## SALAD FANTASIA

Combine in proportions to suit your taste. Toss with Basic Oil and Vinegar Dressing, p. 64.

☐ **BBB + Veg.**

1 tablespoon unflavored gelatin
1¾ cups tomato juice
2 tablespoons sugar
2 tablespoons white distilled vinegar
1 teaspoon grated onion
½ cup diced green pepper
½ cup sliced celery

## FLAVOR TREAT TOMATO ASPIC

Soften gelatin in ¼ cup tomato juice for 5 minutes. Add sugar to 1 cup tomato juice and bring almost to boil. Mix in softened gelatin and stir to dissolve. Add remaining ½cup tomato juice and vinegar. Chill until syrupy. Fold in vegetables. Chill until firm. *Serves 4–6*

☐ **BBB + Fruit + Veg.**

1 tablespoon unflavored gelatin
¾ cup boiling water
2 tablespoons lemon juice
6–8 large ice cubes
½ teaspoon salt
¾ cup chopped raw cauliflower
½ cup sliced radishes
2 teaspoons grated onion

## RED AND WHITE VEGETABLE SALAD

Soften gelatin in ¼ cup water. Add boiling water and stir to dissolve. Add lemon juice and ice. Stir until syrupy and remove unmelted ice. Add salt and vegetables. Spoon into individual molds and chill until they are firm. *Serves 4–6*

☐ **BBB + Fruit + Veg.**

3 cups broccoli flowerets
3 cups cauliflower flowerets
Boiling salted water
½ cup allowed oil
3 tablespoons lemon juice
½ teaspoon salt
1 clove garlic, crushed

## MARINATED POLKA DOT SALAD

Cover and simmer broccoli and cauliflower in ½ inch boiling water 8 minutes or until tender-crisp. Drain. Mix remaining ingredients well and pour over hot vegetables. Chill several hours before serving. *Serves 4–6*

## SPRING PARADE SALAD

**BBB + Fruit + Veg.** ☐

- 1 tablespoon unflavored gelatin
- ½ teaspoon salt
- 1 cup boiling water
- 1 can (6 ounces) frozen unsweetened apple juice concentrate or water
- 1 tablespoon lemon juice
- 1 cup finely shredded carrots
- 1 cup finely shredded cabbage
- 1 cup finely shredded spinach
- 1 teaspoon minced chives

Soften gelatin in ¼ cup water. Add boiling water and salt and stir to dissolve gelatin. Add concentrate or water and lemon juice. Chill until syrupy. Divide gelatin into 3 bowls. Stir carrots into one and pour into 7 x 4 x 3-inch pan. Chill until set, but not firm. Fold cabbage into second portion, pour over carrot mixture, and chill until set. Add spinach and chives to remaining gelatin, pour over cabbage mixture, and chill until firm. Unmold, slice, and serve on lettuce leaves. *Serves 4–6*

## MOLDED CRANBERRY WALDORF

**BBB + Veg.** ☐

- 1 tablespoon unflavored gelatin
- 1 can (8 ounces) unsweetened crushed pineapple, drained, juice reserved
- 2 cups raw cranberries
- ⅓ cup sugar
- ¾ cup finely chopped celery

Soften gelatin in ¼ cup water and set aside. Measure pineapple juice and add water to make 1¼ cups. Cook cranberries in juice for 10 minutes, add sugar, and cook 5 minutes longer. Remove from heat and stir in softened gelatin to dissolve. Cool and chill until syrupy. Fold in pineapple and celery. Add ½ cup chopped nuts, if allowed. **(+ N&S)** Chill until firm. *Serves 4–6*

**Variation: Molded Apple Waldorf**

Omit crushed pineapple, sugar, and cranberries. Dissolve softened gelatin in ¾ cup boiling water. Stir in 1 can (6 ounces) frozen apple juice concentrate, 1 tablespoon lemon juice, 2 red Delicious apples, unpeeled and diced fine, celery, and nuts, if allowed. **(+ N&S)**

## SPINACH SALAD

**BBB + Fruit + N&S** ☐

- 4 cups fresh spinach torn into bits
- ¼ cup allowed oil
- 3 tablespoons lemon juice
- ½ teaspoon salt
- ½ cup sunflower seeds

Toss spinach with oil, lemon juice, and salt. Sprinkle seeds on top. *Serves 4*

**BBB + Fruit + N&S**

## SUNSHINE VEGETABLE SALAD

- ½ head iceberg lettuce, shredded
- 1 cup cauliflower flowerets
- 1 cup shredded carrot
- 1 cup chopped celery
- ¼ cup chopped scallions
- 1 cup bean sprouts
- ¼ cup sunflower seeds

Combine and toss with Ruby French Dressing, p. 66. Serve immediately. *Serves 4–6*

**BBB + Fruit + Veg. + N&S**

## WALDORF SALAD

- 3 unpeeled apples, diced
- 1 can (1 pound 4 ounces) unsweetened crushed pineapple, undrained
- 1 cup diced celery
- 1 banana, diced (optional)
- ½ cup chopped walnuts

Combine and serve. *Serves 6–8*

**BBB + Fruit + TE&A**

## SPICY APRICOT SALAD

- 1 can (1 pound 13 ounces) juice-pack apricot halves, drained, juice reserved
- ¼ cup lemon juice
- 1 teaspoon whole cloves
- 1 4-inch stick of cinnamon
- Hot water
- 1 box (3 ounces) orange-flavored gelatin

Bring apricot juice, lemon juice, and spices to boil. Simmer 10 minutes. Strain into 2-cup measure, add hot water to fill measure, and pour over gelatin. Add apricots while hot so spices will penetrate fruit. Mold and chill until firm. *Serves 6*

**BBB + TE&A**

## GLORIOUS CARROT-PINEAPPLE MOLD

- 1 box (3 ounces) orange-flavored gelatin
- 1 cup boiling water
- 1 can (1 pound 4 ounces) unsweetened crushed pineapple, drained, juice reserved
- 1½ cups finely grated carrots

Dissolve gelatin in boiling water. Measure pineapple juice and add water to make ¾ cup. Add juice and remaining ingredients, stirring until well distributed. Chill until firm. *Serves 4–6*

**Variation:**

Add ⅓ cup chopped pecans, if allowed. (+ **N&S**)

## MOLDED MINT PINEAPPLE

**BBB + Fruit + TE&A** ☐

**1 box (3 ounces) lime-flavored gelatin**
**Pinch of salt**
**¾ cup boiling water**
**6 drops mint extract**
**1½ teaspoons lemon juice**
**1 can (1 pound 4 ounces) unsweetened crushed pineapple, undrained**

Dissolve gelatin and salt in boiling water. Stir in mint extract and lemon juice. Chill until syrupy. Add pineapple, mold, and chill until firm. *Serves 6*

## MOLDED PERSIMMON SALAD

**BBB + Fruit + TE&A** ☐

**1 box (3 ounces) lemon-flavored gelatin**
**1 can (8 ounces) unsweetened crushed pineapple, drained, juice reserved**
**3 large persimmons, peeled, mashed or puréed**
**Grapefruit sections**

Add water to pineapple juice to make 1 cup, bring to boil. Stir in gelatin to dissolve. Chill until syrupy. Add drained pineapple and persimmons. Chill to set. Unmold and garnish with grapefruit sections. *Serves 4*

**Variation:**
Add ½ teaspoon cinnamon and ⅛ teaspoon ground cloves to hot juice for a spicy salad.

## PINK GRAPEFRUIT SALAD

**BBB + Fruit + TE&A** ☐

**1 box (3 ounces) mixed fruit-flavored gelatin**
**¼ teaspoon salt**
**1 cup boiling water**
**¾ cup orange or grapefruit juice or water**
**1½ cups diced pink grapefruit sections**

Dissolve gelatin and salt in boiling water. Add juice and chill until syrupy. Fold in diced grapefruit. Chill until firm. *Serves 4–6*

**Variation: Grapefruit Waldorf Mold**
Use lemon-flavored gelatin and reduce grapefruit sections to 1 cup. Add to syrupy gelatin ½ cup Tofu Dressing I, p. 63, and 1 cup chopped celery along with grapefruit. **(+ Veg.)** Add ½ cup chopped almonds also, if allowed. **(+ N&S)**

## VIVID TOMATO SALAD

**BBB + Veg. + TE&A**

- **6 tomatoes, diced**
- **2 cucumbers, diced**
- **½ green pepper, diced**
- **¼ cup chopped scallions**
- **½ teaspoon salt**
- **Pinch of dried basil and thyme**
- **½ cup Italian Dressing, p. 67**

Combine all ingredients and chill. *Serves 4–6*

## CREATE-A-BEAN SALAD

**BBB + Veg. + TE&A**

- **4 cans (15 or 16 ounces each) beans of your choice, drained: yellow wax beans, cut green beans, French style green beans, French style seasoned green beans, soy beans, garbanzo beans, kidney beans, or limas**
- **1 cup chopped or sliced onions of your choice: scallions, chives, white or red**
- **½ green pepper, chopped or sliced**
- **2 stalks celery, sliced**
- **¼ cup sliced radishes (optional)**
- **1 small cucumber, sliced (optional)**
- **¼ cup chopped parsley (optional)**
- **½ cup allowed oil**
- **½ cup white distilled vinegar**
- **½ teaspoon garlic powder**
- **1 teaspoon salt**
- **Dash of seasoned pepper**

Combine all ingredients and marinate in refrigerator several hours to blend flavors. Stir gently once or twice while marinating. Serve plain or on bed of lettuce. This keeps beautifully. Make ahead for company, or take to a potluck picnic or barbeque. *Makes 8 cups*

## DINER'S CHOICE VEGETABLE SALAD

**BBB + Veg. + TE&A**

- **2 boxes (3 ounces) lemon, lime, lemon-lime, orange, or orange-pineapple-flavored gelatin**
- **¾ teaspoon salt**
- **1½ cups boiling water**
- **2¼ cups cold water**
- **2 tablespoons distilled white vinegar**
- **1-2 cups any vegetable combination already tested and proven friendly. Choose from the following shredded, grated, or chopped vegetables: onion, cabbage. celery, green pepper, pimiento, cauliflower or broccoli flowerets, tomato, cucumber, carrot, parsley, radish**

Dissolve gelatin and salt in boiling water. Stir in cold water and vinegar. Chill until syrupy. Fold in vegetables of your choice and chill until firm in individual molds or flat pan (11¾ x 7½ x 1¾ inches). Unmold on lettuce leaves or shredded lettuce. *Serves 6–8*

## MARINATED POTATO SALAD

**BBB + Veg. + TE&A**

- **6 medium potatoes, unpeeled**
- **¼ cup allowed oil**
- **3 tablespoons white distilled vinegar**
- **2 teaspoons prepared mustard**
- **½ teaspoon salt**
- **Dash of seasoned pepper**
- **1 onion, grated**
- **2 tablespoons finely chopped parsley**

Cover potatoes with water. Bring to a boil, cover, and cook slowly 35 minutes, or until potatoes are just tender. Meanwhile combine oil, vinegar, 2 tablespoons water, and seasonings. When potatoes are done and still hot, peel and slice. Layer in large bowl with onion, parsley, and dressing. Repeat with layers until all ingredients are used. Refrigerate. *Serves 6–8*

**Variation:**

Sprinkle layers with dash of dried dill weed if desired.

☐ **BBB + Fruit + Veg. + TE&A**

## VEGETABLE ORANGE SALAD MOLD

- 1 box (3 ounces) orange-flavored gelatin
- 1 cup boiling water
- 1 tablespoon prepared mustard
- ⅔ cup cold water
- ½ cup chopped celery
- ½ medium cucumber, chopped
- 1½ cups diced oranges or sectioned and seeded tangerines

Dissolve gelatin in boiling water and blend in mustard and cold water. Chill until syrupy. Fold in vegetables and fruit. Chill until firm. *Serves 6*

☐ **BBB + Fruit + Veg. + N&S + TE&A**

## DO-YOUR-OWN-THING SLAW

- 3 cups finely shredded cabbage
- 2 tablespoons minced onion
- ½ cup shredded carrots
- ½ cup chopped green pepper (optional)
- ½ cup peeled diced Jerusalem artichokes (optional)
- 1 cup bean sprouts (optional)
- 3 tablespoons allowed oil
- 2 tablespoons lemon juice
- 1 teaspoon sugar
- ¾ teaspoon dry mustard
- ⅛ teaspoon celery seeds

Combine all ingredients. Chill several hours, stirring once or twice. *Serves 4–6*

**Variation: Quick Basic Slaw**

Prepare slaw, using cabbage, onion, and carrots only. Toss with desired amount of Slaw Dressing, p. 69. *Serves 4*

☐ **BBB + Fruit + Veg. + TE&A**

## PRIZE WINNING SALAD

- 4–6 cups fresh spinach torn into bite-size pieces
- 3 navel oranges, peeled and sectioned
- 1 medium red onion, sliced thin
- 2 ripe avocados
- Imitation bacon bits

Combine all ingredients except bacon bits. Toss lightly with Tangerine Dressing, p. 66. Garnish with bacon bits. *Serves 4–6*

**Variation:**

Omit avocado and replace with 1 cup loquat halves.

## ZESTY MARINATED ASPARAGUS SPEARS

**BBB + Fruit + Veg. + TE&A**

Place asparagus in shallow pan. Mix dressing ingredients and pour over asparagus. Cover tightly and refrigerate several hours.

*To serve:* Slip 4 asparagus spears into each lemon ring, laying each bundle on salad greens. Serve with marinade dressing. Garnish with slivered almonds, optional. **(+ N&S)** *Serves 6*

**Note:* Cut lemon in half, crosswise. Squeeze out juice. From each half of rind cut 3 rings to be used to hold asparagus bundles.

- **24 fresh asparagus spears, cooked tender-crisp, drained**
- **⅓ cup allowed oil**
- **3 tablespoons lemon juice from fresh lemon***
- **1 tablespoon sugar**
- **¼ teaspoon salt**
- **¼ teaspoon dry mustard**
- **¼ teaspoon paprika**
- **Dash garlic powder**
- **Dash pepper**
- **6 lemon rings cut from rind (see note)**

## SPROUT SALAD

**BBB + Fruit + Veg. + TE&A**

Dip avocado slices in lemon juice and arrange with tomato on bed of sprouts. Drizzle on your favorite dressing. Garnish with bacon bits.

- **Avocado, peeled and sliced**
- **Lemon juice**
- **Tomato, cut in wedges or sliced**
- **Fresh alfalfa sprouts**
- **Imitation bacon bits**

## EASY TOMATO ASPIC

**BBB + Fruit + Veg. + TE&A**

Simmer V-8 juice, bay leaf, and cloves 15 minutes. Strain and add lemon juice. Soften gelatin in ½ cup water and add to hot juice. Mold and chill until firm. *Serves 8–12*

- **4 cups V-8 juice**
- **1 small bay leaf**
- **3-4 whole cloves**
- **2 teaspoons lemon juice**
- **2 tablespoons unflavored gelatin**

## SOUTH SEA ISLAND MOLD

☐ **BBB + Fruit + Veg. + N&S + TE&A**

- 1 box (3 ounces) orange-pineapple-flavored gelatin
- ½ teaspoon salt
- 1 cup boiling water
- 1 can (8 ounces) unsweetened crushed pineapple, drained, juice reserved
- 1 teaspoon lemon juice
- ½ cup diced orange sections
- ½ cup chopped celery
- ¼ cup flaked coconut

Dissolve gelatin and salt in boiling water. Measure pineapple juice, adding water to make ¾ cup. Add with the lemon juice to gelatin and chill until syrupy. Fold in pineapple, orange, celery, and coconut. Chill until firm. Unmold on bed of lettuce. *Serves 4–6*

## SUMMER FIESTA SALAD

☐ **BBB + Beef + Fruit + Veg. + TE&A**

- 1 pound lean ground beef
- 2 tablespoons instant chopped onion
- ¼ teaspoon garlic powder
- Salt and pepper
- 1 teaspoon chili powder
- 1 can (8 ounces) tomato sauce
- Leaf or iceberg lettuce, torn
- Scallion, chopped
- Cucumber, peeled and diced
- Radishes, sliced
- Tomato, cut in wedges
- Carrot, grated
- Celery, diced
- Zucchini, sliced
- 1 can (16 ounces) kidney beans, drained
- 1 avocado, peeled and diced
- Santa Barbara Salsa, p. 12

Brown beef and drain off fat. Add onion flakes, garlic powder, salt and pepper to taste, chili powder, and tomato sauce. Stir and cook 5 minutes; set aside. Make salad of size desired from remaining ingredients, except salsa. If salad is for a crowd, the meat mixture can be doubled, tripled, or more. Add meat to salad. Toss and serve immediately. Pass salsa so each person may season own salad. When allowed, natural corn chips may be crushed and tossed with salad. **(+ Corn)**

This salad was a real hit at a Brownie Girl Scout Cookout. Each girl was kept busy with the vegetable and meat preparation—not a cut finger in the process, and they even liked the salad!

## CHICKEN SPECIAL

**BBB + Poultry + Fruit + Veg.**

- 1 tablespoon unflavored gelatin
- ¼ cup lemon juice
- 1 cup boiling water
- ¼ teaspoon salt
- ½ cup unsweetened pineapple juice
- 2 teaspoons grated onion
- ½ cup diced cucumber
- ½ cup diced celery
- 2 tablespoons pimiento
- 1 cup finely diced cooked chicken

Soften gelatin in lemon juice 5 minutes. Add salt to boiling water, add gelatin and stir to dissolve. Add pineapple juice and chill mixture until syrupy. Fold in remaining ingredients. Chill until firm. Unmold on crisp salad greens. *Serves 4–6*

**Variation: Summer Turkey Aspic**

Omit salt, pineapple juice, and grated onion. Soften gelatin in lemon juice. Increase boiling water to 1¾ cups, add softened gelatin and 1 teaspoon Steero Instant Chicken Flavor Bouillon Seasoning and Broth, stirring to dissolve. Replace cucumber with chopped green pepper. Increase chicken to 2 cups. (Or try turkey or tuna. **+ Fish**) Unmold aspic on watercress-lined plate. (**+ TE&A**) *Serves 4*

## CHICKEN-SPINACH SALAD

**BBB + Poultry + Fruit + Veg. + TE&A**

- 3 cups cubed cooked chicken
- 1 can (8½ ounces) water chestnuts, drained and sliced thin
- ½ cup small, thinly sliced scallions
- ½ cup Italian Dressing, p. 67
- 2 quarts fresh spinach leaves, torn into bite-size pieces
- 3 oranges, peeled and sectioned, cut into bite-size pieces

Combine chicken, water chestnuts, and scallions with dressing and chill at least 2 hours. Toss with spinach and oranges. Garnish with ¼ cup toasted sliced almonds, if allowed. (**+ N&S**) *Serves 4 generously*

**Variation:**

Use 4 cups torn spinach and 4 cups thinly sliced Chinese cabbage. Toss salad with 2 tablespoons toasted sesame seeds, if allowed. (**+ N&S**)

## CALIFORNIA CHICKEN SALAD

☐ **BBB + Poultry + Fruit + Veg. + TE&A**

- **2 cups cubed cooked chicken**
- **1 cup diced celery**
- **1 cup seeded grapes**
- **2 cups diced orange sections**
- **½ cup Bev's Salad Dressing, p. 68, or Perfect Cooked Mayonnaise, p. 67**

Combine chicken, celery, and fruits with dressing. Marinate in refrigerator 1 to 2 hours. Serve on crisp iceberg lettuce. Garnish with ½ cup toasted chopped almonds, if allowed. (**+ N&S**) *Serves 6.*

## ENCORE CHICKEN-AVOCADO SALAD

☐ **BBB + Poultry + Fruit + Veg. + TE&A**

- **4 cups diced cooked chicken**
- **¼ cup allowed oil**
- **2 tablespoons lime juice**
- **¼ teaspoon ginger**
- **1 head iceberg lettuce (save 6 nice outer leaves, shred remainder)**
- **1 cup sliced celery**
- **1 or 2 ripe avocados, peeled and sliced**

Chill and marinate chicken with oil, juice, and ginger for several hours. Place large lettuce leaf on each of 6 plates. Toss shredded lettuce with celery and divide evenly on lettuce leaves. Top with marinated chicken and avocado slices. *Serves 6*

## TUNA SPECIAL

☐ **BBB + Fish + Fruit + Veg.**

Follow recipe for Chicken Special, p. 57, substituting for chicken 1 can (6½ ounces) water-pack tuna, drained. *Serves 4–6.*

## CALIFORNIA TUNA SALAD

☐ **BBB + Fish + Fruit + Veg.**

Follow recipe for California Chicken Salad substituting for chicken 1 large can (12½ ounces) water-pack tuna, drained. *Serves 4*

## SALMON RICE SALAD

**BBB + Fish + Veg.**

- **1 can (7¾ ounces) salmon, drained and flaked**
- **2 cups cooked brown or white rice**
- **½ cup sliced celery**
- **2 tablespoons scallion, chopped**
- **½ cup cooked peas**
- **Pineapple Salad Dressing, p. 63 or Basic Oil and Vinegar Dressing, p. 64**
- **Cherry tomatoes (optional)**

Combine all ingredients except cherry tomatoes. Blend with dressing just enough to moisten well. Serve on crisp greens and garnish with cherry tomato halves. *Serves 4*

**Variation: Seaside Vegetable Rice Salad**

Replace salmon with 1 cup shrimp or crab meat. Omit celery, scallion, and peas. Replace with 1 cup finely grated cabbage, ½ cup grated carrot, ¼ cup chopped green pepper, and 2 tablespoons chopped pimiento. Toss with rice and salad dressing. Season with garlic powder or salt, if desired.

## SALMON PINEAPPLE SALAD

**BBB + Fish + Veg.**

- **1 can (7¾ ounces) salmon, drained**
- **1 can (8 ounces) unsweetened crushed pineapple or 1 cup fresh pineapple, cut fine**
- **½ cup seedless grapes, halved**
- **½ cup finely diced celery**
- **½ cup cherry tomatoes, halved (optional)**
- **⅛ teaspoon salt**
- **1 tablespoon white distilled vinegar or lemon juice, if allowed (+ Fruit)**

Combine and chill. Serve on shredded lettuce in scallop shells. Serve with toasted rice cakes. *Serves 2–3*

## SEAFOOD SALAD

**BBB + Fish + Fruit + Veg. + TE&A**

- **¾–1 cup cooked shrimp, lobster, crab, tuna, or salmon**
- **½ teaspoon grated onion**
- **1 tablespoon finely diced green pepper**
- **¼ cup finely diced celery**
- **1 tomato, diced (optional)**
- **Lemon Parsley Fish Marinade, p. 186**
- **Salad greens**

Toss fish with vegetables and dressing to moisten. Marinate several hours, stirring occasionally. Serve on crisp greens, or toss with greens, if preferred. *Serves 4*

## SALMON ON AVOCADO HALF SHELL

☐ **BBB + Fish + Fruit + Veg. + TE&A**

- 1 can (15½ ounces) salmon, chilled
- ½ cup finely diced celery
- 2 tablespoons finely sliced scallion
- 2 avocados, halved

Drain and flake salmon and mix lightly with celery and onion. Place freshly cut avocados on crisp lettuce leaf, fill center with salmon salad, and drizzle with dressing. *Serves 4*

**Variations:**

1. BAKED SALMON AVOCADO—Peel avocados, fill halves with salmon salad, and place in baking dish. Top each with crushed allowed potato chips. Bake in 375° oven 30 minutes. Serve on bed of rice.
2. CRAB AVOCADO TOSSED SALAD—Replace salmon with 1 can (6½ ounces) crab meat, rinsed, drained, and chilled. Omit scallion. Peel and slice avocados. Gently toss crab, celery, and avocados with 6 cups torn salad greens. Drizzle on desired amount of dressing. *Serves 6*

## TOMATO TUNA BOATS

☐ **BB + Fish + Fruit + Veg. + TE&A**

- 2 very large salad tomatoes
- 1 can (20 ounces) unsweetened chunk pineapple, drained
- 1 can (16 ounces) cut green beans
- 1 can (6½-7 ounces) tuna, drained and flaked
- Crisp lettuce

Cut tomatoes in half crosswise, scoop out and reserve pulp and juices, leaving fairly thick shells. Toss pulp with pineapple, green beans and tuna. Add desired amount of dressing. Fill shells and refrigerate. Place on crisp greens and drizzle with additional dressing if desired. Garnish with parsley sprigs and a toothpick glued to a triangular piece of paper to make a "sail" for each boat. *Serves 4*

## GOLDEN MARINATED SALAD

Combine and chill at least 8 hours to allow flavors to blend. *Serves 4*

**BBB + Corn + Veg.**

- **1½ cups canned whole kernel corn or golden hominy, drained**
- **⅓ cup chopped green scallions**
- **1 clove garlic, minced**
- **½ cup chopped green pepper**
- **1 large tomato, peeled, chopped, and drained**
- **2 tablespoons chopped pimiento**
- **1 tablespoon minced parsley**
- **½ teaspoon salt**
- **¼ cup allowed oil**
- **2 tablespoons white distilled vinegar**

## ROYAL NECTAR SALAD

Soften gelatin in cold water. Heat nectar to boiling and add gelatin, stirring to dissolve. Stir in concentrate until melted. Add fruit and chill. Unmold and garnish with watercress. *Serves 6*

**Variation: Apricot Mold**

Omit unflavored gelatin and cold water. Heat nectar to boiling. Dissolve 1 box (3 ounces) lemon-flavored gelatin in nectar. Stir in concentrate to dissolve. Replace grapes and mandarin oranges with ½ cup drained crushed pineapple and 1 diced banana. **(+ TE&A)**

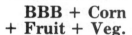

**BBB + Corn + Fruit + Veg.**

- **1 tablespoon unflavored gelatin**
- **¼ cup cold water**
- **1 cup apricot nectar**
- **1 can (6 ounces) frozen unsweetened orange juice concentrate**
- **1 cup seedless grapes, halved lengthwise**
- **1 can (11 ounces) mandarin oranges, drained**
- **Watercress**

## PINK APPLESAUCE MOLD

Soften gelatin in ¼ cup cold water. Bring applesauce, sugar, and candies to boil, stirring constantly. Add gelatin and lime juice and stir to dissolve gelatin. Mold and chill until firm. *Serves 6*

**BB + Corn + Fruit + TE&A**

- **1 tablespoon unflavored gelatin**
- **2½ cups unsweetened applesauce**
- **¼ cup sugar**
- **¼ cup red cinnamon candies**
- **1 teaspoon lime juice**

**BBB + Corn + Fruit + TE&A**

## FROZEN FRUIT SALAD

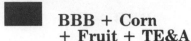

- 1 box (3 ounces) strawberry-flavored gelatin
- 1 cup boiling water
- 1 can (6 ounces) frozen lemonade concentrate
- 1 cup Dsertwhip, whipped, p. 323
- 1 can (16 ounces) Libby's Lite Fruit Cocktail, drained

Dissolve gelatin in boiling water, add concentrate, and stir until melted. Chill to syrupy stage. Whip Dsertwhip and fold into gelatin along with fruit. Pour into 9 x 5-inch bread pan and freeze until firm. Cut into bars or slices. *Serves 6–8*

**BBB + Corn + Fruit + N&S + TE&A**

## PARTY PINK FRUIT SALAD

- 2 boxes (3 ounces each) cherry-flavored gelatin
- 1 cup hot water
- 1 can (16 ounces) cranberry sauce, jellied or whole berry
- 1 cup crushed pineapple, drained, juice reserved
- 4 mashed bananas
- 1 cup Dsertwhip, whipped

Dissolve gelatin in hot water. Add cranberry sauce, blend well, and cool slightly. Measure pineapple juice and add water to make 1 cup. Add juice, pineapple, and bananas to gelatin and chill until syrupy. Fold whipped Dsertwhip into gelatin mixture. Put mixture in a fancy 2-quart mold or shallow baking pan (9 x 12 x 2½ inches). *Serves 8–10*

**BBB + Corn + N&S + TE&A**

## CRANBERRY FANTASY

- 2 cups raw cranberries, ground
- 2 unpeeled apples, diced fine
- ¾ cup sugar
- 1 can (8 ounces) crushed pineapple
- 3 cups miniature marshmallows
- ½ cup walnuts, chopped
- 1 cup Dsertwhip, whipped

Combine all ingredients except nuts and Dsertwhip. Cover and chill overnight. Fold in nuts and whipped Dsertwhip. Serve in lettuce cups. *Serves 8–10*

# SALAD DRESSINGS

## PLAIN APPLE DRESSING

**BBB**

Spoon out desired amount of concentrate. Stir into fruit salad made from canned, drained allowed fruits. When allowed, use as the sweetening and dressing for diced fresh fruit salad. Refreeze any concentrate not used.

**Frozen pure apple juice concentrate, no sugar added**

## PINEAPPLE SALAD DRESSING

**BBB**

Serve on lettuce wedges or on drained allowed fruits. *Makes 1½ cups*

- **⅔ cup allowed oil**
- **¼ cup white distilled vinegar**
- **½ cup unsweetened pineapple juice or unsweetened crushed pineapple**
- **Pinch of salt**

## TOFU DRESSING I

**BBB**

Process tofu, vinegar, and salt in blender until smooth. Add water, 1 tablespoon at a time, until consistency of sour cream. Very soft tofu may not need water at all. Very dry types may require up to 6 tablespoons water. Chilling will help firm up dressing. Serve as dressing, dip, or mayonnaise. *Makes 1½ cups*

**Variation: Tofu Cucumber Dressing**

Peel and chunk one small cucumber and puree in blender. After Tofu Dressing is chilled, fold in cucumber to serve on lettuce wedges or on alfalfa sprouts. *Makes 1¾ cups*

*Note:* Tofu may contain minute amount of lime or lemon. Do not use if highly sensitive to citrus.

- **1⅓ cups tofu (½ of 16–20 ounce package), drained and washed**
- **¼ cup white distilled vinegar**
- **¾ teaspoon salt**

## BASIC OIL AND VINEGAR DRESSING

**BBB**

- **½ cup allowed oil**
- **⅓ cup white distilled vinegar**
- **½ teaspoon salt**

Combine in jar with tight-fitting lid and shake well. *Makes ¾ cup*

## BBB SOYANNAISE

**BBB**

- **¼ cup Ener-G SoyQuik**
- **½ teaspoon salt**
- **½ cup allowed oil**
- **1 tablespoon white distilled vinegar**

Whiz ½ cup water, SoyQuik, and salt in blender. Add oil in fine stream with blender running. Process until thick and all of oil is incorporated. Stir in vinegar or blend briefly. Mixture may thin when you add vinegar, but don't worry. Refrigerate overnight and it will match consistency of real mayonnaise. *Makes 1 cup*

## BBB COOKED MAYONNAISE

**BBB**

- **2 tablespoons rice flour**
- **½ teaspoon salt**
- **½ cup allowed oil**
- **1-2 tablespoons white distilled vinegar to taste**

Stir flour into ¼ cup water in saucepan. Add ¼ cup more water, keeping mixture lump-free. Add salt and heat slowly, stirring constantly, until very thick. Cool and place mixture in mixer bowl. With electric mixer on high setting, add oil in fine stream. Dribble in vinegar, beating between additions, until taste is perfect. Refrigerate. *Makes 1 cup*

## JIFFY OIL AND LEMON DRESSING

**BBB + Fruit**

- **½ cup allowed oil**
- **¼ cup lemon juice**
- **½ teaspoon salt**

Combine in jar and shake well. *Makes ¾ cup*

**Variation:**

When allowed, add to Basic Oil and Vinegar Dressing, p. 64, or to Jiffy Oil and Lemon Dressing any of the following: 1 tablespoon chopped parsley, 1 teaspoon dried thyme, ¼ teaspoon each dried basil and rosemary, ⅛ teaspoon dried oregano, ½ teaspoon dried dill weed. **(+ TE&A)**

## GREEN GODDESS DRESSING

**BBB + Fruit + Veg.** ☐

**Tofu Avocado Dip, p. 11**

Prepare dip and use as is, or thin with water to consistency desired. Serve on salad of choice.

## GARLIC DRESSING

**BBB + Fruit + Veg.** ☐

- **1 cup allowed oil**
- **¼ cup lime juice**
- **¼ cup lemon juice**
- **2 cloves garlic, crushed**
- **½ teaspoon salt**

Mix well and chill. *Makes 1 cup*

## NUT DRESSING

**BBB + Fruit + N&S** ☐

- **½ cup raw nuts (peanuts, cashews, almonds, or pecans)**
- **¼ cup lemon juice**
- **⅛ teaspoon paprika**
- **½ teaspoon salt**

Liquefy nuts with ½ cup water in blender. When smooth, add remaining ingredients. Serve over apple and banana salad or Waldorf salad. *Makes 1 cup*

## POLYNESIAN FRUIT DRESSING

**BBB + Fruit + N&S** ☐

- **2 tablespoons allowed oil or margarine**
- **2 tablespoons rice flour**
- **¼ teaspoon salt**
- **2 tablespoons lemon juice**
- **½ cup unsweetened crushed pineapple, undrained**
- **1 medium banana, mashed**
- **⅓ cup flaked coconut**

Warm oil or margarine and stir in rice flour and salt. Over medium heat, add 1 cup water, a little at a time, stirring constantly. Cook until mixture boils and thickens. Remove from heat, cool, and stir in remaining ingredients. Chill and use on fresh or canned fruit salads. *Makes 2 cups*

## KANSAS SLAW DRESSING

**BBB + TE&A** ☐

- **⅓ cup white distilled vinegar**
- **½ teaspoon salt**
- **½ teaspoon dry mustard**
- **⅔ cup allowed oil**
- **¼ cup sugar**
- **Dash of pepper**

Combine all ingredients in jar, shake well, and chill. *Makes 1 cup*

## TANGERINE DRESSING

☐ **BBB + Fruit + TE&A**

- **⅓ cup freshly squeezed tangerine juice**
- **1 tablespoon freshly squeezed lemon juice**
- **½ teaspoon each salt, dried thyme, and chili powder**
- **2 tablespoons allowed oil**

Combine all ingredients in tightly covered jar and shake well. Serve on tossed salad of torn salad greens, oranges (or other citrus, sectioned and diced), avocado, and red onion or scallions. *Makes ½ cup*

## CITRUS HONEY DRESSING

☐ **BBB + Fruit + TE&A**

- **⅓ cup allowed oil**
- **⅓ cup lime or lemon juice**
- **⅓ cup honey**
- **1 teaspoon grated orange peel**

Mix well and chill. Serve with fruit salad or fruit platter. *Makes 1 cup*

**Variation: Celery Seed Dressing**
Omit orange peel and replace with ½ teaspoon celery seeds. Serve on crisp greens. (+ **N&S**)

## RUBY FRENCH DRESSING

☐ **BBB + Veg. + TE&A**

- **1 can (8 ounces) tomato sauce**
- **½ teaspoon salt**
- **1 teaspoon dry mustard**
- **1 clove garlic, crushed**
- **½ cup allowed oil**
- **⅓ cup white distilled vinegar**
- **1 teaspoon onion powder**
- **½ teaspoon paprika**
- **⅛ teaspoon pepper**

Combine in jar with tight cover. Shake well and chill. *Makes 2 cups*

## DILL DRESSING

☐ **BBB + Veg. + TE&A**

- **⅔ cup allowed oil**
- **¼ cup white distilled vinegar**
- **½ teaspoon salt**
- **¾ teaspoon dried dill weed**
- **½ teaspoon instant minced onion**
- **⅛ teaspoon garlic powder**
- **⅛ teaspoon pepper**

Combine, mix well, and chill. Use on tossed green salad, coleslaw, or lettuce wedges. *Makes 1 cup*

## PERFECT COOKED MAYONNAISE

**BBB + Veg. + TE&A**

**2 tablespoons rice flour**
**¼ teaspoon salt**
**½ teaspoon onion powder**
**¼ teaspoon garlic salt**
**⅛ teaspoon paprika**
**½ teaspoon dry mustard**
**½ cup allowed oil**
**1 tablespoon white distilled vinegar**

Blend flour with ¼ cup water in saucepan, then add ¼cup more water. Add salt and cook over low heat, stirring constantly until very thick. Cool. Place mixture in electric mixer bowl, add seasonings, and beat on high setting while adding oil in fine stream. Mixture should be thick by the time all oil has been incorporated. Add vinegar slowly while continuing to beat. Refrigerate. This has good flavor and can be used in any way that ordinary mayonnaise is used. *Makes 1 cup*

## REMARKABLE SOYANNAISE

**BBB + Veg. + TE&A**

**¼ cup Ener-G SoyQuik**
**¼ teaspoon salt**
**½ teaspoon onion salt**
**¼ teaspoon garlic powder**
**⅛ teaspoon paprika**
**½ teaspoon dry mustard**
**½ cup allowed oil**
**1 tablespoon white distilled vinegar**

Liquefy SoyQuik, ½ cup water, and seasonings in blender. Add oil in fine stream, blender running. When thick, stir in vinegar and refrigerate overnight. *Makes 1 cup*

**Variation:**

This may be made with regular soy powder, but it will have a taste and texture that may not be as pleasing as dressing made with SoyQuik. If you want to try for yourself, increase soy powder slightly, about 1 tablespoon, and decrease water to ⅓ cup.

## ITALIAN DRESSING

**BBB + Fruit + Veg. + TE&A**

**¾ cup allowed oil**
**⅓ cup white distilled vinegar**
**2 tablespoons lemon juice**
**2 cloves garlic, crushed**
**½ teaspoon salt**
**1 teaspoon dry mustard**
**½ teaspoon Italian seasonings, crushed**
**Dash of pepper**

Combine and chill. Shake well before using. *Makes 1¼ cups*

## BEV'S SALAD DRESSING

**BBB + Fruit + Veg. + TE&A**

- ½ cup allowed oil
- 3 tablespoons lemon juice
- ½ teaspoon garlic salt
- 1 teaspoon sugar
- ¼ teaspoon paprika
- ¼ teaspoon salt
- Dash of pepper
- ½ teaspoon dried parsley
- 1 clove garlic, crushed

Combine all ingredients with ¼ cup water in jar with tight cover. Shake well and chill. Shake again before serving on tossed green salad. *Makes ¾ cup*

## TOFU DRESSING II

**BBB + Fruit + Veg. + TE&A**

- 1⅓ cups tofu (½ of 16–20 ounce box), drained
- 2 cloves garlic, crushed
- 1 tablespoon grated onion
- 1 teaspoon dried parsley
- 3 tablespoons lemon juice
- 2 tablespoons allowed oil
- ¼ teaspoon salt
- Dash of pepper
- ¼ teaspoon paprika

Process all ingredients in blender. Add water, 1 tablespoon at a time, only if needed to obtain creamy-thick consistency. Use as dressing, but may be used as a dip also. *Makes 1½ cups*

## POPPY SEED DRESSING

**BBB + Fruit + N&S + TE&A**

- ¾ cup allowed oil
- ⅓ cup fresh lemon juice
- 1 teaspoon dry mustard
- ½ teaspoon salt
- 1 teaspoon finely minced onion
- ½ tablespoon poppy seeds

Combine all ingredients in jar with tight cover. Shake well and chill. *Makes 1 cup*

**Variation:**

Combine all ingredients except oil and seeds in blender. Process until smooth. Add oil in fine stream while blender is running. Add poppy seeds and blend briefly. *Makes 1¼ cups*

## TOASTED SESAME DRESSING

**BBB + Fruit + N&S + TE&A**

- **⅓ cup unsweetened pineapple juice**
- **¼ cup lime juice**
- **2 tablespoons allowed oil**
- **½ teaspoon salt**
- **¼ teaspoon paprika**
- **1 tablespoon toasted sesame seeds**

Combine all ingredients except sesame seeds. Toast seeds in non-stick skillet, stirring constantly until light brown. Add to dressing. *Makes ¾ cup*

## ALMONNAISE

**BBB + Veg. + N&S + TE&A**

- **¼ cup raw blanched almonds**
- **¼ teaspoon instant minced onion**
- **¼ teaspoon garlic powder**
- **¼ teaspoon salt**
- **½ teaspoon dry mustard**
- **½ cup allowed oil**
- **1½ tablespoons white distilled vinegar**

Purée nuts with ¼ cup water and seasonings in blender. Stop motor and scrape lid and sides of blender to push mixture down into blades. With blender set on high setting, add oil in fine stream through feeder tube in lid. When half of oil is used, scrape lid and sides again. Continue adding oil until all is incorporated and almonnaise is thick. Add vinegar and blend briefly. Refrigerate several hours for flavors to blend and mixture to thicken. *Makes 1 cup*

## SLAW DRESSING

**BBB + Fruit + Veg. + N&S + TE&A**

- **1 cup Perfect Cooked Mayonnaise, p. 67**
- **1 tablespoon lemon juice**
- **½ teaspoon whole mustard seeds**
- **¼ teaspoon pepper**
- **¼ teaspoon celery seeds**

Blend all ingredients well. Toss with slaw or potato salad. *Makes 1 cup*

## RICE VINEGAR DRESSING

**BBB + Mold**

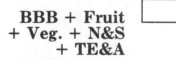

Rice vinegar is fermented and may be substituted for white distilled vinegar only if mold causes no allergic reactions in you. When proven trouble-free, rice vinegar's flavor is distinctive enough to provide taste variety as a change from white distilled vinegar and lemon juice. Dash it on salads and serve, add oil and seasonings as allowed, or substitute it for the tart ingredient in any of the dressing recipes.

## CREAMY GARLIC DRESSING

**BBB + Oats + Corn + Fruit + Veg. + TE&A**

- 3 tablespoons lemon juice
- ¾ cup allowed oil
- ⅔ cup Mocha Mix or Milk-Free Coffee Creamer
- 4 cloves garlic
- ¼ cup oatmeal
- 1 teaspoon salt
- ½ teaspoon sugar
- ¼ teaspoon pepper
- ½ teaspoon paprika

Liquefy all ingredients in blender. Let stand 10 minutes to allow oatmeal to thicken slightly. Process again briefly. Chill. *Makes 1¾ cups*

## CREAMY FRENCH DRESSING

**BBB + Corn + Fruit + Veg. + TE&A**

- 2 teaspoons salt
- 1 tablespoon dry mustard
- ½ teaspoon pepper
- 1 teaspoon paprika
- ¼ cup sugar
- 1 box (1¾ ounces) powdered pectin
- ½ cup lemon juice
- 1 teaspoon Jan-U-Wine Soy Sauce
- 1 teaspoon instant chopped onion
- 1 clove garlic
- 1 can (8 ounces) tomato sauce
- 1½ cups allowed oil

Combine in blender all ingredients except oil. Process until well blended. Add half of oil with blender running. Add remaining oil and process until dressing is creamy. Chill. *Makes 3½ cups*

# Lamb

## ROAST LAMB

**BBB**

Wipe roast with damp cloth or paper towel. Place, fat side up, in roasting pan. Do not add water. Insert meat thermometer in center of roast, making sure thermometer does not touch bone. Roast uncovered in 325° oven until meat thermometer reaches 175° for medium, or 180° for well done. Plan for roast to be done 15 minutes before serving time. Remove and keep warm. During this time make Favorite Rich Gravy, p. 185, using brown lamb drippings in roaster.

Bone-in roasts, allow ¼–½ pound per serving: ¼–⅓ pound for boneless.

Chart times are given for roasts taken from refrigerator. If desired, roast may be rubbed with salt or garlic salt or powder when allowed. Or cut small gashes in roast with point of knife and insert slivers of fresh garlic when allowed. **(+ Veg.)**

Glaze last 15 minutes of roasting time with ¾ cup Homemade Cranberry Jelly, p. 191.

## ROASTING CHART

| Kind | Weight | Hours: medium | Hours: well done |
|---|---|---|---|
| Leg of lamb | 4 to 6 lbs. | 2 to 3 | 2½ to 3½ |
| Leg of lamb | 6 to 8 lbs. | 3 to 4 | 3½ to 4¾ |
| Crown of lamb, rib roast | 3 to 4 lbs. | 2 to 2½ | 2½ to 3 |
| Crown of lamb, rib roast | 4 to 6 lbs. | 2½ to 3½ | 3 to 4 |
| Shoulder roast, bone-in | 4 to 5 lbs. | 2 to 3 | 2½ to 3½ |
| Shoulder or leg roast, boned and rolled | 3 to 4 lbs. | 2 to 2½ | 2½ to 3 |

BBB

## LAMB PILAF

1 tablespoon allowed oil
1½ tablespoons rice flour
1 cup hot water
½ teaspoon salt
1 cup cooked rice (wild, brown, or white)
1 cup finely diced cooked lamb

Blend oil and flour in saucepan and stir over low heat until brown. Mix in hot water and salt. Boil 2 minutes. Add rice and lamb and heat through. *Serves 3*

BBB

## LAMB FRIED RICE

Leftover cooked lamb
Cooked rice
Grated carrots
Frozen green peas
Allowed oil or lamb drippings
Diced tofu (optional)

Mix lamb, rice, carrots, peas, and tofu. Fry in allowed oil or lamb drippings until browned and vegetables cooked. Season with salt. Lamb gravy thickened with rice flour may be added, if desired.

BBB

## LAMB ROLLS

Thin slices lamb from shoulder or leg roast
Whole carrots or strips of sweet potato
Salt to taste
Lamb broth or water
Boiled Brown Rice, p. 245

Wrap lamb slices around whole carrots or sweet potato strips. Tie or secure with wooden toothpicks. Simmer in water or lamb broth until fork barely penetrates carrot when tested or potato is cooked through. Serve on bed of boiled brown rice. Spoon broth over rice.

BBB

## LAMB PATTIES

1 pound ground lamb
1 tablespoons rice flakes (optional)
Salt to taste

Have butcher grind pure lamb or else grind at home. Dealer-prepared lamb sometimes contains wheat, eggs, or milk.

Mix all ingredients, shape into patties, and broil or pan fry in allowed oil. *Makes 4 patties*

## LAMB LOAF I

BBB

Combine all ingredients. Add water if necessary to moisten in order to shape into loaf. Place in loaf pan (7 x 3½ x 2-inch) and bake in 350° oven for 1-1¼ hours. *Serves 2-4*

- **1 pound ground lamb (see Lamb Patties, p. 72)**
- **¼ cup shredded carrot**
- **¼ cup cooked rice or 2 tablespoons rice flour**
- **1 teaspoon salt**

## LAMB LOAF II

BBB

Mix all ingredients with ¾ cup water. Shape into loaf pan (7 x 3½ x 2-inch) oiled with allowed oil and bake in 325° oven 1 hour. Serve hot or cold. *Serves 2-4*

- **1 pound ground lamb (see Lamb Patties, p. 72)**
- **½ teaspoon salt**
- **1 cup grated raw sweet potato**
- **¾ cup Minute Rice**

## BASIC LAMB CASSEROLE

BBB

Brown ground lamb and carrots. Pour off fat. Add salt, 1½ cups water, and rice. Bring to boil, cover, remove from heat and let stand 5 minutes. Pour into 6-cup casserole and set aside. Toast rice flakes in allowed oil until brown. Sprinkle toasted flakes over top of casserole. Bake in 350° oven 45 minutes. *Serves 4-6*

- **1 pound ground lamb (see Lamb Patties, p. 72)**
- **2 carrots, cut in rounds**
- **½ teaspoon salt**
- **1½ cups Minute Rice**
- **½ cup rice flakes**
- **1 tablespoon allowed oil**

## LAMBURGER BROILER SUPPER

BBB

Form lamb, salt, and water into 4 patties. Place on broiler rack along with potato halves. Brush potatoes with oil. Broil 3 inches from flame 5 minutes or until patties are well browned. Turn patties. Brush pears with oil and add to rack. Continue broiling 5 to 10 minutes or until meat is cooked and potatoes and pears are browned. Fill pear centers with jelly. Arrange all on hot platter. *Serves 4*

- **1½ pounds ground lamb (see Lamb Patties, p. 72)**
- **1 teaspoon salt**
- **½ cup water or milk substitute**
- **4 potatoes, cooked in jackets and cut in half**
- **Allowed oil as needed**
- **2 firm pears, cut in half and cored**
- **2 tablespoons Homemade Cranberry Jelly, p. 191**

## LAMB KABOBS

**BBB**

- Lean lamb, cut in 1½-inch cubes
- Sweet potato, cut in cubes
- Carrots, cut in rounds
- Fresh pineapple, cut in chunks, or canned unsweetened chunk pineapple
- Allowed oil

Alternate ingredients on skewers. Roll in allowed oil. Broil 3 inches from flame approximately 25 minutes or until meat is cooked. Season with salt as desired.

## LAMB AND SWEETS

**BBB**

- ½ pound lamb, cut in cubes
- 3 tablespoons rice flour
- ¾ teaspoon salt
- 1 tablespoon allowed oil
- 1½ cups boiling water
- 1½ cups diced peeled sweet potatoes

Roll lamb in mixed flour and salt. Brown in oil. Add water, cover, and simmer 1 hour. Add potatoes, cover, and simmer 25 minutes more or until tender. Make gravy with liquid and rice flour left from dredging lamb. *Serves 3*

## BRAISED LAMB SHANKS

**BBB**

- 2 lamb shanks
- ½ teaspoon salt
- 2 tablespoons allowed oil
- ¾ cup hot water
- 2 tablespoons rice flour
- ½ cup cold water

Sprinkle meat with salt. Brown in oil. Pour off extra fat. Add hot water, cover, reduce heat. Simmer 1½ to 2 hours or until tender. Remove meat from broth, add flour and cold water blended together. Stir constantly until thickened. (Good served with Soy Grits Cereal, p. 248.) *Serves 2*

## ROSY LAMB SHANKS TERRY

**BBB**

- ½ cup rice flour or mixture of rice and potato flours
- 2–3 lamb shanks
- ½–1 teaspoon salt
- 1 cup whole raw cranberries
- 2–3 cups steamed rice (½–¾ cup uncooked rice)

Roll shanks in flour and brown in allowed oil. Arrange in baking dish. Surround and cover with whole raw cranberries. Add 1 cup water, cover and bake in 325° oven 1½ to 2 hours or until meat is tender. Remove fat from drippings. Thicken defatted drippings with rice flour to serve over steamed rice. *Serves 2 or 3*

## BRAISED LAMB HEARTS

**BBB**

**2 lamb hearts**
**½ cup rice flour**
**2 tablespoons potato flour, optional**
**½ teaspoon salt**
**1 tablespoon allowed oil**

Cut hearts in half lengthwise, remove all coarse fibers, and wash hearts in cold water. Combine flours and salt in clean paper bag. Drop hearts into bag, 2 pieces at a time, and shake until meat is completely coated with flour. Heat oil in skillet. Add hearts and brown over high heat until crisp and golden. Lower heat, add ¾ cup water, and cover. Cook over low heat 1 to 1½ hours, checking water occasionally. Add water if necessary. Hearts can be pierced easily with fork when done. If desired, add peeled, quartered potatoes for last 30 minutes of cooking time. *Serves 2*

**Variations:**

1. HASH—Lift hearts from broth, chop, and set aside. Add to remaining broth diced potatoes and carrots. Add water if needed to cook vegetables until done. When vegetables are tender, return chopped heart to pan and mix. If thickening is needed, use seasoned flour from bag in which meat was coated. Mix with a little water and stir into bubbling broth until thickened.
2. SOUP—Lift meat from broth and dice. Add to broth any allowed vegetables and the amount of water desired. Cook covered until vegetables are almost tender. Add diced meat. Thicken, if desired, with mixture from coating bag and adjust seasoning.
3. SALAD—Slice thin or julienne lamb hearts and use on mixed green salad or in sandwiches.
4. SANDWICH SPREAD—Grind cooked lamb hearts. Mix with Tofu Dressing I, p. 63. Spread on toasted allowed bread or on crisp heated rice cakes.

*Note:* Potato flour is used because it makes a lovely brown coating. You may use all rice flour, if you prefer, or use 2 tablespoons soy flour and add rice flour to make ½ cup.

**BBB**

## LAMB CHOPS WITH CRIMSON GRAVY

- 4 lamb shoulder chops, ¾ inch thick
- 1 tablespoon allowed oil
- 2 tablespoons rice flour
- ½ teaspoon salt
- 2 tablespoons Homemade Cranberry Jelly, p. 191

Brown chops in oil, reduce heat, and cook until chops are done, 12 to 15 minutes. Remove from skillet and keep chops hot. Pour excess fat from skillet, retaining 2 tablespoons. Stir in flour and loosen brown bits from bottom of pan. Slowly add 1 cup water, stirring constantly until gravy is thickened and smooth. Add salt and cranberry jelly, stirring until well blended. Remove from heat. Serve chops and gravy with Boiled Brown Rice, p. 245 or with mashed potatoes. *Serves 4*

**BBB**

## LAMB LIVER SLICES

- ½ pound lamb liver sliced thin
- Boiling water
- ½ cup rice flour or ⅓ cup rice flour and 1 tablespoon potato flour
- ¼ teaspoon salt

Scald liver with boiling water, cover, and set aside 12 minutes. Drain. Coat slices with mixture of flour and salt and fry in allowed oil 2 minutes each side or until brown. *Serves 2*

**BBB**

## LAMB STEW

- 2 pounds lamb chops, cut in cubes (save bones for BBB Meat Stock I, p. 18)
- 1 tablespoon allowed oil
- 4 cups hot water
- ½ teaspoon salt
- ½ cup sliced okra or chopped chard
- 3 carrots, cut in rounds
- 2 cups cubed sweet potatoes
- 1 cup frozen green peas
- ¼ cup rice flour

Brown meat in oil, add hot water and salt. Cover, reduce heat, and simmer 1½ hours. Add okra, carrots, and sweet potatoes. Cook another 30 minutes. Add frozen peas and cook 5 minutes more. Mix rice flour with enough water to make thin paste. Add to stew and stir constantly until thickened. *Serves 6*

## LAMB RIBLETS IN SAUCE

**BBB + Fruit + Veg.** ☐

- 1 pound lamb riblets
- Salt to taste
- ¼ cup rice flour
- 1 tablespoon potato flour
- 1 tablespoon allowed oil
- ½ cup orange juice
- 1 teaspoon grated orange peel
- 1 teaspoon sugar
- Cooked lima beans

Drop lamb riblets into paper bag in which you have mixed rice and potato flours and salt. Shake to coat meat well, remove, and reserve remaining flour. Brown riblets in oil. Add orange juice and cover. Simmer 30 minutes. Blend orange peel, sugar, 1 tablespoon of mixed flours, and ½ cup water. Stir into skillet and cook 5 minutes to thicken. Serve with lima beans. *Serves 3–4*

## MARINATED LAMB KABOBS

**BBB + Fruit + Veg.** ☐

- 2 pounds boneless leg or shoulder of lamb, cut in 1-inch cubes
- 2 oranges, sectioned
- 1 can (16 ounces) pearl onions, drained
- 1 clove garlic, crushed
- 2 tablespoons allowed oil
- 1 cup Basic Cranberry Sauce, p. 191
- ½ cup orange juice
- 2 tablespoons lemon juice
- Hot cooked rice

Alternate lamb, orange sections, and onions on 4 to 6 skewers. Blend all other ingredients except rice with ¼cup water. Pour over skewers and let stand 1 hour at room temperature. Broil 3 inches from flame 5 minutes on each side. Heat any remaining marinade and serve over kabobs on rice. *Serves 4–6*

## LAMB SHANK RAGOUT

**BBB + Veg.** ☐

- 4 lamb shanks
- 3 tablespoons allowed oil
- 4 stalks celery cut in 2-inch diagonal slices
- 2 large onions, sliced
- 3 large cloves garlic, crushed or run through press
- 4 medium carrots split and cut in 2-inch diagonal slices
- 1 teaspoon salt
- 2 cups tomato juice
- 1 cup rice

Brown shanks in oil and pour off excess fat. Add celery, onions, garlic, carrots, salt, juice, and 1 cup water. Cover and simmer 1½ hours or until lamb is tender. Stir rice into pan juices, arranging shanks on top. Cover and return to boil. Reduce heat and simmer 25 minutes longer. *Serves 4*

☐ **BBB + Veg.**

## LAMB AND BEAN GOULASH

- **1 pound lamb neck or shank meat (save bones for BBB Meat Stock 1, p. 18)**
- **1 teaspoon salt**
- **¼ cup rice flour**
- **1 tablespoon potato flour**
- **2 tablespoons allowed oil**
- **1 can (16 ounces) tomatoes**
- **1 green pepper, diced**
- **1 can (16 ounces) green beans or 1 package (10 ounces) frozen lima beans**

Cut lamb into 1-inch cubes. Mix salt and flours in paper bag, add lamb, and shake to coat meat. Brown meat in oil and drain off fat. Add tomatoes and pepper. Cover and cook slowly 2 hours. Add water as needed. Combine with beans and continue cooking 15 minutes. *Serves 4*

☐ **BBB + Veg.**

## FAVORITE LAMB LOAF

- **2 pounds ground lamb**
- **½ cup Cream of Rice, uncooked**
- **1 stalk celery, sliced**
- **2 tablespoons diced green pepper**
- **3 tablespoons chopped parsley or 1 tablespoon dried**
- **1 small onion, chopped**
- **1 teaspoon salt**
- **1 can (6 ounces) tomato paste)**

Ask butcher to grind lean lamb especially for you. Ground lamb as packaged may contain wheat, egg, or milk. Combine lamb, Cream of Rice, celery, green pepper, parsley, onion, salt, ⅓ cup tomato paste, and ⅔ cup water. Shape into loaf. Place in 1½-quart loaf pan. With finger, make three diagonal indentations across loaf. Blend remaining tomato paste with ⅔ cup water and pour into indentations. Bake in 350° oven for 1¼ to 1½ hours. *Serves 6*

☐ **BBB + Fruit + Veg. + TE&A**

## MARINATED LAMB CHOPS

- **4 lamb chops 1 inch thick**
- **½ cup lemon juice**
- **¼ cup allowed oil**
- **1 clove garlic, crushed**
- **½ teaspoon salt**
- **½ teaspoon pepper**
- **⅛ teaspoon cinnamon**
- **⅛ teaspoon ground cloves**
- **1 bay leaf**

Marinate lamb chops in a mixture of all other ingredients prepared as follows: Combine juice and oil with seasonings in saucepan over moderate heat. Stir to blend, then simmer 10 minutes. Pour over chops, cover, and refrigerate 4 hours or overnight. Broil chops 3 inches from flame 7 minutes, turn, and broil 6 to 9 minutes longer. If preferred, broil on outdoor grill. Baste with marinade while cooking. *Serves 4*

## GLAZED BAKED LAMB

**BBB + Fruit + TE&A**

- **3 pounds lamb breast, cut in serving pieces**
- **Salt and pepper to taste**
- **1 can (8 ounces) unsweetened crushed pineapple**
- **¼ cup honey**
- **¼ teaspoon cinnamon**
- **Dash of allspice**
- **1 orange, peeled and sliced**

Roast lamb pieces on rack in shallow roasting pan 1 hour at 350°. Drain off drippings. Combine all other ingredients and pour over lamb in roasting pan. Bake 1 hour longer or until lamb is tender and glazed. *Serves 3–4*

**Variation: Glaze II**

Prepare glaze by mixing ¾ cup honey and the juice and peel of 1 orange. Roast lamb 1 hour and drain off fat. Increase oven temperature to 400°. Brush meat with glaze at 15-minute intervals during 1 hour more of roasting time. *Serves 4*

## LAMB BUNDLES

**BBB + Veg. + TE&A**

- **4 lamb chops, trimmed of excess fat**
- **½ teaspoon garlic salt**
- **2 sweet potatoes, peeled and sliced ½ inch thick**
- **4 small zucchini, quartered lengthwise**
- **Paprika to garnish**

Cut 4 large squares of heavy duty aluminum foil. Place chop on each and season with garlic salt. Top with vegetables and sprinkle with paprika. Wrap tightly and place in 9 x 13-inch pan. Bake 1½ hours in 350° oven or until chops are tender. Serve in foil. *Serves 4*

## ITALIAN LAMB STEW

**BBB + Veg. + TE&A**

- **2 pounds boneless lamb shoulder, cubed**
- **1 teaspoon salt**
- **1 teaspoon dried basil**
- **⅛ teaspoon pepper**
- **1 can (16 ounces) stewed tomatoes**
- **1 medium onion, chopped**
- **2 cups sliced celery**
- **1 medium eggplant, cubed**
- **1 pound zucchini, sliced**
- **1 can (16 ounces) green beans**
- **1 package (10 ounces) frozen whole okra**
- **2 medium carrots, sliced**
- **Hot cooked rice**

Brown lamb and add seasonings, stewed tomatoes, onion, and celery. Cover and simmer slowly 1½ hours. Add remaining vegetables and cook 30 to 45 minutes or until lamb and vegetables are tender. Serve on bed of rice. *Serves 4*

# Rabbit

## BBB

1 frying rabbit, cut in serving pieces
¼ cup allowed oil
½ cup rice flour
3 tablespoons potato flour
½ teaspoon salt

## PAN FRIED RABBIT

Blend flours and salt in clean paper bag. Drop in pieces of rabbit and shake to coat. Brown over high heat in allowed oil, reduce heat, cover, and cook 30 to 45 minutes. Uncover to crisp coating. *Serves 4*

**Variation:**

Dip each rabbit piece in oil. Drain. Mix rice and potato flours and salt. Roll oiled rabbit pieces in flour mixture. Arrange in oiled shallow baking dish, leaving space between pieces. Cover tightly with foil. Bake in 400° oven 45 to 60 minutes. Uncover and continue baking 15 minutes or until brown. *Serves 4*

## BBB + Fruit + Veg.

2 pounds rabbit, cut in serving pieces
⅓ cup rice flour
2 tablespoons potato flour
¾ teaspoon salt
2 tablespoons allowed oil
1 can (14½ ounces) unsweetened sliced pineapple, drained, juice reserved
1 large onion, chopped
Vegetable or BBB Meat Stock I, p. 18
1 package (10 ounces) frozen green peas, defrosted enough to separate

## ISLAND HOPPER

Shake rabbit, flours, and ½ teaspoon salt in paper bag to coat rabbit evenly. Brown in oil and remove from skillet. Add pineapple slices and onion separately to oil in skillet and brown. Place rabbit and onion in casserole. Add stock to pineapple juice to make 2 cups, pour into casserole. Sprinkle with ¼ teaspoon salt. Bake in 350° oven 30 minutes. Top with frozen peas, lay pineapple slices on top, and bake another 15 minutes. *Serves 4*

## CONTINENTAL RABBIT

**BBB + Veg. + N&S + TE&A**

- 3–4 pounds rabbit cut in serving pieces
- ⅓ cup rice flour
- 2 tablespoons potato flour
- ½ teaspoon salt
- Dash of pepper
- 2 tablespoons allowed oil
- 2 cups Vegetable Stock, p. 18 or BBB Meat Stock I, p. 18
- 1 tablespoon instant chopped onion
- 1 tablespoon dried parsley
- ¼ teaspoon celery seeds
- ⅛ teaspoon thyme
- 1⅓ cups Minute Rice
- Dash of paprika

Shake rabbit in flours, salt, and pepper in paper bag to coat meat evenly. Brown in oil and remove from skillet. Stir stock, onion, parsley, celery seeds, and thyme into pan. Cook, stirring, to a boil. Spread rice in 6-cup casserole and add seasoned flours from bag. Stir in liquid from skillet until all rice is moistened. Top with browned rabbit pieces. Pour ½ cup water over top and sprinkle on paprika. Cover and bake in 375° oven 30 to 45 minutes or until rabbit is tender. *Serves 4–6*

## RABBIT CONFETTI

**BBB + Veg. + TE&A**

- 3 pounds rabbit, cut in serving pieces
- 2 tablespoons allowed oil
- 1½ teaspoons salt
- ⅛ teaspoon pepper
- ½ cup chopped onion
- 1 clove garlic, minced
- 1 can (16 ounces) tomatoes
- 1 can (8 ounces) tomato sauce
- 1 can (6 ounces) tomato paste
- 2 tablespoons chopped parsley
- 1 teaspoon basil or Italian seasoning
- Cooked brown or white rice or (when corn has been tested and is allowed) wheat-free corn pasta (+ Corn)

Brown rabbit in oil and sprinkle on salt and pepper. Remove rabbit from skillet, add onion and garlic, and sauté until brown. Stir together in large pot all other ingredients except rice. Add browned rabbit pieces, sautéed onion and garlic, and cover. Cook over low heat 1 to 1½ hours or until meat is tender, adding water if necessary during cooking. Serve over rice. *Serves 4–6*

# Beef and Veal

## BASIC POT ROAST

BBB + Beef

3-5 pounds chuck, blade, or round-bone beef roast
1 tablespoon allowed oil or fat cut from meat
Salt to taste

Heat heavy skillet and rub with allowed oil or with fat from roast. Sear meat on both sides, salting if desired. Cover tightly, reduce heat, and cook slowly until tender, 2½ to 3½ hours. Peeled, halved potatoes and quartered carrots may be added for last 30 minutes of cooking. Most meat will make its own liquid, but water may be added if needed. Remove meat and vegetables to platter and keep hot. Pour off all but ¼ cup fat from pan and make Favorite Rich Gravy, p. 185. *Serves 4–6*

**Variation: BBB Brisket**
Brown 2-pound brisket of beef as directed above. Season to taste. Add 2 cups water and continue cooking as directed for Pot Roast. *Serves 4*

## ROAST BEEF

BBB + Beef

Wipe roast with damp cloth or paper towels. Place fat side up in roasting pan. Insert meat thermometer to center of beef, making sure thermometer does not touch bone. Do not season roast. Do not add water. Roast in uncovered pan in 325° oven until meat thermometer reaches 140° for rare, 160° for medium, or 170° for well-done. Plan to remove roast from oven 15 minutes before serving time. Keep warm. This "rest" period makes slicing easier. Garnishes may be found in Condiments section, p. 191 to p. 197. While roast sits, make Favorite Rich Gravy, p. 185. For boneless roast, allow 6 ounces per serving; for bone-in, allow ½ pound per serving.

## ROASTING CHART

| Kind | Weight | Hours: rare | Hours: medium | Hours: well done |
|---|---|---|---|---|
| Standing rib, bone-in | 4 lb. | 1¾ | 2 | 2⅓ |
| Standing rib, bone-in | 6 lb. | 2¼ | 2½ | 3¼ |
| Standing rib, bone-in | 8 lb. | 2½ | 3¼ | 4 |
| Rolled rib (4½″) | 4-5 lb. | 2 | 2½ | 3 |
| Round roast, boneless top or bottom | 5-6 lb. | 2¼ | 2¾ | 3½ |
| Rolled oven roast (3½ to 5″) chuck | 4-6 lb. | 2 | 2½ | 3 |
| Rolled sirloin, boneless | 5 lb. | | | |
| Eye of round | 1½-3 lb. | | 1½ - 1¾ (medium) | |
| Rump, boneless | 3½-5 lb. | | 1½ - 2 (rare)<br>1¾ - 2¾ (medium)<br>2¼ - 3¼ (well done) | |

## BEEF HASH

**BBB + Beef** ☐

**6 small or 3 large potatoes, peeled and diced**
**2 medium carrots, peeled and diced**
**2 tablespoons allowed oil**
**1½ cups leftover beef gravy made with allowed thickening (see Favorite Rich Gravy, p. 185)**
**2 cups diced leftover cooked beef**
**Salt to taste**

Brown potatoes and carrots in oil. Add gravy, beef, ½ cup water and salt. Cover and cook slowly 25 minutes or until vegetables are tender. Stir occasionally during cooking to prevent sticking. Add more water if necessary. *Serves 4*

**Variations:**

1. Sauté 1 small onion with vegetables. (**+ Veg.**)
2. Omit oil if not sautéing vegetables and add diced leftover cooked potatoes and 1 package (10 ounces) frozen green peas and carrots.
3. Omit white potato and replace with sweet potato.
4. BEEF POTATO PIE—Prepare Beef Hash without potatoes. Place hot beef mixture in bottom of casserole. Top with hot mashed potatoes (mashed with allowed margarine and allowed milk substitute). Dot with allowed margarine. Bake in 400° oven 15 minutes or until golden brown. *Serves 4*

BBB + Beef

## BEEF SECOND-TIME-AROUND

Reheat 1 to 2 cups leftover gravy made with allowed thickening. Add 4 slices or 2 cups leftover roast beef chunks and heat through. Serve over mashed potatoes, cooked rice, soy grits, or toasted allowed bread. *Serves 4*

**Variations:**

1. Omit gravy. Prepare thickened beef broth from 2 tablespoons allowed oil, 2 tablespoons rice flour, and 1½ cups homemade Beef Broth, p. 27.
2. When allowed, ½ cup red wine may be added. (+ Mold)

BBB + Beef

## BEEF STRIPS IN GRAVY

**1-1½ pounds round steak**
**Rice flour as needed**
**Allowed oil as needed**
**Salt to taste**

Cut beef into narrow strips 2 inches long. Shake beef and flour in paper bag to coat meat well. Brown meat in allowed oil. Season with salt. Reduce heat and add water to cover meat. Cover and cook slowly 40 minutes or until meat is tender. May be served over rice or mashed potatoes. *Serves 2–3*

BBB + Beef

## SIMPLE SWISS STEAK

**2 pounds round steak**
**Rice flour as needed**
**¼ cup allowed oil**
**1 teaspoon salt**
**1 cup boiling water**
**1 cup chopped carrots**

Trim excess fat from steak and pound in as much flour as possible with meat hammer or edge of heavy plate. Cut into serving pieces. Brown in oil in oven-proof skillet. Add salt, water, and chopped carrots. Cover tightly and bake in 275° oven 2 hours or until meat is tender. Purée pan juices and carrots in blender and reheat. Serve with meat. If thicker gravy is desired, thicken with rice flour. *Serves 6*

BBB + Beef

## PAN BROILED STEAKS

Heat heavy skillet and rub lightly with small piece of beef fat. Brown steaks on both sides in hot skillet. Reduce heat and cook until done. Turn several times to cook evenly. Do not add water or cover pan. Season and serve.

## BROILING CHART

| Kind | Thickness | Minutes per Side | Served |
|---|---|---|---|
| Porterhouse or T-bone | 1 inch | 15 | medium |
| Top round | ¾ inch | 15 | well done |
| Cubed steak | ¼ inch | 2-3 | medium |
| Ground beef patties | ¼-½ inch | 3-5 | medium |

## BROILED STEAKS

**BBB + Beef** ☐

Slash fat edges of steak every 2 inches to prevent curling. Rub pre-heated rack or grill with beef fat or allowed oil. Broil meat 3 inches from flame. Timing for meat taken from refrigerator and broiled in pre-heated broiler or barbeque:

### MINUTES PER SIDE:

| THICKNESS | rare | medium | well done |
|---|---|---|---|
| KIND: fillet, club, rib, T-bone, porterhouse, small sirloin | | | |
| 1 inch | 5 | 6 | 7-8 |
| 1½ inch | 9 | 10 | 12-13 |
| 2 inch | 16 | 18 | 20-21 |
| KIND: large sirloin | | | |
| 1 inch | 10 | 12 | 14 |
| 1½ inch | 12 | 14 | 16 |
| KIND: ground beef patties | | | |
| 1 inch | | 8 | 10 |
| 1½ inch | | 10 | 15 |

## SEASONINGS FOR BROILED STEAKS

**BBB + Veg.**

Blend 1 clove garlic, mashed with ¼ cup allowed margarine. Spread on broiled steak.

Combine allowed oil and 1 to 2 cloves sliced garlic. Allow flavors to blend several hours. Brush on steak.

Sprinkle steak with garlic juice or powder.

**BBB + Fruit + Veg.**

Blend ¼ cup lemon juice, ¼ cup allowed oil, and 1 tablespoon chopped chives. Spread over steak.

**BBB + Veg. + TE&A**

In a shaker, blend 2 tablespoons each salt and paprika with 1 teaspoon each freshly ground pepper, onion powder, and garlic powder. Sprinkle on oiled steak.

**BBB + Corn + Veg. + TE&A**

Sprinkle steaks with Jan-U-Wine Soy Sauce and shake on garlic powder. Turn and repeat on second side. Marinate in refrigerator 8 hours or more. Broil or grill outdoors.

**BBB + Beef**

## TASTY HAWAIIAN MEATLOAF

- **2 pounds lean ground beef**
- **¼ cup Cream of Rice**
- **1 teaspoon salt**
- **1 can ((8 ounces) unsweetened crushed pineapple**
- **¼ cup finely grated carrots**

Combine all ingredients with ¼ cup water. Mix well and pack into pan (9 x 5 x 2¾ inches). Bake in 350° oven 1¼ hours. Let stand 10 minutes before slicing. *Serves 4–6*

*Note:* If desired, shape into 4 small loaves in pans 5¾x 3 x 2 inches. Freeze three and bake one now in 350° oven 45 minutes. Makes a fine sandwich next day on toasted Rice Cake.

## MEATLOAF VERDE

**BBB + Beef** ☐

Mix all ingredients well and shape into loaf, place in 7 x 3½ x 2-inch loaf pan. Bake in 350° oven 1 hour. Let stand a few minutes before slicing. Makes good cold or hot sandwiches next day. *Serves 2–3*

- **1 pound lean ground beef**
- **2 tablespoons shredded carrot**
- **¼ cup mashed potatoes**
- **¾ teaspoon salt**
- **½ cup finely chopped spinach**

## POLYNESIAN BEEF BALLS

**BBB + Beef** ☐

Thoroughly combine beef, cereal, and salt with ¼ cup water. Shape into small balls and brown in hot oil. Remove meatballs and pour off fat. Blend sugar and starch in skillet, then blend in part of pineapple. When mixture is smooth, add remaining pineapple. Slowly add broth, stirring constantly until thickened and clear. Thin with water if necessary. Return meatballs to sauce, cover, and cook slowly 20 to 30 minutes. Serve with rice. *Serves 2–3*

- **1 pound lean ground beef**
- **3 tablespoons Cream of Rice**
- **½ teaspoon salt**
- **2 tablespoons allowed oil**
- **1 tablespoon brown sugar, firmly packed**
- **2 teaspoons tapioca starch *or* 1½ teaspoons potato starch**
- **1 can (8 ounces) unsweetened crushed pineapple**
- **1¼ cup homemade Beef Broth, p. 27**

## BASIC MEATBALLS

**BBB + Beef** ☐

Combine beef, cereal, and salt with ¼ cup water and shape into balls. Brown in hot oil. Add to any sauce or soup allowed and cook until done, 20 to 30 minutes. *Serves 2–3*

- **1 pound lean ground beef**
- **3 tablespoons Cream of Rice**
- **½ teaspoon salt**
- **2 tablespoons allowed oil**

## BEEF STEW PREMIER

**BBB + Beef** ☐

Shake beef with flours in clean paper bag. Brown in hot oil, add salt and 2 cups water. Cover and cook slowly 1½ hours or until meat is tender. Add vegetables and cook 30 minutes longer, adding more water if necessary. *Serves 4*

- **1½ pounds beef stew meat, cut in 1-inch cubes**
- **3 tablespoons rice flour**
- **1 tablespoon potato flour**
- **2-4 tablespoons allowed oil**
- **1 teaspoon salt**
- **2 large potatoes, cut in cubes**
- **2 carrots, sliced**
- **1 cup okra, sliced in thick rings**

**Variations:**

1. Omit stew meat and replace with Basic Meatballs, p. 87.
2. Replace white potato with sweet potato. Omit okra and replace with shredded spinach, adding for last 10 minutes of cooking.
3. Omit okra and replace with fresh asparagus spears.

☐ **BBB + Beef**

## BEEF KABOBS

- 1½ pounds boneless, trimmed beef chuck or round steak, cut in cubes
- ½ cup allowed oil
- ¼ cup white distilled vinegar
- 1 can (20 ounces) unsweetened pineapple chunks, drained, juice reserved
- ½ teaspoon salt
- 2 carrots, cut in chunks and cooked tender-crisp, drained and cooled

Marinate meat cubes 2 to 8 hours in combined oil, vinegar, ⅓ cup reserved pineapple juice, and salt. Thread meat, pineapple chunks, and carrots on skewers. Broil or cook over hot coals until meat is done, about 15 minutes, brushing often with marinade. Turn frequently. Serve on bed of hot rice or soy grits. *Serves 4*

☐ **BBB + Beef**

## BRAISED BEEF HEARTS

- 1½ pounds beef heart
- ½ cup rice flour
- 2 tablespoons potato flour
- ½ teaspoon salt
- 2-4 tablespoons allowed oil
- 2 cups Beef Broth, p. 27 or water
- 1 carrot, chopped

Wash heart and remove veins and thick fibrous parts. Cut into ¾-inch slices and shake with flours and salt in paper bag. Brown in hot oil. Add remaining ingredients, cover, and simmer 1 to 1½ hours or until meat is tender when pierced with fork. *Serves 4–6*

*Note:* This is delicious, but, if you should have leftovers, cube and use in any dish calling for cooked beef. Or grind for sandwich spread.

☐ **BBB + Beef**

## HAMBURGER STROGANOFF OVERTURE

- 1 pound lean ground beef
- 3 tablespoons rice flour
- ½ teaspoon salt
- Tofu Dressing I, p. 63

Brown crumbled beef quickly in hot skillet, stirring constantly. Drain off fat. Stir flour and salt into skillet. Add 2 cups water, stirring constantly until gravy is thickened. Cover and cook slowly 15 minutes. Stir in Tofu Dressing in amount desired. Heat but do not boil. If mixture is too thick, thin with more water. Serve over cooked rice. *Serves 3–4*

## STUFFED VEAL CHOPS

**BBB + Beef + Fruit**

- 4 veal chops, cut 1½ inches thick
- ½ cup Raw Cranberry-Orange Relish, p. 192
- ½ cup rice flour
- 2 tablespoons potato flour
- Allowed oil
- Salt to taste

Make a deep wide slit in each chop, from fat side almost to bone. Fill each pocket with 2 tablespoons relish. Fasten with wooden toothpicks around edges. Dredge chops in blended flours and brown in hot oil. Place in baking dish, and add salt and ½ cup water. Cover, and bake in 300° oven 1 hour. *Serves 4*

## BEEF AND VEGETABLE LOAF

**BBB + Beef + Veg.**

- 2 pounds lean ground beef
- ¼ cup Cream of Rice or ⅓ cup Minute Tapioca
- 1 onion, chopped fine
- 1 stalk celery, sliced thin
- ¼ cup thinly sliced green pepper
- 1 cup grated zucchini
- 1 tablespoon minced parsley
- 1 teaspoon salt
- 1 cup tomato juice

Mix all ingredients well and pack into 1½-quart loaf pan. Bake in 350° oven 1¼ hours. Let stand a few minutes before slicing. Makes good cold or hot sandwiches next day. *Serves 4–6*

## CABBAGE ROLLS

**BBB + Beef + Veg.**

- 12 large cabbage leaves
- Boiling water
- 1½ pounds lean ground beef
- ½ cup minced onion
- ¼ teaspoon garlic powder
- ½ cup Cream of Rice
- ½ teaspoon salt
- 1 cup tomato juice
- 1 cup Beef Broth, p. 27
- ¼ cup chopped parsley

Cover leaves with boiling water and let stand 5 minutes. Drain and cut out heavy core. Set aside. Brown beef and onions together and combine with garlic powder, Cream of Rice, salt, and ¾ cup water. Cook and stir 3 minutes. Divide into 12 parts. Center one part on each leaf. Fold sides to meet, enclosing filling, then fold ends to close. Place rolls, seam side down, in deep kettle, stacking if necessary. Cover with juice and broth. Sprinkle with parsley. Cover and simmer 30 to 45 minutes. *Serves 6*

☐ **BBB + Beef + Veg.**

- **4 cube steaks**
- **2 tablespoons allowed oil**
- **1 medium onion, sliced**
- **1 clove garlic, minced**
- **1 can (16 ounces) stewed tomatoes**
- **1 teaspoon salt**
- **4 small potatoes, peeled and diced**

## CUBE STEAK AND POTATO STEW

Brown steaks quickly in oil, stack on one side of skillet, and sauté onion and garlic until golden. Spread steaks, add tomatoes and salt and cook, covered, 20 minutes. Add potatoes and baste with pan juices. Cover and cook 10 minutes more or until potatoes are tender. *Serves 4*

☐ **BBB + Beef + Veg.**

- **3- pound round steak ½ inch thick**
- **⅓ cup rice flour**
- **1 tablespoon potato flour**
- **Allowed oil**
- **Additional rice flour as needed**
- **Salt to taste**
- **1 large onion, sliced**
- **4-6 potatoes, peeled and halved**

## ROUND STEAK, TATERS, AND GRAVY

Remove outer rim of fat and cut steak into serving size pieces. Blend ⅓ cup rice flour with potato flour and pound into steak with mallet or edge of heavy plate. Brown both sides of floured steak in oil, lift from skillet, and set aside. Measure remaining flour mixture and, if necessary, add rice flour to make 3 tablespoons. Stir into ½ cup water until smooth. Add 3 cups water to skillet, blend in flour-water mixture, and heat, stirring, until thin light brown gravy results. Add salt to taste.

Return meat to gravy, lay onion slices on top, cover, and bake in 350° oven 1½ hours (or simmer on top of stove). Add potatoes for the last 30 minutes of cooking. *Serves 4-6*

☐ **BBB + Beef + TE&A**

- **8- pound rolled boneless rib roast**
- **⅓ cup rice flour**
- **1 tablespoon potato flour**
- **2 teaspoons dried rosemary**
- **2 tablespoons dry mustard**
- **2 teaspoons salt**
- **1 teaspoon pepper**
- **2 teaspoons paprika**

## HERBED BEEF ROAST

Wipe roast with wet paper towel, leaving moist. Blend flours and all seasonings well and pat firmly onto surface of roast. Insert meat thermometer from fat side to center of roast. Bake in shallow roasting pan, fat side up, in 325° oven 3 hours or until thermometer reaches 140° for rare, 160° for medium, or 170° for well done. Let the roast rest 15 minutes before carving across the grain. *Serves 8-10*

## FINE FLAVOR POT ROAST

**BBB + Beef + Veg. + TE&A**

**4-6 pound chuck 7-bone, round bone, or rump roast**
**¼ cup rice flour**
**1 tablespoon potato flour**
**1 tablespoon allowed oil**
**2 teaspoons Steero Instant Beef Flavor Bouillon Seasoning and Broth**
**3 peppercorns**
**1 large onion, sliced**
**1 clove garlic, minced**
**¼ teaspoon celery seeds**
**2 carrots, cut in chunks**

Dredge meat in blended flours. In roasting pan with lid, brown meat on both sides in hot oil. Add all remaining ingredients. Cover tightly and simmer 3 hours or until tender. (Or bake in 325° oven, or put browned roast and remaining ingredients in slow cooker at low setting 12 hours.) Remove meat and vegetables. Thicken cooking liquid with leftover flours stirred into ¼ cup water. Boil 1 minute. *Serves 6–8*

## MAKE AHEAD BARBEQUE BEEF ROAST

**BBB + Beef + Veg. + TE&A**

**4- pound round bone or chuck roast**
**1 tablespoon allowed oil**
**1 can (16 ounces) tomato purée**
**1 teaspoon salt**
**Pepper to taste**
**1 clove garlic, crushed**
**1 large onion, sliced**
**1½ teaspoons dry mustard**
**¼ cup brown sugar**
**¼ cup white distilled vinegar**
**½ teaspoon chili powder (optional)**
**6 whole cloves**
**1 bay leaf**

Brown meat on both sides in oiled roasting pan. Combine all remaining ingredients, add ½ cup water, and cover. Bake in 325° oven 3 hours or until meat is tender. Peek occasionally to see that sauce does not dry out during cooking. Add water if needed. Lift meat, cloves, and bay leaf from juice and discard spices. Chill sauce and meat separately. Lift fat off sauce. Slice beef, cover, and reheat in defatted sauce 30 to 45 minutes in 350° oven. *Serves 4–6*

**Variations:**

1. Use 3-4 pound brisket. Increase baking time as needed.
2. ROAST ITALIANO—Omit seasoning. Add 1 cup sliced celery and 2 cups sliced carrots. Season with ½ teaspoon dried oregano and ¼ teaspoon dried basil. Serve as is or lift out meat and purée liquid and vegeta bles to serve as sauce over meat.

## SAVORY BEEF SHANKS OR SHORT RIBS

☐ **BBB + Beef + Veg. + TE&A**

- 3 pounds beef shanks or short ribs
- 2 tablespoons allowed oil
- 2 tablespoons rice flour
- 1 can (12 ounces) tomato juice
- ½ teaspoon salt
- ⅓ cup chopped celery
- 1 onion, sliced thin
- 1 clove garlic, minced
- ⅛ teaspoon dried basil

Brown ribs on all sides in oil. Remove meat and pour off fat. Return 2 tablespoons fat to skillet, blend in flour, and cook until bubbly. Slowly add juice, stirring constantly until slightly thickened. Add remaining ingredients and ribs. Cook slowly, covered, 2 hours or until ribs are tender. Skim off fat if necessary. Serve with cooked rice. *Serves 4–6*

## CHUCK WAGON STEW

☐ **BBB + Beef + Veg. + TE&A**

- 1½ pounds beef stew meat cut in 1-inch cubes
- 3 tablespoons rice flour
- 1 tablespoon potato flour
- 1 teaspoon chili powder
- ¼ teaspoon garlic powder
- 1 onion, diced
- 2 teaspoons Steero Instant Beef Flavor Bouillon Seasoning and Broth
- 2 cups hot water
- ½ teaspoon salt
- 4 small carrots, sliced
- ½ cup sliced celery
- 3 zucchini, cut in 1-inch pieces
- 2 medium potatoes (sweet or white, cut in 1-inch pieces)
- 1 package (10 ounces) frozen green peas or green beans
- 2 tablespoons chopped parsley
- ½ teaspoon dried oregano

Shake beef with flours, chili powder, and garlic powder in clean paper bag. Brown in hot oiled pot. Push meat to one side and sauté onion. Add bouillon and hot water. Cover and simmer 1 hour. Add carrots, celery, zucchini, and potatoes. Cook 30 minutes or until vegetables are tender. Add peas, parsley, and oregano and cook 5 minutes more. Thin with water if necessary and adjust seasonings to taste. *Serves 4–6*

## VEAL STEW

**BBB + Beef + Veg. + TE&A**

- 2 pounds boneless veal stew meat, cut in 1-inch cubes
- 3 tablespoons rice flour
- 1 tablespoon potato flour
- 2-4 tablespoons allowed oil
- 1 medium onion, sliced thin
- ½ teaspoon salt
- Dash of pepper
- ⅛ teaspoon nutmeg
- 1 teaspoon paprika
- ¼ teaspoon garlic powder
- 1 cup sliced celery
- 1 package (10 ounces) frozen petite green peas

Shake veal in paper bag with flours. Brown in hot oil in dutch oven and remove meat. Sauté onion in drippings. Return meat and add all ingredients except peas. Cover and simmer 1 hour or until meat is tender. Skim off excess fat. Add peas, cover and cook 4 minutes longer. *Serves 6*

## BEEF CHOP SUEY

**BBB + Beef + Veg. + TE&A**

- 1½ pound round steak, cut in 1 x 2-inch strips
- 2 tablespoons allowed oil
- 1½ cups Beef Broth, p. 27, or water
- 1 tablespoon Kitchen Bouquet
- 1 tablespoon sugar
- ¾ teaspoon ginger
- ½ teaspoon salt
- 2 cups sliced onion
- 2 cups sliced celery
- ½ green pepper, cut in strips
- 1 can (16 ounces) Chinese mixed vegetables, drained
- 1 package (6 ounces) frozen Chinese pea pods, thawed
- 1 can (5 ounces) water chestnuts, drained and sliced
- 1 tablespoon tapioca starch

Brown beef in hot oil in skillet or wok, stirring frequently. Add broth and seasonings. Cover and cook over low heat 30 minutes. Add onion, celery, and green pepper. Cook 10 to 15 minutes or until beef is tender. Stir in mixed vegetables, pea pods, and water chestnuts. Blend tapioca starch with ¼ cup water and, tipping pan, blend into liquids. Continue cooking, stirring gently, until vegetables are heated through and sauce is thickened and clear, about 5 minutes. Serve over hot steamed rice. *Serves 6*

**Variation:**

Replace beef with beef liver, cut in ½-inch strips. Coat liver with tapioca starch. Sauté onion, celery, and green pepper in oil. Push vegetables to one side and brown liver. Stir in all remaining ingredients and cook until vegetables are hot and sauce is thickened and clear. Or, replace steak or liver with leftover cooked beef.

☐ **BBB + Beef + Veg. + TE&A**

- **2 onions, chopped**
- **1 clove garlic, minced**
- **2 tablespoons allowed oil**
- **1½-2 pounds boneless beef chuck or stew meat cut in chunks**
- **2 tablespoons paprika**
- **2 teaspoons Steero Instant Beef Flavor Bouillon Seasoning and Broth**
- **1 can (6 ounces) tomato paste**
- **¼ teaspoon salt**
- **Pepper to taste**

## HUNGARIAN GOULASH

Sauté onions and garlic in oil, remove, and reserve. Toss beef with paprika in paper bag. Brown beef in drippings, adding allowed oil if needed. Return onions to pan, add 2½ cups water, and all remaining ingredients, including paprika left in bag. Cover and simmer 1½ to 2 hours or until meat is tender. Stir occasionally. Serve over rice or mashed potatoes, any cooked cereal grain when allowed, or Wheat-Free Corn Pasta. (+ **Corn**) *Serves 4*

**Variation:**

Add ¼ green pepper, sliced, Tabasco sauce to taste, and a pinch of crushed caraway seeds. Add 2 or more cubed potatoes for last ½ hour of cooking.

☐ **BBB + Beef + Veg. + TE&A**

- **1 2-pound boneless round steak**
- **2 teaspoons Steero Instant Beef Flavor Bouillon Seasoning and Broth**
- **1 can (15 ounces) tomato sauce**
- **1 tablespoon instant minced onion**
- **1 clove garlic, crushed**
- **1 tablespoon dried parsley**
- **½ teaspoon salt**
- **½ teaspoon Italian seasoning**
- **¼ teaspoon dried marjoram**
- **2 cups cooked rice (to serve 4) or 3 cups rice (to serve 6)**
- **1⅓ cups hot water**

## STUFFED BEEF ROLLS

Have butcher run steak through tenderizer machine—meat *will* be very thin. To prepare, cut into 4 to 6 pieces. Dissolve bouillon in hot water, pour over meat, let stand 15 minutes, and drain. Combine broth with all ingredients except rice. Place ½ cup rice in each piece of steak. Roll up and fasten with wooden toothpicks. Place all rolls in baking dish, pour sauce over and bake in 375° oven 1 hour, basting often. *Serves 4-6*

## SWISS STEAK HAWAIIAN

**BBB + Beef + Veg. + TE&A**

- 1 2-pound round steak
- ⅓ cup plus 2 tablespoons potato starch or tapioca starch
- 1 teaspoon ginger
- ½ teaspoon paprika
- ½ teaspoon salt
- ¼ cup allowed oil
- 1 onion, sliced and separated into rings
- 2 teaspoons Steero Instant Beef Flavor Bouillon Seasoning and Broth
- 1 can (20 ounces) unsweetened pineapple rings, drained, juice reserved
- 1 green pepper, sliced
- 1 tomato, cut in 8 wedges

Pound into steak blended starch, ginger, paprika, and salt. Brown in hot oil in skillet. Lay onion slices on top. Sprinkle on bouillon mix. Measure pineapple juice and add water to make 2 cups. Pour over meat. Cover and simmer 1 to 1½ hours. Lay pineapple slices, pepper slices, and tomato wedges over steak. Cover and cook another 10 minutes. Remove meat and topping to platter and keep hot. Blend 1 tablespoon starch with ¼ cup water, pour into pan liquid, stirring constantly until thickened. Pour over steak. *Serves 6*

## FLANK STEAK ESPAÑOLE

**BBB + Beef + Veg. + TE&A**

- 1 1½-2-pound flank steak
- ⅓ cup rice flour
- 1 tablespoon potato flour
- 1 teaspoon salt
- Pepper to taste
- ¼ teaspoon garlic powder
- ¼ cup allowed oil
- 1 medium onion, sliced
- ½ green pepper, sliced
- 1 can (16 ounces) stewed tomatoes
- 1 teaspoon chili powder

Have butcher tenderize steak. Combine flours, ½ teaspoon salt, pepper, and garlic powder. Dredge steak in mixture and brown in 2 tablespoons oil. Lay onion and pepper slices over steak. Pour on tomatoes, and add chili powder and ½ teaspoon salt. Cover, and bake in 350° oven 2 hours or until tender. Serve over hot rice, other allowed grain, or corn pasta when allowed. **(+ Corn)** *Serves 4–6*

## QUICK BEEF BALLS IN TOMATO SAUCE

**BBB + Beef + Veg. + TE&A**

- 1 pound lean ground beef
- 3 tablespoons Cream of Rice
- ½ teaspoon salt
- Dash of pepper
- ⅛ teaspoon dried thyme
- ⅛ teaspoon garlic powder
- 2 teaspoons Kitchen Bouquet
- 1 teaspoon Steero Instant Beef Flavor Bouillon Seasoning and Broth
- 1 can (8 ounces) tomato sauce
- 1 teaspoon instant chopped onion
- ¼ teaspoon Italian seasoning
- ⅛ teaspoon garlic powder

Combine beef, Cream of Rice, salt, pepper, thyme, garlic powder, and ¼ cup water. Chill 20 minutes, then form into balls with moist hands. Combine 1 cup water, Kitchen Bouquet, and beef broth in large skillet. Add meatballs and bring to boil. Cover and cook slowly 5 minutes. Turn meatballs, cover, and cook another 5 minutes. Serve over cooked zucchini, well drained, or over cooked spaghetti squash. *Serves 4*

## CURRY BEEF KABOBS (WITH RICE)

**BBB + Beef + Fruit + Veg. + TE&A**

- 1 1½-pounds boneless beef chuck or round steak, trimmed and cut in 1½-inch cubes
- ½ cup chopped onion
- 2 tablespoons allowed oil
- 2 teaspoons curry powder
- ¼ teaspoon garlic powder
- ½ teaspoon salt
- ¾ cup unsweetened pineapple juice
- ½ fresh pineapple
- 2 medium papayas
- 1 green pepper, cut in 1-inch squares
- Cherry tomatoes

Prepare beef and marinade as follows: Sauté onion in oil until tender. Add curry and garlic powders and sauté 1 minute. Stir in salt, pineapple juice, and beef. Refrigerate several hours. Cut pineapple in 1½-inch chunks for skewers. Cut papayas in half lengthwise, peel, and cut into thick slices crosswise. Thread marinated meat, papaya, pepper, cherry tomatoes, and pineapple chunks on skewers. Broil in oven or cook over hot coals, brushing with marinade and turning often, until meat is done, about 15 minutes. Serve kabobs with hot cooked brown rice. *Serves 4*

## PRESTO RANCH STYLE BEANS

**BBB + Beef + Veg. + N&S + TE&A**

- 1 pound lean ground beef
- ½ tablespoon instant chopped onion
- 2 or 3 cans (15 ounces each) Ranch Style Beans

Brown and crumble beef and drain off fat. Add onion and beans and simmer 15 minutes to heat and blend flavors. *Serves 4–6*

## CHILLY PORCUPINES

**BBB + Beef + Veg. + TE&A**

- **1½ pounds lean ground beef**
- **¾ cup rice**
- **1 teaspoon salt**
- **2 cups finely chopped onion**
- **2 cans (8 ounces each) tomato sauce**
- **2 teaspoons Steero Instant Beef Flavor Bouillon Seasoning and Broth**
- **2 teaspoons chili powder**

Combine beef, rice, salt, 1 cup chopped onion, ¼ cup tomato sauce, and ½ cup water. Shape into 6 cone-shaped mounds and place in baking dish. Combine remaining ingredients with 2 cups water and pour over porcupines. Cover tightly with foil and bake in 350° oven 1 hour. Remove cover, increase heat to 375°, and bake 10 to 15 minutes to brown meat. Serve with frozen green peas, crisp salad, and a light gelatin dessert. *Serves 4–6*

## SLOPPY JOE MEAT MIX

**BBB + Beef + Veg. + TE&A**

- **1 pound lean ground beef**
- **1 small onion, chopped**
- **¼ cup chopped green pepper**
- **1 tablespoon chopped parsley**
- **1 can (6 ounces) tomato paste**
- **½ teaspoon salt**
- **1 teaspoon chili powder**
- **Dash of pepper**
- **¼ teaspoon garlic powder**
- **¼ teaspoon dried oregano**
- **2 teaspoons brown sugar**

Brown meat with onion and green pepper. Drain off surplus fat. Add remaining ingredients and ¾ cup water and simmer, covered, 20 minutes. Adjust thickness of mix by cooking uncovered to thicken or by adding water to thin. Serve over cooked zucchini, allowed toasted bread, rice, or corn pasta when allowed. *Serves 4*

## TEXAS CHILI

**BBB + Beef + Veg. + TE&A**

- **1½ pounds lean ground beef**
- **1 onion, chopped**
- **1 clove garlic, crushed**
- **¼ cup chopped green pepper**
- **½ cup chopped celery**
- **1½ teaspoons salt**
- **¼ teaspoon dried oregano**
- **Dash of pepper**
- **1-2 tablespoons chili powder**
- **1 tablespoon honey**
- **1 can (15 ounces) tomato sauce**
- **1 can (6 ounces) tomato paste**

Brown beef with onion, garlic, green pepper, and celery until beef is cooked and vegetables softened. Add remaining ingredients and 1 cup water and cover. Cook slowly 1 hour, stirring occasionally. *Serves 6*

**Variation: Chili with Beans**

Add 2 cans (15 or 16 ounces each) soy beans, small red beans, or kidney beans, drained. Or soak ½ pound dry pinto beans overnight and then cook until tender. Drain and add to chili.

## SPANISH RICE

**BBB + Beef + Veg. + TE&A**

- **1 pound lean ground beef**
- **1 onion, chopped**
- **⅓ cup diced green pepper**
- **1 teaspoon salt**
- **1 teaspoon chili powder**
- **¼ teaspoon garlic powder**
- **Dash of pepper**
- **1 cup rice**
- **1 can (16 ounces) stewed tomatoes**

Brown and crumble beef, then push to one side and sauté onion and green pepper. Add seasonings and rice, stirring to brown. Add tomatoes and 2 cups water. Cover and cook slowly 25 minutes or until liquid is absorbed and rice is tender. *Serves 4–6*

**Variations:**

1. QUICK SPANISH RICE—Omit regular rice and reduce water to 1¼ cups. Combine water with all ingredients except rice after browning meat and vegetables. Simmer, covered, 15 minutes. Stir in 1¼ cups Minute Rice. Cover and let stand 5 minutes.
2. SPANISH RICE STUFFED PEPPERS—Cut off tops and seed 6 medium green peppers. Cook in boiling water to cover 5 minutes and invert to drain. Fill each pepper with 1 serving of Spanish Rice. Place in baking dish with ½ cup water in bottom. Bake in 350° oven 30 minutes. *Serves 6*

## BEEFED-UP ZUCCHINI CASSEROLE

**BBB + Beef + Veg. + TE&A**

- **1 pound lean ground beef**
- **1 clove garlic, crushed**
- **1 cup chopped onion**
- **1⅓ cups tofu, washed and dried**
- **1 teaspoon salt**
- **1 teaspoon dried basil**
- **½ teaspoon dried oregano**
- **¼ teaspoon pepper**
- **2 cups cooked rice (⅔ cup raw)**
- **1 can (15 ounces) tomato sauce or 2 cans (8 ounces each)**
- **4 cups sliced zucchini**

Brown and crumble beef along with garlic, onion, and tofu. Add seasonings, rice, and tomato sauce. Layer zucchini and meat-rice mixture in 2-quart casserole, two layers of each, starting with zucchini. Cover with foil. Bake in 350° oven 45 minutes. *Serves 4–6*

**Variation:**

Omit zucchini and prepare meat-rice mixture. Cut 1 oversize zucchini in half, remove large seeds and parboil until tender-crisp. Scoop out pulp, leaving shell ¼ inch thick. Add pulp to rice mixture and stuff zucchini shells. Place in baking dish of size to accommodate zucchini, cover with foil and bake 30 to 45 minutes at 350° or until squash is tender and meat mixture hot through. Test doneness by piercing zucchini with two-tined fork. *Serves 4 to 6*

## BEEF-VEGETABLE BAKE

**BBB + Beef + Veg. + TE&A**

- **1 pound lean ground beef or 1 pound chopped cooked beef**
- **1 medium onion, chopped**
- **2 tablespoons allowed oil**
- **3 tablespoons rice flour**
- **½ teaspoon salt**
- **1 can (8 ounces) tomato sauce**
- **1 can (16 ounces) cut green beans, drained**
- **2½ cups hot mashed potatoes, prepared with allowed margarine and allowed milk substitute**
- **Allowed margarine**

Cook ground beef in skillet and pour off fat. Sauté onion in oil until transparent. Combine with beef (ground or chopped cooked) and stir in flour and salt. Add tomato sauce and 1 cup water, return to low heat, and stir constantly until thickened. Make layer of green beans in 1½-quart casserole, add layer of beef mixture and a top layer of mashed potatoes. Dot with allowed margarine. Bake in 400° oven 15 minutes or until heated through and potatoes are golden. *Serves 4*

## SAUTÉED CALF LIVER

**BBB + Beef + Veg. + TE&A**

- **1 pound calf liver**
- **½ cup rice flour**
- **2 tablespoons potato flour**
- **1 teaspoon salt**
- **½ teaspoon paprika**
- **1 onion, sliced and separated into rings**
- **1 tablespoon imitation bacon bits**
- **2 tablespoons allowed oil**
- **Parsley sprigs**

Remove skin and membranes from liver and cut in thin slices. Combine flours, salt, and paprika. Dredge liver slices in seasoned flours. Sauté onion and bacon bits in oil, remove, and keep hot. Sauté liver slices 1 to 2 minutes on each side. Top with sautéed onion and bacon bits. Cover and cook 1 more minute. Garnish with parsley sprigs and, if allowed, with lemon wedges. **(+ Fruit)** *Serves 3*

## COMPANY BARBECUE BRISKET

**BBB + Beef + Veg. + TE&A + Mold**

- **1 4-5-pound beef brisket**
- **½ bottle (3½ ounces) Liquid Smoke (Wright's)**
- **Quick Barbecue Sauce, p. 186**

Marinate beef in Liquid Smoke 24 hours, tightly covered and refrigerated, then bake in 300° oven 4 to 5 hours, covered. Lift meat from juice and chill. Discard juice. Slice meat thin across grain. To serve, loosely cover with foil and reheat in Barbecue Sauce in 350° oven 30 to 45 minutes. *Serves 4–6*

**Variations:**

1. Fabulous as cold sandwich meat.
2. Cut bite-size cubes to top green salad on a hot summer evening.

## CEREAL STUFFED PEPPERS

**BBB + Rye + Beef + Veg.**

- **6 medium-large green peppers**
- **1 recipe Cracked Rice and Rye Cereal, p. 250**
- **1½ pounds lean ground beef**
- **¼ teaspoon salt**
- **⅔ cup tomato juice**

Cut tops off peppers and remove seeds. Parboil peppers in water to cover 5 minutes and invert to drain. Prepare cereal. Brown beef and drain off excess fat. Combine meat, cereal, and remaining ingredients. Heat thoroughly. Divide mixture evenly into peppers. Place in baking dish with ½ cup water added around stuffed peppers. Bake in 350° oven 30 minutes. *Serves 6*

## UNIQUE MEATLOAF

**BBB + Rye + Beef + Veg. + TE&A**

- **1½ pounds lean ground beef**
- **1⅓ cups tofu, washed**
- **½ cup Cream of Rye (dry)**
- **1 medium onion, chopped fine**
- **1 stalk celery, sliced thin**
- **2 tablespoons chopped parsley**
- **¼ green pepper, chopped fine (optional)**
- **½ teaspoon chili powder**
- **¾ teaspoon salt**
- **1 can (8 ounces) tomato sauce**

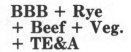

Get your hands into this one! Squeeze hands through all ingredients combined in large bowl. Mix until tofu is well crumbled and distributed. Shape into loaf, place in 2-quart pan and bake in 350° oven 1¼ hours. Let stand 5 to 10 minutes before slicing. Optional garnish: Before baking, press raw sunflower seeds into top of loaf. **(+ N&S)** *Serves 6–8*

## JUICY SIRLOIN STEAKS

**BBB + Rye + Beef + Veg. + TE&A**

- **1 pound lean ground sirloin**
- **½ cup chopped onion**
- **1 teaspoon dried parsley**
- **1 cup finely grated potato**
- **½ cup water or allowed milk substitute**
- **¼ cup Cream of Rye**
- **½ teaspoon salt**
- **⅛ teaspoon pepper**
- **½ teaspoon garlic powder**

Mix all ingredients in large bowl. Chill 20 minutes and shape, with wet hands, into 3 or 4 steak-shaped patties. Broil or grill until done to taste. Serve them with Barbecue Sauce, p. 186, or with "Red Lead" Hamburger Relish, p. 197. *Serves 3–4*

## GLORIA'S TACOS

**BBB + Corn + Beef + Fruit + Veg. + TE&A**

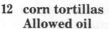

- **12 corn tortillas**
- **Allowed oil**
- **1½ pounds lean ground beef**
- **1 onion, chopped or 1 tablespoon instant chopped onion**
- **1 teaspoon chili powder**
- **Salt and pepper to taste**
- **Avocado slices**
- **Tomato, chopped**
- **Scallions, chopped, (optional)**
- **Lettuce, shredded**
- **1 can (7 ounces) green chili salsa *or* Mild Savory Taco Sauce, p. 187**

Heat each tortilla in a little oil until soft and pliable. Stack and reserve. Brown beef and onion until meat is no longer red and add seasonings. Place large tablespoon of meat on each tortilla, fold in half, and pin shut with 2 wooden toothpicks across top. Fry in small amount of allowed oil until browned and crisp on both sides. Serve remaining ingredients in separate bowls. Let each person fill his own taco and add sauce to taste. (Optional: Include bowl of grated cheese for nonallergic family members.) *Serves 4*

**Variation:**

Grind or shred cooked roast beef, allowing 2 to 3 tablespoons meat per taco. Season as desired. Mix with mashed avocado and salsa or with leftover gravy. Spoon into tortillas and fry until crisp. Add fillings as desired.

## ZESTY TACO

**BBB + Corn + Beef + Fruit + Veg. + TE&A**

- **1 pound lean ground beef**
- **1 can (4 ounces) diced green chilies**
- **¼ cup chopped onion**
- **1 medium clove garlic, minced**
- **1 can (8 ounces) tomato sauce**
- **¼ teaspoon dried oregano**
- **½ teaspoon chili powder**
- **¼ teaspoon salt**
- **12 corn taco shells**
- **Avocado Salsa, p. 12**
- **Lettuce, shredded**

Brown beef in skillet, stirring to crumble. Drain. Stir in chilies, onion, garlic, tomato sauce, and seasonings. Simmer, uncovered, 10 minutes or until desired consistency. Heat taco shells in hot oven until crisp, about 5 minutes. Divide filling into shells. Top each with Avocado Salsa, and shredded lettuce. *Serves 4*

## SLOPPY TOSTADA

**BBB + Corn + Beef + Veg. + TE&A**

- 1½ pounds lean ground beef
- 1 medium onion, diced
- ⅓ cup chopped green pepper
- 1 clove garlic, minced
- Salt to taste
- 1 teaspoon chili powder
- 1 can (8 ounces) tomato sauce
- 12 corn tortillas or tostada shells
- 1 can (17 ounces) Rosarita Vegetarian Refried Beans, heated
- 2 avocados, sliced thin
- Lettuce, shredded
- Santa Barbara Salsa, p. 12

Brown beef, onion, green pepper, and garlic until beef is no longer red. Drain off excess fat. Add salt, chili powder, tomato sauce, and ⅓ cup water. Simmer slowly 10 to 20 minutes, uncovered. In the meantime, fry each tortilla flat and crisp in allowed oil (or heat tostada shells as directed on package). Spread heated beans on each tortilla, top with meat mixture, avocado slices, and lettuce. Pass salsa for each person to doctor his own tostada. *Serves 6–12*

## TAMALE PIE

**BBB + Corn + Beef + Veg. + TE&A**

Filling:

- 1½ pounds lean ground beef
- 1 medium onion, chopped
- 1 cup sliced celery
- ½ green pepper, sliced
- 1 clove garlic, crushed
- 1 can (6 ounces) tomato paste
- 1 can (17 ounces) whole kernel corn
- 2 teaspoons chili powder
- ½ teaspoon salt

Mush:

- 1 cup cornmeal
- ½ teaspoon salt
- ¼ teaspoon garlic powder
- Allowed oil
- Paprika
- Parsley, minced

Brown beef with onion, celery, green pepper, and garlic and pour off excess fat. Stir in ¾ cup water with remaining ingredients and simmer 20 minutes. Meanwhile, prepare mush.

Combine cornmeal, salt, and garlic powder with 3 cups water and bring to boil, stirring constantly. Reduce heat to low and cook 5 minutes.

To assemble pie, press ¾ of mush on bottom and sides of oiled 2-quart casserole, saving remainder for top. Spoon filling into mush shell and top with dollops of mush. If preferred, all mush may be layered on top of pie or mush and filling may be in alternate layers. Bake in 375° oven 30 to 40 minutes. Garnish with paprika and sprinkle of minced parsley. *Serves 6*

**Variations:**

1. Add 1 can (4 ounces) green chilies, chopped, and reduce chili powder to 1 teaspoon .
2. For a different kind of pie, replace corn with 1 can (16 ounces) kidney beans.

## COMPANY POT ROAST

**BBB + Corn**
**+ Beef + Veg.**
**+ TE&A**

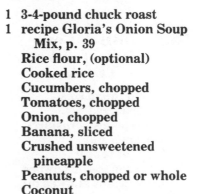

- **1 4-5-pound round-bone or 7-bone roast**
- **½ recipe Gloria's Onion Soup Mix, p. 39**

Place roast in skillet or roasting pan. Sprinkle on soup mix and add 1 cup water. Cover and cook on top of stove or bake in 350° oven 2½ to 3½ hours or until roast tests tender. Potatoes and carrots may be added around roast last 45 minutes of cooking time.

*Onion Gravy:* Pour juices from roasting pan and remove excess fat by spooning off or by chilling long enough for fat to solidify. Combine 3 tablespoons rice flour with ½ cup water, blending until smooth. Add to defatted pan juices and heat, stirring constantly, until thickened.

## MALAYSIAN DINNER

**BBB + Corn**
**+ Beef + Fruit**
**+ Veg. + TE&A**

- **1 3-4-pound chuck roast**
- **1 recipe Gloria's Onion Soup Mix, p. 39**
- **Rice flour, (optional)**
- **Cooked rice**
- **Cucumbers, chopped**
- **Tomatoes, chopped**
- **Onion, chopped**
- **Banana, sliced**
- **Crushed unsweetened pineapple**
- **Peanuts, chopped or whole**
- **Coconut**

Place roast in oven-proof pan, sprinkle with soup mix, and add 2½ cups water. Seal tightly with foil and bake in 350° oven 3 hours or until very tender. Pan juices may be defatted and thickened with rice flour and water paste, if desired. To serve, place rice in center of each plate and top with beef and liquid or thickened sauce. Add accompaniments to plates or display in separate dishes—a divided Lazy Susan is great for this—and allow diners to heap their own plates. Serve with green salad and sherbert. *Serves 4–6*

## NO-WATCH BEEF STEW

**BBB + Corn**
**+ Veg. + TE&A**

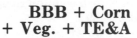

- **2 pounds beef round or chuck, cut in 1-inch cubes**
- **2 tablespoons rice flour**
- **5-6 potatoes, peeled and chunked**
- **½ cup chopped celery**
- **1 package (10 ounces) frozen green beans, partially defrosted**
- **4 carrots, sliced**
- **1 recipe Gloria's Onion Soup Mix, p. 39**

Place beef in 2-quart casserole, sprinkle on flour and stir to coat meat. Add vegetables, soup mix, and 2½ cups water. Seal casserole tightly with foil. Prick a few holes in top with 2-tined fork. Bake in 275° oven 4 to 5 hours or until meat is tender. *Serves 4–6*

**Variation:**

Combine ingredients in large slow cooker. Cook on low setting 10 to 12 hours, or on high 5 to 6 hours.

## SPECIAL BEEF STROGANOFF

**BBB + Corn + Beef + Veg. + TE&A**

- 2 pounds round steak, fat removed, sliced into 1 x 2-inch strips
- ¼ cup rice flour
- 2 tablespoons potato flour
- ¼ cup allowed oil
- 1 recipe Gloria's Onion Soup Mix, p. 39
- 1 cup tofu, washed
- 3 tablespoons white distilled vinegar

Shake meat, several strips at a time, with combined flours in paper or plastic bag, then brown in hot oil. Continue until all meat is coated and browned. Sprinkle on soup mix and add 3 cups water. Cover to cook over low heat 1 hour or until meat is tender. Combine tofu with vinegar and process in blender, adding water a tablespoon at a time, until tofu is creamy smooth and the texture of sour cream. Blend into meat mixture and reheat but do not boil. Serve over cooked rice. *Serves 4–6*

**Variation: Easy Beef Stroganoff**

Use 2 cups leftover cooked beef and 2 cups water. Add soup mix and simmer 10 minutes. Thicken with 3 tablespoons rice flour. Process tofu, vinegar, and water in blender until creamy and stir into meat mixture. Serve over hot rice. *Serves 4*

## BAVARIAN BEEF

**BBB + Corn + Beef + Veg. + TE&A**

- 1½- pound round steak, tenderized
- 2 tablespoons cornstarch
- ½ teaspoon salt
- Dash of pepper
- ¼ teaspoon garlic powder
- 2 tablespoons allowed oil
- 1 large onion, sliced
- 2 cups sliced carrots
- 1 recipe Gloria's Onion Soup Mix, p. 39
- 2½ cups hot water
- ¼ teaspoon chili powder
- 2 tablespoons chopped parsley
- Wheat-free corn pasta

Ask butcher to tenderize (butterfly) round steak. Cut into 1-inch strips. Combine cornstarch, salt, pepper, and garlic powder in paper or plastic bag. Drop in strips of meat and shake to coat. Brown meat in oil. Add all other ingredients except pasta. Cover and cook over low heat 30 to 45 minutes or until meat is tender. Serve over cooked and drained pasta or over hot fluffy rice. Coleslaw accompanies this dish especially well. *Serves 6*

**Variation: Layered Bavarian Casserole**

In 3-quart casserole make layers of the following: browned floured and seasoned steak, sliced onion, and sliced carrots. Sprinkle on dry soup mix, chili powder, and parsley. Pour hot water over all and cover tightly with foil. Bake in 375° oven 1 hour or until meat is tender. If too juicy, uncover last 15 minutes of baking time. If preferred, this may be cooked 8 hours or more in slow cooker on low setting. *Serves 6*

## GLORIA'S SWISS STEAK

**BBB + Corn + Beef + Veg. + TE&A**

- 1 2-pound round steak
- Rice flour
- Allowed oil
- ½ recipe Gloria's Onion Soup Mix, p. 39mc
- ¼ green pepper, sliced
- 1 stalk celery, sliced
- Dash of pepper
- 1 can (8 ounces) tomato sauce

Cut steak into serving pieces or leave whole. Slash fat around edge to prevent curling. Pound as much flour into steak as possible with mallet or edge of heavy plate. Brown meat in oil. Add remaining ingredients and 1½ cups water. Cover and cook 1½ hours or until meat is tender. Add quartered potatoes and carrot sticks last 45 minutes, if desired. *Serves 6*

## GRILLED ONION BURGERS

**BBB + Corn + Beef + Veg. + TE&A**

- 2 pounds lean ground beef
- 1 recipe Gloria's Onion Soup Mix, p. 39
- ½ cup tomato juice or water

Combine all ingredients and mix thoroughly. Form into 8 patties. Broil or grill until done to taste. *Serves 8*

## SPEEDY HOMINY CHILI

**BBB + Corn + Beef + Veg. + TE&A**

- 1 pound lean ground beef
- 1 medium onion, chopped
- ½ teaspoon salt
- 2 teaspoons chili powder
- 1 can (16 ounces) stewed tomatoes
- 1 can (16 ounces) hominy

Brown ground beef and onions and add seasonings. Drain off excess fat. Add remaining ingredients and simmer 15 to 30 minutes. *Serves 4*

## MEATLOAF GLORIOUS

**BBB + Oats + Corn + Beef + Veg. + TE&A**

- 2 pounds lean ground beef
- 1 recipe Gloria's Onion Soup Mix, p. 39
- 1 stalk celery, sliced thin
- ½ large carrot, shredded fine
- 1 tablespoon dried parsley
- ½ cup quick oats
- 1 can (8 ounces) tomato sauce

Combine all ingredients and shape into loaf in 2-quart casserole or loaf pan. Bake in 350° oven 1¼ hours. For lighter seasoning, use only ½ recipe soup mix. Finely sliced green pepper may be added, if desired. This is the loaf we use most often for ourselves and for company dinners. It has a wonderful flavor. Let stand a few minutes after baking to make slicing easier. *Serves 6–8*

## GOURMET MEATBALLS

**BBB + Oats + Corn + Beef + Veg. + N&S + TE&A**

- 1 pound lean ground beef
- ⅓ cup quick oats, uncooked
- 2 tablespoons grated onion
- 2 tablespoons chopped parsley
- ½ teaspoon salt
- 1 tablespoon allowed oil
- ½ recipe Gloria's Onion Soup Mix, p. 39
- Potatoes, peeled, quartered (optional)
- 1½ tablespoons rice flour

Combine meat, oats, onion, parsley, salt and ¼ cup water. Mix well, then refrigerate 20 minutes. Shape into balls with moist hands. Brown balls in hot oil and drain off excess fat. Sprinkle with soup mix and add 1½ cups water. Quartered potatoes may be added at this time, if they are to be used. Cover and cook over low heat 30 minutes. Lift meatballs and potatoes from juices. Blend rice flour with ¼ cup water and add to juices, stirring constantly, until thickened and boiling. If too thick, add more water. Return meatballs and potatoes to gravy and reheat 1 or 2 minutes. *Serves 4*

## SWISS CHARD ROLLS

**BBB + Corn + Beef + Veg. + TE&A**

- 12 large chard leaves
- Boiling water
- 1½ pounds lean ground beef
- 1 cup Quick Brown Rice
- 1 recipe Gloria's Onion Soup Mix, p. 39
- ¼ teaspoon dried oregano

Cover chard leaves with boiling water and let stand 5 minutes. Drain and cut heavy core from each leaf. Brown and crumble beef and drain off excess fat. Stir in rice and 2 tablespoons soup mix. Divide into 12 parts and center 1 portion on each leaf. Roll loosely to allow rice to expand. Fit rolls close together in 2-quart baking dish, seam side down. Combine remaining soup mix, 2½ cups boiling water, and oregano. Pour over rolls. Cover loosely with foil and bake in 350° oven 1 hour or until rice is tender. *Serves 4*

## CREOLE SHORT RIBS

**BBB + Corn + Beef + Veg. + TE&A**

- 3-4 pounds beef short ribs
- 2 tablespoons allowed oil
- 1 recipe Creole Sauce, p. 187
- 1 package (9 ounces) frozen artichoke hearts, thawed
- 2 tablespoons rice flour

Brown ribs on all sides in hot oil. Pour off excess fat and add ½ cup water and all remaining ingredients except flour. Cover and cook over low heat 2 hours or until meat is tender. Lift out ribs and keep hot. Purée pan juices, half at a time, in preheated blender. (Warm container to prevent cracking.) Return to pot and thicken with rice flour and ½ cup water blended and added slowly. Stirring constantly, bring to boil and boil 1 minute. Good served with brown rice. *Serves 4*

## FESTIVE BEEF CASSEROLE

**BBB + Corn + Beef + Veg. + TE&A**

- **1 pound lean ground beef**
- **1 recipe Gloria's Onion Soup Mix, p. 39**
- **1 can (15 ounces) tomato sauce**
- **¾ cup rice**
- **½ cup chopped green pepper**
- **1 cup sliced carrots**
- **1 cup sliced celery**
- **1 can (16 ounces) whole kernel corn, drained**

Brown beef in skillet and drain off excess fat. Add soup mix, 2 cups water, and tomato sauce. Bring to boil. Meanwhile, layer rice, green pepper, carrots, celery, and corn in 2-quart casserole. Pour beef mixture over rice and vegetables. Cover and bake in 350° oven 1¼ hours. *Serves 6*

**Variations:**

1. Omit rice. Bake casserole as directed and then stir in 1⅓ cups Minute Rice. Cover and let stand 5 minutes. Fluff rice with fork.
2. Omit rice and reduce water to ¾ cup. Add 2 cups sliced potato as one layer. Bake, covered, in 350° oven 2 hours.
3. Omit rice and reduce water to ¾ cup. Add 1 package (10 ounces) frozen baby lima beans, 2 cups sliced potato, and 1 teaspoon curry powder. Bake, covered, in 350° oven 2 hours.
4. Omit corn and replace with 1 can (16 ounces) white or golden hominy.
5. Omit corn and replace with 1 can (16 ounces) cut green beans.

## BUSY DAY BRISKET

**BBB + Corn + Beef + Veg. + TE&A**

- **1 3-4-pound beef brisket**
- **1 recipe Gloria's Onion Soup Mix, p. 39**
- **½ cup water or red wine (optional + Mold)**

Line baking pan with heavy duty aluminum foil. Sprinkle half of soup mix on foil and add brisket. Top meat with remaining soup mix. Add liquid and seal tightly with foil. Bake in 325° oven 3½ to 4 hours. Lift out meat and slice thin across grain. Thicken juices with 1 tablespoon rice flour and ¼ cup water. Stir paste into juices and cook until thickened. *Serves 4–6*

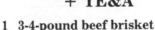

# Poultry

BBB
+ Poultry

## BROILED POULTRY

Begin with skin side of meat toward source of heat—chicken and kabobs 3 inches from heat, turkey and duckling 6 inches from heat. Broil, brushing often with allowed oil or sauce or marinade. Turn and repeat for second side. If preferred, turn and baste often until cooked through and tender.

## BROILING CHART

| Kind | Size | Cut | Time |
|---|---|---|---|
| Any poultry | kabobs | 1 inch cubes | 15-20 minutes |
| Chicken breasts | 12 oz. | half or whole | 40-60 minutes |
| Broiler-fryer | 3 lb. | meaty pieces | 40-60 minutes |
| Broiler-fryer | 2½ lb. | quartered | 40-60 minutes |
| Turkey | 4-5 lb. | split | 1½-2 hours |
| Duckling | 3½-4½ lb. | quartered | 1¼-1½ hours |

BBB
+ Fruit
+ Veg.
+ TE&A

### Variations

1. Marinate and baste in any of the tested and allowed salad dressings in Salad Dressing Section, p. 63.

2. MARINADE—Combine ½ cup allowed oil, 1 teaspoon salt, ½ teaspoon paprika, ¼ cup lemon, lime or orange juice, and ¼ teaspoon garlic powder. Marinate poultry several hours or overnight, covered and refrigerated. Baste with marinade while broiling or baking.

3. BARBECUE—Baste with Barbecue Sauce, p. 186 or with Quick Barbecue Sauce, p. 186.

## ROAST POULTRY

**BBB + Poultry**

Allow ¾ pound poultry per serving. Wash giblets and neck, cover with salted water, and cook until tender. Remove meat, reserve broth, and chill. Use meat in dressings or gravies.

*Unstuffed*—Rinse bird and drain. Rub inside with salt, if desired. When allowed, celery, carrots, onion, parsley, bay leaf, or apple may be placed in cavity for flavoring. **(BBB + Veg. + TE&A)** Bake according to chart, p. 110.

*Stuffed*—Allow 1-1¼ cups stuffing for each pound ready-to-cook poultry weight. Stuff bird with choice of Stuffings from the Vegetables and Side Dishes Section (beginning p. 162). Many of the Meatless Entrees (p. 153), can be used as stuffing also.

Stuff neck cavity loosely, fold neck skin to back, and fasten. Stuff body cavity loosely. Close opening with string laced around metal skewers. Secure around tail. Tie ankles together.

Place prepared bird, breast side up, on rack in shallow roasting pan, or in roasting pan with elevated center to keep bird from swimming in drippings. Twist and fold wings to back so they lie flat. Insert meat thermometer in center of inside thigh muscle, being sure not to touch bone.

Brush poultry with allowed oil or melted milk-free margarine. A small bird or fryer-broiler needs no cover during roasting but should be basted now and then with pan drippings. When larger bird is golden brown, make a foil tent to fit loosely over roasting pan so meat will roast, not steam. Lift tent occa sionally and baste.

For turkey, we use our mothers' method. They dipped cheesecloth (large enough to cover bird) in melted butter. We dip cloth in allowed oil or milk-free margarine to drape over bird at beginning of roasting. As soon as juices drip into pan, baste cloth frequently enough to keep it moist during cooking. What a beautiful golden colored bird!

Cook poultry on rotisserie, if desired. Farberware rotisserie will roast any poultry up to 10 pounds in weight.

Glaze for last 15 to 30 minutes of roasting time. Several glaze recipes follow our roasting chart.

Allow bird to rest at least 15 minutes after removing from heat. This greatly facilitates carving.

Garnish. Use your imagination, but do try Pink Pears for Poultry Pickup, p. 192.

Weight is ready-to-cook weight. Roast to internal temperature of 180-185° on meat thermometer. The chart is a good guide but times will vary according to whether bird is stuffed or unstuffed and according to whether it has been removed from refrigerator immediately prior to baking. Unstuffed turkey requires ½ hour less cooking time than that given for stuffed.

*Note:* If using turkey parts or half turkey, secure skin at edges of meat to keep meat moist during cooking.

# ROASTING CHART

| Kind | Weight | Prepared | Temp. | Time |
|---|---|---|---|---|
| Cornish game hen | 1 lb. | hollow | 350° | 45-60 minutes |
| Cornish game hen | 1 lb. | stuffed | 350° | 1-1¼ hours |
| Broiler-fryer | 2½ lb. | hollow | 400° | 1 hour |
| Broiler-fryer | 2½ lb. | stuffed | 375° | 1½ hours |
| Roasting hen | 5 lb. | hollow | 350° | 2 hours |
| Roasting hen | 5 lb. | stuffed | 325° | 2½-3 hours |
| Capon | 6 lb. | hollow | 325° | 2½ hours |
| Turkey parts | 5-8 lb. | | 325° | 2½-3 hours |
| | 8-10 lb. | | 325° | 3-3½ hours |
| | 10-12 lb. | | 325° | 3½-4 hours |
| Half turkey | 6 lb. | | 325° | 2½-3 hours |
| Whole turkey | 6-8 lb. | stuffed | 325° | 3-3½ hours |
| | 8-12 lb. | stuffed | 325° | 3½-4½ hours |
| | 12-16 lb. | stuffed | 325° | 4½-5½ hours |
| | 16-20 lb. | stuffed | 325° | 5½-6½ hours |
| | 20-24 lb. | stuffed | 325° | 6½-7½ hours |

☐

**BBB**
**+ Fruit**
**+ TE&A**

## GLAZES

1. Combine lemon rind and juice of 1 lemon and ¼ cup honey. Add 2 tablespoons melted allowed margarine.

2. Combine ¼ cup honey, ¼ cup sugar, 1 cup orange juice and a pinch of salt.

3. Combine ⅓ cup Clair's Lemon Marmalade, p. 242, or any other allowed jam and 2 tablespoons allowed margarine or pan drippings.

4. Combine ¼ cup orange juice, ½ cup BBB Brown Sugar Syrup, p. 205, ¼ teaspoon ginger, and 1 tablespoon grated orange peel.

5. Combine 1 can (7 ounces) jellied cranberry sauce, 2 tablespoons melted allowed margarine or pan drippings, and ½ teaspoon marjoram. **(+ Corn + TE&A)**

6. Combine ¼ cup apricot jam, ¼ cup lemon juice, ¼ teaspoon ginger, and ½ teaspoon salt. **(+ Corn)**

7. Combine 1 can (6 ounces) frozen orange juice concentrate, thawed, and 2 tablespoons Jan-U-Wine Soy Sauce. **(+ Corn)**

## CHICKEN PREMIER

**BBB + Poultry** ☐

- **3 chicken breasts, each cut in half**
- **⅓ cup plus 3 tablespoons rice flour**
- **1 tablespoon potato flour (optional)**
- **Allowed oil**
- **1½ cups peeled and chunked carrots**
- **¾ teaspoon salt**
- **2½ cups water or allowed milk substitute or Cooked Chicken-Seasoned Stock, p. 117**
- **3 cups hot cooked rice, brown or white**

Shake chicken breasts, one at a time, in bag with ⅓ cup rice flour and potato flour to coat. Brown well in hot oil and remove to baking pan. Purée carrots, salt, 3 tablespoons rice flour, and 1 cup liquid in blender or food processor. Add remaining liquid. Pour into skillet and cook, stirring constantly, until thickened and boiling. Be sure to scrape up brown bits from bottom of pan. Pour this thin sauce over chicken in baking pan. Cover tightly and bake in 350° oven 45 minutes or until tender. Serve on bed of hot cooked rice. *Serves 3–6.*

## YAMMY CHICKEN

**BBB + Poultry** ☐

- **2 cups cooked chicken**
- **2 cups chicken gravy made with allowed thickening**
- **4–5 sweet potatoes, boiled until tender, drained**
- **2 tablespoons allowed margarine**
- **Salt to taste**
- **Unsweetened apple or pineapple juice or allowed milk substitute**

Heat chicken and gravy to boil, thinning with water if too thick. Mash potatoes with margarine, salt, and juice to desired consistency. Place chicken mixture in 1½-quart casserole and top with potatoes. Bake in 400° oven 25 minutes or until piping hot. *Serves 3–4*

## SKINNY CHICK

**BBB + Poultry** ☐

- **2½ pound broiler-fryer or equivalent in parts**
- **Salt to taste**

Place chicken pieces, skin side down, in non-stick skillet. Salt to taste, cover tightly and cook over low heat 20 minutes. Turn pieces and tilt lid of skillet to allow liquid to cook off. Continue cooking until tender and browned, 20 to 30 minutes. *Serves 4*

**Variation:**

Season with garlic or onion powder and herbs as allowed. **(+ Veg. + TE&A)**

☐ **BBB + Poultry**

- 1 2½–3-pound broiler-fryer, cut up, or equivalent in parts
- ¼ cup allowed oil
- 1 cup rice flour
- 3 tablespoons potato flour (optional, but aids browning)
- 1 teaspoon salt

## FRIED CHICKEN

Roll chicken pieces in oil and drain. Shake pieces one at a time in paper or plastic bag with seasoned flours.

*Skillet method*—Brown coated chicken in hot oil, cover, and cook slowly 20 to 40 minutes or until tender. Hide liver under back or ribs to keep from spattering grease. Remove lid and fry until coating crisps. Serve with Southern Chicken Gravy, p. 189. *Serves 4*

*Oven methods*—Brown coated chicken in hot oil. Remove pieces to baking pan or onto wire rack above shallow pan and bake in 350° oven 45 minutes.

Coated chicken may also be baked at 400° 1 hour without being first browned in skillet.

**Variations:**

1. When tested and allowed, add choice of seasonings to flour mixture: pepper, paprika, seasoned salt, onion or garlic powder, dried thyme, rosemary, marjoram, curry powder, or poultry seasoning **(+ Veg. + TE&A).**
2. Halved Cornish game hens or parts of small turkey may be prepared by same methods, extending cooking time for turkey parts.

☐ **BBB + Poultry**

- 1 cup brown rice, rinsed and drained
- 3 tablespoons allowed oil
- 3 cups hot Chicken Stock, p. 30
- ½ teaspoon salt
- 1½ cups cubed chicken breast meat
- 2 cups diced carrots
- 1 package (9 ounces) frozen artichoke hearts or 1 package (10 ounces) frozen spinach, cooked and drained
- 1 can (8 ounces) unsweetened pineapple slices, drained, juice reserved

## BEGINNERS CASSEROLE

Brown rice in 2 tablespoons oil in ovenproof 1½-quart baking pan. Add stock, salt, and chicken and bring to boil. Cover and bake in 250° oven 30 minutes. Sauté carrots in remaining oil and add to casserole along with artichoke hearts or spinach. Add reserved pineapple juice. Toss well. Top with sliced pineapple. Continue baking 20 minutes. *Serves 4–6*

## POULTRY À LA KING

## BBB + Poultry

**2 cups Chicken Stock, p. 30, or substitute other poultry if desired**
**¼ cup allowed margarine or congealed chicken fat**
**3 tablespoons rice flour**
**½ teaspoon salt**
**2½ cups diced or sliced cooked poultry**

Prepare Chicken Stock the day before or early in the day. Refrigerate broth and poultry separately. Pick poultry from bones and dice or slice. Melt margarine or fat, blend in flour, and cook until bubbly. Slowly add stock, stirring constantly until thickened. Boil 1 minute. Stir in salt and prepared poultry and heat through. Serve over hot rice or allowed toast. *Serves 4*

**Variations:**

1. ASPARAGUS HOLLANDA—Cook and drain frozen asparagus spears and frozen green peas (1 package each, 10 ounces). Place spears on allowed toast, ring with peas, and cover with poultry and sauce.
2. ARTICHOKE SPECIAL—Cook frozen artichoke hearts (9 ounces) and drain. Add to poultry in sauce and serve over Soy-Potato Waffles, p. 200.
3. INDIVIDUAL POULTRY PIES—Line 4 chicken pie tins with mashed sweet or white potatoes. Cook and drain frozen peas-carrots (10 ounces) and add to poultry mixture. Turkey goes well in sweet potato shells. Chicken is better with white potatoes. Fill shells and bake in 400° oven until hot through and potato edges are golden. If preferred, bake empty potato shells 30 minutes in 400° oven, then fill with hot bubbling poultry-vegetable mixture.
4. SAVORY POULTRY À LA KING—Sauté 1 tablespoon grated onion and ¼ cup diced celery in margarine. Add sautéed vegetables and 1 tablespoon each chopped parsley and diced pimiento to poultry mixture. **(+ Veg.)**
5. CREAMED CHICKEN—Replace Chicken Stock with allowed milk substitute. Serve over rice, allowed toasted bread, waffle, or Soy Grits Cereal, p. 248.
6. POULTRY SUPREME—Sauté 1 chopped onion and ½ cup sliced celery in allowed margarine to add to original recipe. Then, just before serving, add 1 sliced avocado to sauce. Serve over fluffy rice garnished with chopped nuts, if allowed. **(+ Fruit + Veg. + N&S)**

**BBB + Poultry**

- 2 small turkey thighs (1½–2 pounds each), boned
- Salt to taste
- 2 medium carrots, peeled
- 1 tablespoon allowed margarine
- ¼ cup allowed oil

## BRAISED STUFFED TURKEY THIGHS

Have butcher bone turkey or do it yourself with sharp knife. Sprinkle lightly with salt inside and out. Replace each bone with carrot dotted with 1½ teaspoons margarine. Fold meat around carrots and tie. Brown in hot oil all around and drain off excess fat. Add ½ cup water, cover, and bake in 325° oven 1½ hours or until tender. Serve sauce as is or thicken with small amount of rice flour. *Serves 4–6.*

**Variations:**

1. Remove meat from juice when done. Measure liquid. Bring to boil and add equal amount Minute Rice. Remove from heat, cover, and set aside 5 minutes.
2. When allowed, stuff with celery and onion. Season with garlic powder, dash of white pepper, and 1 teaspoon Steero Instant Chicken Flavor Bouillon Seasoning and Broth. (optional **+ Veg. + TE&A**) Sprinkle 1 tablespoon dried parsley over turkey before baking.

**BBB + Poultry**

- 3 cups hot steamed rice
- 1 package (10 ounces) frozen asparagus, cooked and drained or 1 package (9 ounces) frozen artichoke hearts, cooked and drained
- 1 pound cooked chicken slices
- 3 tablespoons rice flour
- 2½ cups allowed milk substitute
- 2 tablespoons allowed oil
- ½ teaspoon salt

## SIMPLY DIVINE

Layer rice, asparagus or artichoke hearts, and chicken in 2-quart oiled casserole. Blend flour with ½ cup milk substitute to smooth paste, add remaining milk substitute, oil, and salt. Cook slowly, stirring constantly until thickened. Pour over casserole. Bake in 400° oven for 25 minutes or until hot through. *Serves 4*

**Variation: Rice-Chicken Almondine**

Omit asparagus or artichoke hearts. Sauté 1 tablespoon minced onion and ½ cup slivered almonds in 2 tablespoons additional oil. Add to sauce along with 2 tablespoons diced pimiento and 1 tablespoon minced parsley. If desired, top with coconut and bake until bubbly. Serve with fresh pineapple slices. **(+ Veg. + N&S)**

## POLYNESIAN CHICKS DEBUT

**BBB + Poultry** ☐

- **1 3-pound broiler-fryer or equivalent in parts**
- **⅓ cup rice flour**
- **2 tablespoons potato flour**
- **Salt**
- **2–4 tablespoons allowed margarine**
- **1 can (20 ounces) pineapple chunks, drained, juice reserved**
- **1 package (10 ounces) frozen green peas**

Shake chicken pieces in paper bag with flours and 1 teaspoon salt, and set aside. Brown drained pineapple chunks in 1 tablespoon margarine, stirring often. Remove. Add margarine necessary to brown coated chicken. Measure reserved juice and add water to make 1½ cups. Pour over chicken, add salt to taste, and return pineapple chunks. Cover and cook slowly 30 minutes or until chicken is tender. Add peas, return to boil, cover, and cook 5 minutes. Serve over cooked brown rice. *Serves 4*

**Variations:**

1. If desired, blend part of coating flour with cold water to a thin paste and stir into simmering liquid to thicken.
2. CASSEROLE—Sauté ¾ cup white rice with pineapple. Pour into casserole. Bring liquid and peas to boil and add to casserole. Season to taste. Top with browned chicken. Cover and bake in 350° oven 45 to 60 minutes or until rice and chicken are tender.
3. SKILLET DINNER—Remove chicken when regular recipe is done. Keep hot. Stir 1⅓ cups Minute Rice into juices. Cover and let stand 5 minutes. Stir and serve topped with chicken.

## YAMMY TURKEY

**BBB + Poultry + Fruit + Veg.** ☐

- **½ cup sliced onion**
- **2 tablespoons allowed oil**
- **1½ cups leftover roast turkey**
- **1½ cups leftover turkey gravy, made with allowed thickening**
- **4–5 sweet potatoes, boiled, drained, and peeled**
- **1 can (8 ounces) unsweetened crushed pineapple**
- **Salt to taste**
- **2 tablespoons orange juice**
- **1 teaspoon grated orange peel**

Sauté onion in oil, add turkey and gravy, and heat to boil. Thin gravy with water as necessary. Mash potatoes with remaining ingredients. Place turkey mixture in 2-quart baking dish and top with mashed sweets. Bake in 400° oven 30 minutes or until hot through. *Serves 3 or 4*

☐ **BBB + Poultry + Fruit**

## ROAST DUCK

Rub 5-pound duck with lemon juice outside and salt inside. Refrigerate at least 4 hours or overnight. Stuff with desired allowed stuffing, close cavity, and insert meat thermometer in thickest part of thigh. Roast in 325° oven until thermometer reaches 180° to 185°. Time will be approximately 2½ to 3 hours. Serve with Fruited Gravy, p. 190.

Duck may also be roasted on rotisserie, using longest cooking time. Glaze last 15 to 30 minutes, if desired. To spur your imagination, see California Sunshine Chicken, p. 127, and then create your own glaze from tested and allowed fruits and seasonings. *Serves 5*

**Glaze Variations:**

1. Simmer ½ cup orange juice, ½ cup honey, and 1 tablespoon pan drippings to meld flavors. Serve duck garnished with orange slices. **(+ TE&A)**

2. Blend 1½ teaspoons cornstarch with 1 tablespoon water. Combine with ½ cup red currant jelly, ½ cup orange juice, 2 tablespoons lemon juice, and dash of ginger. Boil 1 minute, stirring constantly. **(+ Corn + TE&A)**

3. Combine 1 can (6 ounces) frozen tangerine juice concentrate, thawed, and ½ cup lime juice. **(+ Corn)**

☐ **BBB + Poultry + Veg.**

## POULTRY NESTS

- **5 cups allowed bread crumbs or 100% White Rye Bread when allowed (+ Rye)**
- **¼ cup minced onion**
- **1 teaspoon celery salt**
- **½ cup allowed margarine**

Combine and press into bottom and sides of 6 oiled individual casseroles, custard cups, or pie tins. Bake in 375° oven 20 minutes. Fill with Poultry à la King or a variation, p. 113.

## COOKED CHICKEN-SEASONED STOCK

**BBB + Poultry + Veg.**

- 1 broiler-fryer (about 3 pounds)
- 2 carrots, chunked
- 1 tablespoon instant chopped onion
- 2 teaspoons dried parsley
- 2 stalks celery with leaves, chunked
- 1 teaspoon salt

Bring all ingredients to boil, cover and reduce heat. Simmer 45 to 60 minutes or until chicken is tender. Cool and lift out chicken. Remove skin and bones and cut meat into desired-size pieces or slices. (Meat may be packaged in measured amounts and frozen for later use.) Strain stock and chill. Next day, remove fat from stock. (Freeze stock by the cupful, if desired.) Purée vegetables with small amount of stock and reheat for a quick lunch for the cook, perhaps. Use prepared chicken stock in recipes of your choice.

**Variation:**

This may be prepared in slow cooker on low setting 7 to 10 hours or on high 2½ to 3½ hours. Why not let it cook while you sleep? Next morning, debone chicken and chill broth for later use.

## TURKEY GUMBO

**BBB + Poultry + Veg.**

- 1 onion, chopped
- 1 clove garlic, minced
- 1 cup rice
- 2 tablespoons allowed oil
- 2½ cups Cooked Chicken-Seasoned Stock (make by substituting turkey for chicken, if desired)
- 1 package (10 ounces) frozen cut okra, or 2 cups fresh okra, sliced
- 2 cups diced cooked turkey
- ½ teaspoon salt

Sauté onion, garlic, and rice in oil. Add remaining ingredients. Cover and cook slowly 25 minutes or until rice is tender. *Serves 4–6*

**Variation:**

Sliced green pepper may be sautéed with onion. Replace stock with 1 can (16 ounces) stewed tomatoes and 1 cup water. Add dash of hot pepper sauce to taste. **(+ TE&A)**

**BBB + Poultry + Veg.**

- 1 recipe Cooked Chicken-Seasoned Stock, p. 117
- 1 cup cooked chicken meat, minced
- ¼ cup finely minced celery
- ¼ cup minced green pepper
- 1 tablespoon allowed oil or margarine
- 1 teaspoon instant minced onion
- 1 teaspoon dried parsley
- ¼ teaspoon paprika
- 1 cup Cream of Rice
- ⅓ cup rice flour
- 1 tablespoon potato flour

## SAUTÉED POULTRY-RICE SLICES

Prepare chicken and stock in advance and defat stock. Sauté celery and green pepper in oil until soft. Add onion, parsley, paprika, and 3 cups stock. Bring to boil. Sprinkle in Cream of Rice, stirring constantly 30 seconds. Remove from heat, cover, and let stand 5 minutes. Stir in minced chicken, pour mixture into oiled 8 x 4 x 2-inch loaf pan and chill several hours. Unmold, cut into slices, coat with blended flours, and fry in small amount allowed oil until browned and hot through. *Serves 3 to 4*

**Variations:**

1. POULTRY-GRITS SLICES—Replace Cream of Rice with ¼ cup Quick Grits when corn is allowed. Sprinkle grits into boiling stock, stirring constantly. Cover and cook slowly 4 to 5 minutes. Add chicken, mold, and chill. Slice, coat in cornmeal, and fry in allowed oil. **(+ Corn)**
2. POULTRY-CORN SLICES—Reduce Seasoned Stock to 2 cups. Replace Cream of Rice with 1 cup white or yellow cornmeal blended with ¾ cup cold water. Add cornmeal mixture slowly to boiling stock, stirring constantly. Cook and stir over low heat 5 minutes. Continue as in original recipe. **(+ Corn)**

**BBB + Poultry + TE&A**

- 1 3-4 pound duckling, cut in pieces
- ¾ cup rice flour
- ¼ cup potato flour
- 1 teaspoon salt
- ¼ teaspoon pepper
- 2 teaspoons paprika
- Allowed oil

## FRIED DUCKLING

Shake duckling pieces in flours and seasonings mixed in paper bag. Fry pieces, skin side down, in ¼ inch hot oil in skillet. When brown, turn and brown second side. Add ½ cup water and cover. Cook over low heat or bake in 350° oven 1 hour. Uncover and continue cooking ½ hour to crisp coating. If desired, serve with Favorite Rich Gravy, p. 185. *Serves 4-6*

## ROAST GOOSE

**BBB + Poultry + Fruit + TE&A**

Rub 8- to 10-pound goose inside and out with lemon juice, salt, pepper and ½ teaspoon ginger. Insert meat thermometer in thickest part of thigh. Oven roast, breast side up, on rack in shallow pan as follows: Uncovered, at 400° 1 hour, then reduce heat to 325° and continue baking 1½ hours or until thermometer reaches 185°. Spoon off fat or remove with baster every 30 minutes of baking time.

If desired, add for last ½ hour of cooking ¼ cup each chopped onion, carrots, and celery. **(+ Veg.)** When bird is done, you may wish to purée vegetables with pan juices and serve as gravy or you may thicken juices with rice or potato flour.

*Stuffed*—Rub goose with lemon and seasonings. Fill cavity with stuffing of your choice as allowed. Roast at 325° 3¼ hours or until thermometer reaches 185°.

*Note:* Do not rub goose with oil and do not baste. It bastes itself.

## SWEET ORANGE CHICKEN

**BBB + Poultry + Fruit + TE&A**

**4 chicken legs with thighs**
**2 tablespoons allowed oil**
**¼ cup mild honey**
**¾ cup orange juice**
**½ teaspoon salt**
**½ teaspoon dry mustard**
**½ teaspoon paprika**
**Orange cartwheels**

*Skillet Method*—Brown chicken in oil beginning with skin side, turn until all brown, and drain fat. Cover and cook slowly 20 minutes. Mix remaining ingredients, pour over chicken, and turn to coat with sauce. Cook uncovered 15 to 20 minutes or until chicken is tender, basting often. Add orange cartwheels last 5 minutes. *Serves 4*

*Oven Method*—Marinate chicken in honey-orange mixture several hours. Bake, uncovered, skin side down, 30 minutes in 400° oven. Turn meat and bake another 30 minutes or until tender, adding cartwheels last 5 minutes. Thicken sauce with 1½ teaspoons tapioca starch blended with ¼ cup water. Add to pan juices, stirring constantly until thickened. Boil 1 minute. *Serves 4*

☐ **BBB + Poultry + Fruit + TE&A**

- 2 pounds poultry, cut in ½-inch cubes
- 2 tablespoons allowed oil
- ½ cup honey
- ¼ cup prepared mustard
- ⅓ cup lemon juice
- 1 teaspoon curry powder
- ½ teaspoon salt
- Green pepper
- Fresh pineapple chunks

## CURRY KABOBS

Marinate meat cubes several hours, refrigerated, in mixture of oil, honey, mustard, lemon juice, curry powder, and salt. Thread on skewers with green pepper and pineapple. Broil or barbeque 15 minutes or until meat is tender. Brush often during cooking with curry marinade. *Serves 4*

**Variation:**

Use curry mixture to marinate 3 pounds chicken parts overnight in refrigerator. Next day, bake, uncovered, in 375° oven 1 hour or until tender and richly glazed.

☐ **BBB + Poultry + Veg. + TE&A**

- 1 broiler-fryer, quartered
- 1 tablespoon allowed oil
- Salt and pepper
- 1 cup brown rice
- ½ cup chopped onion
- 1 cup sliced celery
- 3 cups Cooked Chicken-Seasoned Stock, p. 117
- ½ teaspoon poultry seasoning

## BAKED CHICKEN AND RICE

Brown chicken in oil and season. Remove from skillet and add brown rice, onion, and celery. Add stock and poultry seasoning and bring to boil. Transfer to 1½-quart baking dish and top with chicken. Bake, covered, in 350° oven 45 to 60 minutes or until rice and chicken are tender. *Serves 4 big eaters*

☐ **BBB + Poultry + Veg. + TE&A**

## BAKED BARBECUE CHICKEN

Arrange 3-5 pounds chicken pieces in shallow oiled baking dish. Coat chicken well with Barbecue Sauce, p. 186, or Quick Barbecue Sauce, p. 186. Bake in 400° oven 45 to 60 minutes or until chicken is fork tender. *Serves 6–8*

## BRAISED CORNISH GAME HENS

**BBB + Poultry + Veg. + TE&A**

- **2-4 Cornish game hens, halved or whole**
- **2-4 tablespoons allowed oil**
- **1 small onion, chopped**
- **¾ cup chopped celery**
- **½ cup sliced carrots**
- **1 tablespoon chopped parsley**
- **½ teaspoon salt**
- **1 bay leaf**
- **Dash of pepper**
- **1½ tablespoons rice flour**
- **½ teaspoon Kitchen Bouquet**

Brown hens in oil on all sides and set aside. Sauté onion, celery, and carrots in oil until soft. Stir in seasonings and 1¼ cups water. Return hens to kettle, breast side down. Cover and cook slowly 30 to 45 minutes or until tender. Remove hens and keep hot. Purée vegetables, flour, and small amount of pan juices. Return mixture to kettle and combine with pan juices. Cook, stirring constantly, until broth is thickened. Stir in Kitchen Bouquet.

For light eaters, have butcher halve hens. For growing boys of any age, serve 1 hen each. *Serves 2–8*

## CHICKEN CONTINENTAL

**BBB + Poultry + Veg. + TE&A**

- **1 3-4-pound frying chicken, cut in pieces**
- **⅓ cup rice flour**
- **1 tablespoon potato flour**
- **1 teaspoon salt**
- **¼ teaspoon pepper**
- **¼ cup allowed oil**
- **3 teaspoons Steero Instant Chicken Flavor Bouillon Seasoning and Broth**
- **1 tablespoon minced parsley**
- **2 teaspoons chopped celery leaves**
- **⅛ teaspoon dried thyme**
- **2 teaspoons instant minced onion**
- **1⅓ cups Minute Rice**
- **Dash of paprika**
- **Parsley sprigs**

Shake chicken pieces in paper bag with combined flours, salt and pepper. Brown in oil and remove. Combine 2½ tablespoons coating flours with ⅓ cup water and stir to blend well. Add bouillon, 2 cups water, flour paste, dried herbs and onion to skillet, stirring constantly until sauce is thickened and boiling. Place rice in 3-quart casserole. Pour ¾ sauce over rice and stir to moisten. Top with chicken pieces and pour on remaining sauce. Cover and bake in 375° oven 45 to 60 minutes or until chicken is tender. Garnish with dash of paprika and parsley sprigs. A delicious company casserole. *Serves 6*

## CHICKEN JAMBALAYA

**BBB + Poultry + Veg. + TE&A**

Follow Pork Jambalaya, p. 139, replacing pork with cooked chicken.

## TURKEY STEW

☐ **BBB + Poultry + Veg. + TE&A**

- **3 pounds turkey thighs or breast, cut in chunks**
- **2 tablespoons allowed oil**
- **Salt and pepper to taste**
- **6 small whole boiling onions**
- **6 small red new potatoes, scrubbed**
- **2 carrots, peeled and cut in thick diagonal slices**
- **1 cup sliced celery**
- **1 teaspoon Steero Instant Chicken Flavor Bouillon Seasoning and Broth**
- **2 tablespoons minced parsley**
- **1 teaspoon dried basil**
- **1 package (10 ounces) frozen green peas**

Brown turkey pieces in oil and season to taste. Push turkey to one side and sauté onions, potatoes, carrots, and celery in drippings. Add 1 cup water and all ingredients except peas. Cover and cook slowly 1½ hours or until turkey is done. Add peas, cover and cook 5 minutes. Serve with juices or thicken with rice flour if desired. *Serves 4–6*

## ARROZ CON POLLO

☐ **BBB + Poultry + Veg. + TE&A**

- **3 pounds broiler-fryer parts**
- **1 onion, chopped**
- **2 cloves garlic, minced**
- **1 can (16 ounces) stewed tomatoes**
- **1 teaspoon salt**
- **1 teaspoon chili powder**
- **½ medium green pepper, diced**
- **1 cup rice**
- **1 jar (2 ounces) pimiento, sliced**

Brown chicken in non-stick skillet, skin side first. Remove and sauté onion and garlic in drippings. Add tomatoes, 1 cup water, salt, chili powder, and chicken. Cover and simmer 20 minutes. Add remaining ingredients. Cover and cook 30 minutes longer or until rice and chicken are tender. *Serves 4–6*

**Variation:**

Replace tomatoes and water with 2½ cups Cooked Chicken-Seasoned Stock, p. 117. Replace chili powder with 1 teaspoon dried rosemary, ½ teaspoon dried thyme, and 1 bay leaf. Add 1 box (10 ounces) frozen baby limas when rice is added.

## CHICKEN CASSEROLE

Shake chicken with flours and salt in paper bag. Brown in hot oil and remove from skillet. Sauté onion and pepper in remaining drippings until soft. Add tomatoes, breaking them up, and add beans. Heat thoroughly, stirring brown bits from bottom of skillet. Transfer to 3-quart casserole and stir in remaining ingredients. Place browned chicken on top. Cover and bake in 375° oven 45 to 60 minutes or until chicken is done and casserole bubbly. *Serves 4–6*

**BBB + Poultry + Veg. + TE&A** ☐

- 1 broiler-fryer or equivalent in parts
- ⅓ cup rice flour
- 1 tablespoon potato flour, optional
- 1 teaspoon salt
- 2 tablespoons allowed oil
- 1 small onion, chopped
- ½ green pepper, diced
- 1 can (16 ounces) stewed tomatoes
- 1 can (15-16 ounces) garbanzo beans, drained
- 1 can (1 pound 12 ounces) Loma Linda Boston Style Soybeans
- 1½ cups cooked brown rice
- ¾ teaspoon dried basil
- Pinch of pepper
- 1 tablespoon imitation bacon bits

## SAUCY LIVERS

Sauté livers in margarine 3 to 5 minutes, remove and reserve. Sauté onion and pepper until soft. Blend in flour and seasonings. Add 2 cups water, stirring constantly until thickened. Cover and cook slowly 15 minutes. Remove bay leaf, add livers, and heat 5 minutes. Spoon over allowed toast or waffles, cooked grits, or rice. May also be spooned into Mashed Potato Shells, p. 166 or into Poultry Nests, p. 116. *Serves 4*

**BBB + Poultry + Veg. + TE&A** ☐

- 1 pound chicken livers, halved
- ¼ cup allowed margarine
- 1 onion, chopped
- ¼ cup chopped green pepper
- 2½ tablespoons rice flour
- ¼ teaspoon dried thyme
- 2 teaspoons Steero Instant Chicken Flavor Bouillon Seasoning and Broth
- 1 bay leaf
- 1 tablespoon imitation bacon bits

## CHICKEN LIVERS ITALIANO

☐ **BBB + Poultry + Veg. + TE&A**

- 1 pound chicken livers, halved
- ¼ cup rice flour
- ½ teaspoon salt
- ¼ teaspoon pepper
- 4 tablespoons allowed oil
- 1 onion, chopped
- 1 cup rice
- 2 teaspoons Steero Instant Chicken Flavor Bouillon Seasoning and Broth
- 1 teaspoon dried basil
- 1 bay leaf
- 1 tablespoon imitation bacon bits
- Chopped parsley

Shake chicken livers in combined flour, salt, and pepper in paper or plastic bag. Brown livers in 2 tablespoons oil. Remove and reserve. Add remaining oil and sauté onion and rice. Stir in seasonings and 2½ cups water. Bring to boil, cover, and cook over low heat 15 minutes. Top with browned livers and bacon bits. Continue cooking 10 to 15 minutes or until rice is tender. Remove bay leaf and garnish with parsley. *Serves 4–6*

## CHICKEN CREOLE

☐ **BBB + Poultry + Veg. + TE&A**

- 2 whole chicken breasts, boned, skinned, and cut in 1-inch pieces
- 3 tablespoons allowed oil
- Salt, paprika, garlic powder, and cayenne pepper to taste
- 1 medium onion, sliced
- ½ green pepper, sliced
- 1 cup sliced celery
- 1 can (8 ounces) tomato sauce
- 1 can (16 ounces) stewed tomatoes
- ½ teaspoon dried thyme
- Dash of Tabasco sauce
- 1 tablespoon tapioca starch

Sauté chicken in oil and season with salt, paprika, garlic powder, and cayenne while browning. Push to one side of skillet and sauté onion, pepper, and celery until soft. Add all remaining ingredients except starch. Cover and cook over low heat 25 minutes. Blend starch with ¼ cup water and add to pan juices, stirring constantly until clear and thickened. Serve over rice. *Serves 4–6*

## CHICKEN GUMBO

**BBB + Poultry + Veg. + TE&A**

- 1 recipe Chicken Creole, p. 124, omitting starch
- 1 cup rice
- 1 package (10 ounces) frozen okra, cut or whole

Prepare Chicken Creole recipe. Add 1 cup water, rice, and okra with tomatoes and tomato sauce. Bring to boil, cover, and cook over low heat 25 minutes or until rice and okra are tender. *Serves 4–6*

## CHICKEN CACCIATORE

**BBB + Poultry + Veg. + TE&A**

- 2 pounds meaty chicken parts
- ½ cup rice flour
- 1 tablespoon potato flour
- 1 teaspoon paprika
- Allowed oil
- ½ medium green pepper, chopped
- 1 medium onion, diced
- 1 clove garlic, crushed
- ½ teaspoon Italian seasonings
- 1 tablespoon dried parsley
- 1 can (16 ounces) stewed tomatoes
- 1 teaspoon salt
- ¼ teaspoon pepper

Coat chicken pieces by shaking in blended flours and paprika in paper bag. Brown in large skillet with as little oil as possible. Remove and reserve. Drain off excess fat and sauté green pepper, onion, and garlic in skillet. Add ½ cup water and remaining ingredients and bring to boil, stirring to loosen brown bits from bottom of pan. Return chicken and spoon sauce over pieces. Cover and cook slowly 40 to 60 minutes or until chicken is tender. *Serves 4–6*

**Variations:**

1. *Prepare ahead method*—Brown chicken and make sauce. Pour sauce on chicken in casserole and refrigerate. Remove and let stand 30 minutes before baking. Bake, covered, in 350° oven 1½ hours or until tender.
2. Serve cacciatore over steamed rice, cooked spaghetti squash, or zucchini. After corn has been tested and is allowed, try the treat of Wheat-Free Corn Pasta (spaghetti or shells). **(+ Corn)**
3. Replace Italian seasoning with 1 teaspoon chili powder and add 1 tablespoon imitation bacon bits.
4. Replace water with Burgundy wine. **(+ Mold)**

## CHICKEN PILAF

**BBB + Poultry + Veg. + TE&A**

Follow recipe for Chicken Cacciatore but with the following changes: Omit garlic and Italian seasoning. Add 1 cup additional water and 1½ cups white rice. Cook as recipe directs.

## CHICKEN CURRY

**BBB + Poultry + Veg. + TE&A**

- **3 pounds broiler-fryer parts**
- **1 tablespoon curry powder**
- **1 cup chopped onion**
- **1 cup chopped celery**
- **Dash of ginger**
- **2 teaspoons Steero Instant Chicken Flavor Bouillon Seasoning and Broth**
- **Dash of pepper**
- **¼ teaspoon garlic powder**
- **2 tablespoons rice flour**

Brown chicken, skin side down, until golden. Turn and brown second side. Remove chicken from pan and set aside. Stir in curry powder and cook 1 minute. Add and sauté onion and celery until soft. Stir in remaining seasonings and flour and blend. Add 2 cups water slowly, stirring until thickened and boiling. Return chicken to sauce, cover, and cook slowly 30 to 45 minutes or until chicken is tender. Serve over hot cooked rice. *Serves 4*

**Variation:**

As allowed, top with any or all of the following: orange or grapefruit sections, onion, green pepper, cucumber, cantaloupe, banana, peanuts, coconut.

## FRUITED CHICKEN BREASTS

**BBB + Poultry + Fruit + Veg. + TE&A**

- **½ cup short-grain brown rice**
- **1½ cups Cooked Chicken-Seasoned Stock, p. 117 or water + ½ teaspoon salt**
- **2 teaspoons instant minced onion**
- **½ teaspoon ginger**
- **4 whole chicken breasts, boned**
- **2 teaspoons Steero Instant Chicken Flavor Bouillon Seasoning and Broth**
- **1½ tablespoons tapioca starch**
- **2 tablespoons lemon juice**
- **Dash of paprika**
- **1 navel orange, sectioned**
- **1 cup seedless grapes, halved**

Simmer rice in stock, covered, 45 minutes or until tender. Stir in onion and ¼ teaspoon ginger. Spoon ¼ of mixture into each chicken breast, fold over, secure edges with wooden toothpicks, and set aside. Blend bouillon, starch, and remaining ginger in large skillet. Slowly add 2 cups water and lemon juice. Stirring constantly, bring to boil and cook until thick and clear. Place stuffed breasts in sauce, spoon sauce over, and sprinkle with paprika. Cover and simmer 30-45 minutes or until tender. Add orange sections and grapes and barely heat through. *Serves 4*

## CHICKEN ROSEMARY

**BBB + Poultry + Fruit + Veg. + TE&A**

- **4 pounds meaty chicken parts**
- **1 medium onion, chopped**
- **2 tablespoons allowed oil**
- **1 can (8 ounces) tomato sauce**
- **¼ cup lemon juice**
- **1 teaspoon salt**
- **¼ teaspoon garlic powder**
- **¼ teaspoon dry mustard**
- **1 teaspoon dried rosemary**

Place chicken, skin side down, in shallow baking dish. Sauté onion in oil, add remaining ingredients, and bring to boil. Pour over chicken and bake in 400° oven 30 minutes. Turn chicken and continue baking 30-40 minutes or until tender and well glazed. *Serves 4–6*

**Variations:**

1. Replace rosemary with 1½ teaspoons fresh marjoram leaves, minced.
2. Replace rosemary with 2 tablespoons honey for easy barbequed chicken.

## CALIFORNIA SUNSHINE CHICKEN

**BBB + Poultry + Fruit + TE&A**

- **8 chicken thighs**
- **2 tablespoons tapioca starch**
- **2 tablespoons brown sugar**
- **½ teaspoon salt**
- **½ teaspoon ginger**
- **⅛ teaspoon pepper**
- **1½ cups orange juice**
- **2 oranges, peeled and sectioned**

Brown chicken, skin side down to start, in non-stick skillet, and remove to 2-quart casserole. Blend starch, sugar, and seasonings and add to skillet. Slowly stir in orange juice mixed with ½ cup water. Cook until mixture is thickened and clear. Boil 1 minute. Pour over chicken, cover, and bake 40 minutes in 350° oven. Add orange sections and continue baking 20 minutes. If allowed, top with ½ cup slivered almonds, uncover, and bake at 400° 5 minutes to brown nuts. (+ N&S) *Serves 4–6*

## SLIM YOUNG CHICK

**BBB + Poultry + Fruit + Veg. + N&S + TE&A**

- **1 broiler-fryer, quartered**
- **Garlic salt to taste**
- **⅓ cup lemon, orange or lime juice**
- **½ teaspoon ginger**
- **1 teaspoon chopped parsley**
- **Paprika**
- **Sesame seeds**

Rub garlic salt into chicken. Blend juice of your choice, ½ cup water, ginger, and parsley, and pour over fryer placed skin side down in shallow baking dish. Sprinkle with paprika and seeds. Bake, uncovered, in 400° oven 30 minutes, basting occasionally. Turn, baste, sprinkle with paprika and seeds, and continue baking 30 minutes longer. *Serves 4*

**BBB + Poultry + Fruit + Veg. + TE&A + Mold**

- 2 pounds chicken breasts, cut in bite-size pieces
- 2 tablespoons allowed oil
- 1 package (16 ounces) frozen Oriental Vegetables (green beans, broccoli, onions, and mushrooms)
- 2 teaspoons Steero Instant Chicken Flavor Bouillon Seasoning and Broth
- 1 can (20 ounces) unsweetened pineapple chunks, drained, juice reserved
- ½ teaspoon ginger
- ¼ teaspoon dry mustard
- 2 teaspoons tapioca starch
- 1 tablespoon lemon juice

## CHICKEN-VEGETABLE LUAU

Stir-fry chicken in oil in large skillet or wok 10 minutes to brown all sides. Add vegetables and bouillon seasoning. Measure and add pineapple liquid with water to make 1¼ cups. Bring to boil, reduce heat, and let steam 5 minutes. Add pineapple chunks. Blend spices and starch with lemon juice and stir into mixture until juice thickens. Let boil 1 minute. Serve over hot fluffy rice. *Serves 4–6*

**BBB + Rye + Poultry**

- 3 pounds chicken parts
- Allowed oil
- Salt to taste
- Cream of Rye Cereal

## CHICKEN-IN-THE-RYE

Roll chicken pieces in oil and drain. Sprinkle with salt and roll in cereal to coat. Place in shallow baking dish and bake in 400° oven 45 to 60 minutes or until tender. *Serves 4*

**BBB + Corn + Poultry**

- 1 3-pound broiler-fryer, cut in pieces or 3 pounds chicken parts
- ½ cup Mocha Mix or other allowed milk substitute
- 1 cup yellow cornmeal
- 1 teaspoon salt
- Allowed oil

## IOWA FRIED CHICKEN

Dip chicken parts in liquid, then shake pieces, one at a time, in paper bag containing cornmeal and salt. Wait 5 minutes to let coating set. Fry in ½ inch oil until golden brown on all sides. Cover and cook 45 minutes until tender. Uncover and cook 10 minutes until crisp. Drain on paper towel. *Serves 4*

**Variation:**

For more flavor, add ½ teaspoon garlic powder and ¼ teaspoon pepper to cornmeal when allowed. (**+ TE&A**)

## TERIYAKI CHICKEN

**BBB + Corn + Poultry + TE&A**

- **3 pounds chicken parts**
- **Jan-U-Wine Soy Sauce**
- **Garlic powder**
- **Dried rosemary**

Place chicken in shallow baking pan. Sprinkle with soy sauce, garlic powder and rosemary. Turn and repeat. Marinate several hours, covered and refrigerated. Bake in marinade, uncovered, in 400° oven 45 to 60 minutes. *Serves 4*

**Variation:**

Omit rosemary, add ½ cup lemon juice, ¼ cup water and ⅛ teaspoon ginger. Combine with soy sauce and garlic powder to marinate chicken. (**+ Fruit**)

## PEACHY CHICK

**BBB + Corn + Poultry + Fruit + TE&A**

- **3 whole chicken breasts, split in half**
- **3 chicken legs with thighs**
- **1 can (16 ounces) cling peach halves, drained, juice reserved**
- **2 tablespoons lemon juice**
- **2 tablespoons Jan-U-Wine Soy Sauce**
- **½ teaspoon garlic salt**
- **1 teaspoon prepared mustard**
- **1 unpeeled orange, cut in cartwheels**

Place chicken in shallow baking dish. Combine peach juice with all ingredients except peaches and orange. Pour over chicken. Bake in 400° oven 45 to 60 minutes or until tender, basting often. Tuck orange slices and peach halves around chicken pieces. Baste and bake 5 minutes longer to heat fruit through. *Serves 6*

**Variation: Laetril Chick**

Replace peaches with 1 can whole apricots!

## CHICKEN FLAUTA

**BBB + Corn + Poultry + Fruit + Veg. + TE&A**

- **Corn tortillas**
- **Allowed oil**
- **Chopped cooked chicken**
- **Tofu Dressing I, p. 63 or Perfect Cooked Mayonnaise, p. 67**
- **Shredded lettuce**
- **Avocado**
- **1 teaspoon lemon juice**
- **1 can (7 ounces) green chili salsa**

Heat number of tortillas desired in small amount of oil until limp and pliable. Combine chicken with enough dressing to hold together. Place small roll of mixture down center of tortilla and top with shredded lettuce. Roll filled tortilla and place, seam side down, in baking dish. Whir in blender avocado with dressing and lemon juice to consistency of guacamole. Spread on each roll in pan and spoon on a little salsa. Bake in 400° oven 20 to 25 minutes or until topping bubbles. Serve with remaining salsa.

**BBB + Corn + Poultry + Fruit + Veg. + TE&A**

8 corn tortillas
2 cups diced cooked chicken
2 tablespoons rice flour
½ teaspoon salt
2 tablespoons tomato paste
2 teaspoons Steero Instant Chicken Flavor Bouillon Seasoning and Broth
2 cups Mocha Mix or other allowed milk substitute
1 can (7 ounces) green chilies, chopped
2 tablespoons instant minced onion

## GLORIOUS CHICKEN CASSEROLE

Cut tortillas into 1-inch strips and place half in 8 x 12-inch baking pan. Top with 1 cup chicken. In saucepan, combine flour, salt, tomato paste, and bouillon and stir to blend. Slowly add 1 cup water and milk substitute, stirring constantly over low heat until thickened. Add chilies and onion. Pour half of sauce over casserole, and add another layer of tortillas, chicken, and sauce. Cover tightly and refrigerate 24 hours. Cover and bake in 300° oven 1 to 1½ hours. *Serves 4*

**BBB + Corn + Poultry + Fruit + Veg. + TE&A**

2 chicken breasts, halved, boned, and skinned
2 tablespoons allowed margarine
Salt to taste
Paprika to taste
1 can (8 ounces) sliced pineapple, drained, juice reserved
1 can (16 ounces) yams in syrup, drained, juice reserved
1½ tablespoons tapioca starch or arrowroot powder
¼ teaspoon dry mustard
¼ teaspoon ginger
2 tablespoons lemon juice
1 teaspoon instant chopped onion

## GLAZED CHICKEN BREASTS

Brown chicken in margarine and season with salt and paprika. Remove and reserve. Add pineapple and yam juices to pan. Blend starch, mustard, ginger, lemon juice, and onion. Add to juices and heat, stirring constantly until thickened. Slip 1 chicken piece through each of 4 pineapple rings and place in baking dish. Arrange yams around chicken. Chunk any remaining pineapple and add to baking dish. Pour sauce over, cover, and bake in 350° oven 20 to 30 minutes or until chicken is tender. Bake, uncovered, 10 minutes longer, basting potatoes and chicken with sauce. *Serves 4*

## SOUTHERN CHICKEN FRICASSEE

**BBB + Corn + Poultry + TE&A**

- 3 pounds broiler-fryer parts
- ¾ cup rice flour
- 2 tablespoons potato flour (optional)
- 1 teaspoon salt
- ⅛ teaspoon pepper
- ¼ cup allowed oil
- 1½ cups boiling water
- 1 cup milk-free coffee creamer (Mocha Mix; Lucerne Non-Dairy Product-Cereal Blend; or any other allowed milk substitute)

Shake chicken pieces in mixture of flours, salt, and pepper in paper or plastic bag. Fry in oil, removing pieces as they are well browned. When all are browned, return pieces to skillet, pour on boiling water, and cover tightly. Simmer 30 minutes. Blend remaining coating flour into milk substitute until smooth. Push chicken to side and add flour-milk mixture to broth while stirring constantly until thickened and bubbly. *Serves 4–6*

**Variation: Chicken n' Dumplings**

Sauté in oil chicken, 1 sliced onion, 1 sliced stalk celery with leaves, and 1 sliced carrot. Omit milk substitute and increase water to 2½ cups. Cover and cook chicken as directed, but do not thicken juices. Add Knorr Raw Potato Dumplings, following mix directions on package. Cook with chicken, uncovered, 20 minutes. *Serves 4–6*

## KOREAN CHICKEN AND VEGETABLES

**BBB + Corn + Poultry + Fruit + Veg. + TE&A**

- 2 chicken breasts, boned, skinned, cut in bite-size pieces
- ¼ cup Jan-U-Wine Soy Sauce
- ½ teaspoon paprika
- 1 medium onion, chopped
- 2 teaspoons cornstarch
- 2 tablespoons allowed oil
- 1 teaspoon Steero Instant Chicken Flavor Bouillon Seasoning and Broth
- 1 cup sliced celery
- 1 cup sliced carrots
- 2 small zucchini, sliced
- ½ medium green pepper, sliced
- 1 can (20 ounces) pineapple chunks, drained, juice reserved
- 1 package (6 ounces) frozen Chinese pea pods, thawed
- 1 recipe Sweet Sour Sauce, p. 190

Combine chicken, soy sauce, paprika, onion, and cornstarch and let stand ½ hour. Stir and brown marinated chicken slowly in oil. Add bouillon seasoning, ¾ cup water, celery, carrots, and any marinade left. Cover and cook slowly 5 minutes. Add zucchini, pepper, pineapple chunks, and pea pods. Cover to steam 5 to 10 minutes or until chicken is tender and vegetables tender-crisp. Meanwhile, prepare Sweet Sour Sauce with reserved pineapple juice. Toss with chicken and vegetables. Serve over hot rice. *Serves 4–6*

## QUICK CHICKEN TACO

**BBB + Corn + Poultry + Fruit + Veg. + TE&A**

- **2 cups chopped cooked chicken**
- **1 teaspoon instant chopped onion**
- **Chicken gravy or thickened broth**
- **¼ teaspoon garlic salt**
- **1 can (4 ounces) green chili salsa**
- **Sliced avocado (optional)**
- **Tomato wedges**
- **Shredded lettuce**
- **6 taco shells, heated**

Combine and heat chicken, onion, just enough gravy to bind mixture, garlic salt, and ¼ cup chili salsa. Fill each taco shell with ⅓ cup chicken mixture. Top with avocado, tomato, and shredded lettuce. Pass extra chili salsa at table. *Makes 6 tacos*

**Variation:**

Omit taco shells and double other recipe ingredients. Oil skillet and heat, one at a time, 12 corn tortillas until pliable. Fill each with ⅓ cup chicken mixture, fold, and fasten edges with wooden toothpicks. Fry in allowed oil. Serve with avocado, tomato, lettuce, and salsa on the side to be added to taste by each diner.

## CHICKEN MEXICALI

**BBB + Corn + Poultry + Veg. + TE&A**

- **1 3-pound broiler-fryer, cut in pieces**
- **Allowed milk substitute**
- **⅓ cup cornmeal**
- **½ teaspoon salt**
- **Dash of pepper**
- **4 tablespoons allowed oil**
- **½ large green pepper, sliced**
- **½ large sweet red pepper, sliced**
- **½ cup chopped scallions**
- **¼ teaspoon garlic powder**
- **1 teaspoon chili powder**
- **1 tablespoon chopped parsley**
- **¼ teaspoon dried oregano**
- **½ teaspoon salt**
- **1 can (8 ounces) tomato sauce**
- **1 can (4 ounces) chopped green chilies**

Dip chicken pieces in milk substitute. Shake chicken in cornmeal, salt, and pepper in paper or plastic bag. Fry pieces in 2 tablespoons hot oil until brown on all sides. Remove to 1½-quart casserole. Using 2 tablespoons of fat remaining in frying pan, sauté peppers and scallions until soft. Add remaining ingredients and ½ cup water and bring to boil. Pour over chicken and bake casserole in 350° oven 1¼ hours or until chicken is tender. Serve with Cornbread, p. 230. *Serves 4–6*

## CHICKEN CHOP SUEY

**BBB + Corn + Poultry + Veg. + TE&A**

Follow Quick Chop Suey recipe, p. 141, replacing pork with cooked chicken.

## ISLANDER GAME HEN CASSEROLE

**BBB + Corn + Poultry + Veg. + N&S + TE&A**

Marinate game hen halves 1 hour in soy sauce, bouillon seasoning, ⅓ cup water, and garlic powder. Lift hens out (reserving marinade) and brown in oil. Remove and set aside. Brown onion, rice, and green beans in oil. Add 1⅓ cups water and all remaining ingredients except paprika and almonds. Transfer to 3-quart baking dish and top with browned hens. Sprinkle with paprika. Cover and bake in 350° oven for 45 to 60 minutes or until rice and hens are tender. Uncover, garnish with nuts, and bake 5 to 10 minutes longer. *Serves 4*

- **2 Cornish game hens, halved**
- **⅓ cup Jan-U-Wine Soy Sauce**
- **2 teaspoons Steero Instant Chicken Flavor Bouillon Seasoning and Broth**
- **¼ teaspoon garlic powder**
- **2 tablespoons allowed oil**
- **1 large onion, chopped**
- **¾ cup rice**
- **1 cup sliced green beans**
- **2 small yellow crookneck squash, sliced**
- **1 package (6 ounces) frozen Chinese pea pods, thawed**
- **1 can (5 ounces) water chestnuts, drained and sliced**
- **¼ teaspoon ginger**
- **Dash of paprika**
- **Toasted slivered almonds**

## OVEN CRISP CHICKEN

**BBB + Barley + Corn + Poultry + N&S + TE&A + Mold**

Dip washed and dried chicken pieces in oil or milk substitute. Shake, 1 piece at a time, with seasonings and crushed flakes in paper or plastic bag. Place in shallow baking pan and bake in 400° oven 1 hour or until tender and golden. For less greasy chicken, place on rack in shallow pan to bake. *Serves 4*

- **1 3-pound broiler-fryer, or equivalent in parts or 4 game hens, halved**
- **Allowed oil or milk substitute**
- **1 teaspoon paprika**
- **Dash of pepper**
- **½ teaspoon onion salt or garlic salt**
- **Crushed cornflakes, Corn Chex, or Nutri-Grain Corn—Whole Grain Cereal**

# Pork

☐
BBB
+ Pork

## FRESH PORK ROAST

Place roast in open roasting pan and insert meat thermometer in thickest part of meat. Make sure tip of thermometer does not touch bone. Roast, uncovered, at 325° for 30 to 45 minutes per pound or to an internal temperature of 185°. Meat may be rubbed with salt before roasting, if desired. After roasting, let meat rest 15 minutes before carving. Prepare gravy while meat rests.

### ROASTING CHART

| Kind | Weight | Hours: well done | Temperature |
|---|---|---|---|
| Leg, fresh ham | 5-7 pounds | 4½ hours | 185° |
| Loin, end | 4 pounds | 2½-3 hours | 185° |
| Loin, center | 5 pounds | 3-3½ hours | 185° |
| Boneless, rolled | 4 pounds | 3-3½ hours | 185° |
| Crown | 7 pounds | 4 hours | 185° |

☐
BBB
+ Pork
+ Veg.
+ TE&A

## SEASONINGS FOR ROAST PORK WHEN ALLOWED

Silvered garlic (make tiny cuts in meat and insert garlic)
Garlic salt
Garlic powder
Dried sage, thyme, or rosemary
Dry mustard

## PORK CHOPS AND ISLAND RICE

**BBB + Pork**

Brown chops in oil and sprinkle with salt. Add pineapple, cover and simmer 20 minutes or until chops are tender. Move chops to side of skillet, add 1 cup water, and bring to boil. Stir in rice. Cover and remove from heat. Let stand 5 minutes. *Serves 4*

- **6 pork chops, ½-inch thick**
- **2 tablespoons allowed oil**
- **½ teaspoon salt**
- **1 can (8 ounces) unsweetened crushed pineapple, undrained**
- **1½ cups Minute Rice**

## HOT PIG (PORK CHILI)

**BBB + Pork + Veg. + TE&A**

Brown pork in oil and add salt. Pour off excess fat, pushing pork to side of pot. Sauté onion and garlic in remaining fat and add chilies, tomato sauce, 1 cup water, and chili powder. Reduce heat, cover, and simmer 45 minutes or until pork is tender. Remove lid and simmer another 15 minutes to thicken sauce. Chili may be used as follows: Over cooked white or brown rice; with added canned or home-cooked soybeans, pinto beans, white beans, pink beans, or garbanzos; over cooked spaghetti squash or cooked zucchini; over cooked barley **(+ Barley)**; with added fresh or canned corn or canned hominy **(+ Corn)**; or over cooked 100% corn pasta **(+ Corn)**. *Serves 6–8*

- **2 pounds lean pork, cut in 1-inch cubes**
- **2 tablespoons allowed oil**
- **½ teaspoon salt**
- **1 medium onion, diced**
- **2 cloves garlic, crushed**
- **2 cans (4 ounces each) green chilies, diced**
- **2 cans (8 ounces each) tomato sauce**
- **1 teaspoon chili powder**

## HONEYED PORK CHOPS

**BBB + Pork + TE&A**

Pour over chops in baking dish combined honey, pineapple, mustard, and ginger. Bake, uncovered, in 350° oven 1½ hours, basting occasionally with honey sauce. *Serves 4*

- **4 double thick loin pork chops**
- **½ cup honey**
- **1 can (8 ounces) packed-in-own-juice pineapple chunks**
- **1 teaspoon prepared mustard**
- **⅛ teaspoon ground ginger**

**Variations:**

1. Use canned apricot halves or sliced peaches instead of pineapple.
2. Substitute 1 cup orange juice for pineapple. Top each chop with thin slice of orange. **(+ Fruit)**

☐ **BBB + Pork + TE&A**

- 1 4-pound pork loin
- ¾ cup brown sugar, firmly packed
- ⅓ cup unsweetened pineapple juice
- 2 tablespoons white distilled vinegar
- 1 teaspoon dry mustard
- ⅛ teaspoon ginger or ground cloves

## GLAZED PORK LOIN ROAST

Place meat, fat side up, in shallow roasting pan. Combine all other ingredients and coat roast. Roast in 325° oven 2½ to 3 hours or until meat thermometer reaches 185°. Brush occasionally during cooking with sauce and pan juices. *Serves 6*

☐ **BBB + Pork + Fruit + TE&A**

- 3 pounds country-style pork ribs
- 1 tablespoon allowed oil
- ¾ cup orange juice
- 3 tablespoons lemon juice
- ⅓ cup honey
- 1 bay leaf
- 1½ teaspoons garlic powder
- ½ teaspoon ginger
- ¼ teaspoon ground cloves
- 1 teaspoon grated lemon peel
- 1 teaspoon salt
- ⅛ teaspoon pepper

## GLAZED RIBS

Cut ribs into single serving portions. Brown in oil over high heat on all sides. Place in shallow baking dish. Meanwhile combine glaze ingredients and simmer 15 minutes. Lift out bay leaf and pour glaze over ribs. Bake in 400° oven 1½ hours or until done through. Turn once during baking. *Serves 4*

☐ **BBB + Pork + Veg. + TE&A**

- 3 pounds country-style pork ribs

Sauce:

- 1 can (8 ounces) tomato sauce
- 2 tablespoons brown sugar, firmly packed
- ¼ cup white distilled vinegar
- 1 teaspoon garlic powder
- 1½ teaspoons dry mustard
- ¼ teaspoon ginger
- ¼ teaspoon barbecue spice
- ½ teaspoon salt

## GARLIC BARBECUE PORK RIBS

Simmer sauce ingredients with ½ cup water 15 minutes, then cool. Pour over ribs in baking dish and cover tightly with foil. Marinate 8 hours or overnight, refrigerated. Bake in 325° oven 2 hours. Uncover and bake at 400° 15 to 20 minutes to brown. *Serves 4*

## SKILLET PORK CHOPS WITH RICE

**BBB + Pork + Veg. + TE&A**

- **4 pork chops or steaks cut ½inch thick**
- **1 tablespoon allowed oil**
- **½ teaspoon salt**
- **Dash of pepper**
- **½ teaspoon garlic powder**
- **½ teaspoon dried basil**
- **1 small onion, diced**
- **½ cup sliced celery**
- **1 can (16 ounces) stewed tomatoes**
- **1 cup rice**
- **1 package (10 ounces) frozen green peas**

Brown chops in oil and add seasoning. Remove from skillet and sauté onion and celery. Drain off surplus fat. Add 1¼ cups water and stewed tomatoes. Bring to boil, stir in rice, and place chops on top. Cover, reduce heat, and simmer 25 to 35 minutes. Add frozen peas and simmer 5 minutes longer or until rice and meat are tender. *Serves 4*

## CHOP-TOP CASSEROLE

**BBB + Pork + Veg. + TE&A**

- **1 pound dried blackeye peas or 1½ cups dried white beans, soaked overnight**
- **4 lean pork steaks or chops, cut 1 inch thick**
- **2 tablespoons allowed oil**
- **½ teaspoon garlic salt**
- **Salt and pepper to taste**
- **1 large onion, chopped**
- **1 can (16 ounces) stewed tomatoes**
- **1 bay leaf**
- **½ teaspoon dried rosemary or thyme**

After soaking peas or beans, cook as directed for Cooked Dried Beans, p. 172. Brown pork in oil and season with garlic salt, salt, and pepper. Lift out chops or push aside to sauté onions. Mix all other ingredients including cooked peas or beans in 3-quart casserole, top with chops, cover and bake in 350° oven 1 hour or until chops are very tender. *Serves 4*

## DOUBLE "A" PORK CHOPS

**BBB + Pork + Fruit + Veg. + TE&A**

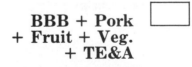

- **1 acorn squash, peeled and cut in ½-inch slices**
- **2 tablespoons allowed oil**
- **4 pork chops, cut 1-inch thick**
- **½ teaspoon salt**
- **Dash of pepper, (optional)**
- **3 apples, cored and cubed**
- **3 tablespoons honey**
- **1 tablespoon lemon juice**

Prepare squash, brown in oil, and remove from skillet. Brown pork chops and lay browned squash on top. Season with salt and pepper. Combine apples, honey, and lemon juice and spoon between chops. Cover and cook over medium heat 20 minutes or until pork and squash are tender. Stir apples once to glaze during cooking. *Serves 4*

## HERBED PORK ROAST

**BBB + Beef + Pork + Veg. + TE&A**

- 1 6-pound pork roast
- 1 teaspoon salt
- ½ teaspoon pepper
- 1 teaspoon dried thyme
- ½ teaspoon dried rosemary
- 1 tablespoon dried parsley
- 1 teaspoon garlic powder
- ½ cup sliced celery
- 2 carrots, sliced
- 1 medium onion, sliced
- 4 whole cloves
- 3 bay leaves
- 2 Steero Instant Beef Flavor Bouillon and Broth Cubes
- 1½ cups boiling water

Rub meat with mixture of salt, pepper, thyme, rosemary, parsley, and garlic powder. Bake in 450° oven 25 minutes to brown. Reduce heat to 350°. Place vegetables, cloves, and bay leaves around meat. Dissolve bouillon cubes in 1½ cups boiling water and add to roasting pan. Continue roasting, uncovered, 2 hours or more. Meat thermometer should register 185°. Transfer roast to platter. Discard cloves and bay leaves and skim fat from liquid. Purée vegetables in preheated blender, adding ¼ cup liquid from pan if needed. Return to pan and reheat to serve unthickened with roast. *Serves 8–10*

## PORK STEAKS AND GRAVY

**BBB + Poultry + Pork + Fruit + Veg. + TE&A**

- 2 medium onions, sliced
- 2 tablespoons allowed oil
- 4 pork steaks, cut ½ inch thick
- 2 Steero Instant Chicken Flavor Bouillon and Broth Cubes
- 2 tablespoons lemon juice
- ⅛ teaspoon pepper
- 3 tablespoons rice flour
- Lemon slices
- Parsley sprigs

Sauté onions in oil until transparent and remove from skillet. Brown pork steaks in same skillet and top with sautéed onions. Add bouillon cubes, lemon juice, pepper and 1½ cups water. Reduce heat, cover, and simmer 25 to 30 minutes or until steaks are cooked through. Lift meat from skillet and keep warm. Skim fat from pan juices. Blend rice flour and ½ cup water and, stirring constantly, thicken juices in pan. Garnish meat and serve with gravy. *Serves 4*

*Note:* Halved potatoes and whole baby carrots may be cooked slowly along with meat for a delicious meal-in-a-pan.

## PORK JAMBALAYA

**BBB + Poultry + Pork + Veg. + TE&A**

- 1 small onion, chopped
- ¼ cup sliced green pepper
- ¼ cup chopped celery
- 2 tablespoons allowed oil
- 3 teaspoons Steero Instant Chicken Flavor Bouillon Seasoning and Broth
- 2 cups boiling water
- 1 tablespoon imitation bacon bits
- 1 cup long grain rice
- 1 can (16 ounces) stewed tomatoes
- 1 cup leftover cooked pork
- 2 tablespoons chopped parsley

Sauté onion, pepper, and celery in oil. Add chicken flavor seasoning and boiling water. Combine with all other ingredients in 1½-quart casserole. Bake, uncovered, in 375° oven 45 minutes or until rice is tender. If desired, cook on top of stove 25 minutes or until rice is tender. *Serves 4*

## SWEDISH RYE MEAT BALLS

**BBB + Rye + Beef + Pork + Veg. + TE&A**

- ¾ pound lean ground beef
- ¼ pound lean ground pork
- 1 tablespoon soy flour
- ¼ teaspoon onion powder
- ¼ teaspoon ground allspice
- ⅓ cup Cream of Rye cereal, uncooked
- ¼ cup rice flour
- 1 tablespoon potato flour
- 2-4 tablespoons allowed oil
- ¼ teaspoon salt
- 1 teaspoon instant minced onion
- 1 teaspoon dried parsley

Combine first 6 ingredients with ½ cup water and form into tiny balls. Combine flours, roll each meatball in flour, and brown in oil. Drain off surplus fat. Add 2 cups water and remaining ingredients, cover, and simmer 10 to 15 minutes or until meatballs are cooked through. Remove meatballs with slotted spoon and keep hot. If thicker gravy is desired, make thin paste from flours remaining with ¼ to ½ cup water. Add to pan liquid, stirring constantly until thickened. Boil 1 minute, adjusting thickness with water. Return meatballs to gravy to reheat. Serve over rice. *Serves 4*

## MARINATED GRILLED PORK CHOPS OR STEAKS

**BBB + Corn + Pork + Veg. + TE&A**

**Pork chops or steaks, 1 for each person or 2 for big eaters**
**Jan-U-Wine Soy Sauce**
**Garlic powder**

Coat chops with soy sauce and sprinkle lightly with garlic powder. Turn and repeat on other side. Cover container tightly and refrigerate 8 to 24 hours. Turn chops over once or twice during marinating. Grill on outdoor barbeque until cooked through. Serve with corn grilled in husks or with baked beans, green salad, and fresh fruit on a hot summer day.

## SWEET AND SOUR PORK

**BBB + Corn + Pork + Fruit + N&S + TE&A**

- **¼ cup brown sugar, firmly packed**
- **3 tablespoons cornstarch**
- **1 can (20 ounces) pineapple chunks, drained, juice reserved**
- **2 teaspoons Jan-U-Wine Soy Sauce**
- **½ teaspoon salt**
- **¼ cup lemon juice**
- **¼ cup slivered almonds**
- **2 pounds cooked boneless pork, cut into 1½-inch cubes**

Combine brown sugar and cornstarch in large saucepan. Measure juice from pineapple and add water to make 2 cups. Add liquid to saucepan. Cook, stirring constantly, until thick and glossy. Add soy sauce, salt, lemon juice, meat, and pineapple chunks. Cover and cook slowly 30 minutes. Garnish with slivered almonds. Serve over cooked rice. *Serves 4*

## PORK AND PEANUT CASSEROLE

**BBB + Corn + Pork + Fruit + N&S + TE&A**

- **1 pound lean ground pork**
- **½ cup chopped onions**
- **2 cloves garlic, minced**
- **1 can (8 ounces) pineapple slices, drained, juice reserved**
- **1 tablespoon cornstarch**
- **½ cup peanuts, chopped**
- **¼ cup chopped parsley**
- **1 teaspoon salt**
- **½ teaspoon ginger**
- **Dash of seasoned pepper**
- **2-3 cups cooked rice**

Brown pork, onions, and garlic, stirring so meat breaks up into fine pieces. Add water to pineapple juice to make 1 cup. Blend, a little at a time, into cornstarch, then stir into meat mixture along with all other ingredients except cooked rice. Cook, stirring, until thickened and boiling. Spoon rice into casserole. Arrange pineapple slices over rice, reserving 1 slice for garnish. Pour meat sauce over rice, garnish with pineapple slice, and bake in 350° oven 30 to 40 minutes. Add extra chopped or whole peanuts for final garnish. *Serves 4*

## QUICK CHOP SUEY

Brown meat, onion and celery in oil. Add all other ingredients except cornstarch. Reduce heat, cover, and simmer 10 minutes. Blend cornstarch with ¼ cup cold water and add to pork and vegetables, stirring constantly until thickened. Serve over hot cooked rice. *Serves 4*

**BBB + Corn + Beef + Pork + Veg. + TE&A**

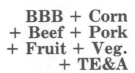

- **1½ cups leftover cooked pork, cut in small pieces**
- **1 medium onion, sliced**
- **1 cup chopped celery**
- **1 tablespoon allowed oil**
- **1 can (5 ounces) water chestnuts, drained and sliced**
- **1 can (16 ounces) bean sprouts, drained, or 2 cups fresh sprouts**
- **1 teaspoon Steero Instant Beef Flavor Bouillon Seasoning and Broth**
- **2 tablespoons Jan-U-Wine Soy Sauce**
- **1¼ cups boiling water**
- **2 tablespoons cornstarch**

## PORK CHOPS AND ONION RICE

Brown chops in non-stick skillet, lift out and sauté green pepper and celery in drippings from meat. Reserve 1 tablespoon soup mix and blend all remaining ingredients in 2-quart casserole. Stir in peppers and celery and place chops on top. Sprinkle reserved soup mix over top and cover tightly. Bake in 350° oven 1 hour or until chops and rice are tender. *Serves 4*

**BBB + Corn + Beef + Pork + Fruit + Veg. + TE&A**

- **4 pork chops, 1 inch thick**
- **½ cup chopped green pepper**
- **½ cup sliced celery**
- **1 recipe Gloria's Onion Soup Mix, p. 39**
- **1 cup rice**
- **2 tablespoons lemon juice**
- **2 tablespoons diced pimiento**
- **3 cups hot water**

**BBB + Corn + Poultry + Pork + Fruit + Veg. + TE&A**

- 1½ pounds boneless pork loin, cut in thin strips
- 2 tablespoons allowed oil
- 1 medium onion, sliced
- ½ teaspoon salt
- ⅛ teaspoon pepper
- 2 teaspoons Steero Instant Chicken Flavor Bouillon Seasoning and Broth
- 2 tablespoons Jan-U-Wine Soy Sauce
- 2 tablespoons brown sugar, firmly packed
- ¼ cup lemon juice
- 2 carrots, grated
- 1 can (16 ounces) cut green beans, drained
- 1 tablespoon cornstarch

## PORK AND VEGETABLES

Brown meat in oil, then push to one side and sauté onion. Add seasonings, brown sugar, lemon juice, and 1½ cups water. Reduce heat, cover, and simmer 40 minutes. Add grated carrots and green beans. Cook, covered, another 15 minutes or until carrots are barely tender. Blend cornstarch with ½ cup water and add slowly to hot mixture, stirring constantly until thickened. Serve plain or on cooked rice. This has a delicious flavor. *Serves 4*

# Fish

## FOILED FISH AND VEGETABLES

**BBB + Fish** ☐

- **4 small new potatoes, sliced thin**
- **1½-2 pounds fish fillets cut in 1-inch cubes**
- **1 package (10 ounces) frozen asparagus spears, thawed**
- **4 baby carrots, sliced thin**
- **2 tablespoons allowed margarine**
- **Salt to taste**

Evenly divide potatoes, fish, asparagus, and carrots onto 4 heavy aluminum foil sheets. Dot each bundle with 1½ teaspoons margarine and sprinkle with salt. Double fold foil on top, roll up ends for a long flattish package. Put bundles in baking dish and bake in 400° oven 20 to 25 minutes or until vegetables and fish are done—open one package to test. These may also be cooked on an outdoor grill for same amount of time. *Serves 4*

**Variation:**

Use other allowed vegetable combinations later (after testing) along with lemon juice, parsley, paprika, and pepper. **(+ Fruit + Veg. + TE&A)**

## CREAMED TUNA

**BBB + Fish** ☐

- **1 can (6½-7 ounces) tuna, drained and crumbled**
- **2 cups BBB White Sauce, p. 183 or Cream of Rice White Sauce, p. 184**
- **1 package (10 ounces) frozen green peas or peas-carrots, cooked and drained (optional)**

Combine tuna with white sauce, heat and add peas or peas-carrots, if desired. Serve over any hot crisp waffle coded **BBB** or allowed toasted bread. *Serves 2-4*

**Variation:**

When tested and allowed, add any one or more of the following: 1 teaspoon instant chopped onion, 1 teaspoon dried parsley, dash of pepper, or chopped pimiento. **(+ Veg. + TE&A)**

**BBB + Fish**

**Creamed Tuna, p. 143 with allowed vegetables added**
**Mashed Potatoes, p. 165**
**Allowed margarine**

## TUNA PIE

Place creamed tuna with allowed vegetables in large pie tin or in individual tins. Top with hot mashed potatoes and dot with margarine. Bake in 400° oven until tops of potatoes brown and creamed tuna bubbles. *Serves 4*

**Variation: Tuna boats**

Place creamed tuna and vegetables in Poultry Nests, p. 116, or in Mashed Potato Shells, p. 166.

**BBB + Fish**

## BROILED FISH

Preheat broiler. Place small whole fish, thick steaks, or fillets on oiled grill. Brush non-fatty fish with allowed oil or melted allowed margarine. Season with salt. Cook 3 inches from source of heat. Thin fillets need no turning. Turn others once during cooking, brushing second side with oil or margarine. Cook until fish flakes when fork tested. Allow 20 to 30 minutes for whole split fish up to 4 pounds, 10 to 15 minutes for 1-1½-inch steaks, and less time for fillets.

**Variations:**

1. When allowed, brush with lemon or lime juice. (**+ Fruit)**
2. Marinate in Lemon Parsley Fish Marinade, p. 186. (**+ Fruit + Veg.)**
3. Season with Seasoned Salt Blend. p. 176. (**+ Veg. + TE&A)**

**BBB + Fish + Fruit + Veg. + TE&A**

**¼ cup melted allowed margarine**
**Juice and grated peel of ½ lemon**
**½ teaspoon garlic powder**
**1 tablespoon finely chopped chives (optional)**
**Dash of pepper**

## LEMON BASTING SAUCE FOR BROILED FISH

Blend and baste fish during broiling or grilling.

**Variation:**

Barely soften margarine and blend with remaining ingredients. Shape into roll, wrap, and chill. Slice and serve on cooked fish. *Makes ⅓ cup.*

## TUTTI FRUITY FISH STEAKS

**BBB + Fish + Fruit**

- 4 fish steaks 1 inch thick
- 2 cups boiling water
- 2 tablespoons lime juice
- 1 teaspoon salt
- 2 tablespoons allowed margarine
- 1 tablespoon tapioca starch or arrowroot powder
- 1 cup orange juice
- 2 teaspoons grated orange peel
- 1 can (11 ounces) mandarin oranges, drained
- 1 cup seedless grapes, halved

Cover and simmer fish in hot water, lime juice, and salt 10 minutes. Melt margarine, add starch, and blend. Add orange juice, stirring constantly until thickened and boiling. Boil 1 minute, add orange peel and fruits. Allow fruits to heat through. Place cooked fish on warm serving platter and cover with sauce. *Serves 4*

## SALMON PATTIES

**BBB + Fish + Fruit + Veg.**

- 1 can (15½ ounces) salmon, drained, liquid reserved
- 1½ teaspoons instant minced onion
- 1 tablespoon minced celery
- 2 tablespoons chopped parsley
- ¼ teaspoon salt
- 2 tablespoons rice flour or tapioca starch or potato starch
- 1 cup cold mashed potatoes
- ½ cup mashed cooked zucchini or other mashed allowed vegetable

Mix all ingredients well, using salmon liquid as necessary to moisten enough to form into patties. Fry over medium heat in allowed oil until golden brown on both sides. *Serves 4–5*

## SHRIMP CREOLE

**BBB + Fish + Veg. + TE&A**

- Creole Sauce, p. 187
- 1 bay leaf
- ¼ teaspoon dried thyme
- 1 pound small cooked shrimp
- 3 cups hot cooked rice

Prepare Creole Sauce as directed with bay leaf, thyme, and shrimp added. Serve over hot rice in individual bowls. *Serves 4–6*

☐ **BBB + Fish + optional Fruit + Veg.**

## BAKED FISH IN CHIPS

- 4 fish fillets
- 2 tablespoons allowed oil
- 1 tablespoon lemon juice (optional)
- 1 teaspoon onion powder or garlic powder
- 1 teaspoon dried parsley
- 1½ cups crushed potato chips (See Munchies available in markets, p. 351)

Dip fish in blended oil, lemon juice, onion powder and parsley. Roll in crushed chips and lay on rack in shallow pan. Bake in 425° oven 20 minutes or until fish flakes easily.

☐ **BBB + Fish + Fruit + Veg. + TE&A**

## FRIED FISH FILLETS

- 4 fish fillets (6-8 ounces each)
- Lemon Parsley Fish Marinade, p. 186
- ¼ cup rice flour
- 1 tablespoon potato flour, (optional)
- ½ teaspoon paprika
- 2-4 tablespoons allowed oil
- Lemon slices
- Parsley sprigs

Place fillets in marinade for 30 minutes, turning once. Blend flours and paprika and coat fillets with mixture. Fry in oil 3 to 4 minutes on each side or until lightly browned and fish flakes easily. Garnish with lemon slices and parsley. *Serves 4*

☐ **BBB + Fish + Veg + TE&A**

## SEAFARERS NEWBURG

- 2 cups BBB White Sauce of choice, p. 183, or Cream of Rice White Sauce, p. 184
- 1 teaspoon dry mustard
- ⅛ teaspoon paprika
- 1 cup diced cooked lobster
- Dash of pepper
- 1 cup small cooked shelled shrimp
- 1 cup cooked flaked fish of choice
- Salt to taste

To prepared white sauce, add seasonings and fish. Adjust salt as desired. Bake in 1½-quart casserole in 350° oven until bubbling hot, 25 to 30 minutes. Serve over hot cooked rice or crisp BBB Waffle.

**Variation:**

Replace lobster with crab meat, top casserole with allowed crushed potato chips, and bake.

## SEAFOOD SUPREME

**BBB + Fish + Veg + TE&A** ☐

- 1 pound small raw shelled and deveined shrimp
- 2 tablespoons allowed margarine
- ¼ cup minced onion
- 2 tablespoons minced green pepper
- ¼ cup minced celery
- 1 tablespoon minced parsley
- ½ cup Perfect Cooked Mayonnaise, p. 67 or Remarkable Soyannaise, p. 67
- Dash of garlic salt
- Pinch of dried basil
- Crushed allowed potato chips or allowed crumbs, p. 232
- Dash of paprika

Combine all ingredients except potato chips and paprika and place in oiled 1½-quart baking dish, or divide among 4 scallop shells. Top with chips or crumbs and sprinkle with paprika. Bake in 400° oven 25 minutes. *Serves 4*

## SOLE MILANO

**BBB + Fish + Veg + TE&A** ☐

- ½ cup chopped onion
- ½ cup finely sliced celery
- ¼ cup diced green pepper
- 2 tablespoons allowed oil
- 1 can (16 ounces) tomatoes
- ½ teaspoon salt
- Dash of pepper
- 1 bay leaf
- ½ teaspoon dried basil or oregano
- 2 tablespoons chopped parsley
- 4 sole fillets, or other white fish
- 2 tablespoons rice flour

Sauté onion, celery, and pepper in oil until soft. Add and chop tomatoes with seasonings and parsley. Bring to boil and simmer, covered, 10 minutes. Bury fish in sauce, cover, and simmer 10 minutes or until fish flakes easily. If desired, lift out fish and keep hot. Thicken sauce with rice flour blended with ¼ cup water. Stir into sauce over low heat until thickened. *Serves 4*

**Variation:**

Bake thick steaks or a 2½-pound piece of halibut, shark, bass, or other fish in sauce, covered, at 375° for 20 minutes. Uncover and bake another 20 minutes, basting occasionally until fish flakes easily.

☐ **BBB + Fish + Fruit + Veg. + TE&A**

- 4 fish fillets (sole, flounder, cod, or red snapper)
- 2 tablespoons lemon juice
- Salt and white pepper
- ½ teaspoon grated lemon peel
- 1 tablespoon minced parsley
- 4 tablespoons allowed margarine

## TANGY BAKED FISH

Place fish in oiled baking dish, sprinkle with lemon juice and seasonings. Dot with allowed margarine. If desired, lay lemon slice on each and sprinkle with paprika. Bake in 325° oven 20 minutes or until fish flakes easily. *Serves 4*

☐ **BBB + Fish + Fruit + Veg. + TE&A**

- 1 medium avocado, sliced
- 2 tablespoons lemon juice
- 1 pound sole fillets
- Salt and pepper to taste
- 2 cups cooked white or brown rice
- 2 tablespoons minced chives
- ½ teaspoon curry powder
- ½ lemon, cut in cartwheels
- 2 tablespoons melted allowed margarine

## BAKED SOLE CASSEROLE

Drizzle avocado slices with lemon juice to coat and set aside. Arrange fish in baking dish and season with salt and pepper. Blend rice well with chives and curry powder, spoon over fish, and arrange avocado slices and lemon slices on top. Drizzle with melted margarine. Sprinkle with almonds, if allowed. **(+ N&S)** Cover and bake in 350° oven 20 minutes or until fish flakes with a fork. *Serves 4*

☐ **BBB + Fish + Fruit + TE&A + Mold**

- 2 cups cooked rice
- 1 teaspoon grated lemon peel
- 1 teaspoon prepared mustard
- ⅛ teaspoon cayenne pepper
- ⅛ teaspoon black pepper
- 2 tablespoons lemon juice
- 1½ cups medium white sauce, p. 183
- 2 cups fresh steamed or canned crab meat
- ¼ pound fresh mushrooms, sliced
- 2 tablespoons allowed oil
- ½ cup waffle or soy bread crumbs (soft crumbs, see pp. 200 and 232)

## CRAB CASSEROLE

Combine cooked rice with lemon peel and spread over bottom of oiled 2-quart baking dish. Add mustard, cayenne and black pepper to cream sauce. Stir in crab meat. Sauté mushrooms in 1 tablespoon oil until lightly browned and add lemon juice. Stir into crab mixture and spread over rice. Drizzle remaining oil over crumbs and toss with fork. Top casserole with crumbs and bake, uncovered, in 400° oven 20 minutes or until heated through and lightly browned. *Serves 6*

## COMPANY PAELLA

**BBB + Poultry + Fish + Veg. + TE&A**

- 1 recipe Cooked Chicken-Seasoned Stock, p. 117
- 1 cup short grain brown rice
- 2 cloves garlic, crushed
- 2 tablespoons allowed oil
- 1 jar (2 ounces) pimiento, sliced
- ½ teaspoon dried oregano
- Pinch of saffron
- ¼ teaspoon dried rosemary
- ½ teaspoon salt
- 1 cup tomato sauce
- ¾ pound raw shelled and deveined shrimp
- 6½-10 ounces canned tuna, salmon, clams, or oysters, undrained
- 2 cups diced cooked chicken
- 1 package (9 ounces) frozen artichoke hearts or frozen green peas

Prepare chicken and stock a day ahead. Bone and dice chicken. Chill chicken and stock separately.

Sauté rice and garlic in oil. Add pimiento, seasonings, tomato sauce, 2 cups defatted stock, and shrimp. Cover and cook slowly until rice is tender, 40 to 50 minutes. Stir in fish, diced chicken, and vegetable. Heat thoroughly. *Serves 6*

**Variation:**

Sauté rice and garlic in oil. Combine with all other ingredients in slow cooker. Cook 8 to 10 hours on low setting or 3 to 4 hours on high or until rice is tender.

## SALMON POTATO CASSEROLE

**BBB + Poultry + Fish + Veg. + TE&A**

- 4 medium potatoes, peeled and sliced thin
- 1 teaspoon instant minced onion
- 3 tablespoons parsley, chopped fine, reserving 1 tablespoon for top of casserole
- 1 can (7¾ ounces) salmon, drained
- 1 package (10 ounces) frozen green peas
- 3 tablespoons allowed oil or margarine
- 2 tablespoons rice flour
- 2 teaspoons Steero Instant Chicken Flavor Bouillon Seasoning and Broth
- Dash of paprika

Make layers of potatoes, onion, parsley, fish, and peas in oiled 2-quart casserole. Start and end with potatoes (3 layers potatoes, 2 each of others). Make thin sauce by stirring flour into oil, adding 2 cups water and bouillon seasoning. Cook, stirring constantly, until thickened. Pour over casserole, lifting ingredients slightly to allow sauce to run in and around potatoes. Sprinkle top with paprika and chopped parsley. Cover and bake in 350° oven 1 hour or until potatoes are soft. *Serves 4-6*

**Variation:**

Omit bouillon seasoning and water and replace with allowed milk substitute.

☐ **BBB + Poultry + Fish + Veg. + TE&A**

## SALMON-VEGETABLE SKILLET MEAL

- **¾ cup chopped onion**
- **½ cup sliced celery**
- **1 clove garlic, crushed**
- **2 tablespoons allowed oil**
- **1 cup rice**
- **¼ teaspoon each salt, dried thyme, dried marjoram**
- **2 cups Chicken Stock, p. 30**
- **1 package (10 ounces) frozen green peas, thawed**
- **1 can (7¾ ounces) salmon, drained**
- **1 cup diced cooked chicken (optional)**
- **1 tablespoon chopped pimiento**

Sauté onion, celery, and garlic in oil until soft. Add rice to pan and stir until brown. Add seasonings and stock. Cover and cook over low heat 25 minutes or until rice is tender. Add peas, salmon, chicken if used, and pimiento. Cover and cook 2 or 3 minutes or until peas are done and fish and chicken hot. *Serves 4–6*

☐ **BBB + Poultry + Fish + Veg. + TE&A**

## BAYOU GUMBO

- **1 recipe Creole Sauce, p. 187, omitting tapioca starch**
- **2 cups small shelled shrimp**
- **2 cups diced cooked poultry**
- **1 package (10 ounces) frozen cut okra**
- **1 tablespoon imitation bacon bits**

Combine sauce with remaining ingredients. Cover and cook over very low heat 2 hours or until sauce is thickened. Serve over hot cooked rice. *Serves 6-8*

**Variation: Bayou Casserole**

Prepare sauce, add remaining ingredients and heat to boil. Pour into casserole and stir in 1 cup rice. Cover and bake in 350° oven 1 to 1½ hours or until rice and okra are tender.

## SOUTHERN FRIED FISH

**BBB + Corn + Fish**

**4 fish fillets (6-8 ounces each)**
**Allowed milk substitute**
**Cornmeal or crushed allowed corn chips**
**Salt if desired for cornmeal coating (omit for corn chips)**
**2 tablespoons allowed oil**

Dip fish in milk substitute and roll in cornmeal. Fry in allowed oil 3 to 4 minutes per side until light brown and fish flakes easily. If allowed, sprinkle with paprika. (+ **TE&A**) *Serves 4*

## TUNA TACO

**BBB + Corn + Fish + Fruit + Veg. + TE&A**

**2 cans (6½-7 ounces each) tuna in spring water, undrained**
**1 tablespoon instant minced onion**
**¼ teaspoon garlic powder**
**1 can (8 ounces) tomato sauce**
**½ teaspoon chili powder**
**1 medium avocado**
**1 tablespoon lemon juice**
**Tomato, diced**
**Lettuce or spinach, shredded**
**8 corn taco shells, heated**
**1 can (4 ounces) green chili salsa or Mild Savory Taco Sauce, p. 187**

Combine tuna, onion, garlic powder, tomato sauce, and chili powder. Stir and cook, crumbling tuna, until mixture thickens and holds together. Pop taco shells into 400° oven 5 minutes, remove, and fill. Mash avocado with lemon juice. Top tuna mixture with avocado, then layer on tomatoes and lettuce. Pass the salsa. *Serves 4 (2 tacos each)*

## TERIYAKI FISH STEAKS

**BBB + Corn + Fish + Fruit + Veg. + TE&A**

- 4 fish steaks (shark, halibut, salmon, or bass)
- ¼ cup allowed oil
- 2 tablespoons Jan-U-Wine Soy Sauce
- ¼ teaspoon dry mustard
- 2 tablespoons lemon or lime juice
- ½ teaspoon ginger
- ⅛ teaspoon garlic powder

Marinate steaks in combination of all remaining ingredients 1 hour, turning once. Broil or grill 3 inches from flame 3 to 5 minutes on first side, brushing often with marinade. Turn, brush with marinade, and broil or grill 5 to 7 minutes on second side or until fish flakes easily. *Serves 4*

## CHINESE SHRIMP

**BBB + Corn + Poultry + Fish + Veg. + TE&A**

- 1 pound raw shrimp, peeled, deveined, halved lengthwise
- 2 tablespoons allowed oil
- ½ medium onion, sliced
- ½ medium green pepper, sliced
- 1 cup diagonally sliced celery
- 1 package (6 ounces) frozen Chinese pea pods, thawed
- 1 can (5 ounces) water chestnuts, drained and sliced
- 4 cups fresh spinach or bok choy, coarsely chopped
- 3 cups fresh bean sprouts
- 1½ cups Chicken Stock, p. 30
- ¼ cup Jan-U-Wine Soy Sauce
- ¼ teaspoon salt
- ⅛ teaspoon pepper
- 1½ tablespoons cornstarch
- 3 cups hot cooked rice

Sauté shrimp in large skillet in oil 1 minute. Add and stir-fry 2 minutes onion, green pepper, and celery. Layer on remaining vegetables and ½ cup stock, soy sauce, salt, and pepper. Cover and steam 3 to 5 minutes or until vegetables are tender-crisp. Blend cornstarch with ¼ cup stock until smooth, and stir in remaining ¾ cup stock. Add to vegetables, stirring constantly until liquid is thickened and clear. Serve over hot fluffy rice. *Serves 6*

# Meatless Entrees

## TIPS N' TOAST

**BBB**

Prepare asparagus tips and white sauce separately. Toast bread and spread with margarine. Place 6 asparagus tips on each slice of toast or on a bed of cooked rice. Cover with ½ cup sauce. *Serves 4*

- **24 asparagus tips, cooked tender-crisp**
- **2 cups BBB White Sauce, p. 183, or Cream of Rice White Sauce, p. 184**
- **4 slices allowed bread or cooked rice**
- **Allowed margarine**

## VEGETABLE-RICE BBB CASSEROLE

**BBB**

Bring liquid, margarine, and salt to boil. Add rice, cover, and steam for 25 minutes. Place ⅓ of rice in bottom of 1½-quart casserole, spread ½ of vegetables over rice, then ½ of pineapple. Repeat, ending with rice. Pour ¾ cup pineapple juice or additional water or stock over casserole. Bake in 350° oven, covered, 45 minutes or until hot through and vegetables are tender.

**Variation:**

1. Sauté tofu cubes in allowed margarine and make layer on vegetables for protein-rich casserole.
2. Cooked, diced lamb or rabbit may be added, if desired. (+ **BBB Meat**)

- **2 cups water or Vegetable Stock, p. 18**
- **1 tablespoon allowed margarine**
- **½ teaspoon salt**
- **1 cup rice**
- **Vegetables, choice of following in desired amounts: soybean sprouts, grated carrots, chopped spinach or chard, fresh or frozen green peas.**
- **1 can (20 ounces) unsweetened crushed pineapple, drained, juice reserved**

☐ **BBB + Veg.**

## QUICK STUFFED TOMATOES PILAU

- 6 large tomatoes
- ½ teaspoon salt
- 1 teaspoon instant minced onion
- ⅛ teaspoon garlic powder
- 1 tablespoon chopped parsley
- 1 cup Minute Rice
- 1 tablespoon allowed oil

Cut tops from tomatoes and reserve. Core tomatoes and scoop pulp and juice into saucepan. Add 1 cup water and all remaining ingredients except rice and oil. Bring to boil and add rice. Cover and let stand 5 minutes. Spoon rice mixture into tomato shells. Place stuffed tomatoes in baking dish, replace tops and brush with oil. Bake in 400° oven 30 minutes, spooning juices over tomatoes two or three times during baking. Serve hot or at room temperature. *Serves 6*

☐ **BBB + Veg.**

## FRIED RICE

- ½ medium green pepper, diced fine
- 2 stalks celery, sliced thin
- 1 medium onion, diced fine
- ¼ cup allowed oil
- 1 large tomato, peeled and chopped
- 3-4 cups cooked brown rice
- ½ teaspoon salt

Sauté green pepper, celery, and onion in oil until tender. Add remaining ingredients. Stir and fry until hot throughout. *Serves 6*

☐ **BBB + Veg. + TE&A**

## STUFFED ZUCCHINI BOATS

- 4 medium zucchini, halved lengthwise
- 1 recipe Boston Baked Soybeans with Rice, p. 158
- Toasted Rice Flakes, p. 247

Parboil zucchini in salted water 5 minutes or until tender-crisp. Carefully lift out squash and drain on paper towels. When cool enough to handle, scoop out seeds and pulp, leaving ½-inch thick shell. Mash pulp and add to soybeans. Spoon mixture into boats and top with flakes. Bake in shallow loaf pan in 375° oven 30 minutes or until topping is golden and shells heated through. *Serves 4–8*

☐ **BBB + Veg. + TE&A**

## SPAGHETTI SQUASH

- 1 spaghetti squash (2–3 pounds)
- 1 recipe Italian Sauce, p. 188

Cut squash in half lengthwise and remove seeds. Add 2 tablespoons water to each half and cover with foil or turn cut side down in shallow baking dish and add 1 inch water. Bake in 400° oven 45 minutes and test for doneness. When done, run fork over inside of squash to remove spaghetti-like strands from shell. Heap on plates and serve covered with Italian Sauce. *Serves 4–6*

## SAUCY VEGETABLE MEDLEY

**BBB + Veg. + TE&A**

- 1 recipe Boiled Brown Rice, p. 245
- 4 cups fresh vegetables, sliced or diced (squash, green beans, okra, carrots, broccoli, or whatever is allowed)
- 1 clove garlic, crushed
- 2 tablespoons allowed margarine
- ⅛ teaspoon paprika
- 2 tablespoons chopped parsley
- 2 cans (8 ounces) tomato sauce
- 2 tablespoons instant chopped onion
- 1 bay leaf
- ¼ teaspoon dried basil
- ¼ teaspoon dried oregano
- Salt and pepper to taste

Cook rice as directed and place in bottom of oiled 2-quart casserole. Sauté vegetables of choice and garlic in margarine and sprinkle with paprika. Spoon vegetables over rice. Meanwhile, combine ½ cup water and all other ingredients, simmer 15 minutes and pour over casserole. Bake, covered, in 375° oven 30 to 45 minutes. *Serves 4–6*

**Variations:**

1. Replace rice with Rye Cereal, p. 250. (+ **Rye**)
2. Replace rice with Quick Barley Cereal, p. 254 or with Whole Grain Barley Cereal, p. 254. (+ **Barley**)
3. Replace rice with Buckwheat Groats, p. 261. (+ **Buckwheat**)

## TOFU STUFFED PEPPERS

**BBB + Veg. + TE&A**

- 4 green peppers
- 1 medium onion, chopped
- ½ cup thin sliced celery
- 1 clove garlic, crushed
- 3 tablespoons allowed oil
- 1 package (16–19 ounces) tofu, washed, dried, and cubed
- 1 can (8 ounces) tomato sauce
- ½ teaspoon dried oregano
- 1 teaspoon dried basil
- ½ teaspoon salt
- ⅛ teaspoon pepper

Cut tops from peppers, remove seeds and membrane, and parboil in salted water 5 minutes. Sauté onion, celery, and garlic in oil until transparent. Add tofu cubes and continue cooking, turning gently until cubes are crusty. Add tomato sauce and seasonings. Stuff peppers and place in baking dish with ¼-inch water in bottom. Bake in 375° oven 30 to 40 minutes. *Serves 4*

☐ **BBB + Veg. + TE&A**

## FANTASTIC RICE

- ½ cup onion, chopped
- 1 cup brown or white rice
- 3 tablespoons allowed oil
- ½ teaspoon salt
- ⅛ teaspoon pepper
- 1 cup frozen petite green peas
- 1 jar (4 ounces) pimiento, diced
- 1 teaspoon paprika
- 1 tablespoon imitation bacon bits (optional)

Sauté onion and rice in oil. Season with salt and pepper and add water or broth required—2 cups for white rice, 2½ to 3 cups for brown rice. Bring to boil, cover, and cook over low heat 25 minutes for white rice, 40 minutes for brown. Toss lightly with peas and pimiento. Garnish with paprika and imitation bacon bits. *Serves 6*

☐ **BBB + Veg. + TE&A**

## SAVORY BEANS

- 1 medium onion, cut in rings
- ½ medium green pepper, sliced
- 1 clove garlic, minced
- 2 tablespoons allowed oil
- 1 can (16 ounces) stewed tomatoes
- ½ teaspoon salt
- Dash of pepper
- ½ teaspoon Italian seasoning
- 4 cups cooked navy, lima, or garbanzo beans (See p. 172)

Sauté onion, green pepper, and garlic in oil. Add tomatoes and seasonings and simmer 10 minutes to blend flavors. Add cooked beans and bake in 350° oven 1 hour. If casserole gets dry, add water as necessary. *Serves 4–6*

☐ **BBB + Veg. + TE&A**

## SAHARA FALAFEL MIX

Look for this mix in the specialty section of your market. The ingredients are garbanzo beans, yellow peas, onion, parsley, herbs, spices, and sea salt—no preservatives, artificial flavorings, or colorings. This may be fried as patties in allowed oil, following package directions. Teaspoon-size patties are nice for hors d'oeuvres. This mix may also be used dry as breading for meats or it may be combined with ground beef for hamburger patties or meat loaf.

## BAKED BEANS

**BBB + Veg. + TE&A**

- **1 small onion, chopped**
- **2 tablespoons allowed oil**
- **3 cups cooked navy or lima beans, see p. 172 or 2 cans (16 ounces each) soy beans**
- **⅛ teaspoon garlic powder**
- **¼ cup brown sugar, firmly packed**
- **2 tablespoons honey**
- **1 teaspoon dry mustard**
- **1 cup tomato juice**
- **¼ teaspoon salt**
- **⅛ teaspoon pepper**
- **1 tablespoon imitation bacon bits**
- **1 teaspoon Kitchen Bouquet**

Sauté onion in oil. Combine ½ cup water with all other ingredients in bean pot. Bake, covered, in 300° oven 2 to 3 hours. Stir occasionally. Uncover and bake 1 hour longer, adding water if too dry. *Serves 4*

**Variation: Picnic Pot-o-beans**

Replace beans with 2 cans (15 ounces each) Loma Linda Boston Style Soybeans, undrained, and 1 can (15-17 ounces each) red kidney beans and lima beans, drained. Sauté ½ cup sliced celery with onion. Omit water and Kitchen Bouquet. Replace with 2 tablespoons lemon juice. Combine all ingredients in 2-quart casserole and bake at 375° 30 to 45 minutes or until beans are hot and bubbly. **(+ Fruit)** *Serves 8*

## ITALIAN TOFU CASSEROLE

**BBB + Veg. + TE&A**

- **¼ cup allowed oil**
- **1 cup Minute Rice**
- **1 medium onion, diced**
- **½ medium green pepper, diced**
- **1 clove garlic, minced fine**
- **1 package (19 ounces) tofu, washed, dried, and cubed**
- **½ teaspoon dried oregano**
- **1 teaspoon dried basil**
- **1 teaspoon salt**
- **⅛ teaspoon pepper**
- **2 cans (8 ounces each) tomato sauce**
- **1½ pounds small zucchini, sliced thin**

Bring 1 cup water and 1 tablespoon oil to boil and stir in rice. Cover and set aside. Sauté onion, green pepper, garlic, and tofu in remaining oil. Season, remove from heat, and stir in tomato sauce. Place ½ zucchini slices in bottom of 8 x 10-inch oiled loaf pan. Spread all of rice over squash. Top with ½ tofu mixture. Repeat zucchini and tofu layers. Cover tightly with foil. Bake in 350° oven 45 to 60 minutes until zucchini is tender. *Serves 6*

☐ **BBB + Veg. + TE&A**

**1 can (15 ounces) Loma Linda Boston Style Soybeans**
**2 cups cooked brown rice**
**1 can (8 ounces) stewed tomatoes or 1 cup cooked fresh tomatoes**
**2 scallions, sliced**
**½ teaspoon dried basil**
**½ teaspoon salt**

## BOSTON BAKED SOYBEANS WITH RICE

Mix all ingredients in oiled 1½-quart casserole. Bake in 350° oven 30 minutes or until hot throughout. *Serves 4–6*

☐ **BBB + Veg. + TE&A**

**1 cup rice**
**2 tablespoons allowed oil**
**1 medium onion, minced**
**1 clove garlic, minced**
**½ medium green pepper, chopped**
**1 teaspoon salt**
**1-2 teaspoons chili powder**
**1 cup tomatoes or 1 can (8 ounces) tomato sauce**

## MEXICAN RICE

Brown rice in oil, add and sauté onion, garlic, and green pepper. Add seasonings, tomatoes, and 2 cups water. Cover and cook over low heat 30 minutes or until rice is tender. Uncover to allow moisture to cook off. Avoid stirring. *Serves 4*

**Variation:**
Omit chili powder and serve as Spanish rice.

☐ **BBB + Veg. + N&S +TE&A**

**½ cup chopped onion**
**½ cup sliced celery**
**½ cup slivered almonds**
**½ cup brown rice**
**½ cup wild rice**
**2 tablespoons allowed oil**
**3 cups boiling water or Vegetable Stock or BBB Meat Stock I or II, p. 18**
**1 teaspoon salt**
**¼ teaspoon garlic powder**
**⅛ teaspoon pepper**
**1 tablespoon chopped parsley**

## WILD RICE ALMONDINE

Sauté vegetables, nuts, and rice in oil until rice is lightly browned. Add seasonings and parsley and mix well. Pour into 1½-quart oiled casserole and add boiling liquid. Stir to mix evenly. Cover and bake in 325° oven 1 hour or until water is absorbed and rice is tender. *Serves 4–6*

**Variations:**

1. Sauté 4 to 6 chicken livers with vegetables and rice. Omit almonds and replace with 1 large tomato, peeled and cut in wedges. (**+ Poultry**)

2. Sauté sliced mushrooms with vegetables and rice. Use ½ cup white wine to replace ½ cup liquid. (**+ Mold**)

## POT-O-VEGETABLES

**BBB + Veg. + TE&A**

- 1 cup chopped onion
- 1 clove garlic, crushed
- ¼ cup allowed oil
- ½ medium green pepper, cut in strips
- 1 can (16 ounces) stewed tomatoes
- 2 cups zucchini cut in ½-inch slices
- 1 small eggplant, peeled and cut in 1-inch cubes
- 1 cup diced potatoes
- 1 tablespoon chopped parsley
- 1 teaspoon salt
- ⅛ teaspoon pepper
- ½ teaspoon dried basil
- 1 teaspoon rice flour, optional

Sauté onion and garlic in oil in deep kettle. Add all remaining ingredients except flour. Cover and cook 25 minutes, or until vegetables are tender-crisp. Thicken juices if desired with 1 teaspoon rice flour blended with 1 tablespoon water. Add and cook 1 minute. Serve over cooked rice or as is. *Serves 4–6*

## TROPICAL RICE

**BBB + Fruit + Veg. + N&S + TE&A**

- 1⅓ cup Minute Rice
- 1⅓ cup boiling water
- 2 teaspoons curry powder
- 3 tablespoons allowed oil
- 2 large bananas, cut in ½-inch slices
- ¼ cup finely chopped onion
- ¼ cup slivered almonds
- ¼ cup flaked coconut
- ½ teaspoon salt

Stir rice into boiling water, cover, and set aside. Cook curry powder with oil until bubbly, add bananas, and sauté. Remove bananas and keep warm. Add onion and almonds and sauté. Stir rice and remaining ingredients except bananas into onion mixture. Stir and heat thoroughly. Add bananas and toss lightly. *Serves 6*

## BEAN TOSTADA

**BBB + Corn + Fruit + Veg.**

- Corn tortillas or packaged tostada shells
- Allowed oil
- Rosarita Vegetarian Refried Beans
- Sliced avocado
- Lettuce, shredded fine
- Tomato, sliced

Fry corn tortillas in hot oil until crisp (or heat packaged tostada shells as directed on package). Spread beans on each shell and slip under broiler to heat. Top each tostada with avocado slices, large pile of shredded lettuce, and tomato slices. Tastier if served with purchased green chili salsa or Mild Savory Taco Sauce, p. 187. (+ **TE&A**) Serve 1 or 2 tostadas per person.

## SALAD STUFFED TOMATOES

**BBB + Corn + Veg.**

- 4 large ripe tomatoes, chilled
- 1 recipe Golden Marinated Salad, p. 61

Make thick tomato shells by removing tops and pulp. Invert to drain, then slice in wedges to within ½ inch of bottom. Add reserved pulp to Marinated Salad. Spoon salad into each tomato. Serve on salad greens. Top with dollop of BBB Cooked Mayonnaise, p. 64 or with Perfect Cooked Mayonnaise, p. 67 if spices are allowed. *Serves 4*

## HOMINY STUFFED PEPPERS

**BBB + Corn + Veg. + TE&A**

- 4 large green peppers
- ⅓ cup chopped onion
- 1 clove garlic, minced
- 2 tablespoons allowed oil
- 1 can (16 ounces) golden hominy, drained
- 1 tomato, peeled and chopped
- 2 tablespoons chopped pimiento
- 1 tablespoon chopped parsley
- ½ teaspoon salt
- 1 tablespoon imitation bacon bits or ½ teaspoon chili powder

Cut tops from peppers and remove seeds and membrane. Parboil in salted water 5 minutes and turn to drain. Sauté onion and garlic in oil. Add all other ingredients and cook 10 minutes to blend flavors. Stuff peppers with mixture and place in baking dish. Pour ½ inch water around peppers and bake in 375° oven 30 minutes. *Serves 4*

**Variation:**

For Stuffed Tomatoes, core and remove center pulp from medium-large tomatoes, leaving thick shell. Use tomato pulp in place of tomato called for in recipe. Cut tomato shells in wedges almost to bottom, stuff, and bake as for peppers.

## CREAMED VEGETABLE CASSEROLE

**BBB + Corn + Veg. + TE&A**

- 1 small onion, chopped
- ½ cup sliced celery
- 2 tablespoons allowed oil
- 2 cups White Sauce, p. 183
- ¼ teaspoon summer savory
- 1½ cups cooked vegetables (green beans, peas, squash, carrots, etc.)
- ½ package (12 ounces) wheat-free corn pasta—ribbons, cooked as directed

Sauté onion and celery in oil. Stir in white sauce, seasonings, and cooked vegetables. Heat, but do not boil. Combine with drained ribbons and place in 2-quart casserole. Top with oiled crumbs, p. 232 and bake in 375° oven 25 minutes or until hot through. *Serves 4*

## MEXICAN CASSEROLE

**BBB + Corn + Veg. + TE&A**

Sauté onion, green pepper, and garlic in oil. Add all ingredients except pasta. Bring to boil, cover, and simmer slowly 10 minutes. Combine with pasta shells in 2-quart baking dish. Bake in 375° oven 30 minutes or until hot and bubbly. *Serves 4*

**1 medium onion, chopped**
**½ cup diced green pepper**
**1 clove garlic, crushed**
**¼ cup allowed oil**
**1 tablespoon chopped parsley**
**1 teaspoon salt**
**2 teaspoons chili powder**
**Dash of pepper**
**1 can (16 ounces) stewed tomatoes**
**1 can (16 ounces) kidney beans, drained**
**½ package (12 ounces) wheat-free corn pasta—shells, cooked as directed.**

## SAVORY ONION RICE

**BBB + Corn + Veg. + TE&A**

Sauté rice and onion in oil until golden. Add boiling water. Simmer, covered, 25 minutes or until rice is tender. Stir in chopped parsley and pimientos. Cook 5 minutes longer, uncovered. *Serves 4–6*

**1 cup long grain white rice**
**1 medium onion, chopped**
**1 tablespoon allowed oil**
**2 cups boiling water**
**2 tablespoons chopped parsley**
**1 jar (2 ounces) pimientos, chopped**

## VEGETABLE RICE CASSEROLE

**BBB + Corn + Veg. + TE&A**

Sauté onions and celery in oil. Blend all ingredients with ½ cup water in 2-quart casserole. Bake, covered, in 350° oven or until hot through and potatoes and carrots are tender. *Serves 4*

**1 cup chopped onions**
**½ cup chopped celery**
**3 tablespoons allowed oil**
**1 cup shredded potato**
**2 cups shredded carrot**
**1 can (8 ounces) whole kernel corn**
**1 can (15 ounces) Hain Soybeans**
**1 cup cooked rice**
**1 cup tomato juice**
**½ teaspoon salt**
**¼ teaspoon paprika**
**½ teaspoon brown sugar**

# Vegetables and Side Dishes

## VEGETABLES

Only a few simple cooking instructions for vegetables are included in this book. We presume that the food preparer who works with us understands basic vegetable cookery. We have tried to give imaginative ideas, especially for preparing the limited number of vegetables included in the Basic Building-Block Foods.

We ourselves love fresh vegetables and prepare them with as little water as possible, cooking until barely tender-crisp. This retains vitamins and color and happy textures for the teeth to enjoy. If you have questions about the plain cooking of vegetables, you will find them answered in many other books.

Use canned or frozen vegetables as long as they have nothing added except salt. In markets, look in the regular canned vegetable department as well as in the diet section for water-pack vegetables. Some products have added ingredients such as dextrose (usually corn sugar). Look at varieties and labels in your local health food store.

For the cook in a hurry who can't manage the schedule for soaking and cooking soybeans, try canned soybeans (Hain and Loma Linda in our area). We like their taste and they provide good protein. These are especially helpful in the beginning of food testing while kinds of meat are limited.

When allowed, try Rosarita Vegetarian Refried Beans (made with soya oil rather than pork lard), Libby's Solid Pack Pumpkin, and some brands of tomato paste (making sure they contain tomatoes only or tomatoes and salt). Later, try tomato sauces containing tomatoes, other vegetables, spices, and salt. Beware of the addition of dextrose until you are sure of your tolerance for corn.

Poultry and meat stuffings are included in this section. For side dishes of rice, barley, and other grains, see the Meatless Entrees section. Those recipes can be used alone as entrees as well as to accompany a plain meat entree.

## BOILED ARTICHOKES

**BBB**

Wash artichokes thoroughly, slice stem off near base and clip sharp points with shears. Remove small bottom leaves and discard. Stand artichokes upright in deep pot and add salt and oil to each. Pour in 2 to 3 inches boiling water, cover pot, and simmer 35 to 45 minutes or until base is tender when pierced. Remove artichokes and drain upside down. Serve with BBB Cooked Mayonnaise, p. 64 or with BBB Soyannaise, p. 64. *Serves 4*

**4 medium artichokes**
**¼ teaspoon salt per artichoke**
**1 teaspoon allowed oil for each artichoke**
**Boiling water**

## CARROT FRIES

**BBB**

Cook carrots in boiling water 10 minutes or until tender-crisp. Drain and dry. Place in oiled baking pan, brush tops with oil and sprinkle with salt. Bake in 375° oven 10 minutes to crisp and brown.

**Large carrots, peeled and scrubbed, quartered lengthwise, and cut into 3-inch lengths**
**Allowed oil**
**Salt to taste**

## CARROTS AND ASPARAGUS PAS DE DEUX

**BBB**

Cook carrots in small amount of salted water, covered, until almost tender. Add asparagus and cook until asparagus is done. If using fresh asparagus, cook all the time with carrots. Drain. Drizzle margarine over vegetables. *Serves 4–6*

**2 cups sliced carrots**
**1 package (10 ounces) frozen cut asparagus or 1 pound fresh asparagus**
**Salt**
**Allowed margarine, melted**

**Variation:**

Sprinkle chopped fresh parsley over vegetables. (+ **Veg.**)

## PEAS AND CARROTS

**BBB**

Cook each vegetable separately and drain. Toss gently with allowed margarine. Salt to taste if desired. *Serves 4*

**8 tiny baby carrots or 1 cup carrot slices**
**1 package (10 ounces) frozen petite peas**
**Salt (optional)**

## BASIC CREAMED SPINACH

**BBB**

- **1 package (10 ounces) frozen spinach, cooked and drained**
- **1 cup White Sauce prepared with allowed thickening, p. 183**

Stir spinach and sauce gently together and heat. Prepare with fresh cooked and drained spinach if desired. *Serves 2–3*

## HARVARD BEETS

**BBB**

- **1½ tablespoons tapioca starch or arrowroot powder**
- **½ teaspoon salt**
- **¼ cup white or brown sugar**
- **¼ cup white distilled vinegar**
- **¾ cup beet liquid or water**
- **2 cups cooked beets, sliced or diced or 1 can (16 ounces) beets, drained, juice reserved**

Blend starch or arrowroot, salt, and sugar in saucepan. Add vinegar and liquid slowly, stirring constantly to keep smooth. Bring to boil, stirring until thickened. Add cooked beets and reheat. If desired, 1 tablespoon allowed margarine may be stirred into sauce. *Serves 4*

**Variations:**

1. Replace vinegar with lemon or lime juice **(+ Fruit)**
2. Replace sugar with honey. Add a few whole cloves to sauce. **(+ TE&A)**
3. ORANGE BEETS—Replace sugar with honey. Replace vinegar with lemon or lime juice. Replace beet juice with orange juice and add ½ teaspoon each grated orange peel and ground ginger. **(+ Fruit + TE&A)**

## PICKLED BEETS

**BBB**

- **1 can sliced or whole beets, drained, juice reserved, or cooked fresh beets**
- **Beet juice, measured**
- **White distilled vinegar, ½ amount of beet juice**

Combine beets, beet juice, and vinegar. Marinate in refrigerator in jar with tight fitting lid. *Serves 4*

*Note:* I, Gloria, have no food allergies and love pickled eggs like the ones my mother made when I was a child. Just add shelled, hard-cooked eggs to the pickled beets and marinate at least 24 hours. The longer eggs are marinated, the deeper the colored juice penetrates and flavors. I confess that I sometimes divide the family's beet mixture and use half for my eggs.

## GOLDEN NEW POTATOES

**BBB**

**16 small new potatoes**
**Boiling water to cover**
**Allowed margarine, melted**
**Salt to taste**

Cook potatoes, covered, in boiling water 20 to 30 minutes or until tender. Cool and remove skins. Roll potatoes in enough melted margarine to coat well. Sprinkle with salt and fry to reheat and brown slightly. *Serves 4*

**Variation:**

When allowed, place oiled potatoes in baking dish. Sprinkle with salt and paprika. Add finely chopped parsley, mint, or chives and bake in 375° oven 30 minutes or until crispy and brown. **(+ Veg. + TE&A)**

## CREAMED NEW POTATOES

**BBB**

**16 small new potatoes or chunks of other thin-skinned peeled potatoes**
**Boiling water**
**2 cups Cream of Rice White Sauce, p. 184**

Cook potatoes, covered, in boiling water to cover 20 to 30 minutes or until tender. Cool and peel. Add to prepared sauce and cover. Place over low heat 5 minutes. *Serves 4*

**Variations:**

1. Cook 1 package (10 ounces) frozen green peas as directed. Drain and add to potatoes in white sauce just before serving. Delicious!
2. Sauté ½ cup chopped celery and ¼ cup chopped onion in 2 tablespoons allowed margarine. Add to potatoes or to potatoes and peas in white sauce. Add 1 tablespoon chopped fresh parsley to garnish. **(+ Veg.)**
3. Add 2 teaspoons Steero Instant Chicken Flavored Bouillon Seasoning and Broth to white sauce. Combine with vegetables. **(+ Poultry + Veg. + TE&A)**

## MASHED POTATOES

**BBB**

**6 medium potatoes, peeled and cut in cubes**
**2 tablespoons allowed margarine**
**1 teaspoon salt**
**⅓ cup allowed milk substitute**

Simmer potatoes in water to cover until tender, 15 minutes. Drain, reserving potato water to use later in gravy, sauces, or breads. Mash potatoes with margarine, salt, and milk substitute by hand or electric mixer. Mixer makes them smooth and fluffy with little effort. *Serves 4*

BBB

## MASHED POTATO SHELLS

Prepare Mashed Potatoes, p. 165 or amount needed for desired size casserole or pie pan. Spread potatoes over bottom and sides of oiled baking dish, building side walls as high as possible. Drizzle melted allowed margarine over potatoes. Bake in 400° oven 30 to 40 minutes or until crispy, brown, and firm. Fill with hot creamed vegetables, meat, or meat in gravy or sauce.

BBB

## STUFFED BAKED POTATOES

- 4 russet potatoes, scrubbed
- 2 tablespoons allowed margarine
- ⅓ cup allowed milk substitute
- ½ teaspoon salt
- 1 cup frozen green peas, cooked and drained

Bake potatoes in 400° oven 1 hour. Slice off center top and scoop out potato, being careful not to break shell. Mash potato with margarine and milk substitute and salt. Fill shell half full with mashed potato, add ¼ cup peas and top with remaining potato. Return to oven and bake at 375° 15 minutes. *Serves 4*

**Variation:**
Refrigerate prepared stuffed potatoes and bake next day at 375° 30 to 45 minutes.

BBB

## SCALLOPED POTATOES

- 6 medium potatoes, peeled or unpeeled
- ⅓ cup rice flour or ½ cup potato starch
- Salt to taste
- Allowed milk substitute
- Allowed margarine

Cut potatoes into thin slices. Layer ⅓ potatoes in bottom of well oiled baking dish. Sprinkle with ½ flour or starch. Repeat another layer of each, and top with final ⅓ potatoes. Pour on enough milk substitute to come to top layer of potatoes and both coming an inch from top of baking dish to prevent boiling over. Dot with allowed margarine. Bake, covered, in 350° oven 1 to 1¼ hours or until tender. Uncover and bake 15 minutes more to brown slightly. *Serves 4*

**Variation:**
Add ½ teaspoon instant minced onion in each layer of flour. Sprinkle top of casserole with paprika and a little finely chopped parsley. **(+ Veg. + TE&A)**

BBB

## POTATO PANCAKE

- 2 medium potatoes, peeled and grated
- ¼ cup potato starch
- ½ teaspoon salt

Combine all ingredients and form into patties. Fry in allowed oil until brown and potato is cooked through. *Serves 3-4*

## BROILED POTATO RINGS

**BBB**

**New potatoes**
**Allowed oil or margarine**
**Salt, if desired**

Chill scrubbed new potatoes. Cut unpeeled potatoes in thin slices, place on greased baking sheet. Brush with allowed oil and season with salt, if desired. Broil 10 minutes without turning until brown or until potatoes are done.

**Variation:**

Sprinkle with garlic salt or Seasoned Salt Blend, p. 176 or Herb Blend Seasoning, p. 177. **(+ Veg. + TE&A)**

## FRIED POTATOES

**BBB**

4 **large scrubbed potatoes, cut in thin strips or ¼-inch rounds, peeled or unpeeled**
**Allowed oil**
**Salt**

Soak strips or rounds in ice water to cover for 10 minutes. Drain and dry thoroughly between toweling. Fry by your choice of methods. *Serves 4*

*Method 1*—Fry in electric deep fry pan as recommended. Drain on paper towel. Salt while hot.

*Method 2*—Fry in skillet until brown on one side and turn to brown second side. Cook until tender. Season.

*Method 3*—Place potatoes on greased cookie sheet, brush with oil and sprinkle with salt. Bake in 425° oven until crisp and golden, but tender inside.

## TOASTED POTATO PEELS

**BBB**

Don't ever throw away another potato peel! These are too good! Potatoes should be well scrubbed and peeled with knife or peeler. It doesn't matter whether you peel a potato for the peels or for the potato. Cover the peels with cold water and refrigerate until ready to use. Drain and dry peels thoroughly. Pour 2 to 4 tablespoons allowed oil in baking pan. Press peels in single layers in oil. Flip each to oil other side (or brush with oil). Season with salt if desired. Bake in 400° oven 10 to 20 minutes, depending on thickness of peel. Chilled peels may take longer. Bake until browned and crisp. Lift peels onto paper towel and drain. Serve immediately while crisp. When allowed, season with Seasoned Salt Blend, p. 176. **(+ Veg. + TE&A)**

BBB

## HASH BROWN POTATOES

- 4 medium potatoes, grated, peeled or unpeeled
- Allowed oil
- Salt to taste

Grate potatoes on a double fold of paper toweling to absorb potato water. Spread over bottom of well-oiled skillet and season. Cover and cook slowly until crispy brown on bottom. Lift with wide spatula, add more oil for second side. Turn carefully to avoid oil spatters. Brown well on second side. Serve hot. *Serves 4*

**Variations:**

1. Use grated leftover cooked potatoes or canned whole potatoes.

2. HASH BROWN CARROTS—Grate carrots coarsely and place 1 inch thick in well-oiled frying pan. Cook over medium heat, uncovered, until brown crust forms on bottom. Serve crusty side up. Needs no seasoning. A great favorite. Sugar in carrots forms a kind of caramelized crust.

3. CRUSTY HASH BROWNS—Cut leftover boiled potatoes in small cubes (2½ cups). Stir with 2½ tablespoons rice flour, 3 tablespoons allowed milk substitute and ½ teaspoon salt. Pour into hot oiled skillet, press down hard with spatula to form crusty brown underside. Remove from pan, add small amount of oil, and return, crust side up. Press down to brown second side.

BBB

## BAKED SWEET POTATOES OR YAMS

Scrub sweets or yams and bake at 400° 50 to 60 minutes. Serve with peel on, merely cutting into serving size lengths. Serve hot, room temperature, or cold. If chilled, potato skin can be peeled back like that of bananas. Sweet potatoes are at their best served plain, without seasoning.

**Variation:**

Add a surprise by cutting a cross in skin of each serving length. Insert 1 teaspoon allowed margarine and 1 tablespoon Peach-Apricot Jam, p. 235.

## FRENCH FRIED SWEET POTATOES

BBB

Cut potatoes in ¼-inch slices for chips or in 3 x 4-inch lengths for fries. Chill in ice cold vinegar water to cover for 30 minutes. Drain and dry thoroughly. Preheat oil in skillet to 360°. Fry potatoes, single layer at a time, 3 to 5 minutes, or until dark golden brown. Yams will take less time than sweets. Drain on paper towel, sprinkle with salt while warm. Store in airtight container.

**2 pounds sweet potatoes or yams, peeled**
**1 tablespoon white distilled vinegar**
**Allowed oil**
**Salt**

## CANDIED SWEET POTATOES

BBB

Arrange potato slices flat to cover bottom of large skillet. Add water to half cover, ½ to ¾ cup sugar, and 1 tablespoon or more allowed margarine. Boil, covered, until potatoes are half cooked. Remove lid and allow water to boil off, then continue cooking until potatoes are caramelized.

**Sweet potatoes, peeled and cut in 1-inch rounds**
**Brown sugar, firmly packed**
**Allowed margarine**

## BAKED SWEETS AND PINEAPPLE

BBB

Slice half of potatoes into oiled baking dish. Cover with drained pineapple chunks and top with remaining sliced potatoes. Combine oil, thickening chosen, and ½ cup reserved pineapple juice. Stirring constantly, cook until boiling and thickened. Pour over casserole. Sprinkle on brown sugar and Rice Flakes. Bake in 375° oven 20 minutes or until hot through. *Serves 4–6*

### Variation:

Replace pineapple with precooked apple slices. Make sauce with liquid in which apples were cooked.

**1 can (1 pound, 12 ounces) sweet potatoes, drained**
**1 can (20 ounces) unsweetened chunk pineapple, drained, juice reserved**
**1 tablespoon allowed oil**
**1 tablespoon rice flour or 1½ teaspoon tapioca starch**
**Brown sugar**
**1 recipe Toasted Rice Flakes, p. 247**

## FESTIVE SWEET POTATOES

**BBB**

- **2 sweet potatoes, 8-10 inches long**
- **Apple or pineapple juice, if desired**
- **1 can (16 ounces) water-pack peach halves**

Wash potatoes and bake in jackets at 400° 1 hour or until tender. Remove potato from jacket. Whip until fluffy, adding juice if desired. Be sure to keep mixture stiff. Arrange 4 to 6 peach halves in baking dish. Mound potatoes on each peach half. Bake in 375° oven 15 minutes or until heated through. *Serves 4–6*

**Variation:**

Bake mound of mashed sweets on pineapple slices. Dot with allowed margarine, if desired.

## TRIO OF POTATO STUFFINGS FOR POULTRY

**BBB**

I—Stuff bird with cold mashed potatoes made with allowed margarine, milk substitute, and salt.

II—Parboil thin potato slices 6 minutes. Drain, saving liquid for gravy. Toss potatoes with allowed oil, salt, and rice flour or potato starch. Chill. Stuff bird.

III—Dice cooked potato. Sauté in allowed oil. Season with salt. Chill and stuff bird.

## SWEETS AND APPLE STUFFING

**BBB**

- **2 cups chopped cooked or canned sweet potatoes or yams**
- **1 tart apple, grated**
- **¼ cup brown sugar, firmly packed**
- **⅛ teaspoon salt**
- **¼ cup liquid from canned sweet potato or apple juice or water**

Combine all ingredients. Chill. Stuff bird just before baking.

**Variation:**

Omit liquid and add 1 can (8 ounces) unsweetened crushed pineapple.

## BBB STUFFING (2½-POUND BIRD) BBB

Sauté apple in oil. Combine with other ingredients, toss, and chill. Stuff bird just before baking.

**Variation:**

Add cooked giblets to sautéed apple and cook 2 minutes. Replace apple juice with chicken broth.

**(+ Poultry)**

- **1 large cooking apple, chopped**
- **2 tablespoons allowed oil or margarine**
- **1½ cups allowed soft bread crumbs**
- **½ teaspoon salt**
- **3 tablespoons apple juice or water**

# PLAIN COOKED RICE

## (4 to 6 servings) BBB

| Kind of Rice | Quantity | Liquid | Salt | Oil | Timing |
|---|---|---|---|---|---|
| Long grain white | 1 cup | 2 cups | ½ tsp. | 1 Tbsp. | 25 minutes |
| Short grain brown | 1 cup | 3 cups | ½ tsp. | 2 Tbsp. | 45 minutes |
| Long grain brown | 1 cup | 4 cups | 1 tsp. | 1 Tbsp. | 60 minutes |
| Wild rice | 1 cup | 4 cups | 1 tsp. | | 40 minutes |
| Minute Rice | 1½ cups | 1½ cups | ½ tsp. | 1 tsp. | 5 minutes |
| Quick Brown Rice | 1 cup | 1½ cups | ½ tsp. | | 15 minutes |

*White Rice*—Bring liquid, salt, and oil to boil and add rice. Cover and cook slowly for time given.

*Brown Rice*—Place all ingredients in saucepan (oil may be omitted). Bring to boil. Cover and cook slowly. Rice may be browned in oil, then boiling water and salt added, and cooked as directed.

*Wild Rice*—Cover rice with water, bring to boil. Cover and cook slowly. When rice is fully fluffed, drain off any excess water, add salt and serve.

*Minute Rice*—Bring water, salt, and oil to boil. Stir in rice, cover and let stand 5 minutes. Fluff with fork.

*Quick Brown Rice*—Bring liquid and salt to boil. Stir in rice. Cover and cook slowly 15 minutes.

*Note:* Liquid may be water or any allowed meat stock. Do not lift lid while steaming rice.

**BBB**

## COOKED DRIED SOYBEANS

Cover 1 cup soybeans with hot water and let soak 12 hours. Drain and rinse several times. Cover with cold water and add 1 tablespoon allowed oil. Bring to boil, cover, and cook slowly 2½ hours. Add 1 teaspoon salt near end of cooking time. *Makes 2½ cups*

**BBB**

## BASIC FRIED OKRA

- **4 cups ½-inch slices fresh okra**
- **½ cup rice flour**
- **3 tablespoons potato flour**
- **½ teaspoon salt**
- **Allowed oil**

Mix flours and salt. Toss enough flour mixture with okra to coat cut edges well. Heat oil in skillet, add okra and cover. Fry over medium heat, stirring occasionally to brown evenly. When nearly fork tender, uncover and continue frying to crisp coated edges. *Serves 4*

**Variation: Fried Okra and Potatoes:**
Cut and coat okra as above. Combine with desired amount of cubed cold boiled potatoes and fry as directed. Season with salt.

☐ **BBB + Veg.**

## COOKED DRIED BEANS

*Pink Beans, Baby Limas, Garbanzos, Navy (small white)*—Cover 1 cup beans with 3½ cups water, bring to boil, and boil 2 minutes. Cover, remove from heat, and set aside 1 hour. Bring to boil, simmer slowly, covered, 1 to 1½ hours or until beans are tender. Add salt (½ to ¾ teaspoon) near end of cooking time. When tender, drain. Makes 2½ cups

*Black-eyed Peas*—Cover 1 cup beans with 3½ cups water; bring to boil. Cook slowly, covered, for 45 to 60 minutes or until beans are just tender. Add salt (½ to ¾ teaspoon) near end of cooking time. Makes 2½ cups.

*Lentils*—Bring 1 cup lentils, 2½ cups water, and ¾ teaspoon salt to boil. Simmer gently 20 to 30 minutes. Makes 2 cups.

*Split Peas*—For mashed or purée, bring 1 cup peas and 2 cups water to boil, cover, and simmer slowly 45 to 60 minutes. Add salt (½ to ¾ teaspoon).

For split peas to retain shape, bring 4¾ cups water to boil. Add 1 cup split peas, bring to boil again, and boil 2 minutes. Remove from heat. Cover and soak ½ hour. Add ½ to ¾ teaspoon salt.

## REFRIED BEANS

**BBB + Veg.** ☐

**2 cups dried pink beans**
**1 teaspoon baking soda**
**1 small onion, minced fine**
**1 clove garlic, crushed**
**½ cup allowed oil**
**Salt to taste**

Soak beans overnight in 5 cups water. Next morning, drain, add 5 cups fresh water and soda, bring to boil, then simmer, covered, 1½ to 2 hours or until tender. Stir occasionally while cooking. Drain and reserve liquid. Sauté onion and garlic in oil, add 1 cup beans, and mash well. Add a little bean liquid. Repeat bean and bean liquid additions until both are used. Add salt. Cook again over low heat until thickened. This requires frequent stirring. May be chilled and reheated in allowed oil as needed. *Serves 8*

*Refried Beans, Canned*—Rosarita Vegetarian Refried Beans (17 ounces) can save effort without recoding. Contains no fat except soy oil. When pork has been proven friendly, regular Rosarita or other brands of refried beans may be used, but we urge reading labels.

## CROOKNECK SQUASH AND PEA PODS

**BBB + Veg.** ☐

**3 cups small tender yellow crookneck squash**
**1 package (6 ounces) frozen Chinese pea pods**
**1 tablespoon allowed margarine**
**Salt to taste**

Cook squash in small amount of salted water, covered, until tender-crisp. Drain. Cook peas as directed on package. Combine and toss with margarine. *Serves 4–6*

## ZUCCHINI PLUS

**BBB + Veg.** ☐

**½ cup chopped onion**
**¼ cup sliced green pepper**
**2 tablespoons allowed oil**
**½ teaspoon salt**
**1 pound zucchini, sliced**
**1 can (16 ounces) garbanzo beans, drained**
**1 tablespoon chopped parsley**

Sauté onion and green pepper in oil and add salt. Add zucchini and ¼ cup water, cover, and simmer 10 minutes or until only tender-crisp. Add garbanzos and parsley. Heat through and drain. *Serves 4–6*

**Variations:**

1. Omit water, garbanzos, and parsley. Sauté 2 cloves garlic, crushed, with onion and add 3 medium tomatoes, peeled and chopped. Cook with squash 10 minutes, covered. Uncover and cook off liquid.

2. Replace garbanzos and parsley with 1½ cups whole kernel canned corn and 1½ teaspoons dried dill weed. (**+ Corn + TE&A**)

☐ **BBB + Veg.**

## ACORN SQUASH MEDLEY

**2 small acorn squash**
**Allowed margarine**
**Brown sugar to taste**

Cut squash in half lengthwise and scoop out seeds and strings. Steam over boiling water 30 minutes, keeping tightly covered, or bake 30 minutes, cut side down, in oiled baking dish in 375° oven. Turn squash right side up, coat edges and cavity with allowed oil or margarine, sprinkle with brown sugar and bake at 375° 15 to 20 minutes. *Serves 4*

**Variations:**

1. CRANBERRY SQUASH—Omit brown sugar and fill cavity with Basic Cranberry Sauce, p. 191, during last 15 minutes of baking time.
2. NUTTY ORANGE—Sprinkle squash with grated orange peel and chopped nuts. (+ **Fruit + N&S)**
3. SPICED SQUASH—Sprinkle with nutmeg and white sugar or omit sugar and fill cavity with Peach-Apricot Jam, p. 235. (+ **TE&A)**

☐ **BBB + Veg.**

## SPINACH TANGO

**½ cup chopped onion**
**¼ cup chopped green pepper**
**1 tablespoon diced pimiento**
**⅓ cup allowed oil**
**3 pounds fresh spinach, washed and drained**
**1 teaspoon salt**
**2 tablespoons white distilled vinegar**

Sauté onions, pepper, and pimiento in oil 3 to 5 minutes. Add spinach and salt. Cover and cook 10 minutes or only until spinach is tender-crisp. Add vinegar and serve. *Serves 6*

☐ **BBB + Veg.**

## PARTY CAULIFLOWER

**½ pound cauliflower (small head or 2½ cups)**
**2 tablespoons allowed margarine**
**1 cup cherry tomatoes**
**Salt to taste**

Break cauliflower into small flowerets. Cook in boiling water 5 minutes or until tender-crisp, covered. Drain, add margarine, cherry tomatoes, and salt. Cook and toss gently until tomatoes are hot. *Serves 4*

☐ **BBB + Veg.**

## PILAU STUFFING (10 to 12 lb. bird)

Prepare Fried Rice, p. 154 and chill. Stuff bird just before baking.

## BEETS AND GREENS

**BBB + Veg.**

- **3-6 beets with tops**
- **1 small onion, chopped**
- **2 tablespoons allowed oil**
- **Salt to taste**

Cut 2 inches above tops of beets and reserve leaves. Wash beets and cover with boiling water. Cook 45 to 60 minutes or until tender. Cool enough to handle and slip skins off, then slice or dice beets. Wash leaves, chop, and set aside. Sauté onion in oil and add leaves. Cover and cook until wilted—water clinging to leaves should be sufficient for cooking. Add beets and salt and reheat. *Serves 4–6*

## PEAS AND CABBAGE DUO

**BBB + Veg.**

- **½ large head cabbage, chopped**
- **1 package (10 ounces) frozen petite peas**
- **¼ teaspoon salt**
- **1 tablespoon allowed margarine**

Cook cabbage in small amount of water, covered, until tender-crisp. Cook peas as directed on package. Combine the two vegetables, add salt, and toss with margarine. *Serves 4*

## SWEET-SOUR CABBAGE

**BBB + Veg.**

- **2 tablespoons finely chopped onion**
- **2 tablespoons allowed oil**
- **⅓ cup brown sugar, firmly packed**
- **¼ cup white distilled vinegar**
- **½ teaspoon salt**
- **2 pounds red cabbage, shredded**

Sauté onion in oil and add all ingredients except cabbage. Cook briefly until sugar is dissolved, then add cab bage. Cook and stir 15 to 18 minutes. If allowed, add 1 teaspoon caraway seeds. **(+ N&S)** Serve very hot. *Serves 8*

## GOURMET CARROTS

**BBB + Fruit + Veg. + TE&A**

- **2-3 cups sliced carrots**
- **1 tablespoon lemon juice**
- **¼ teaspoon salt**
- **3 tablespoons allowed margarine**
- **1 tablespoon tapioca starch or arrowroot powder**
- **⅓ cup orange juice**
- **2 tablespoons mild honey**
- **1 tablespoon minced chives**

Cook carrots in ⅓ cup water, lemon juice, salt, and margarine until just tender-crisp. Blend starch with juice and honey. Remove carrots from saucepan, saving cooking water and keeping carrots hot. Add starch mixture to carrot water, stirring constantly until thickened. Pour over carrots and sprinkle with chives. *Serves 4*

## SAUCY BROCCOLI-FLOWER

☐ **BBB + Fruit + Veg. + TE&A**

- **1 package (10 ounces) frozen cauliflower**
- **1 package (10 ounces) frozen broccoli spears**
- **2 tablespoons allowed margarine**
- **½ teaspoon salt**
- **1½ tablespoons rice flour**
- **½ teaspoon dry mustard**
- **1¼ cups allowed milk substitute**
- **2 teaspoons lemon juice**
- **1 tablespoon chopped pimiento**
- **1 tablespoon chopped parsley**

Steam vegetables in steamer basket above boiling water 8 minutes, tightly covered. Combine margarine, salt, flour, and mustard and cook until bubbling. Add milk substitute slowly, stirring constantly until mixture thickens. Add remaining ingredients to sauce and pour sauce over vegetables arranged in large serving bowl. *Serves 4–6*

## ANN'S JAZZY GREEN BEANS

☐ **BBB + Fruit + Veg. + TE&A**

- **1-2 pounds green beans, cut in small diagonal slices**
- **1 onion, chopped**
- **1 stalk celery, chopped**
- **¼ cup allowed margarine**
- **1 teaspoon curry powder**
- **½ teaspoon paprika**
- **1 tablespoon imitation bacon bits**
- **1 tablespoon lemon juice**
- **1 tablespoon chopped parsley**
- **Salt to taste**
- **Dash of pepper**

Sauté beans, onions, and celery in margarine 15 minutes. Add remaining ingredients and stir. Add 1 cup water, cover, and cook over low heat 45 to 60 minutes or until beans are tender-crisp. *Serves 4*

## SEASONED SALT BLEND

☐ **BBB + Veg. + TE&A**

- **⅓ cup salt**
- **½ teaspoon dried thyme**
- **½ teaspoon dried marjoram**
- **½ teaspoon garlic powder**
- **2¼ teaspoons paprika**
- **½ teaspoon curry powder**
- **1 teaspoon dry mustard**
- **¼ teaspoon onion powder**
- **⅛ teaspoon dill weed**

Blend all ingredients well and place in a shaker bottle with tight fitting lid. When not in use, keep bottle covered to keep mixture from absorbing moisture from the air. This is good on salads. vegetables, in soups, on Toasted Potato Peels, p. 167, and many other things. If allowed, add ½ teaspoon celery seeds. **(+ N&S)** *Makes about ½ cup*

## HERB BLEND SEASONING (NO SALT)

**BBB + Veg. + TE&A**

**2 tablespoons paprika**
**2 tablespoons dry mustard**
**2 tablespoons garlic powder**
**3 tablespoons onion powder**
**1 teaspoon white pepper**

Blend all ingredients well and store in a shaker bottle with tight-fitting lid (to keep moisture out). Use this blend when you want to avoid salt. If allowed, add ½ teaspoon celery seeds. **(+ N&S)** *Makes ½ cup*

## HONEYED ONIONS

**BBB + Veg. + TE&A**

**¼ cup allowed oil or margarine**
**¼ cup honey**
**2 teaspoons white distilled vinegar**
**½ teaspoon salt**
**1 teaspoon dry mustard**
**1 pound small white boiling onions, cooked tender-crisp**
**Dash of paprika**
**1 tablespoon chopped parsley**

Combine oil, honey, vinegar, salt, and mustard in skillet. Heat to blend well. Add onions and cook over low heat, turning gently occasionally to glaze. Just before serving, add paprika and parsley. *Serves 6*

**Variation:**

Replace onions with crisp cooked carrot slices. Garnish with slivered toasted almonds. **(+ N&S)**

## GREEN BEAN BAKE

**BBB + Veg. + TE&A**

**½ cup rice**
**1 onion, sliced thin**
**2 tablespoons allowed oil**
**1 can (16 ounces) cut green beans, drained**
**½ teaspoon salt**
**⅛ teaspoon pepper**
**⅛ teaspoon Tabasco sauce**
**2 cans (8 ounces each) tomato sauce or 1 can (16 ounces) tomatoes**

Spread rice over bottom of oiled 1½-quart casserole. Sauté onion in oil and spoon over rice. Add layer of green beans. Bring ½ cup water and all remaining ingredients to boil in onion sautéeing pan, mashing tomatoes, if used. Pour over casserole, cover and bake in 350° oven 30 to 40 minutes or until rice is tender. *Serves 6*

**Variation:**

Omit rice and oil. Sauté onion with 1 pound lean ground beef and drain off excess fat. Add ½ cup water and remaining ingredients and simmer 15 minutes. Transfer to unoiled casserole and top with mashed potatoes. Dot with allowed margarine and bake as directed or until potatoes are brown and casserole hot through. Serve with crisp green salad for a complete meal. **(+ Beef)**

**BBB + Veg.**
**+ TE&A**

- **3-4 cups (1 pound) fresh green beans**
- **½ teaspoon salt**
- **Pepper to taste**
- **1 tablespoon imitation bacon bits**
- **1 teaspoon instant chopped onion**

## TASTY GREEN BEANS

Remove ends and break beans into 1-inch pieces. Add 1 cup water and bring quickly to boil. Cover, reduce heat, and simmer 35 to 50 minutes. Add remaining ingredients and cook another 10 minutes to blend flavors. *Serves 4*

**Variations:**

1. QUICK TASTY GREEN BEANS—Heat 2 cans (16 ounces each) green beans in ½ cup of their own juice. Do not add water. Add seasonings, cover, and simmer 10 minutes to blend flavors.
2. BEANS AND VEGIES—Prepare fresh green beans as directed but omit bacon bits and instant onion. Before beans are done, sauté 1 tablespoon minced onion, 1 clove garlic (whole), 1 tablespoon minced celery, and 1 tablespoon minced green pepper in 2 tablespoons allowed oil. Add 1 cup diced tomato and cook 8 to 10 minutes. Discard garlic clove and add mixture to beans.
3. DILLY BEANS—Omit bacon bits. After cooking beans, season with dash of garlic powder and ½ teaspoon dill weed.

**BBB + Veg.**
**+ TE&A**

- **½ cup chopped onion**
- **½ cup finely chopped celery**
- **¼ cup allowed oil**
- **2 cans (16 ounces each) soybeans, drained or 1 package (16-20 ounces) tofu, drained, washed, and dried**
- **2 tablespoons chopped parsley**
- **¼ teaspoon dried sage or thyme**
- **½ teaspoon salt**

## SOYBEAN OR TOFU STUFFING

Sauté onion and celery in oil. Crumble tofu and add, if used. Combine all ingredients (either canned soybeans or tofu) and chill. Stuff poultry immediately before baking. *Makes 4–5 cups*

**Variations:**

1. CASSEROLE—Combine all ingredients with 1 can (16 ounces) stewed tomatoes. Bake in 350° oven 25 minutes or until heated through. *Serves 4*
2. Add 1 can (8½ ounces) water chestnuts, sliced. Rice may replace soybeans or tofu. Use enough cooked rice to serve 4.

## SWEET POTATO GLAZES

**BBB + Fruit + N&S + TE&A**

- **4 medium sweet potatoes or yams, cooked and peeled *or* 2 cans (1 pound, 2 ounces each) small whole yams, drained**
- **Glaze of choice**

GLAZE I—Blend 2 tablespoons allowed margarine with 1 tablespoon tapioca starch and ⅓ cup brown sugar, firmly packed. Cook until bubbly. Add ¾ cup orange juice and, stirring constantly, cook until thick and clear. Season with ¼ teaspoon salt and ½ teaspoon cinnamon. Pour over potatoes arranged in oiled baking dish. Sprinkle with 1 teaspoon grated orange or lemon peel and ⅓ cup chopped pecans. Bake in 350° oven 30 minutes.

If desired, replace sugar with ¼ cup honey. Blend honey with orange juice and add to starch. Reduce baking temperature to 325°. *Serves 6–8*

GLAZE II—Combine ¼ cup allowed margarine, ¾ cup brown sugar, firmly packed, and ½ cup apricot nectar. Cook until syrupy, about 5 minutes. Pour over potatoes and sprinkle with ⅓ cup chopped pecans. Bake as in Glaze I. (+ **Corn**) *Serves 6–8*

GLAZE III—Combine ¼ cup allowed margarine, ⅔ cup Gold Medal Marmalade, p. 243, ¼ teaspoon salt and 2 tablespoons lemon juice in large skillet. Cook briefly, stirring constantly, until thickened. Add potatoes to sauce and cook over low heat, turning frequently, until well glazed. (+ **Corn**) *Serves 6–8*

## WILD RICE STUFFING (3-pound bird)

**BBB + Veg. + N&S + TE&A**

- **½ cup chopped onion**
- **½ cup finely diced celery**
- **½ cup pine nuts or slivered almonds**
- **2 tablespoons allowed oil**
- **1 cup cooked wild rice, prepared as directed, p. 171**
- **2 tablespoons chopped parsley**
- **¼ teaspoon sage or thyme**
- **½ teaspoon salt**

Sauté onion, celery, and nuts in oil. Combine with cooked rice and remaining ingredients. Chill. Stuff small bird just before baking. This goes especially well with duckling.

## RICE STUFFING (3½-pound bird)

☐ **BBB + Poultry**

**Giblets and necks from 1 or 2 small birds or 1 set turkey giblets and neck**
**1 teaspoon salt**
**1 cup cooked white or wild or brown rice**
**2 tablespoons allowed oil**
**½ cup grated carrots**

Boil giblets and neck over low heat, covered, in 5 cups salted water until tender. Remove meat from neckbones, chop giblets and set aside. Brown rice in oil. Add and sauté carrots. Add reserved giblet broth in suggested amounts, bring to boil, cover and simmer as follows:

| Kind of Rice | Broth | Cooking Time |
|---|---|---|
| 1 cup white rice | 2 cups broth | 25 minutes |
| 1 cup wild rice | 4 cups broth | 40 minutes |
| 1 cup brown rice | 2½ cups broth | 40 minutes |
| 1 cup Quick Brown Rice | 1½ cups broth | 15 minutes |
| 1½ cups Minute Rice | 1½ cups broth, boiling, add cover and let stand | 5 minutes |

Add giblets to stuffing and chill. Stuff bird just before baking.

**Variation:**

When allowed, sauté 2 tablespoons chopped onion and ½ cup diced celery with 1 tablespoon chopped parsley and add to stuffing. **(+ Veg.)** Add ¼ teaspoon poultry seasoning, when allowed. **(+ TE&A)**

## CREAMED ONIONS

☐ **BBB + Poultry + Veg. + TE&A**

**½ cup sliced celery**
**2 tablespoons allowed oil or margarine**
**1½ tablespoons rice flour**
**1 teaspoon instant Chicken Flavored Bouillon Seasoning and Broth**
**Pepper to taste**
**1 cup allowed milk substitute**
**¼ cup reserved onion juice**
**1 can (16 ounces) small whole onions, drained, juice reserved**
**1 tablespoon chopped parsley**

Sauté celery in oil or margarine. Blend in flour and seasonings. Slowly add liquids, stirring constantly until thickened. Add onions and parsley. Cook over low heat 10 minutes but do not boil. *Serves 4*

## RYE STUFFING (3-pound bird)

**BBB + Rye + Veg. + TE&A**

- ½ teaspoon salt
- ¾ cup Cream of Rye
- ½ cup chopped onion
- ½ cup finely diced celery
- ¼ cup allowed oil
- 2 tablespoons chopped parsley
- ¼ teaspoon sage

Bring 2¼ cups water and salt to boil and, stirring constantly, slowly sprinkle in Cream of Rye. Boil 3 minutes. Cover and let stand 3 minutes. Sauté onion and celery in oil. Combine with all other ingredients. Chill. Stuff bird just before baking.

**Variations:**

1. Replace water, salt, and Cream of Rye with 24 RyKrisp wafers, broken and soaked in ¾ cup hot water.
2. Replace cooked Cream of Rye cereal with cooked Rye Cereal, p. 250.
3. Replace cooked Cream of Rye cereal with 2 cups torn 100% White Rye Bread from market. Add ½ teaspoon salt. Sauté ½ cup grated carrots with onion and celery. Moisten mixture with small amount of water, milk substitute, or allowed vegetable stock.

## SUCCOTASH HOE-DOWN

**BBB + Corn + TE&A**

- 1 package (10 ounces) frozen whole kernel corn
- 1 package (10 ounces) frozen baby lima beans
- 2 tablespoons allowed margarine
- ½ teaspoon salt
- 1 tablespoon chopped parsley

Cook vegetables separately as directed on packages. Combine and toss with remaining ingredients. *Serves 4*

## CHILI CORN

**BBB + Corn + Veg. + TE&A**

- 1 large onion, chopped
- 1 clove garlic, crushed
- ½ large green pepper, chopped
- 2 tablespoons allowed oil
- 1 teaspoon chili powder
- ½ teaspoon salt
- Dash of pepper
- 1 can (16 ounces) tomatoes
- 1 can (16 ounces) whole kernel corn, drained
- 1 can (16 ounces) kidney beans, drained

Sauté onion, garlic, and pepper in oil. Add all remaining ingredients. Cover and simmer 15 minutes to blend flavors. *Serves 4–6*

**BBB + Corn + Veg. + TE&A**

## CORN SHOW-OFF

- 1 medium onion, chopped
- ½ medium green pepper, sliced
- 1 clove garlic, crushed
- 2 tablespoons allowed oil
- ½ teaspoon salt
- Freshly ground pepper to taste
- 2 cans (16 ounces each) whole kernel corn, drained
- 1 tablespoon honey
- 1 jar (2 ounces) chopped pimiento
- 1 tablespoon imitation bacon bits

Sauté onion, green pepper, and garlic in oil. Season with salt and pepper and add corn and honey. Cook over low heat, covered, 10 minutes. Add pimiento and bacon bits and toss. *Serves 6*

**BBB + Corn + Veg. + TE&A**

## KNORR RAW POTATO DUMPLING MIX

Purchase and prepare as directed on package. Mix contains dehydrated potatoes, potato gratings, cornstarch, salt, and onion powder and is preserved by sodium sulfite. *Makes 8 dumplings*

**BBB + Rye + Corn + Poultry + Veg. + TE&A**

## HOLIDAY TURKEY STUFFING (12-pound bird)

- 3 cups Cornbread, p. 230, crumbled
- Turkey giblets and neck
- 3 cups 100% White Rye Bread
- 1 medium onion, chopped
- 4 stalks celery with leaves, sliced
- ½ cup allowed margarine
- 1 tablespoon dried parsley
- 1 teaspoon salt
- 1 teaspoon paprika
- 1 teaspoon dried sage or poultry seasoning
- Pinch of dried basil

On day before, bake cornbread. Cover turkey giblets and neck with salted water and simmer, covered, until tender. Refrigerate broth and giblets separately. Next day, crumble cornbread and tear rye bread into small pieces, using your largest bowl to facilitate mixing. Sauté onion and celery in oil and add to breads along with seasonings and desired amount chopped giblets. Remove fat from chilled broth and discard. Heat 1 cup broth and use to moisten, but not soak, stuffing. Mix well and chill. Stuff neck and cavity of turkey immediately before baking.

**Variation:**

Rice or Soya Potato wheat-free breads may be used in place of 100% White Rye. Toast bread and cube or tear into small pieces. (+ **Rye**)

# Sauces and Gravies

## WHITE SAUCE CHART

1 cup allowed milk substitute
1–3 tablespoons allowed oil or milk-free margarine, melted
¼ teaspoon salt or salt to taste

| Thickeners | Thin sauce | Medium sauce | Thick sauce | Code |
|---|---|---|---|---|
| Potato starch | 1 teaspoon | 2 teaspoons | 1 tablespoon | **BBB** |
| Tapioca starch | 1½ teaspoons | 1 tablespoon | 1½ tablespoons | **BBB** |
| Arrowroot | 1½ teaspoons | 1 tablespoon | 1½ tablespoons | **BBB** |
| Potato flour | 1½ teaspoons | 1 tablespoon | 2 tablespoons | **BBB** |
| Rice flour | 1 tablespoon | 1½ tablespoons | 2 tablespoons | **BBB** |
| Rye flour | 1 tablespoon | 2 tablespoons | 3 tablespoons | **BBB + Rye** |
| Oat flour | 1 tablespoon | 2 tablespoons | 3 tablespoons | **BBB + Oats** |
| Barley flour | 1 tablespoon | 2 tablespoons | 3 tablespoons | **BBB + Barley** |
| Cornstarch | 1½ teaspoons | 1 tablespoon | 1½ tablespoons | **BBB + Corn** |

**Method 1:** Combine thickener and oil or margarine in saucepan. Cook until mixture is bubbly. Slowly add liquid, stirring constantly until thickened. Season, reduce heat, and simmer 1 minute. If sauce is lumpy, beat with wire whisk.

**Method 2:** Blend thickener with only enough liquid to make smooth paste. Add remaining liquid, little at a time, keeping smooth. Or place thickening agent and liquid in jar with tight-fitting lid and shake vigorously until smooth. Stir in oil or margarine and salt. Place over medium heat and stir constantly until sauce reaches boil. Reduce heat and simmer 1 minute. *Makes 1 cup*

**Seasonings for 1 Cup Sauce:**

1 teaspoon minced onion (+ **Veg.**)
1 tablespoon chopped parsley (+ **Veg.**)
½ cup sautéed celery (+ **Veg.**)
Celery salt (+ **Veg.**)
2 tablespoons toasted almonds (+ **N&S**)
Vegetable salt (+ **Veg.** + **TE&A**)
Mixture of herbs (+ **TE&A**)
Paprika
1 teaspoon Steero Instant Chicken Flavor Bouillon and Seasoning Broth (+ **Poultry** + **Veg.** + **TE&A**)

## BBB MINUTE TAPIOCA WHITE SAUCE

- **2 cups milk substitute**
- **½ teaspoon salt**
- **5 teaspoons Minute Tapioca for medium sauce; 3 teaspoons for thin; 7 teaspoons for thick**

Mix all ingredients and let stand 5 minutes. Bring to boil, stirring constantly. Remove from heat, cover, and let stand 5 minutes. Reheat. If desired, purée in blender for smoother sauce.

## BBB CREAM OF RICE WHITE SAUCE

- **2 cups allowed milk substitute**
- **½ teaspoon salt**
- **3 tablespoons Cream of Rice for medium sauce; 2 tablespoons for thin; ¼ cup for thick**

Combine and bring to boil, stirring constantly. Reduce heat and, still stirring, simmer 1 minute. Cover and set aside 4 minutes. Purée in blender until smooth, taking care not to splash hot mixture. Reheat as needed. *Makes 2 cups*

**Variations:**

1. For seasoned white sauce, add 1 tablespoon chopped parsley and 1 tablespoon chopped chives after blending. (+ **Veg.**)
2. Add 1 cup chopped celery and ½ cup chopped onion sautéed in 2 tablespoons allowed margarine or oil. Especially good as a cream sauce for vegetables, such as new potatoes and peas. (+ **Veg.**)

## FAVORITE RICH GRAVY

**BBB**

**¼ cup lamb or rabbit pan drippings, excess fat poured off**
**3 tablespoons rice flour**
**2½ cups cooled broth from matching meat or water**
**Salt to taste**

Shake flour and liquid vigorously in jar with tight lid. When free of lumps, stir into hot pan drippings over low heat until gravy thickens. Loosen and incorporate browned meat crusts from pan for rich flavor. Boil gently 1 or 2 minutes and salt to taste. *Makes 2¾ cups.*

*Note:* As beef, poultry, and pork are tested and added, their pan juices from roasting or frying will yield tasty gravies by this method. They will, of course, be coded **+ Beef, + Poultry,** or **+ Pork.** Baked fish juices will also tempt you to create gourmet sauces, perhaps by adding white wine. **(+ Fish + Mold)**

**Variations:**

1. Another method: Stir flour directly into fat in pan. Heat and brown. Add liquid, stirring constantly to keep smooth, and continue as directed in recipe.

2. Other **BBB** flours may be used for 2½ cups liquid as follows:

*a.* 5 teaspoons potato starch

*b.* 2½ tablespoons tapioca starch or potato flour

*c.* 5 teaspoons Minute Tapioca (see Minute Tapioca White Sauce, p. 184)

3. After testing, other flours may be used and gravies recoded as follows:

*a.* 5 tablespoons rye flour **(+ Rye)**

*Note:* Soy milk teams well with rye for cream gravy.

*b.* 5 tablespoons oat flour **(+ Oats)**

*Note:* Teams well with poultry. **(+ Poultry)**

*c.* 5 tablespoons barley flour **(+ Barley)**

*Note:* Especially good with beef. **(+ Beef)**

4. Water in which potatoes have been boiled should not be discarded. Use as part of liquid in any gravy recipe. Potato water contains some starch and will assist in thickening gravy. Adjust as desired.

5. GIBLET GRAVY—Add boiled neck meat and giblets, minced, to poultry gravy after thickening. Reheat to serve. **(+ Poultry)**

6. SOUTHERN CHICKEN GRAVY—Blend 2 tablespoons potato flour into fried chicken skillet drippings and crumbs. Add 2 cups allowed milk substitute or liquid milk-free coffee creamer. **(+ Corn + TE&A)**

## LEMON PARSLEY FISH MARINADE

**BBB + Fruit + Veg.**

- **½ cup parsley sprigs**
- **1 medium onion**
- **½ cup lemon juice**
- **½ teaspoon salt**

Liquefy all ingredients in blender. Brush on fish while baking, broiling, or barbecuing. *Makes ½ cup*

## QUICK BARBECUE SAUCE

**BBB + Veg. + TE&A**

- **1½ tablespoons brown sugar, firmly packed**
- **1½ teaspoons dry mustard**
- **1½ cups commercial catsup or homemade Catsup, p. 197**
- **2 tablespoons white distilled vinegar**
- **3 tablespoons allowed margarine**

Blend sugar and mustard. Add ¼ cup water and remaining ingredients and simmer slowly 10 minutes. This is delicious on thin slices of roast or brisket of beef. Add 2 tablespoons Worchestershire sauce, if allowed. (+ **Corn + Fish**) *Makes 2 cups*

## BARBECUE SAUCE

**BBB + Veg. + TE&A**

- **¼ cup allowed oil or margarine**
- **1 small onion, minced**
- **1 clove garlic, crushed**
- **1 can (8 ounces) tomato sauce**
- **2 tablespoons brown sugar, firmly packed**
- **1½ teaspoons dry mustard**
- **1 tablespoon white distilled vinegar**
- **¼ teaspoon chili powder**
- **⅛ teaspoon cayenne pepper**
- **½ teaspoon salt**

Sauté onion and garlic in oil or margarine until tender. Add ½ cup water and all other ingredients. Cook gently 30 minutes, covered. *Makes 2 cups*

## CREOLE SAUCE

**BBB + Veg. + TE&A**

- **1 cup sliced onions**
- **1 green pepper, sliced**
- **1 clove garlic, crushed**
- **2 tablespoons allowed oil**
- **2 cans (16 ounces each) whole tomatoes**
- **1 teaspoon sugar**
- **¾ teaspoon salt**
- **Dash of pepper**
- **¼ teaspoon chili powder**
- **Pinch of celery salt**
- **2 tablespoons tapioca starch**

Sauté onions, pepper, and garlic in oil. Add all remaining ingredients except tapioca starch. Cook slowly 30 minutes, stirring occasionally. Blend starch with ¼ cup water and stir slowly into sauce. Cook until sauce is thickened and boil 1 minute. Serve over hot fluffy rice. *Serves 4*

**Variation:**
Add Tabasco sauce to taste for hotter sauce.

## HOMEMADE TOMATO SAUCE

**BBB + Veg. + TE&A**

- **3 cups peeled chopped fresh tomatoes**
- **1 large onion, quartered**
- **1 stalk celery, diced**
- **½ large green pepper, sliced**
- **1 carrot, cut in pieces**
- **3 sprigs parsley**
- **1 bay leaf**
- **1 teaspoon brown sugar**
- **½ teaspoon salt**
- **½ teaspoon dried basil**
- **Dash of pepper**
- **¼ teaspoon garlic powder**

Liquefy tomatoes, onion, celery, green pepper, carrot, and parsley in blender. Combine all ingredients and simmer 40 minutes or until thick, stirring occasionally to prevent scorching. Cock lid loosely over kettle to keep spatters within bounds. Freeze in 1-cup batches for future use. *Makes 4 cups*

## MILD SAVORY TACO SAUCE

**BBB + Veg. + N&S + TE&A**

- **1 medium onion, quartered**
- **1 can (16 ounces) whole tomatoes**
- **1 can (4 ounces) green chilies**
- **2 tablespoons allowed oil**
- **1 teaspoon mustard seeds**
- **1 teaspoon coriander seeds**
- **½ teaspoon salt**
- **Dash of cayenne pepper**

Purée onion, tomatoes, and green chilies in blender. Combine in saucepan with other ingredients and bring to boil. Simmer 5 to 10 minutes. Thin with water if sauce is too thick. *Makes 2½ cups*

**Variation:**
For those who like it hot, add Tabasco sauce to taste.

## MOUNT ST. HELEN'S TACO SAUCE (HOT)

☐ **BBB + Veg. + TE&A**

- **1 can (16 ounces) tomatoes or stewed tomatoes**
- **1 teaspoon instant minced onion**
- **1 can (3.5 ounces) Ortega Hot Peppers**

Purée all ingredients in blender. Pour into saucepan and cover. Simmer 30 minutes. Chill. Add another can of tomatoes for milder sauce. *Makes 2½ cups; 4½ cups with tomatoes*

## ITALIAN SAUCE

☐ **BBB + Veg. + TE&A**

- **1 large onion, chopped**
- **½ green pepper, chopped**
- **1 stalk celery, sliced**
- **2 tablespoons allowed oil**
- **2 cloves garlic, mashed**
- **1 can (16 ounces) whole tomatoes**
- **1 can (8 ounces) tomato sauce**
- **1 can (6 ounces) tomato paste**
- **1 teaspoon chopped parsley**
- **½ teaspoon dried oregano**
- **1 teaspoon dried basil**
- **½ teaspoon dried marjoram**
- **1 teaspoon salt**
- **Dash of pepper**
- **½ teaspoon chili powder**

Sauté onion, pepper, and celery in oil. Add 2 cups water and all remaining ingredients and bring to boil. Simmer, stirring frequently, 30 to 60 minutes or until thickened. Cock lid loosely over kettle to prevent spattering. *Makes 5 cups*

**Variations:**

1. Brown 1 pound lean ground beef, drain well, and add to sauce. **(+ Beef)**
2. Omit green pepper, celery, and whole tomatoes. Replace with 1 can (16 ounces) stewed tomatoes.
3. Sauté ½ cup mushrooms with other vegetables. Also replace ½ cup water with same amount of red wine. **(+ Mold)**
4. CHILI SAUCE—Omit herbs and increase chili powder to 2 teaspoons. Add ⅛ teaspoon cayenne pepper and 1 teaspoon dry mustard. Simmer 30 to 35 minutes while flavors blend and sauce thickens. Serve over rice or Wheat-Free Corn Pasta when allowed **(+ Corn)** or use as enchilada sauce. *Makes 5 cups*

## BROWN SAUCE

☐ **BBB + Beef**

- **3 tablespoons allowed margarine**
- **2½ tablespoons rice flour**
- **½ teaspoon salt**
- **2 cups Beef Soup Stock, p. 27**

Cook margarine, flour, and salt until bubbly. Slowly add stock, stirring constantly until mixture boils and thickens. Continue cooking 1 minute. *Makes 2 cups*

**Variation:**

Prepare quick beef stock with 2 teaspoons Steero Instant Beef Flavor Bouillon Seasonings and Broth and 2 cups hot water. Omit salt from Brown Sauce recipe. **(+ Veg. + TE&A)**

## MY FAVORITE QUICK SPAGHETTI SAUCE

**BBB + Beef + Veg. + TE&A**

Brown and crumble beef along with onion and garlic in large skillet. Drain off excess fat. Add 1½ cups water and all remaining ingredients. Bring to boil, reduce heat, and simmer slowly, uncovered, for at least 30 minutes to blend flavors. Serve over cooked zucchini, spaghetti squash, rice or other cooked cereal, or wheat-free corn pasta, when allowed. **(+ Corn)** *Makes 6½ cups*

- **1 pound lean ground beef**
- **1 medium onion, chopped or 1 tablespoon instant chopped onion**
- **1 clove garlic, crushed or ¼ teaspoon garlic powder**
- **¾ teaspoon salt**
- **Pepper to taste**
- **½ teaspoon Italian seasoning**
- **½ teaspoon dried parsley**
- **1 teaspoon chili powder**
- **1 can (16 ounces) stewed tomatoes**
- **2 cans (8 ounces each) tomato sauce**

## SOUTHERN CHICKEN GRAVY

**BBB + Poultry + TE&A**

Blend flour into drippings. Add liquid slowly, stirring constantly until thickened. If gravy seems lumpy, beat with wire whisk. Stir up browned crust from bottom of pan. Delicious. *Makes 2¼ cups*

- **2 tablespoons potato flour**
- **¼ cup pan drippings from fried chicken**
- **2 cups allowed milk substitute or liquid milk-free coffee creamer (+ Corn)**
- **Salt and pepper to taste**

## CHICKEN CURRY SAUCE

**BBB + Poultry + Veg. + TE&A**

Blend oil, starch, and seasonings in saucepan. Over medium heat, gradually add 2½ cups water. Stir constantly until mixture thickens and comes to boil. Boil 1 minute. *Makes 2⅔ cups*

**Variation:**

Use, instead of bouillon and water, 2½ cups homemade Chicken Stock, p. 30, or Cooked Chicken-Seasoned Stock. p. 117.

- **¼ cup allowed oil**
- **2½ tablespoons tapioca starch**
- **2 teaspoons Steero Instant Chicken Flavor Bouillon Seasoning and Broth**
- **½ teaspoon curry powder**
- **Dash of pepper**

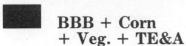

**BBB + Corn + Veg. + TE&A**

- 2 cans (8 ounces each) tomato sauce
- 1 jar (10 ounces) Heinz Piccallili Relish or Hamburger Relish

## LEONA'S MEATLOAF SAUCE

Combine and simmer slowly 5 to 10 minutes. This is delicious sauce to spoon over meatloaf slices, or in which to reheat leftover slices. *Makes 3 cups*

**BBB + Corn + Fruit + TE&A**

- ⅓ cup brown sugar, firmly packed
- 3 tablespoons cornstarch
- 1 cup pineapple juice
- 3 tablespoons lemon juice
- 3 tablespoons Jan-U-Wine Soy Sauce
- 1 tablespoon allowed margarine

## SWEET SOUR SAUCE

Blend sugar and cornstarch well. Add remaining ingredients, stirring in a little at a time. Heat, stirring constantly until sauce thickens and boils 1 minute. Stir in margarine. Combine with cooked poultry, pork, or vegetables. *Makes 1½ cups*

**BBB + Corn + Poultry + Fruit + TE&A**

- 2-4 tablespoons poultry pan juices (duckling is especially delicious)
- 2 tablespoons tapioca starch or cornstarch
- 2 teaspoons Steero Instant Chicken Flavor Bouillon Seasoning and Broth
- ⅓ cup Gold Medal Marmalade, p. 243

## FRUITED GRAVY

To hot pan drippings add starch mixed in ¼ cup water. Stir rapidly and cook until smooth. Add instant seasoning and 1¾ cups water, stirring constantly until thick and clear. Continue boiling 1 minute. Stir in marmalade until melted. *Makes 2 cups*

**BBB + Corn + Beef + Veg. + TE&A**

- 1 recipe Gloria's Onion Soup Mix, p. 39
- 2 cups boiling water
- 3 tablespoons rice flour

## ONION GRAVY

Stir soup mix into boiling water and simmer, covered, 10 minutes. Blend flour with 1 cup water until smooth. Add slowly to soup, stirring constantly until thickened. Simmer 1 minute. *Makes 3 cups*

# Condiments and Accompaniments

## BASIC CRANBERRY SAUCE **BBB**

- 1 cup sugar
- 2 cups raw cranberries

Bring sugar and 1 cup water to boil and continue boiling 5 minutes. Add cranberries and cook until skins pop, approximately 5 minutes more. Chill. *Makes 3 cups*

## HOMEMADE CRANBERRY JELLY **BBB**

- 2 cups raw cranberries
- 1 cup boiling water
- 1 tablespoon (1 envelope) unflavored gelatin
- ⅔ cup sugar

Cook cranberries in boiling water until skins pop. Drain, measure juice, and add boiling water to make 1 cup. Soften gelatin in ½ cup cold water. Add gelatin and sugar to hot liquid and stir to dissolve. Press cranberries through sieve and add pulp to gelatin mixture. Pour into 1-quart mold and chill until firm. *Makes 2–3 cups*

## MOLDED CRANAPPLE SAUCE **BBB**

- 1 tablespoon (1 envelope) unflavored gelatin
- 1 cup raw cranberries
- ¾ cup frozen unsweetened apple juice concentrate

Soften gelatin in ¼ cup cold water. Cook cranberries in 1 cup water until skins pop. Remove from heat, add softened gelatin, and stir to dissolve. Add frozen concentrate and stir until thawed. Chill until syrupy. Pour into lightly oiled (allowed oil) vegetable can (2-cup size) to mold. Chill overnight or until very firm. To serve, open bottom of can, push sauce up from bottom ¾ inch at a time, and slice into rounds, using top of can as guide. Lay each slice on bed of lettuce or serve roll uncut in glass bowl to pass at table. *Makes 2 cups*

**Variation:**

Prepare as above but purée in blender after adding concentrate.

**BBB + Fruit**

## PINK PEARS FOR POULTRY PICKUP

- **1 cup Basic Cranberry Sauce, p. 191**
- **¼ cup orange juice**
- **2 Anjou pears**

Melt cranberry sauce in small saucepan over low heat and blend in orange juice. Halve pears lengthwise and remove core. Dip cut side of pears in cranberry-orange glaze and arrange, skin down, in baking dish. Bake in 325° oven. Baste with remaining glaze during baking. *Serves 4*

**BBB + Fruit**

## RAW CRANBERRY-ORANGE RELISH

- **1 pound raw cranberries, washed and stemmed**
- **2 unpeeled oranges, quartered, seeds removed**
- **2 apples, quartered and cored**
- **1 lemon, quartered, seeds removed**
- **2 cups sugar or honey**

Grind fruits in food grinder with medium or large-holed grinder plates. Or, if preferred, chop cranberries, 1 cup at a time, in blender. Purée fruits and sugar or honey in blender and combine with chopped cranberries. Chill 24 hours. Or, spoon into 1 cup containers and freeze for future use. *Makes 4–5 cups*

**Variation:**

Add 1 teaspoon cinnamon and ½ teaspoon ground cloves. (+ **TE&A)**

**BBB + Fruit**

## CRANAPPLE RELISH

- **1 cup unsweetened crushed pineapple, drained, juice reserved**
- **1 cup raw cranberries, cut in half**
- **⅓ cup sugar or honey**
- **1 tablespoon lemon juice**

Measure pineapple juice, add water to make ½ cup. Combine with all ingredients and chill overnight. Excellent with poultry. *Makes 2½ cups*

**BBB + Fruit**

## RUBY RELISH

- **¼ cup sugar**
- **1 teaspoon grated orange peel**
- **3 tablespoons Sunny Morning Marmalade, p. 236, or Apricot-Pineapple Jam, p. 236**
- **¼ cup lemon juice**
- **1 can (16 ounces) julienne beets, drained**

Combine sugar, orange peel, marmalade or jam, and lemon juice. Add beets and mix gently. Refrigerate several hours. Drain and serve as relish with meat or poultry. *Makes 2 cups*

## NEW POTATO TASTE TEASER

**BBB + Fruit + Veg.**

- 4 tablespoons allowed margarine
- 1 lemon, grated peel and juice
- 1 teaspoon rice flour
- Salt to taste
- ¼ cup chopped parsley
- 2 tablespoons chopped chives

Melt but don't brown margarine in saucepan. Add grated peel, flour and salt. Stir and heat enough to cook flour, then remove from heat. Add lemon juice, parsley, and chives and pour over new potatoes boiled in their jackets until barely tender. Stir gently to coat potatoes with sauce. *Makes ½ cup*

## LEMON PATTIES

**BBB + Fruit + Veg.**

- 1 cup allowed margarine
- 1 tablespoon grated lemon peel
- 2 tablespoons lemon juice

Soften and cream margarine and work in lemon peel and juice. Stir in additional seasonings as allowed and desired. For example: chopped parsley, minced onion, or chives for fresh additions. Or use dried marjoram, oregano, basil, tarragon, or paprika to taste. Or use as is. Shape into 1 x 5-inch roll and place in refrigerator to harden. Slice roll into patties and serve on allowed vegetables. *Makes 10 ½-inch slices*

**Variation: Lime Patties**

Substitute lime peel and juice for lemon. Add dash of cayenne and serve on steak or fish.

## TARRAGON TEASER

**BBB + Fruit + Veg.**

- 2 tablespoons allowed margarine, melted
- ¼ teaspoon dried tarragon
- 1 teaspoon lemon juice

Blend and serve with spinach, green beans, broccoli, or with your choice of allowed vegetables. *Serves 2–3*

## PINEAPPLE CARTWHEELS

**BBB + Veg.**

- 1 can (20 ounces) sliced unsweetened pineapple, drained and towel dried
- ¼ cup rice flour
- 1 tablespoon potato flour
- 2 tablespoons allowed oil
- 2 tablespoons parsley or mint leaves, minced

Dip pineapple slices in well-mixed flours and sauté in oil in hot skillet. Decorate with minced parsley or mint and use to garnish any meat or poultry platter. *Makes 10–12*

**Variation:**

Dip slices in allowed oil and brown sugar. Broil in toaster-broiler or in 400° oven until sugar melts and bubbles. Add parsley or mint to serve, if desired. **(+ TE&A)**

☐ **BBB + Fruit + N&S**

- **¼ cup allowed margarine**
- **½ cup slivered almonds**
- **3 tablespoons lemon juice**

## ALMOND SAUCE

Melt margarine slowly in heavy skillet and add slivered almonds. Heat and stir until almonds are toasted. Add lemon juice and serve over asparagus. When vegetables such as broccoli, cauliflower, or green beans have been tested and are allowed, this sauce is also delicious on those. (**+ Veg.**) *Serves 4–6*

☐ **BBB + Fruit + N&S**

- **½ cup sesame seeds**
- **1 tablespoon allowed oil**
- **1 tablespoon allowed margarine**
- **¼ cup lemon juice**

## SESAME SAUCE

Stirring constantly, brown sesame seeds in oil. Add margarine and lemon juice. Serve hot over asparagus, chard, or spinach. *Serves 4*

☐ **BBB + Veg. + N&S**

- **1 cup thinly sliced scallions**
- **1 cup milk substitute**
- **2 tablespoons rice flour**
- **2 teaspoons white distilled vinegar**
- **½ teaspoon dill seeds**
- **2 tablespoons allowed margarine**
- **1 medium cucumber, peeled and chunked**

## CUCUMBER SAUCE

Blend all ingredients except cucumber in blender and cook until thickened. Return to blender and add cucumber. Blend until smooth. Serve over cooked vegetables of choice, as allowed. *Makes 2½ cups*

☐ **BBB + TE&A**

- **1 tablespoon allowed margarine**
- **2 tablespoons chopped mint leaves**

## MINT SAUCE FOR VEGETABLES

Melt margarine, add mint and serve over cooked peas, fresh or frozen. Good also with boiled potatoes or steamed carrots. *Serves 4*

☐ **BBB + TE&A**

- **3 tablespoons dry mustard**
- **½ teaspoon salt**
- **1 teaspoon sugar**
- **1½ teaspoons vinegar**
- **½ cup allowed oil**

## HOT SWEET MUSTARD

Stir mustard, salt, sugar, vinegar, and 2 tablespoons water together in small mixer or processor bowl. With mixer on high setting, add oil in fine stream until mixture is thick and glossy. Refrigerate. *Makes ⅔ cup*

## HOLIDAY ORANGES

**BBB + Fruit + TE&A**

- **3 navel oranges**
- **1 box (3 ounces) orange-flavored gelatin**
- **1 cup boiling water**
- **Lettuce (optional)**

Cut oranges in half lengthwise, from stem end to navel. Carefully scoop out and reserve pulp and juice, leaving shells whole. Dissolve gelatin in boiling water. Add ¾ cup reserved orange juice and pulp. Chill until syrupy and spoon into orange shells. Chill several hours or overnight. Gelatin should be extra firm. To serve, cut each shell into 3 wedges and arrange on crisp dry lettuce and treat as salad with dollop of Tofu Dressing I, p. 63 or omit lettuce and serve as garnish with poultry or meat. *Serves 6 as salad*

## JELLIED CRANBERRY SAUCE

**BBB + Fruit + TE&A**

- **2½ cups raw or frozen cranberries**
- **1 box (3 ounces) orange or lemon-flavored gelatin**
- **⅓ cup sugar**

Cook cranberries in 1⅔ cups water until skins pop. Drain and measure juice. Using 1½ cups hot liquid, dissolve gelatin and sugar. Combine with cranberries and purée in blender. Mold and chill until firm. *Serves 6–8*

## GLAZED BARTLETT PEAR HALVES

**BBB + Fruit + TE&A**

- **1 can (29 ounces) unsweetened Bartlett pear halves, drained, juice reserved**
- **1 cup orange sections**
- **⅓ cup juice from pears**
- **¼ cup honey**
- **2 tablespoons Sunny Morning Marmalade, p. 236**
- **2 tablespoons lemon juice**
- **1 teaspoon whole cloves or ⅛ teaspoon ground cloves**

Arrange pears and orange sections in shallow baking dish and drizzle with honey. Combine pear juice, orange marmalade, lemon juice, cloves and nutmeg in small saucepan. Heat to boiling and pour over pears and orange sections. Bake in 325° oven 25 minutes, basting 3 or more times. Serve hot or cold with poultry or pork. *Serves 6–8*

☐ **BBB + TE&A**

## BROILED PEACHES

- 1 can (29 ounces) unsweetened peach halves
- ⅓ cup sugar
- 1 teaspoon allowed oil
- ½ teaspoon cinnamon

Drain peaches and dry on paper towels. Place, cut side up, in baking dish. Work sugar, oil, and cinnamon together. Divide mixture evenly to fill peach hollows with mixture and broil until hot and freckled. Serve to accompany any meat dish. Especially good with lamb. *Makes 6–8*

☐ **BBB + Veg. + TE&A**

## HERB PATTIES

- 1 cup (2 cubes) allowed margarine
- 1 teaspoon dried dill weed
- ¼ cup chopped chives
- ½ teaspoon dried tarragon

Soften margarine and blend in seasonings. Reshape into sticks or roll, refrigerate to harden, and cut into patties to serve with corn-on-the-cob, lamb or pork chops. Also good on baked potatoes or on other vegetables of choice as allowed. *Makes 10–12 patties.*

☐ **BBB + Fruit + Veg. + TE&A**

## FRESH TOMATO CATSUP (NO VINEGAR)

- 12 ripe tomatoes (4-5 cups)
- 2 tablespoons lemon juice
- ½ teaspoon ground allspice
- ½ teaspoon ground cloves
- ½ teaspoon onion salt
- ¼ teaspoon onion powder
- 1 teaspoon sugar
- ¼ teaspoon pepper
- ½ teaspoon dry mustard
- 1 teaspoon salt

Wash, core, and quarter tomatoes. Place in vegetable steamer rack over boiling water and steam until soft and mushy. Press through colander or sieve to remove skin and seeds. Combine purée with remaining ingredients and bring to boil. To prevent spattering, cock lid over pot. Reduce heat and simmer until desired consistency. Stir occasionally to prevent spices settling to bottom and scorching. Cool, pour into small containers, and freeze for future use. *Makes 3–4 cups*

☐ **BBB + Fruit + Veg. + TE&A**

## TANGY ORANGE SAUCE

- 4 tablespoons allowed margarine
- 1 teaspoon dry mustard
- ½ cup orange juice
- 1 tablespoon chopped fresh parsley or dried parsley
- Grated peel of 1 orange

Melt margarine in small saucepan and stir in mustard until smooth. Add remaining ingredients and serve hot over asparagus, carrots, or mashed sweet potatoes or yams. Good also on other green vegetables when they are allowed or on meatloaf. *Makes ¾ cup*

## CATSUP

**BBB + Veg. + TE&A**

Purée onion, garlic, and tomatoes in blender. Combine with remaining ingredients and simmer 30 to 60 minutes, stirring occasionally. Cook until desired consistency. To prevent spattering, cock lid over pan. *Makes 3 cups*

- **1 large onion, quartered**
- **1 clove garlic**
- **1 can (16 ounces) whole or stewed tomatoes**
- **1 can (15 ounces) tomato paste**
- **⅓ cup white distilled vinegar**
- **2 tablespoons honey**
- **1 teaspoon ground allspice**
- **½ teaspoon ground cloves**
- **1 teaspoon dry mustard**
- **¼ teaspoon ground cumin**
- **¼ teaspoon pepper**
- **½ teaspoon dried basil**
- **1 teaspoon salt**

## "RED LEAD" HAMBURGER RELISH

**BBB + Veg. + N&S + TE&A**

Bring purée, vegetables, apples, and 1½ cups water to boil. Tie whole spices in cheesecloth bag. Add vinegar, spice bag, and remaining ingredients to boiling tomato mixture. Cook slowly, stirring occasionally until mixture is thick and tasty, 45 to 60 minutes. To prevent spattering during cooking, cock lid loosely over top of kettle. Remove spice bag, cool mixture. Freeze relish in small containers for use later as desired. Store in the refrigerator after thawing. *Makes 4–5 cups*

- **3 cans (16 ounces each) tomato purée**
- **1 large onion, chopped fine**
- **1 green pepper, chopped fine**
- **1 stalk celery, sliced thin**
- **1½ cups chopped apples**
- **1 teaspoon whole cloves**
- **1 2-inch stick cinnamon, broken**
- **¼ teaspoon whole allspice**
- **½ teaspoon celery seeds**
- **⅓ cup white distilled vinegar**
- **⅛ teaspoon cayenne pepper**
- **1 teaspoon dry mustard**
- **⅓ cup honey**
- **2 teaspoons salt**

# Breads

## SOME THOUGHTS ON WHEATLESS BAKING

Different grains, beans, roots, and such produce flours with varying advantages and disadvantages. Experience has taught us to select among the flours to best suit the usage, keeping in mind the following:

Rice flour gives a graininess to baked products, so we suggest combining it with other flours for a better baked product.

Potato and soy flours are also best used in combination. I, Gloria, frequently combine rice, soy, and potato flours, blending well before adding any liquid. Otherwise, the potato flour in the combo balls up in hard lumps.

When using rye flour for cakes, add 1 tablespoon cornstarch for each cup of rye. Use only after passing both *rye* and *corn* in your testing program, of course. When making cookies or biscuits of rye flour, add 2 teaspoons cornstarch per cup of flour in recipes, again, only when *corn* is allowed.

Rye, oat, barley, and buckwheat flours contain slight amounts of gluten. Wheat also contains gluten, as you know. None of these are for celiacs.

Tapioca, potato, soy, rice, corn, and millet are gluten-free.

## PANCAKES AND WAFFLES

A blender is a necessity for most of our waffle batters. Blending liquefies presoaked grains and beans. It also grinds nuts. Best of all, a blender incorporates air into batters. Air is hard to come by and to retain with no help from eggs and usually none from gluten. Believe us, air is the breath of life to a waffle, and you are about to become an expert in hydrokinetics.

If batter is too thin, waffles are next-to-impossible to remove from waffle iron in one piece. If iron is not precisely preheated, try to keep yourself cool. Few mishaps are fatal and most kitchen reverses are reversible. When in trouble, run a check on your production line.

## Measurements

Remember, level not beveled for a cup or spoonful. Use all flours unsifted. Just fluff with fork before measuring. Presoaked grains and beans (see "Plan Ahead" paragraph below) are measured after soaking and with excess water drained and retained. Include drained water in liquid for recipe for added nutrition and taste.

## Timing

Recipe timing is based on waffle iron set at Medium. Most of our waffles require 8 to 10 minutes cooking time. Be patient. Don't force lid open unless you like split waffles. Leave lid closed an extra 2 minutes or until opening requires no muscle. I, Gloria, set a timer. This is my biggest help in waffle baking.

## Plan Ahead

Before retiring for the night, set grain or beans to soak for morning waffles. Measure in proportions of 1 cup grain or beans to 2 cups water. On an unhurried day, you may decide to set several different kinds of beans to soak, each in a separate bowl or jar. After soaking 8 to 12 hours, drain each, label, and freeze separately. For a spur-of-the-moment waffle craving, measure frozen grain or beans and proceed with recipe. Baking time may need to be lengthened if batter is chilly.

## Salvage Mishaps

If, after measuring and mixing just-so and preheating a well-seasoned iron, waffles persist in a sticky mood, resort to Pam. **(BBB + TE&A)** If Pam has not been tested and proven friendly for the allergy sufferer, serve that first neat waffle to an allergy-free family member. The second waffle will probably behave, and will not be so saturated with the aerosol oil product. If all else fails, stir in slightly more of your favorite dry ingredient to thicken batter, or add a bit of water and serve pancakes instead.

## Cool and Keep

Extra waffles need to cool on racks where air circulates on all sides. Then freeze 1 hour on cookie sheet (single layer). When stiff, stack with waxed paper between layers and slip into freezer bag. Label and store in freezer. These are as handy as a credit card. They are ideal under fruit (sweetened with sugar or unsweetened) for shortcake. For entrees, top them with creamed or sauced meats or vegetables.

Or, dry waffles on racks and grind in blender into crumbs for breading meats or to sprinkle on casseroles.

Or, tear leftover waffles into small pieces for use instead of bread in Holiday Turkey Stuffing, p. 182.

Or, make garlic bread. Spread waffle with Garlic Spread, p. 12, or with allowed margarine and garlic powder or garlic salt. Toast in broiler until crisp and brown. **(+ Veg.)**

Or, make cinnamon toast. Spread waffle with allowed margarine, sugar, and cinnamon. **(+ TE&A)**

### Reheat

Pop cool or frozen waffle sections into toaster or place whole waffles on cookie sheets in 400° oven. Heat uncovered for crisp or covered with foil for soft waffles. For extra crispy, heat directly on oven rack. Guard against burning.

**BBB**

## SOY-POTATO PANCAKES OR WAFFLES

- **¼ cup potato starch**
- **⅔ cup soy flour**
- **2 teaspoons cereal-free baking powder**
- **¼ teaspoon salt**
- **3 tablespoons allowed oil**

Blend dry ingredients well before stirring in oil and 1 cup water. Cook pancakes on medium-hot griddle. Makes 8 pancakes that brown and turn easily. Or bake in preheated waffle iron 8 to 10 minutes. Makes amazingly light, crisp waffles.

**Variation:**

1. SOY-TAPIOCA PANCAKES OR WAFFLES—Replace potato starch with ⅓ cup tapioca starch (sometimes called tapioca starch flour). Allow batter to stand 2 minutes before using.
2. SOY-RICE-POTATO WAFFLE—Replace soy flour with equal amount soy milk powder. Add 6 tablespoons rice flour to recipe.

**BBB**

## CREAM OF RICE WHITE LACE WAFFLE

- **1 cup Cream of Rice**
- **2 cups boiling water**
- **¼ cup allowed oil**
- **¾ teaspoon salt**

Pour boiling water over Cream of Rice and let stand 10 minutes. Stir in ½ cup cold water, oil, and salt. Bake in preheated iron 10 minutes for waffles almost like white lace.

PANCAKES: Thin batter slightly and spoon onto preheated griddle or non-stick pan. *Makes 4 waffles or 16 pancakes*

## RICE FLAKE SOLO WAFFLE

**BBB**

Liquefy rice flakes in 2 cups water in blender until smooth. Let stand 10 minutes to thicken. Add remaining ingredients and ½ cup water and blend briefly. Bake in preheated waffle iron 10 minutes. These are light brown, delicate waffles. *Serves 4*

- **2 cups Arrowhead Rice Flakes**
- **3 tablespoons allowed oil**
- **1 teaspoon salt**

## RICE DUET WAFFLE

**BBB**

Liquefy all ingredients in 2¼ cups water in blender until smooth and let stand 10 minutes to thicken. Blend again briefly. Pour batter into preheated waffle iron and bake 8 minutes plus 2 minutes if necessary. These do not brown but are light and good. *Serves 3*

- **1½ cups Arrowhead Rice Flakes**
- **⅓ cup Cream of Rice**
- **2 tablespoons allowed oil**
- **¾ teaspoon salt**
- **1 tablespoon cereal-free baking powder**

**Variation: Triple Trio Rice Waffle**

Reduce Cream of Rice to 3 tablespoons and water to 2 cups. Add ¾ cup presoaked rice. (See "Plan Ahead," p. 199, for presoaking directions.)

## RICE-SOY PANCAKES OR WAFFLES, OPUS I

**BBB**

Place all ingredients in blender, add 2¼ cups water, and liquefy. Let stand 10 minutes to thicken, then blend again briefly. For pancakes, spoon circles of batter on preheated griddle, smoothing with back of spoon so cakes won't be too thick. Brown on both sides. For waffles, bake in preheated waffle iron 8 to 10 minutes. *Makes 12–16 pancakes or 3–4 waffles*

- **1½ cups presoaked brown rice (See "Plan Ahead," p. 199)**
- **¾ cup soy grits or ⅓ cup soy granules**
- **3 tablespoons allowed oil**
- **½ teaspoon salt**

## RICE-SOY WAFFLES, OPUS II

**BBB**

Liquefy all ingredients in 2¼ cups water in blender. Let stand at least 5 minutes, then blend again briefly. Bake in preheated waffle iron 8 to 10 minutes. *Makes 3 large waffles*

- **1 cup presoaked soybeans (See "Plan Ahead," p. 199)**
- **1½ cups Arrowhead Rice Flakes**
- **2 tablespoons allowed oil**
- **½ teaspoon salt**

## RICE POLISH PANCAKES OR WAFFLES

**BBB**

- **⅓ cup rice flour**
- **¼ cup rice polish**
- **½ teaspoon salt**
- **1 tablespoon cereal-free baking powder**
- **3 tablespoons allowed oil**

Add 1 cup water to dry ingredients, mixing until smooth. If necessary, thin batter with 1 or 2 tablespoons water for pancakes. Bake waffles in preheated waffle iron 8 to 10 minutes. *Makes 8 pancakes or 2 waffles*

## RICE-GARBANZO-CASHEW WAFFLES

**BBB + Veg. + N&S**

- **1½ cups presoaked brown rice, drained (See "Plan Ahead," p. 199)**
- **¾ cup presoaked garbanzos, drained (See "Plan Ahead")**
- **⅓ cup raw cashews**
- **2 tablespoons allowed oil**
- **½ teaspoon salt**

Add to liquid drained from presoaking rice and beans enough water to make 1½ cups. Use to liquefy all ingredients in blender. Let stand 10 minutes to thicken, then blend again briefly. Pour into preheated waffle iron and bake 8 to 10 minutes. These are delicious. *Makes 3 large waffles*

## RYE SOLO WAFFLES OR PANCAKES

**BBB + Rye**

- **2¼ cups Cream of Rye**
- **¼ cup allowed oil**
- **¾ teaspoon salt**
- **¾ teaspoon synthetic vanilla**

Place 3 cups water in blender, then add all other ingredients. Liquefy until light and smooth. Let stand 10 minutes to thicken. Bake in preheated iron 10 minutes. *Makes 3 waffles or 9–12 pancakes*

## RICE AND RYE PANCAKES OR WAFFLES

**BBB + Rye**

- **1½ cups presoaked brown rice (See "Plan Ahead," p. 199)**
- **¾ cup Cream of Rye**
- **3 tablespoons allowed oil**
- **½ teaspoon salt**

Liquefy all ingredients in 2 cups water in blender until smooth and let stand 10 minutes. Bake waffle 10 minutes. Bake 2 more minutes if lid is hard to open. These don't get very brown, but are tasty and light. *Makes 12 pancakes or 3 waffles*

## RYE-SOY-CASHEW WAFFLE

**BBB + Rye + N&S**

- **1½ cups presoaked soybeans (See "Plan Ahead," p. 199)**
- **⅓ cup raw cashews**
- **1 cup rye flour**
- **3 tablespoons allowed oil**
- **¾ teaspoon salt**
- **¾ teaspoon synthetic vanilla**

Liquefy beans and cashews with 1½ cups water in blender. Add flour, 1 cup water, oil, salt, and vanilla. Blend until light and creamy. Bake in preheated waffle iron 10 to 12 minutes. If iron is hard to open, leave waffle in another 2 minutes. *Makes 3 waffles*

## SIMPLE OAT SOLO WAFFLE

**BBB + Oats**

- **2 cups quick oats**
- **¼ cup allowed oil**
- **½ teaspoon salt**

Liquefy all ingredients with 2 cups water in blender until smooth. Let stand 10 minutes, then blend again briefly. Bake in preheated waffle iron 8 to 10 minutes. *Makes 3 waffles*

## FABULOUS OAT WAFFLE DELIGHT

**BBB + Oats + N&S**

- **1 cup boiling water**
- **⅓ cup Cream of Rice**
- **2 cups rolled oats**
- **½ cup coconut**
- **¼ cup allowed oil**
- **½ teaspoon salt**

Pour boiling water over Cream of Rice, stir to moisten well, and set aside. Liquefy other ingredients with 1¾ cups water in blender. Add Cream of Rice and blend again. Let batter stand to thicken (or, if too thick, add 1 or 2 tablespoons water). Pour into preheated waffle iron and bake 8 to 10 minutes. These are delicious. *Makes 4*

## FAVORITE RYE-OAT PANCAKES OR WAFFLES

**BBB + Rye + Oats**

- **1 cup rye flour**
- **2 tablespoons soy milk powder**
- **½ cup quick oats**
- **4 teaspoons cereal-free baking powder**
- **1 tablespoon sugar**
- **½ teaspoon salt**
- **¼ cup allowed oil**

Combine dry ingredients. Add 1⅔ cups water and oil and blend well. Bake on hot oiled griddle. For waffles, set batter aside 5 minutes to thicken. Bake 8 to 10 minutes in preheated waffle iron. These brown beautifully, are easy to handle, and have a good texture. *Makes 12 small pancakes or 3 waffles*

## BARLEY SOLO PANCAKES OR WAFFLES

**BBB + Barley**

- **1 cup barley flour**
- **2 teaspoons cereal-free baking powder**
- **¼ teaspoon salt**
- **3 tablespoons allowed oil**

Blend dry ingredients. Add oil and 1¼ cups water and beat until smooth. Let stand 2 minutes to thicken. Bake pancakes on hot griddle. Bake waffles in preheated iron 8 to 10 minutes. *Makes 8 pancakes or 2 large waffles*

## BARLEY-GARBANZO WAFFLE

**BBB + Barley + Veg.**

- **1 cup presoaked garbanzos** **(See "Plan Ahead," p. 199)**
- **1½ cups Arrowhead Barley Flakes or 1¼ cup barley flour**
- **2 tablespoons allowed oil**
- **¾ teaspoon salt**

Liquefy presoaked beans with 1¼ cups water in blender. Add 1 cup water and all other ingredients. Blend until light and creamy and let stand 10 minutes to thicken. Bake in preheated waffle iron 10 minutes to brown slightly. These are large, light, barley-flavored waffles. *Makes 3*

**BBB + Corn**

- 1½ cup boiling water
- ¾ cup cornmeal
- 3 tablespoons allowed oil
- ¾ teaspoon salt

## BEAUTIFUL CORN SOLO PANCAKES OR WAFFLES

Pour boiling water over cornmeal and stir until well blended. Place oil and salt in blender and add hot cornmeal. Blend until light and smooth. Let stand 10 minutes. Batter should be extra thick for waffles. For pancakes, thin batter with 1 or 2 tablespoons water. Bake pancakes on hot griddle or in preheated waffle iron 8 to 10 minutes. *Makes 8–10 pancakes or 2–3 large golden waffles*

*Note:* We advise eating with corn syrup for a lovely corn duet. Or make it a trio by decorating your table with cornflowers.

**BBB + Corn**

- 2 cups boiling water
- 1 cup regular corn grits or hominy quick grits
- ¼ cup allowed oil
- ½ teaspoon salt

## NITTY-GRITTY PANCAKES OR WAFFLES

Pour boiling water over grits and let soak 10 minutes. Add oil and salt. Liquefy in blender until smooth and creamy. Bake in preheated waffle iron 10 minutes. *Makes 16 pancakes or 4 large waffles*

**BBB + Corn**

- 1½ cups boiling water
- ¾ cup corn grits
- 1 cup presoaked brown rice (See "Plan Ahead," p. 199)
- 1 cup presoaked soybeans (See "Plan Ahead," p. 199)
- 3 tablespoons allowed oil
- ¾ teaspoon salt

## CORN GRITS-RICE-SOY WAFFLE

Pour boiling water over grits and let stand 10 minutes. Liquefy rice and soybeans in ¾ cup water. Add grits, oil, and salt. Blend until smooth. Let stand 5 to 10 minutes to thicken. Bake in preheated waffle iron 8 to 10 minutes. *Makes 3 golden light waffles*

**Variation: Cornmeal-Garbanzo Waffle**

Omit corn grits and replace with 1¼ cups cornmeal. Omit brown rice and replace soybeans with equal amount of presoaked garbanzo beans. **(+ Veg.)**

## CORN FLOUR PANCAKE OR WAFFLE

**BBB + Corn**

- **1 cup corn flour**
- **$\frac{1}{2}$ cup soy flour**
- **1 tablespoon cereal-free baking powder**
- **$\frac{1}{2}$ teaspoon salt**
- **3 tablespoons allowed oil**

Combine dry ingredients and blend well. Add oil and $1\frac{2}{3}$cups water and mix well. Bake on preheated griddle or waffle iron 8 to 10 minutes. These waffles are rather dry but provide a perfect base for creamed meats or vegetables. Can also be used as stuffing for fowl, garlic toast, or croutons, as suggested on p. 232. *Makes 2–3 firm waffles or 8–12 pancakes.*

## GLORIOUS GOLDEN WAFFLES

**BBB + Rye + Oats + Corn**

- **1 cup boiling water**
- **$\frac{1}{4}$ cup cornmeal**
- **$\frac{1}{2}$ cup rolled oats**
- **$\frac{1}{2}$ cup soy milk powder**
- **$\frac{1}{2}$ cup rye flour**
- **$\frac{1}{4}$ cup allowed oil**
- **$\frac{1}{2}$ teaspoon salt**

Pour boiling water over cornmeal, stir, and set aside. Place $1\frac{1}{2}$ cups water in blender, add all other ingredients, and process until well mixed. Add cornmeal and blend until light and creamy. Let stand 5 minutes. Bake in preheated waffle iron 8 to 10 minutes plus 2 minutes more if needed. These are large golden waffles. *Makes 3–4 waffles*

# PANCAKE AND WAFFLE TOPPINGS

## BBB BROWN SUGAR SYRUP

**BBB**

Bring 2 cups brown sugar, firmly packed, and 1 cup water to boil while stirring. Simmer 5 minutes over low heat. When allowed, add dash of cinnamon. **(+ TE&A)** *Makes $1\frac{1}{2}$ cups*

## HAWAIIAN PINEAPPLE SAUCE

**BBB**

- **$1\frac{1}{2}$ teaspoons tapioca starch**
- **$\frac{1}{4}$ cup brown sugar, firmly packed**
- **1 can (1 pound 4 ounces) unsweetened crushed pineapple**
- **2 tablespoons allowed margarine or oil**

Blend starch and brown sugar. Add $\frac{3}{4}$ cup water and pineapple. Bring to boil, stirring constantly. Simmer slowly 3 minutes. Stir in margarine. This sauce goes well on broiled chicken also. *Makes $2\frac{3}{4}$ cups*

**BBB**

**1½ cups brown sugar, firmly packed**
**1 cup unsweetened apple juice**

## BBB APPLE SYRUP

Bring sugar and apple juice to boil, stirring constantly. Simmer slowly 5 minutes. White sugar may be substituted if desired. When allowed, add 1 stick cinnamon and 2 whole cloves. (+ **TE&A**) *Makes 1½ cups*

**BBB**

## DOMINO'S LIQUID BROWN SUGAR

Purchase Domino's Liquid Brown Sugar and use, as is, for syrup.

☐ **BBB + Fruit**

**2 cups blackberries or strawberries**
**2 cups sugar**

## BLACKBERRY OR STRAWBERRY SYRUP

Mash blackberries or strawberries with sugar, add 1 cup water, and bring to boil, stirring until sugar is melted. Simmer 15 minutes. *Makes 2½ cups*

☐ **BBB + Fruit**

**1 cup unsweetened grape juice**
**1¾ cups sugar**
**1½ tablespoons lemon juice**

## GRAPE SYRUP

Bring grape juice and sugar to boil, stirring constantly. Add lemon juice. *Makes 1½ cups*

☐ **BBB + TE&A**

**2 cups white or brown sugar, firmly packed**
**1 teaspoon imitation maple flavor**

## MAPLE FLAVORED SYRUP

Bring sugar and 1 cup water to boil, stirring constantly. Reduce heat and simmer 5 minutes. Remove from heat and stir in flavoring. *Makes 1½ cups*

**Variations:**

1. RUM FLAVORED SYRUP—Omit maple flavor and stir in ½ to 1 teaspoon imitation rum flavor.
2. MAPLE-CINNAMON SYRUP—Stir in ¼ teaspoon cinnamon.
3. MAPLE-NUT SYRUP—Stir in ¼ cup toasted chopped almonds. (+ **N&S**)

## HONEY SYRUP

**BBB + TE&A** ☐

**½ cup allowed margarine**
**½ cup honey**

Melt margarine, remove from heat and stir in honey. Add ½ cup water and mix well. Reheat but do not let syrup boil. *Makes 1½ cups*

**Variations:**

1. ORANGE-HONEY SYRUP—Replace water with orange juice. (+ **Fruit**)
2. SPICED-HONEY SYRUP—Add 1 tablespoon lemon juice, ⅛ teaspoon cinnamon, dash of nutmeg, and ground cloves. (+ **Fruit**)

## WHIPPED HONEY SPREAD

**BBB + TE&A** ☐

**½ cup allowed margarine, softened**
**⅓ cup honey**

Whip margarine, adding honey, little at a time, until all is incorporated. Refrigerate. *Makes ¾ cup*

**Variations:**

1. SPICY WHIPPED HONEY SPREAD—Add 1 teaspoon cinnamon.
2. ORANGE or LEMON WHIPPED HONEY SPREAD—Add 2 tablespoons orange or lemon juice and blend well. (+ **Fruit**)
3. CRUNCHY WHIPPED HONEY SPREAD—Add ¼ cup toasted chopped almonds and dash of ginger. (+ **N&S**)

## STRAWBERRY SPREAD

**BBB + Fruit + TE&A** ☐

**½ cup allowed margarine, softened**
**⅓ cup mashed strawberries**
**2 tablespoons honey**

Add strawberries and honey, little at a time, to softened margarine, beating hard between additions. Spread on hot waffle. *Makes 1 cup*

**BBB + Fruit + TE&A**

- 1⅓ cups sugar
- ½ teaspoon cinnamon
- Dash of ground cloves
- 1 tablespoon lemon juice
- 2 apples, peeled and chopped
- 2 tablespoons allowed oil or allowed margarine

## SPICY APPLE SYRUP

Combine 2 cups water with all ingredients except oil or margarine. Bring to boil, stirring constantly. Simmer 5 minutes or until apples are tender. Stir in oil or margarine. Serve warm. *Makes 2¾ cups*

**BBB + Corn + TE&A**

- 2 cups sugar
- 1 cup apricot nectar
- 2 tablespoons allowed margarine
- 1 teaspoon imitation maple flavoring

## MAPLE-APRICOT SYRUP

Bring sugar, 1 cup water, and nectar to boil. Simmer 5 minutes. Stir in margarine and maple flavoring. *Makes 2½ cups*

*Note:* Prepared "maple syrups" on your market shelf (unless you are a Vermonter) usually contain corn syrup. Read ingredients and buy only if you have tested corn and found it friendly.

**BBB + Corn + TE&A**

- ½ cup sugar
- 1 tablespoon cornstarch
- ⅛ teaspoon salt
- 2 tablespoons allowed margarine
- 2 tablespoons lemon juice
- 1 teaspoon grated lemon peel
- Dash of nutmeg

## LEMON SYRUP

Combine sugar, cornstarch, and salt. Stir to blend. Add 1½ cups water and bring to boil, stirring constantly until thickened. Simmer 3 minutes, remove from heat, and add remaining ingredients. Serve warm. *Makes 1½ cups*

# MUFFINS AND BISCUITS

I, Gloria, got carried away. Like a bloodhound on the trail of a prize fox—in this case, a prize muffin—I kept following clues until I had finally scared up 30 muffins and a few biscuits. I hated to give up while I had things going my way.

I've tried to make muffins using each grain. Muffins provide an especially delicious way to introduce each new grain into your food testing program. Easy to make and best served hot, muffins supply perfect bread when wheat-free breads are hard to find. Besides, no purchased bread can ever be nearly as fresh and tempting as the muffins you quick-stir and serve hot from the oven.

*Warning:* Muffins may be habit forming. Those in the BBB code are so tasty that you may never want to go on to other grains. Muffins coded white are all gluten free. So are Rise and Shine Muffins, p. 218, and Soy-Cornmeal Muffins, p. 218.

If gluten is not an enemy to you, brave the rye, oats, barley, and buckwheat sections, one at a time, during your test periods. Just beware of combinations containing grains not yet tested. Read the +'s in each code.

All dry ingredients are measured unsifted. Dip in proper measure and level off with knife or finger. Be sure that flour is not packed into measure. Rice flour in recipes is white rice flour unless otherwise indicated.

The amount of water added to muffin batter is critical. If batter is too thick, it doesn't stand a chance of rising because it has a weight problem. If too thin, it may rise and then fall. Just-right batter will produce a slightly rounded or peaked muffin when done.

Reheat leftover muffins in a closed paper bag in the oven set at 425°. Leave about five minutes and, like magic, hot muffins again!

## SUNSHINE MUFFINS — BBB

**1¼ cups rice flour**
**3 tablespoons soy flour**
**2 teaspoons potato flour**
**¼ cup sugar**
**4 teaspoons cereal-free baking powder**
**½ teaspoon salt**
**1 cup finely grated carrots, loosely packed**
**2 tablespoons allowed oil**

Blend dry ingredients and toss with grated carrots. Add oil and ¾ cup water and stir well. Add 1 to 2 tablespoons more water if needed. Spoon oiled muffin tins ¾ full. Bake in preheated 400° oven 15 minutes. These are exceptional muffins—gorgeous texture, color and flavor. Sure to receive raves! *Makes 12*

**Variation:**

For a bonus treat, top each muffin with whole or chopped roasted and salted sunflower seeds. **(+ N&S)**

## MORNING-JOY RICE MUFFINS

**BBB**

- **1⅓ cups white rice flour**
- **⅓ cup soy flour**
- **1 tablespoon potato flour**
- **¾ teaspoon salt**
- **¼ cup sugar or 2 tablespoons honey**
- **4 teaspoons cereal-free baking powder**
- **2 tablespoons allowed oil**

Blend dry ingredients, stir in oil and 1¼ cups water, and blend well. Spoon into oiled muffin tins, filling ¾ full. Bake in preheated 400° oven 20 minutes. These are lightly browned good muffins. *Makes 10–12*

**Variation:**

When allowed, add 1 tablespoon grated orange or lemon peel. **(+ Fruit)**

## APPLE HARVEST MUFFINS

**BBB**

- **1 recipe Morning-Joy Rice Muffins (above)**
- **½ cup grated apples, drained (use juice as part of water called for in recipe)**
- **Brown sugar**

Prepare Morning-Joy Rice Muffin recipe. Stir in grated apples. Spoon into oiled muffin tins and sprinkle on brown sugar. Bake in preheated 400° oven for 20 minutes. Bake these muffins in oiled miniature muffin tins for 15 minutes if desired. *Makes 10–12 regular or 28–32 party muffins.*

**Variation:**

When allowed, sprinkle cinnamon on each sugared muffin before baking. **(+ TE&A)**

## HIGH PROTEIN TOFU MUFFINS

**BBB**

- **1⅓ cups rice flour**
- **⅓ cup soy flour**
- **1 tablespoon potato flour**
- **2 teaspoons cereal-free baking powder**
- **1 teaspoon baking soda**
- **½ teaspoon salt**
- **2 tablespoons sugar**
- **1 cup tofu, washed, dried, crumbled, and loosely packed**
- **2 tablespoons allowed oil**
- **1 tablespoon white distilled vinegar**

Blend dry ingredients in bowl. Add crumbled tofu and toss well. Add oil, vinegar, and 1 cup water. Beat into stiff dough. If too stiff, beat in more water, 1 tablespoon at a time. Spoon into oiled muffin tins and bake in preheated 400° oven 20 minutes. *Makes 10–12*

## PINEAPPLE TEA MUFFINS

**BBB**

Blend dry ingredients and add oil and pineapple. Stir well. Add 2 tablespoons water, beat, then add 1 or 2 tablespoons more water if batter seems too thick. Spoon into oiled miniature muffin tins and bake in preheated 400° oven 15 minutes (or in regular tins for 20 minutes). *Makes 28–32 tea-size muffins.*

- **1 cup rice flour**
- **¼ cup rice polish**
- **1 teaspoon potato flour**
- **½ teaspoon salt**
- **¼ cup brown sugar, firmly packed**
- **4 teaspoons cereal-free baking powder**
- **2 tablespoons allowed oil**
- **1 cup unsweetened crushed pineapple**

## RICE POLISH MUFFINS

**BBB**

Blend dry ingredients, stir in oil, and 1¼ cups water. Beat well and spoon into oiled muffin tins. Bake in preheated 400° oven 15 to 20 minutes. These do not brown well, but have a delicate light texture inside. *Makes 10*

- **1 cup white rice flour**
- **½ cup rice polish**
- **2 tablespoons sugar**
- **4 teaspoons cereal-free baking powder**
- **½ teaspoon salt**
- **2 tablespoons allowed oil**

## RICE FLOUR BISCUITS

**BBB**

Blend dry ingredients with margarine, using back of spoon or fingertips, until mixture resembles cornmeal. Add milk substitute or water and stir into a ball. Work ball in hands briefly. Pat out ½ inch thick on lightly rice-floured board. Cut with biscuit cutter (or shape with hands). Place on oiled baking sheet and brush tops with allowed oil or margarine. Bake in preheated 425° oven 15 to 18 minutes or until done through. These do not brown well nor rise much. Rather than try cutting biscuit apart, spread allowed margarine on top and enjoy their delicacy. These are also fine for fruit shortcake. *Makes 8*

- **1 cup rice flour**
- **⅛ teaspoon salt**
- **2 teaspoons cereal-free baking powder**
- **2 tablespoons allowed margarine**
- **½ cup allowed milk substitute or water**

## FLAKY BISCUITS

**BBB**

- **1⅓ cups white rice flour**
- **½ cup soy flour**
- **1 teaspoon potato flour**
- **4 teaspoons cereal-free baking powder**
- **½ teaspoon salt**
- **¼ cup allowed margarine**

Mix all dry ingredients. Reserve small handful of this mixture to use later. With tips of fingers, pinch margarine into dry ingredients until texture of coarse sand. Make hole in middle, add ¾ cup water all at once, and stir with fork, quickly gathering all into damp ball. Spread reserved flour mixture on board and turn out dough. Pat or roll to ½ inch thick and cut with 2-inch round cookie cutter. Handle dough as little as possible. Bake in well-greased pan in preheated 425° oven 12 minutes or until cooked through and lightly browned. Take two and eat them while they're hot! *Makes 10–12*

**Variations:**

1. *BISCUIT STICKS*—Pat dough ½ inch thick on rice-floured board. Cut into strips ½ inch wide and 3 inches long. Brush with melted allowed margarine and bake as for biscuits. *Makes 20 to 24*
2. CINNAMON ROLLS—Pat dough ½ inch thick, spread with softened allowed margarine, sprinkle with brown sugar and cinnamon, and roll jelly-roll fashion. Cut roll into 1-inch slices. Lay slices (cut side down and separated) on oiled pan and bake in preheated 425° oven 15 to 20 minutes (**+ TE&A**). *Makes 5–6*
3. SUPER-DUPER CINNAMON ROLLS—Nuts and/ or raisins may also be spread in center of Cinnamon Rolls, when you have reached these rungs on your food additions ladder. When rolls cool, drizzle on Powdered Sugar BBB Glaze, p. 271, or Powdered Sugar Glaze, p. 272 (**+ Corn + TE&A**). If you use nuts (**+ N&S**). If you use raisins (**+ Mold**). *Makes 5–6*

## BEST-OF-THE-MORNING BLUEBERRY MUFFINS

**BBB + Fruit**

- **1⅓ cups rice flour**
- **⅓ cup soy flour**
- **1 tablespoon potato flour**
- **¾ teaspoon salt**
- **¼ cup sugar**
- **4 teaspoons cereal-free baking powder**
- **2 tablespoons allowed oil**
- **½ cup fresh or frozen whole blueberries**
- **1 tablespoon grated orange peel**

Blend dry ingredients in bowl and stir in oil and 1¼ cups water. Blend well. Quickly mix in blueberries and orange peel and spoon into oiled muffin tins. Bake in preheated 400° oven 20 minutes. You'll want these often. They are our favorite of all the muffins. *Makes 10–12*

**Variation:**

Bake these for a buffet table in oiled miniature muffin tins. Bake 15 minutes at 400°. *Makes 25-30*

## BROWN SESAME TOPPED MUFFINS

**BBB + N&S**

- **¾ cup brown rice flour**
- **¾ cup rice bran**
- **¼ soy flour**
- **¼ cup brown sugar, firmly packed**
- **½ teaspoon salt**
- **4 teaspoons cereal-free baking powder**
- **2 tablespoons allowed oil**
- **Toasted sesame seeds**
- **Brown sugar**

Blend dry ingredients, stir in oil and 1¼ cups water, mixing well. Spoon into oiled muffin tins. Sprinkle on toasted sesame seeds and top with brown sugar. Bake in preheated 400° oven 15 minutes. These muffins are a rich brown inside and out. *Makes 10–12*

## ZUCCHINI MUFFINS

**BBB + Veg. + N&S + TE&A**

- **1⅓ cups rice flour**
- **⅓ cup soy flour**
- **1 tablespoon potato flour**
- **½ teaspoon salt**
- **¼ cup brown sugar, firmly packed**
- **4 teaspoons cereal-free baking powder**
- **1 cup finely grated zucchini, drained and patted dry on paper toweling**
- **2 tablespoons allowed oil**
- **½ teaspoon synthetic vanilla**
- **¼ teaspoon cinnamon**
- **⅓ cup chopped nuts**

Combine dry ingredients and toss with zucchini. Add 1¼ cups water and remaining ingredients, beating well. Spoon into oiled muffin tins. Bake in preheated 400° oven 18 to 20 minutes. *Makes 12*

## CREAM OF RYE MUFFINS

**BBB + Rye**

- **½ cup Cream of Rye cereal**
- **1 cup rice flour**
- **2 tablespoons brown sugar, firmly packed**
- **4 teaspoons cereal-free baking powder**
- **½ teaspoon salt**
- **2 tablespoons allowed oil**

Blend dry ingredients, add oil and 1 cup water, and mix well. Batter will seem too thin, but will thicken if left to stand only a couple of minutes. Spoon into oiled muffin tins. Bake in preheated 400° oven 15 minutes. These muffins have a wonderful flavor and are slightly crunchy inside, almost as if they contained nuts. They rise beautifully and have a crispy brown crust. *Makes 8*

## RYE MUFFINS

**BBB + Rye**

- **1 cup rye flour**
- **¾ cup rice flour**
- **4 teaspoons cereal-free baking powder**
- **½ teaspoon salt**
- **2 tablespoons brown sugar, firmly packed**
- **2 tablespoons allowed oil**

Blend dry ingredients and stir in oil and 1¼ cups water. Beat until well mixed. Spoon into oiled muffin tins, filling ⅔ full. Bake in preheated 400° oven 15 to 20 minutes. *Make 10–12*

## RYE-SOY GRITS MUFFINS

**BBB + Rye**

- **¾ cup soy grits**
- **½ cup rye flour**
- **2 tablespoons sugar**
- **½ teaspoon salt**
- **4 teaspoons cereal-free baking powder**
- **2 tablespoons allowed oil**

Blend dry ingredients and stir in oil and 1¼ cups water. Beat well. Spoon into oiled muffin tins and bake in preheated 400° oven 20 minutes. *Make 8*

## RYE BISCUITS

**BBB + Rye**

- **1 cup rye flour**
- **¼ teaspoon salt**
- **1 tablespoon cereal-free baking powder**
- **1 tablespoon sugar**
- **2 tablespoons allowed margarine**

Blend dry ingredients with margarine until mixture resembles cornmeal. Measure ½ cup water and take out 1 tablespoon. Add water to dry mixture and stir in. Gather dough into a ball. Place on rye-floured board and flip over to flour top side. Pat out ½ inch thick. Keep dough rather loose. Instead of adding flour to stiffen, use just enough to keep dough from sticking to hands. Cut into biscuits with cookie or biscuit cutter. Place on ungreased baking sheet. Bake in preheated 425° oven 15 to 20 minutes. *Makes 8*

## CRANBERRY FRUIT MUFFINS

**BBB + Rye + Fruit + N&S**

- **2 cups rye flour**
- **1 cup sugar**
- **2½ teaspoons cereal-free baking powder**
- **½ teaspoon baking soda**
- **1 large orange, seeded**
- **2 tablespoons allowed oil**
- **Boiling water**
- **1½ cups raw cranberries**
- **½ cup chopped nuts**

Combine dry ingredients. Grind orange and peel in blender, then measure. Add boiling water to orange to make 1 cup, add oil and another 2 tablespoons water. Mix with dry ingredients. Chop cranberries and nuts separately and add to batter, blending lightly. Place in greased muffin tins. Bake in preheated 350° oven 25 minutes. *Makes 12*

## OATMEAL MUFFINS

**BBB + Oats**

- **⅔ cup rice flour**
- **¼ cup soy flour**
- **1½ teaspoons potato flour**
- **1 tablespoon cereal-free baking powder**
- **½ teaspoon salt**
- **¼ cup sugar**
- **1 cup rolled oats**
- **3 tablespoons oil**
- **1 cup plus 2 tablespoons allowed milk substitute**

Blend all dry ingredients. Add oil and milk substitute at once, stirring to blend. Spoon into oiled muffin tins and bake in preheated 400° oven 15 to 20 minutes. *Makes 12*

## OAT-SOY GRITS MUFFINS

**BBB + Oats**

- **½ cup soy grits**
- **¾ cup oat flour**
- **1 tablespoon cereal-free baking powder**
- **2 tablespoons sugar**
- **1 teaspoon salt**
- **2 tablespoons allowed oil**

Blend dry ingredients; add oil and ¾ cup water, and stir briefly. Spoon into oiled muffin tins. Bake in preheated 400° oven 15 minutes. *Makes 8*

## ROLLED OAT MUFFINS

**BBB + Oats**

- **2 cups rolled oats, ground***
- **½ teaspoon salt**
- **2 tablespoons cereal-free baking powder**
- **2 tablespoons sugar**
- **¼ cup allowed margarine**

Blend dry ingredients and margarine with fingertips until mixture resembles coarse cornmeal. Stir in 1 cup water. Spoon into oiled muffin tins. Bake in preheated 400° oven 15 minutes. *Makes 8–10*

**Note:* Grind rolled oats in blender, a cup or two at a time, until you have 2 cups ground oats. It will be almost like oat flour.

## RICE-OAT MUFFINS

**BBB + Oats**

- **3 tablespoons oat flour**
- **¾ cup rice flour**
- **1 tablespoon cereal-free baking powder**
- **1 tablespoon sugar**
- **½ teaspoon salt**
- **2 tablespoons allowed oil**

Blend dry ingredients and stir in oil and ½ cup water. Spoon into oiled muffin tins, filling ⅔ full. Bake in preheated 400° oven 15 to 20 minutes. These don't brown much but are crispy good outside, and fine textured inside. *Makes 6 small muffins*

## BLUEBERRY OAT MUFFINS

**BBB + Oats + Fruit + N&S**

- **1 recipe Rolled Oat Muffins, p. 215**
- **½ cup blueberries, fresh or frozen**
- **½ cup nuts, chopped**

Add blueberries and nuts to Rolled Oat Muffins batter. Bake as directed. It's a fine treat! *Makes 8–10*

## CRUNCH TOPPED OAT MUFFINS

**BBB + Oats + TE&A**

- **1 recipe Rolled Oat Muffins, p. 215**
- **2 tablespoons sugar**
- **2 teaspoons rice flour**
- **1 teaspoon cinnamon**
- **1 teaspoon allowed margarine**

Prepare muffin batter and place in oiled muffin tins. Blend remaining ingredients to crumbly stage, sprinkle evenly over each muffin before baking. Bake in preheated 400° oven 15 minutes for a muffin with a sweet crunchy topping. *Makes 8–10*

## HONEY BANANA MUFFINS

**BBB + Oats + Fruit + N&S + TE&A**

- **1¼ cups rice flour**
- **3 tablespoons soy flour**
- **1 tablespoon potato flour**
- **4 teaspoons cereal-free baking powder**
- **½ teaspoon baking soda**
- **½ teaspoon salt**
- **1 cup quick oats**
- **¼ cup chopped nuts**
- **½ cup honey**
- **¼ cup allowed oil**
- **1½ cups mashed ripe bananas**

Blend all dry ingredients. In another bowl, mix honey, oil, ¼ cup water, and mashed banana. Combine with dry ingredients, mixing well. Spoon into oiled muffin tins. Bake in preheated 350° oven 25 to 30 minutes or bake in miniature muffin tins for 18 to 20 minutes for a party table. *Makes 10–12 regular size or 25–30 small*

**Variation: Loaves**

Pour batter into 7⅜ x 3½ x 2¼-inch oiled loaf pan. Bake in preheated 350° oven 45 minutes or until done in center when tested. Cool 10 minutes in pan before turning out. Cool completely, then wrap in foil. Refrigerate for easy slicing. This dough may also be baked in 2 5¼ x 3¼ x 2¼-inch pans. The little remaining dough may be baked in muffin tins.

## RYE-OATMEAL MUFFINS

**BBB + Rye + Oats**

- **2 cups quick oats**
- **1 cup rye flour**
- **¼ cup sugar**
- **½ teaspoon salt**
- **2 tablespoons cereal-free baking powder**
- **¼ cup allowed oil**

Blend dry ingredients. Add oil and 1 cup water. Stir well, adding up to ¼ cup additional water if needed. Try adding 1 tablespoon water at a time until good muffin batter consistency is reached. Fill oiled muffin tins ⅔ full. Bake in preheated 400° oven 15 minutes. *Makes 12*

## HIGH-RISE RICE BARLEY MUFFINS

**BBB + Barley**

- **2/3 cup rice flour**
- **1 1/3 cups barley flour**
- **2 tablespoons cereal-free baking powder**
- **1/4 cup sugar**
- **1/2 teaspoon salt**
- **2 tablespoons allowed oil**

Blend dry ingredients in bowl and stir in oil and 1 1/2 cups water. Spoon into oiled muffin tins, filling 2/3 to 3/4 full. Bake in preheated 400° oven 15 minutes. These beautiful muffins have good texture and flavor. Serve to company along with roast pork or beef. *Makes 12*

**Variation: Surprise Muffin**

Fill muffin tins only half full to begin. Center on each 1/2 teaspoon allowed jam, cold from refrigerator. Top with more batter, sealing jam inside. Bake as directed. *Makes 12*

## BARLEY BISCUITS

**BBB + Barley**

- **2 1/2 cups barley flour**
- **1 tablespoon cereal-free baking powder**
- **1/2 teaspoon salt**
- **1 tablespoon sugar**
- **1/3 cup allowed margarine**

Blend dry ingredients and pinch or cut in margarine until mixture resembles cornmeal. Stir in 3/4 cup water. Place on barley-floured board and work with hands just until dough is no longer sticky. Pat or roll out 1/2 inch thick and cut into 2-inch biscuits. Place in oiled pan, flip over so top is oiled (or brush tops with oil). Bake in preheated 450° oven 12 to 15 minutes or until lightly browned. These remain quite flat but have a lovely delicate texture. If desired, make biscuits double decker after oiling and before baking and they will easily pull apart. *Makes 20*

**Variations:**

1. COCONUT OR SESAME STICKS—Add 1 cup flaked coconut or 1/2 cup sesame seeds to dough. Roll or pat out 1/2 inch thick. Cut into sticks about 1/2 inch wide x 3 inches long. Bake as for biscuits. **(+ N&S)** *Makes 40*
2. CINNAMON ROLLS—Pat dough 1/2 inch thick. Spread with softened allowed margarine. Sprinkle with sugar and cinnamon. **(+ TE&A)** Add raisins, if allowed. **(+ Mold).** Roll up jelly-roll fashion, pressing dough together if it tears. Cut into 3/4-inch slices. Place cut side down on oiled pan or cookie sheet and bake in preheated 450° oven 12 to 15 minutes. If desired, drizzle warm rolls with Powdered Sugar BBB Glaze, p. 271, or with Powdered Sugar Glaze, p. 272. **(+ Corn)** *Makes 12–15*

## LAVA DOME RYE-BARLEY MUFFINS

**BBB + Rye + Barley**

- **1 cup rye flour**
- **1 cup barley flour**
- **½ teaspoon salt**
- **4 teaspoons cereal-free baking powder**
- **2 tablespoons sugar**
- **2 tablespoons allowed oil**

Blend dry ingredients and stir in oil and 1¼ cups water. Spoon into oiled muffin tins ⅔ to ¾ full. Bake in preheated 400° oven 15 to 20 minutes. These rise well and crack on the lumpy top. They reminded us of Mount St. Helens' developing lava dome. *Makes 8–10*

## RISE AND SHINE MUFFINS

**BBB + Corn**

- **¾ cup rice flour**
- **¼ cup soy flour**
- **¾ cup cornmeal**
- **2 tablespoons sugar**
- **4 teaspoons cereal-free baking powder**
- **½ teaspoon salt**
- **2 tablespoons allowed oil**

Blend dry ingredients in bowl and stir in oil and 1 cup water. Spoon into oiled muffin tins. Bake in preheated 400° oven 15 minutes. Delicious muffins—worth getting up for! *Makes 8*

## SOY-CORNMEAL MUFFINS

**BBB + Corn**

- **1 cup cornmeal**
- **1 cup soy flour**
- **2 tablespoons sugar**
- **2 tablespoons cereal-free baking powder**
- **½ teaspoon salt**
- **¼ cup allowed oil**

Blend dry ingredients and stir in oil and 1 cup water. Quickly spoon into oiled muffin tins, filling ⅞ full. Bake in preheated 400° oven 15 minutes. These muffins have delicious flavor and texture. *Makes 10*

## GRAIN ENSEMBLE MUFFINS

**BBB + Rye + Corn**

- **1 cup rice flour**
- **½ cup cornmeal**
- **½ cup rye flour**
- **4 teaspoons cereal-free baking powder**
- **2 tablespoons sugar**
- **½ teaspoon salt**
- **2 tablespoons allowed oil**

Blend dry ingredients and stir in oil and 1¼ cups water. Spoon into oiled muffin tins, filling ⅔ to ¾ full. Bake in preheated 400° oven 15 minutes. *Makes 10–12*

**Variation:**

Replace rye flour with oat flour or oats ground in blender. (+ **Oats**) Replace rye with barley flour for variety in flavor. (+ **Barley**)

## RYE-CORNMEAL MUFFINS

**BBB + Rye + Corn + TE&A**

- ½ cup cornmeal
- ¾ cup rye flour
- 1 tablespoon cereal-free baking powder
- ½ teaspoon salt
- 2 tablespoons allowed oil
- 2 tablespoons honey

Combine dry ingredients, stir in oil, honey, and ¾ cup water. Spoon into oiled muffin tins. Bake in preheated 400° oven 15 minutes. *Makes 8*

## MILLET-OAT DUO MUFFINS

**BBB + Oats + Millet**

- 1½ cups oat flour
- ½ cup millet flour
- ½ teaspoon salt
- 4 teaspoons cereal-free baking powder
- 3 tablespoons brown sugar, firmly packed
- 2 tablespoons allowed oil

Combine dry ingredients in bowl. Blend 1¼ cups water with oil and stir into dry mixture. Spoon batter into oiled muffin tins, filling ⅔ full. Bake in preheated 400° oven 15 to 20 minutes. *Makes 12*

## TRI-GRAIN MUFFINS

**BBB + Barley + Millet**

- ½ cup millet flour
- ½ cup barley flour
- ¼ cup soy flour
- 4 teaspoons cereal-free baking powder
- ¼ cup brown sugar, firmly packed
- 2 tablespoons allowed oil

Blend dry ingredients in bowl, combine ⅔ cup water with oil and stir into dry ingredients. Spoon into oiled muffin tins, filling ⅔ full. Bake in preheated 375° oven 20 to 25 minutes. These are nice textured muffins with crispy outsides. *Makes 12*

**BBB + Barley + Millet**

- ¼ cup millet flour
- ¼ cup barley flour
- ½ cup rice flour
- ¼ cup soy flour
- ½ teaspoon salt
- 4 teaspoons cereal-free baking powder
- ¼ cup brown sugar, firmly packed
- 2 tablespoons allowed oil

## HARMONIOUS QUARTET MUFFINS

Blend dry ingredients and stir in oil and ¾ cup water. Spoon into oiled muffin tins, filling ¾ full. Bake in preheated 400° oven 15 minutes. These muffins are crispy brown outside, nicely textured inside. *Makes 8*

**BBB + Corn + Buckwheat**

- 1 cup buckwheat flour
- ½ cup white cornmeal
- 4 teaspoons cereal-free baking powder
- ½ teaspoon salt
- 2 tablespoons brown sugar, firmly packed
- ¼ cup allowed oil

## BUCKWHEAT-CORNMEAL MUFFINS

Blend dry ingredients in mixing bowl. Combine 1¼ cups water with oil and stir into dry ingredients. Spoon into oiled muffin tins, filling ⅔ full. Bake in preheated 400° oven 15 minutes or until done. These muffins are unusual in color and texture—fascinating and flavorful. *Makes 12*

**Variation:**

When allowed, add ¼ cup raisins. **(+ Mold)**

# CRACKERS

Crackers require time and patience. We use unsifted dry ingredients. Cracker dough needs generous amounts of allowed margarine to facilitate easy handling and produce a crispy finished product. Blend margarine with dry ingredients before adding liquid. Stir dough until it looks satiny smooth and pulls away from sides of bowl in a ball. Most of our cracker recipes are plain, but later in your food testing you might like to season with onion or garlic powder or vegetable salt **(+ Veg.)**; top with poppy, sesame, or anise seeds **(+ N&S)**; or sprinkle with Seasoned Salt Blend, p. 176.

Gently knead dough in hands—no extra flour should be required. If, however, dough is sticky, work in 1 tablespoon extra flour. Divide dough into small portions to pat or roll thin on smooth surface lightly floured with recipe-matching flour. A Tupperware pastry sheet works well, but try heavy foil or waxed paper. Pick up as little additional flour from board as possible when gathering dough left from first cutting. If dough becomes dry and crumbly, add a few drops of water and work in. Pat or roll and cut again.

These cracker doughs are too delicate for lifting cutouts by hand, particularly rice doughs. Slide a sharp cutting knife under each cutout and lift onto free hand, then transfer to baking sheet.

If desired, cut "crispy critter crackers" for children from animal cookie cutters. The little critters are extra trouble but are also fun.

Crackers available in markets are listed for the convenience of the cook in a hurry.

## Crackers available in markets — BBB

Chico-San Rice Cakes, salted or unsalted (whole grain brown rice, no preservatives)
Arden Rice Cakes, salted or unsalted (whole brown rice, no preservatives)
Hol-Grain Natural Rice Wafer-ets, salted or unsalted (brown rice, water, salt)
Kitanihon Plain Rice Crunch Crackers (rice, soybean oil, salt)

## DELICIOUS BROWN RICE CRACKERS — BBB

**2 cups cooked brown rice, loosely packed**
**¼ cup rice flour**
**½ teaspoon cereal-free baking powder**
**¼ teaspoon salt**
**¼ cup allowed margarine**

Mash rice with fork until all grains are broken up and mat together. Add remaining ingredients, blending into a smooth ball that pulls away from sides of bowl. Pick up dough and knead briefly. Place half the dough on very lightly rice-floured board, roll gently with floured rolling pin or pat with hands ⅛ to ¼ inch thick. Cut with cookie cutter and place on ungreased baking sheet. Salt if desired. Repeat with remaining dough. Bake in preheated 375° oven 20 to 22 minutes or until delicately browned and crisp. Cool on racks. *Makes 40–45*

## CRISPY CREAM OF RICE CRACKERS — BBB

**2 tablespoons Cream of Rice cereal**
**¾ cup rice flour**
**1 teaspoon cereal-free baking powder**
**¼ teaspoon salt**
**¼ cup allowed margarine**

Sprinkle Cream of Rice into ½ cup boiling water, cook 30 seconds, cover and let stand 3 minutes. Cool cereal and stir into remaining ingredients until dough forms smooth ball that pulls away from sides of bowl. Pick up and knead gently. If still too moist, add 2 tablespoons rice flour and work in. Place half of dough on rice-floured board, roll ⅛ to ¼ inch thick with floured rolling pin. Cut crackers with 2-inch cookie cutter, run sharp knife under each, and transfer to unoiled baking sheet. Salt if desired. Repeat with remaining dough. Bake in preheated 325° oven 30 minutes or until barely browned. Cool on racks. *Makes 36*

## Crackers available in markets

**BBB + Veg.**

Edward and Sons Baked Brown Rice Snaps, Onion–Garlic (brown rice, onion powder, garlic powder, sea salt)

**BBB + N&S**

Arden Rice Cakes with Sesame, salted or unsalted (brown rice, sesame seeds, no preservatives)

Chico-San Rice Cakes with Sesame (brown rice, sesame seeds, no preservatives)

Soken Brown Rice Petals (brown rice flour, black sesame seeds, salt, water)

Edward and Sons Baked Brown Rice Snaps (brown rice, sesame)

**BBB + Fish + Veg.**

Kitanihon Seaweed Flavored Rice Crunch Crackers (rice, seaweed, shrimp, sea salt, soybean oil)

**BBB + Fish + N&S**

Kitanihon Sesame Flavored Rice Crackers (rice, soybean oil, sesame seeds, shrimp, sea salt)

**BBB + Rye**

Natural RyKrisp (whole rye and salt)
Master Old Country Hardtack (rye, small amount of water, salt)

**BBB + Rye**

## RICE AND RYE CRACKERS

- **½ cup rice flour**
- **½ cup rye flour**
- **¼ teaspoon salt**
- **1 teaspoon cereal-free baking powder**
- **¼ cup allowed margarine**

Blend dry ingredients into margarine. Add ¼ cup water and stir into smooth ball of dough. Pick up and knead briefly. Roll out dough, half at a time, on lightly rye-floured surface to ⅛ to ¼ inch thick. Cut crackers with 2-inch cookie cutter, or cut into squares. Slip sharp knife under each cracker and lift to ungreased baking sheet, assisting with free hand. Continue with remaining dough. Salt if desired. Bake in preheated 375° oven 8 to 10 minutes or until delicately browned. Remove crackers to cooling rack. *Makes 42*

## CREAM OF RYE CRACKERS

**BBB + Rye**

- **¼ cup Cream of Rye cereal**
- **¾ cup rye flour**
- **1 teaspoon cereal-free baking powder**
- **½ teaspoon salt**
- **¼ cup allowed margarine**

Sprinkle Cream of Rye into ¾ cup boiling water and cook 3 minutes. Cover and set aside 3 minutes. Uncover and, when cool, mix with all other ingredients. Stir until mixture pulls away from sides of bowl. Knead briefly and divide dough in half. Roll, half at a time, on lightly rye-floured board ⅛ to ¼ inch thick with rye-floured rolling pin. Cut into squares with sharp knife or cut rounds with 2-inch cookie cutter. Slide thin knife under each cracker and transfer to unoiled baking sheet. Salt as desired. Bake in preheated 325° oven 30 minutes or until thoroughly dry. *Makes 36*

## Crackers available in markets

**BBB + Rye + N&S**

Rye-ce Caraways (brown rice, whole rye, caraway seeds, sea salt, no preservatives)

**BBB + Rye + N&S + TE&A**

Sesame RyKrisp (whole rye, coconut oil, sesame seed, salt, BHA)
Seasoned RyKrisp (whole rye, coconut oil, salt, caraway, BHA)

**BBB + Rye + Mold**

Kavli Norwegian Flatbread, Thick and Thin (whole rye, yeast, salt)
Finn Crisp, Light or Dark (rye, yeast, salt)
Finn Crisp, Dark with Caraway (rye, yeast, salt, caraway) **(+ N&S)**
Rytak Knackebrod (rye, yeast, salt)
Siljans Knacke—Swedish Dark Rye Crispbread (rye flour, yeast, salt)
Ryvita—Crisp Rye Bread (whole rye flour, salt, and yeast)
Bahlsen Rogga—Thin Whole Rye Cracker (whole rye flour, sourdough, salt)

### BBB + Oats

## OAT CRACKERS

- **2 cups rolled oats**
- **1 cup boiling water**
- **1 teaspoon baking soda**
- **1 teaspoon salt**
- **3 tablespoons allowed oil**

Grind oats into a flour in blender, pour boiling water over, and set aside 5 minutes. Stir in other ingredients. When thick enough to handle, knead on oat-floured board or between sheets of waxed paper. Batter will become easy to handle and non-sticky. Roll thin and cut into squares. Slide sharp knife under each cracker and lift to unoiled baking sheet. Salt if desired. Bake in preheated 350° oven 20 to 30 minutes or until whole cracker is dry and edges begin to brown and curve. Cool on racks. *Makes 16*

### BBB + Barley

## BARLEY CRACKERS

- **⅓ cup allowed margarine**
- **1 cup barley flour**
- **¼ cup soy flour**
- **1 teaspoon cereal-free baking powder**
- **¼ teaspoon salt**

Blend margarine with dry ingredients. Add ¼ cup water and stir into smooth ball that pulls away from sides of bowl. Knead briefly in hands. Roll dough out on lightly floured surface to ⅛ to ¼ inch thick. Cut with fancy cookie cutters or sharp knife pressed into dough. Slide knife along underside of cracker and lift to ungreased baking sheet. Salt if desired. Bake in preheated 350° oven 12 to 15 minutes. *Makes 20*

### BBB + Corn

## Crackers available in markets

Arden Rice Cakes with Corn (brown rice, corn, salt, no preservatives)

### BBB + Millet + N&S

Chico-San Rice Cakes with Millet, salted or unsalted (brown rice, millet, sesame seeds, no preservatives)

Arden 5 Grain Rice Cakes (whole brown rice, rye, millet, caraway seed, flaxseed, sea salt) (+ **Rye**)

### BBB + Buckwheat

Arden Rice Cakes with Buckwheat (brown rice, buckwheat, no preservatives)

### BBB + Buckwheat + N&S

Chico-San Rice Cakes with Buckwheat added, salted or unsalted (brown rice, buckwheat, sesame seeds, no preservatives)

# LOAF BREADS

For me, Gloria, it is almost impossible, without wheat flour, to make a good-textured sandwich bread that holds together when sliced. Also, when dealing with flours acceptable on our program, I'd give my eyeteeth if eggs were not taboo. So, the breads in the following section are mostly snack or tea breads, using vegetable or fruit additions to help hold them together and keep them moist.

For many years we depended on Guisto's Vita-Grain Soy Buns for Beverly's bread for toast and sandwiches. Then, a few years ago, disaster struck. These buns as well as Guisto's Millet-Soya Bread, Rice Bread, Lima-Soya Bread, Lima-Potato Bread and Soya Hot Dog Buns were all taken off the market.

When we wrote Guisto's, they replied that theirs is a whole-grain bakery and that baking specialty breads in a wheat-filled environment could result in slight contamination. Since any stray gluten can cause some people problems, Guisto's recommended the use of Bray's breads: Soya Potato Bread, Rice Bread, and Lima Bean Bread.

Bray's is a handmade product developed by a leading allergy doctor, we were told, and their breads are totally gluten free. Look for such scrupulous bakers in your health food stores and for brands listed for purchase within our bread section.

We are able to order Orowheat Wheat-Free 100% Rye Bread from our Orowheat Bakery outlet.

Guisto's have now returned their products to the health food store near us with new labeling, and we continue to use the Soy Buns even though wheat is listed as an ingredient. The chance that these buns really contain wheat is slight and they produce no allergic reaction in Bev.

Each bun is made like an uncut hamburger bun. We cut them into three slices that slip easily into the toaster. They are of good texture and hold together well for sandwiches for the brown bagger in the family.

Baking mixes that do not contain wheat are available. We have listed those with their ingredients under Baking Mixes available in markets, p. 371. Their packages give recipes for breads, muffins, cookies, and other baked goods, with or without egg. Look for these in your health food stores.

Many good bread recipes using egg and sometimes milk products appear in books written by Marion N. Wood. All her breads are gluten-free. Her books are *Gourmet Food on a Wheat-free Diet* and *Delicious and Easy Rice Flour Recipes* (Charles C. Thomas, Publishers, Bannerstone House, 301-327 East Lawrence Avenue, Springfield, Illinois). Another book of gluten-free recipes is *Good Food, Gluten-free* by Hilda Cherry Hills, (Keats Publishing, Inc., New Canaan, Connecticut).

In our recipes, dry ingredients are usually measured unsifted. Occasionally, we specify and recommend sifting. These are exceptions where things went a little better for us if we sifted. Unless a recipe suggests that you sift, simply fork fluff flours a bit before spooning them into your measuring cup.

**BBB**

## Breads available in markets

*Note:* The leavening used in these breads is grain free.

Bray's Soya Potato Bread (soya flour, potato starch, water, soya oil, cereal-free leavening, sugar, salt)

Bray's Rice Bread (rice flour, potato starch, soya flour, water, soya oil, sugar, cereal-free leavening, salt)

**BBB**

## APPLESAUCE BREAD

**1⅓ cups rice flour**
**½ cup soy flour**
**1 tablespoon potato flour**
**¾ cup sugar**
**3 teaspoons cereal-free baking powder**
**1 teaspoon salt**
**½ teaspoon baking soda**
**1 cup Gloria's Applesauce, p. 344**
**2 tablespoons allowed oil**

Mix dry ingredients. Blend applesauce, oil, and 2 tablespoons water and add to dry ingredients. When mixed, batter should be thin enough to fall readily off spoon. If it requires hard shaking or pushing off with a scraper, stir in 1 to 2 tablespoons more water. Spoon batter into 2 oiled 5½ x 3 x 2-inch loaf pans. Bake in preheated 350° oven 35 to 45 minutes and test with toothpick stuck into center of one loaf. Continue cooking until pick comes out clean. Turn out on racks and cool. Wrap and refrigerate. This will slice well the next day. *Makes 2 loaves*

**Variations:**

1. COFFEE CAKE—prepare batter as above. Pour into 2 oiled 8-inch cake pans. Make several indentations in batter with back of spoon. Fill depressions with applesauce. Sprinkle entire coffee cake with brown sugar and toasted rice flakes. Bake at 350° 20 to 25 minutes or until done when tested. *Serves 12*
2. Add to above recipe ½ teaspoon cinnamon and ½ cup chopped nuts or use to top coffee cake when allowed. **(+ N&S + TE&A)**
3. Drizzle on cooled coffee cake glaze made of confectioners powdered sugar and enough water to run in stream from spoon. **(+ Corn)**

## BANANA BREAD

**BBB + Fruit**

- 1 cup rice flour
- ½ cup soy flour
- 2 tablespoons tapioca or potato starch
- 4 teaspoons cereal-free baking powder
- ¾ cup sugar
- Pinch of salt
- ¼ cup allowed oil
- ¾ cup mashed ripe banana

Sift dry ingredients together and set aside. Blend oil, banana, and ¼ cup water. Combine with dry ingredients and mix well. Bake in 2 oiled 5¾ x 3 x 2¼-inch pans 45 minutes or in 7¼ x 3½ x 2-inch loaf pan in preheated 350° oven 1 hour or until bread tests done when toothpick in center of loaf comes out clean or when finger pressed in center leaves no impression. *Makes 1 medium loaf or 2 small loaves*

**Variation:**

Add ⅛ teaspoon nutmeg and ¼ teaspoon cinnamon, when allowed. (+ **TE&A**)

## CRANBERRY ORANGE BREAD

**BBB + Fruit + N&S**

- 1⅓ cups rice flour or 1 cup rice and ⅓ cup rice bran or polish
- ½ cup soy flour
- 1 tablespoon potato flour
- 1 cup sugar
- 2 teaspoons cereal-free baking powder
- ½ teaspoon baking soda
- ½ teaspoon salt
- 2 cups fresh cranberries, minced in blender
- ½ cup chopped nuts
- 1 tablespoon grated orange peel
- ¾ cup orange juice or juice of 1 orange + water to equal ¾ cup
- ¼ cup allowed oil

Measure all dry ingredients into large bowl. Flours do not need sifting. Stir well. Add minced cranberries, nuts and orange peel and mix well. Blend orange juice and oil and add, all at once, to dry mixture. If batter is too dry to mix well, add 1 to 2 tablespoons more water. Pour into oiled tins and bake in preheated 350° oven as follows: Miniature Tea Muffins—about 20 minutes; regular size muffins—about 25 minutes; 5¾ x 3¼ x 2¼-inch loaf pans—35 to 45 minutes; 8½ x 4½ x 2¾-inch loaf pan—1 hour.

The little tea muffins are pretty and delicious. They do more than justice to any tea table or morning coffee get-together. Not one guest will ever suspect them of not being "normal people" treats. *Makes 24 tea muffins, 8 regular muffins, 2-3 small loaves, and 1 large loaf*

## Bread available in markets

**BBB + Veg.**

Bray's Lima Bean Bread (soya flour, potato starch, lima bean flour, water, sugar, cereal-free leavening, and salt.

**BBB + Veg. + N&S + TE&A**

## ZUCCHINI BREAD

- 1 cup sugar
- 1 cup allowed oil
- ¼ cup allowed milk substitute
- 2 cups finely grated zucchini
- 1 teaspoon synthetic vanilla
- 2 cups rice flour
- ⅔ cup soy flour
- 2 tablespoons potato flour
- ½ teaspoon salt
- 1 teaspoon baking soda
- 2 teaspoons cereal-free baking powder
- ½ teaspoon cinnamon
- ¼ cup chopped nuts or sunflower seeds

Mix first 5 ingredients in large bowl. Stir all dry ingredients together until well blended. Add to zucchini mixture and stir until all ingredients are well mixed. Stir in nuts. Spoon batter into 3 oiled 5½ x 3⅛ x 2-inch pans. Bake in preheated 325° oven 40 to 45 minutes, or bake in 1 large loaf pan, 8½ x 4½ x 2¾ inch for 1 hour. Cool. Wrap in foil or plastic, refrigerate, and slice the next day. This is delicious. Holds together well and good flavor. *Makes 3 small loaves or 1 large loaf*

**BBB + N&S + TE&A + Mold**

## Bread available in markets

Food for Life Rice Bread (rice flour, water, soya oil, natural fiber, cottonseed, yeast, salt)

**BBB + Rye + Fruit + N&S + TE&A**

## BANANA NUT BREAD

- ⅓ cup allowed margarine
- 3 tablespoons molasses
- ¼ cup honey
- ¼ cup allowed milk substitute
- 1 cup mashed bananas (2 medium)
- ½ teaspoon salt
- 4 teaspoons cereal-free baking powder
- ¼ cup soy flour
- 1¾ cups rye flour
- ½ cup nuts, chopped
- 1 teaspoon grated lemon peel

Preheat oven to 350°. Oil large 8½ x 4½ x 2¾-inch loaf pan. In large mixing bowl cream margarine, molasses, and honey. Beat in milk substitute and bananas. Add remaining ingredients and mix thoroughly. Pour into oiled loaf pan and bake 50 to 60 minutes or until done when tested with toothpick. This rises high and slices beautifully. Perfect! *Makes 1 large loaf*

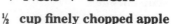

## QUICK APPLE NUT BREAD

**BBB + Rye + N&S + TE&A**

- ½ cup finely chopped apple
- ½ cup chopped walnuts
- 2 cups sifted rye flour
- 1 tablespoon cereal-free baking powder
- ½ teaspoon salt
- ½ teaspoon cinnamon
- ½ cup honey
- 2 tablespoons allowed oil
- ½ cup allowed milk substitute

Mix chopped apple and nuts. Sift flour, shaking portion over apple and nuts. Add remaining flour to baking powder, salt, and cinnamon. Mix honey, oil, and 2 tablespoons water in large mixing bowl. Add dry ingredients alternately with allowed milk substitute, beating after each addition. Stir in apple and nuts last. Turn into oiled 8½ x 4½ x 2¾-inch loaf pan and bake in 350° oven 1 hour. After removing from oven, let stand in pan a few minutes, then remove to cake rack and cool.

Scrumptuous! Slices well. Great for teas or gifts. If giving away, you may wish to bake in 2 oiled 5¾ x 3¼ x 2¼-inch pans 40 to 45 minutes. Give one away and keep one for the family. *Makes 1 large loaf or 2 small loaves*

## Bread available in markets

**BBB + Rye + Mold**

Orowheat Wheat-Free 100% Rye Bread (rye flour, water, raw cane syrup, partially hydrogenated vegetable shortening, soybean oil, fresh yeast, salt)

## CARROT PINEAPPLE BREAD

**BBB + Oats**

- 1 cup rice flour
- ⅓ cup rice bran or polish
- ½ cup soy flour
- 1 tablespoon potato flour
- 4 teaspoons cereal-free baking powder
- ½ teaspoon baking soda
- 1 teaspoon salt
- ¾ cup sugar
- 1 cup quick oats
- 1 cup finely shredded carrots, loosely packed
- ¼ cup unsweetened pineapple
- ¼ cup allowed oil
- 1 cup allowed milk substitute

Put all dry ingredients in a large bowl—no need to sift. Add shredded carrots and stir. Mix remaining ingredients and add, all at once, to dry ingredients. Mix well until all dry ingredients are moistened. Pour into oiled 8½ x 4½ x 2¾-inch loaf pan or into 3 smaller 5¾ x 3¼ x 2¼ pans. Bake in preheated 350° oven 1 hour for the larger loaf or until done when tested; 35 to 45 minutes for the smaller loaves. Cool loaf in pan 5 minutes, then remove to rack. When cool, wrap in foil or plastic and refrigerate overnight. This is easier to slice when cold, if you can keep away from it while hot. It really is yummy hot with allowed margarine. *Makes 1 large loaf or 3 small loaves*

## Bread available in markets

**BBB + Rye + Barley + TE&A + Mold**

The Original White Rye Bread—100% wheat-free (white rye flour, water, soya oil, honey, molasses, salt, yeast, malt, lecithin, no preservatives)

**BBB + Corn**

- 1 cup cornmeal
- ½ teaspoon salt
- 2 teaspoons softened allowed margarine, melted
- 1 cup boiling water

## QUICK CORNBREAD

Blend cornmeal, salt, and margarine. Add boiling water, stirring to form stiff dough. Shape into 2 round cakes ½ inch thick. Place on oiled pan or sheet and brush with additional melted margarine. Bake in preheated 450° oven 20 minutes. Break into pieces and serve while hot. *Serves 4*

**BBB + Corn + TE&A**

- 2½ cups cornmeal
- 3 tablespoons soy flour
- 2 tablespoons honey
- 1 teaspoon salt
- 1 tablespoon cereal-free baking powder
- ¼ cup allowed oil

## CORNBREAD

Blend dry ingredients, add oil and 1¼ cups water. Mix well. If very dry, add 1 to 2 tablespoons water. Pour batter into oiled 9-inch round baking dish or heavy 9-inch skillet. Bake in preheated 350° oven 35 to 45 minutes. For muffins, fill tins ¾ full and bake 20 to 25 minutes. *Makes 8 wedges or 12 muffins*

**BBB + Corn + Fruit**

## Bread available in markets

Corn Tortillas (*Note:* Read package list of ingredients. Corn may be soaked in lime water. Avoid if you are very sensitive to citrus.

**BBB + Rye + Corn + TE&A**

- 1½ cups soy flour
- 1½ cups rye flour
- 1 cup cornmeal
- ½ cup sugar
- 1 teaspoon baking soda
- 1 tablespoon cereal-free baking powder
- ½ teaspoon salt
- 2 cups allowed milk substitute
- ½ cup honey or half honey and half molasses. (+ Mold)

## BROWN BREAD

Preheat oven to 375°. Oil five 16-ounce fruit or vegetable cans. Mix flours, cornmeal, sugar, soda, baking powder, and salt. Add milk substitute and blend well. Add honey and mix. Pour about 1 cup batter into each can. Bake 30 minutes or until cake tester inserted in center comes out clean, about 35 minutes. Remove from oven. Let stand 5 minutes. Remove bread from cans onto rack covered with double thickness of paper toweling. Cool, wrap tightly, and store in refrigerator.

Try a slice with margarine and nut butter spread. Out of this world! *Makes 5 loaves, about 10 slices each*

## STEAMED BROWN BREAD

**BBB + Rye + Oats + Corn + TE&A**

**1 cup yellow cornmeal**
**1 cup rye flour**
**1⅓ cups quick oats**
**2 teaspoons baking soda**
**1 teaspoon salt**
**¼ cup Ener-G SoyQuik**
**1 tablespoon white distilled vinegar**
**½ cup honey**

Mix cornmeal, rye flour, oats, soda, and salt. Blend SoyQuik and 2 cups water until smooth and add vinegar. Let this pseudo buttermilk stand 5 minutes. Combine dry ingredients, liquid, and honey. Blend well and let stand 5 minutes while oiling two 1-pound coffee cans and putting 1 inch of water in large kettle with trivet. Stir batter and pour into coffee cans. Set on trivet and cover kettle. Bring water to boil. When steam begins to escape, reduce heat. Steam 1½ to 2 hours.

Remove cans to rack, allowing bread to cool in cans 30 minutes to 1 hour. Top will dry in this time. Invert can over palm of hand, rap bottom to loosen bread, and shake out gently as you support loaf with hand. Continue cooling bread on rack. Wrap and refrigerate for easy slicing—that is, if you can stay out of it long enough. This is a special company bread—good for teas or served with Loma Linda Soy Beans Boston Style. *Makes 2 round loaves*

**Variation:**

Add ⅓ cup raisins when allowed. (+ **Mold**)

## BARLEY BROWN BREAD

**BBB + Rye + Barley + Corn + TE&A**

**1 cup rye flour**
**1 cup barley flour**
**1 cup yellow cornmeal**
**½ teaspoon baking soda**
**1 tablespoon cereal-free baking powder**
**1 teaspoon salt**
**¼ cup allowed oil**
**½ cup honey**

Mix dry ingredients. Add 2 cups water and stir into smooth batter. Add oil and honey and beat hard. Pour into 2 well-oiled 1-pound coffee cans or into 3 oiled 5¾ x 3¼ x 2¼-inch loaf pans. Place on center rack of preheated 350° oven with shallow pan of water on rack below. Bake 40 to 45 minutes for coffee cans, slightly less for smaller pans. This batter also makes great hot muffins that rise tall and hold. Bake muffins 20 to 25 minutes. *Makes 2 round loaves, 3 small loaves, or 12 muffins*

# WHEAT-FREE BREAD CRUMBS, MEAT COATINGS, AND CROUTONS

These can be made from any bread, muffin, waffle, cracker, snack food, cereal, or flour that has acceptable ingredients for your diet. There are many prepackaged crackers, snack foods, and cereals that make beautiful meat coatings and save you time. They are listed with their ingredients within the chapters of the book.

## Bread Crumbs

Be alert! Read ingredients lists. Even crumbs can produce unhappy results. Use only those that contain ingredients you have tested. Many of our muffins and waffles make excellent crumbs. Use as allowed.

Soft crumbs can be made by tearing any allowed bread, muffin, or waffle into small pieces or by chopping coarse in a blender. Use in Holiday Turkey Stuffing, p. 182, to replace rye bread or use in meatloaves or meatballs, see guide p. 276. Combine 1 cup soft crumbs with 2 tablespoons melted allowed margarine and sprinkle on top a favorite casserole before baking.

Fine dry crumbs are made from soft crumbs, baked in 300° oven until very dry, then crushed fine (¾ cup soft crumbs will equal about ¼ cup fine dry crumbs). Use our guide, p. 276, for amounts to be used in meatloaves or meatballs or combine 1 cup dry crumbs with ¼ cup melted allowed margarine for casserole toppings. Dry crumbs make excellent coatings for breading meats and vegetables. Season as allowed. Perhaps you'll want to try our Savory Seasonings that follow.

☐ **BBB + Veg. + TE&A**

## SAVORY SEASONING I

- **1 cup fine dry crumbs**
- **2 teaspoons onion powder**
- **½ teaspoon salt**
- **Dash of pepper**
- **½ teaspoon garlic salt**
- **¼ teaspoon paprika**
- **¼ teaspoon dried thyme, rosemary, *or* basil**

Combine all ingredients. Use as desired for meat or vegetable coating or casserole topping. *Makes 1 cup*

## SAVORY SEASONING II

**BBB + Veg. + TE&A**

**1 cup fine dry crumbs**
**2 teaspoons onion powder**
**½ teaspoon salt**
**½ teaspoon garlic salt**
**1 teaspoon chili powder**
**Dash of pepper**
**1 tablespoon dried parsley**
**¼ teaspoon paprika**

Combine all ingredients. Use as desired for meat or vegetable coating or casserole topping. *Makes 1 cup*

## Thoughts on Breading Meat

It is helpful to dip meat in milk substitute, allowed oil, or allowed margarine before rolling in fine dry crumbs.

Bake puffed rice **(BBB)**, puffed corn **(+ Corn)**, or puffed millet **(+ Millet)** at 400° for 10 minutes. Crush fine. Season as allowed.

Coat chicken or chops with crushed natural style unpeeled potato chips. **(BBB)**

Combine ½ cup rice flour, 2 tablespoons potato flour, and ½ teaspoon salt in clean paper bag. Drop meat in bag. Shake carefully until meat is coated. The small amount of potato flour makes meat brown beautifully. Experiment with other flours and seasonings allowed. Barley flour goes well with beef **(+ Barley)**. The rice and potato flour combination is a favorite of ours for coating chicken to be fried. **(BBB)**

Cornmeal makes a crunchy coating for chicken or fish. **(+ Corn)**

Crush and use Kellogg's Nutri-Grain Rye, Barley or Corn cereals as well as Rice Krispies, Rice Chex, Corn Chex or cornflakes after each of your choices has been tested and accepted. Add seasonings as allowed. The list of ingredients for these cereals is found in our cereal section.

For a zesty chicken coating, dip chicken in allowed margarine that has been seasoned with chili powder, garlic powder, pepper and dried parsley. Roll in crushed natural style corn chips. **(+ Corn + Veg. + TE&A)**

## Croutons

Cut firm bread into ½-inch cubes. We find an electric knife helpful for this because it does not mash the cut edges. It helps also if the bread is cold and firm from the refrigerator and is not too fresh. Spread cubes on a cookie sheet. Bake in 300° oven 30 minutes or until cubes are dry and golden.

For garlic croutons, add ⅛ teaspoon garlic powder and ¼ cup melted allowed margarine to 3 cups unbaked cubes. Toss until evenly coated. Bake, cool, and store in the refrigerator, covered.

Our waffle recipes using soaked grains and beans are great for croutons. Cut leftover waffles into cubes while they are still crisp from the iron. Lay on cookie sheets, bake, cool, and store in the refrigerator, covered.

# Jams, Jellies, and Marmalades

Fruits that contain pectin can be made into jelly provided the proper amounts of sugar and heat are added. "The proper amounts" sometimes frighten or baffle those who prepare these sweet treats. Fortunately for us, apples, a fruit allowed on our basic food program, are high in pectin and can lend their jelling properties to pectin-poor fruits. When necessary, we can add pectin concentrate to fruits requiring major help in order to jell. Best of all, the fruits that may be used freely by almost everyone are those most prized for jams and jellies. No need for deprivation in this area. We merely need to learn the jelling tricks.

The old spoon method of testing for the jelly stage of boiling fruit and sugar is still valid. While the mixture boils, pour a tablespoonful back into the kettle by holding it above the steam and watching carefully. When two drops form at the bottom of the tipped spoon and then run together to form one drop before falling, the jelly stage has been reached. This is called "sheeting."

If you prefer to use a candy, deep-fat, or jelly thermometer, you can discover the exact jelly stage for the altitude at which you live, and you'll never again have a jelly failure. Using your thermometer, heat it in water to the point of boiling. Make a note of the temperature on the thermometer when the water boils and then add 8°. When the proper fruit and sugar reach boiling + 8°, jelly will result even at the peak of the Rockies.

Jams may be thick or loose according to luck, intention, or preference. The longer they cook, the thicker they become. Remember that they thicken as they cool. Remove from heat and test with a spoonful on a plate set in the freezer five minutes. If too thin, cook longer and test again. If too thick, add a little water and reheat.

Fruits vary so much in ratio of pulp to juice, and tastes vary so much in desired looseness or tightness in "a little jam for the bread," that we must leave the exact yield from each recipe to the individual food preparer and the family's preference. We recommend trying recipes that sound good and personalizing favorite successes with notes in your book regarding texture enjoyed and amounts obtained.

## PEACH-APRICOT JAM

**BBB**

- **1 pound peaches**
- **2 pounds apricots**
- **6 cups sugar, approximately**

Peel and slice fruits. Measure and add 1 cup sugar for each cup fruit. Adjust sugar down to ¾ cup, if fruit is especially ripe. Allow sugared fruit to stand 1 to 2 hours. Then place over heat and, stirring constantly, bring to boil. Reduce heat and simmer, stirring occasionally, 20 to 30 minutes, depending on thickness desired. Seal in sterilized jars with lids or melted paraffin. *About 3 pints*

## CARROT MARMALADE

**BBB**

- **5 large carrots, cut in chunks**
- **4 cups sugar, approximately**

Grind half the carrots in blender with 1 cup water. Pour into kettle and repeat with remaining carrots and another 1 cup water. Boil ground carrots until soft, measure, and add equal amount of sugar. Stir until sugar melts, then simmer 30 minutes or until as thick as desired. Seal in sterilized jars with lids or melted paraffin. *About 2 pints*

## PEAR HONEY

**BBB**

- **5 pounds Seckel or Kieffer pears (20 medium)**
- **2 cups unsweetened crushed pineapple**
- **10 cups sugar, approximately**

Peel and core pears and grind, using coarse blade of grinder or food processor. Measure pears and pineapple and add equal amount of sugar. Cook, stirring frequently, until mixture is as thick as desired and pears are clear. Seal in sterilized jars with lids or melted paraffin. *About 7 pints*

## SUGAR-FREE BBB JAM

**BBB**

- **1 or 2 large cans canned-in-juice allowed fruits**

Use favorite fruit or combinations such as: apricots and pineapple; peaches and white grapes; pears and purple plums; or whatever suits your fancy among allowed fruits. Purée fruit or fruits in blender. Pour into flat pyrex baking dish and bake at lowest oven setting until of consistency desired. Refrigerate.

## APRICOT-PINEAPPLE JAM

**BBB**

- **4 cups diced fresh apricots**
- **4 cups sugar**
- **1 can (20 ounces) unsweetened crushed pineapple**

Mix apricots and sugar and boil 20 minutes. Add pineapple and bring again to boil. Seal in jars with lids or melted paraffin. *About 3 pints*

## PEACHY EASY BUTTER

**BBB**

- **5 pounds ripe peaches, peeled and sliced**
- **4 cups sugar**

Cook peaches with ½ cup water, stirring occasionally until soft, about 20 minutes. Press through sieve or ricer or purée in blender and stir in sugar. Pour into 9 x 13-inch pan and bake in 350° oven about 1½ hours or until of desired consistency. Stir twice during baking. Seal in jars with lids or with melted paraffin. *About 3 pints*

## CLARA'S APRICOT JAM

**BBB**

- **3 pounds ripe apricots (25-30)**
- **5 cups sugar**
- **10 apricot pits**

Peel, pit, and chop apricots. Crack pits and remove kernels. Pour 2 cups sugar over apricots and let stand 8 hours. Add remaining sugar and boil gently with kernels until of desired consistency. Seal, allowing 1 or 2 kernels to each jar, and cover with melted paraffin. *About 2½ pints*

## PEACH-PLUM JAM

☐ **BBB + Fruit**

- **3 pounds peaches (7 cups)**
- **3 pounds red plums (7 cups)**
- **12 cups sugar**
- **1 lemon, sliced thin**

Peel and pit peaches, pit plums, and cut fruit into small chunks. Crush lightly, add sugar and lemon and cook, stirring occasionally, until desired consistency. Seal in sterilized jars with lids or with paraffin. *About 6 pints*

## SUNNY MORNING MARMALADE

☐ **BBB + Fruit**

- **2 grapefruit**
- **2 lemons**
- **2 oranges**
- **¼ teaspoon salt**
- **Sugar equal to fruit pulp**

Peel fruit and prepare peel by removing most of white inner layer and slicing peel into very thin strips. Simmer prepared peel in 2 cups water 20 minutes. Drain off water. Purée fruit pulp in blender or food processor and measure. Stir in equal amount of sugar and add to cooked peel. Add salt and bring to boil, stirring to prevent sticking. Simmer until thick and clear, about 20 minutes. Seal in sterilized jars with lids or melted paraffin. *About 2 pints*

## PLUM-RASPBERRY JAM

**BBB + Fruit**

- **3 pounds purple plums (7 cups)**
- **6 cups sugar**
- **1½ cups raspberries**

Pit plums and grind, using medium blade. Measurement should be about 5 cups. Combine plums and sugar, add raspberries, and stir. Bring to boil, stirring frequently, reduce heat and simmer about 40 minutes or until of desired consistency. Seal in sterilized jars with lids or melted paraffin. *About 3½ pints*

## PINEAPPLE-CARROT MARMALADE

**BBB + Fruit**

- **4 pounds carrots**
- **3 lemons**
- **1 can (20 ounces) unsweetened crushed pineapple**
- **4 cups sugar**
- **1 cup orange juice**

Peel carrots and grind with unpeeled lemons, using fine or medium blade. Add pineapple, sugar, and orange juice. Bring to boil, reduce heat, and simmer, stirring occasionally, until clear and of desired consistency. Seal in sterilized jars with lids or melted paraffin. *About 4½ pints*

## SIMPLEST PLUM JAM

**BBB + Fruit**

- **4 cups red plums**
- **4 cups sugar**

Pit and chop or grind plums. Add sugar and let stand at least 1 hour. Simmer over low heat until of desired consistency. Seal in sterilized jars with lids or melted paraffin. *About 2 pints*

## STRAWBERRY PRESERVES

**BBB + Fruit**

- **5 cups strawberries**
- **5 cups sugar**
- **¼ cup lemon juice**

Wash and hull strawberries. Sprinkle on sugar and mix gently. Heat slowly in large kettle until juice covers berries. Boil 7 minutes. Add lemon juice and boil 3 minutes more. Skim. Remove from heat and pour into large flat pan. Cover pan with cloth and let stand 8 hours or overnight. Seal without reheating in sterile jars, using melted paraffin. *About 2 pints*

## LIME-PEAR HONEY

**BBB + Fruit**

- **3 pounds pears (12 medium)**
- **1 can (8½ ounces) unsweetened crushed pineapple**
- **Juice and grated peel of 1 lime**
- **5 cups sugar**

Peel and core pears and chop. Add other ingredients and boil gently 20 minutes, stirring frequently. Test for desired consistency and, when reached, seal in sterilized jars. *About 3 pints*

☐ **BBB + Fruit**

## LOQUAT JAM

- **1 pound loquats, partially ripe**
- **1½ cups sugar**
- **Grated lemon peel**

Wash loquats, scald, and remove seeds. Peel if desired. Chop fruit in blender or food processor or by grinding, using coarse blade. Add sugar, lemon peel, and 1 cup water. Bring to boil and boil rapidly until juice sheets from spoon or until desired consistency. Seal in sterilized jars with lids or melted paraffin. *About 1 pint*

**Variation:**
Cook pulp until very soft and press through jelly bag. Return to heat and boil until juice is thick and pink. Measure and add equal amount of sugar. Test as above and seal.

☐ **BBB + Fruit**

## RASPBERRY-PEAR JAM

- **3 pounds pears (12 medium)**
- **5 cups sugar**
- **Juice of 1 lemon**
- **1 package (16 ounces) frozen unsweetened red raspberries**

Peel, core, and chop pears. Add sugar and lemon juice and boil gently 20 minutes. Add raspberries and continue cooking until desired consistency. Seal in sterilized jars with lids or melted paraffin. *About 3 pints*

☐ **BBB + Fruit**

## JAM SESSION FOR TRIO

- **9 cups sugar**
- **5 cups tart green apples, peeled and chopped**
- **2 cups unsweetened crushed pineapple**
- **4 cups fresh red raspberries**

Combine sugar and 2 cups water and boil until mixture spins a thread. Add fruits and boil about 30 minutes, but stir and test frequently and remove from heat when of desired consistency. Seal in sterilized jars with lids or paraffin. *About 2½ pints*

☐ **BBB + Fruit**

## CHERRY-LOGANBERRY JAM

- **5½ cups pitted tart red cherries (2 pounds)**
- **7 cups sugar**
- **7 cups loganberries (2 pounds)**

Pit cherries and cover with 2 cups sugar. Add loganberries and cover with 2 cups sugar. Allow to stand 1 to 2 hours in cool place. Add remaining 3 cups sugar. Stir and cook to desired consistency. Seal in sterilized jars with lids or melted paraffin. *About 2 pints*

## ORANGE-FIG JAM

**BBB + Fruit**

- **2 cups sugar**
- **3½ cups fresh figs, peeled and chopped**
- **1 large orange**
- **3 tablespoons lemon juice**

Add sugar to figs. Cut orange peel into fine strips. Chop orange pulp, discarding seeds. Mix figs, orange peel and pulp, and ¼ cup water. Cook slowly about 30 minutes, stirring frequently until desired thickness. Add lemon juice, stir, and remove from heat. Seal in sterilized jars with lids or melted paraffin. *About 1½ pints*

## PEACH-APPLE JAM

**BBB + Fruit**

- **2 cups peaches, peeled, pitted, and chopped**
- **2 cups apples, peeled, cored, and chopped**
- **3 tablespoons lemon juice**
- **2 teaspoons grated lemon peel**
- **3½ cups sugar**

Mix all ingredients in large kettle. Cook slowly, stirring frequently until thick and transparent, about 1 hour. Seal in sterilized jars with lids or melted paraffin. *About 2 pints*

## APPLE-RASPBERRY JAM

**BBB + Fruit**

- **9 cups sugar**
- **2 pounds tart apples, peeled and chopped fine**
- **3 cups red raspberries, fresh or frozen unsweetened**

Combine sugar and 2 cups water. Boil until syrup spins a thread. Stir in apples and boil 2 minutes. Add raspberries and boil 20 minutes, stirring frequently. Seal in sterilized jars with lids or melted paraffin. *About 5 pints*

## PEACH-PINEAPPLE JAM

**BBB + Fruit**

- **12 large peaches, peeled and mashed**
- **Juice and grated peel of 1 orange**
- **1 cup unsweetened crushed pineapple**
- **9 cups sugar**

Mix all ingredients and cook rapidly 30 minutes or until desired consistency. Seal in sterilized jars with lids or melted paraffin. *About 4 pints*

## PEACH HONEY

**BBB + Fruit**

- **12 large peaches, peeled**
- **1 large orange**
- **Sugar**

Chop peaches and orange, including peel, in food processor or grinder. Measure and add equal amount of sugar. Cook rapidly 20 minutes or until desired consistency. Seal in sterilized jars with lids or melted paraffin. *About 5 pints*

☐ **BBB + Fruit**

- 4 **large tangerines**
- 1 **large grapefruit**
- ½ **cup lemon juice**
- **Sugar**

## TANGERINE-GRAPEFRUIT MARMALADE

Wash fruit and trim thin slice from each end. Cut into halves, then slice as thin as possible. Remove any seeds and measure fruit. Add 4 times as much water as fruit and bring to full boil. Continue boiling until reduced by half, about 1 hour. Measure cooked fruit and divide in half. Place each half in separate kettle. To each add 1 cup sugar and ¼ cup lemon juice for each cup fruit. Boil hard, stirring frequently, until juice sheets from spoon or reaches your jell temperature on thermometer. Remove from heat and skim. Seal in sterilized jars with lids or melted paraffin. *About 3 pints*

☐ **BBB + Fruit**

- 6 **medium persimmons, very ripe**
- 4 **cups sugar**
- ½ **cup lemon juice**

## PERSIMMON JAM

Wash persimmons and remove calyx. Cut into small pieces and measure. If less than 4 cups, add only as much sugar as fruit and boil gently with lemon juice and 1 cup water until desired consistency. Seal in sterilized jars with lids or melted paraffin. *About 2 pints*

☐ **BBB + Fruit + Veg.**

- 4 **cups apple juice**
- 3 **cups sugar**
- **Juice of 1 lemon**
- 3 **tablespoon white distilled vinegar**
- 2 **sweet red peppers, sliced thin**
- 1 **clove garlic, mashed**

## RED PEPPER JELLY

Combine apple juice, sugar, lemon juice, and vinegar in large kettle. Add red peppers and garlic and bring to boil. Boil until mixture spins a thread. Remove from heat and skim. Seal in sterilized jars with lids or with melted paraffin. *About 2 pints*

☐ **BBB + Fruit + Veg.**

- 2 **pounds zucchini, peeled, seeded, and cubed**
- 2 **cups sugar**
- 2 **oranges, quartered and sliced fine**
- **Juice of 1 lemon**

## ZUCCHINI MARMALADE

Mix zucchini with sugar and add oranges. Let stand overnight. Next day, add lemon juice and bring to boil. Remove from heat and set aside another 24 hours. Third day, boil again and continue cooking over low heat until desired consistency. Seal in sterilized jars with lids or with melted paraffin. *About 2½ pints*

## GOLDEN SUN MARMALADE

Combine fruit with lemon juice and honey in large kettle and bring to boil. Cook over medium heat, stirring frequently until fruit is clear and mixture thickens to desired consistency. Remove from heat, skim, and stir 7 minutes. Stir in walnuts. Seal in sterilized jars with lids or with melted paraffin. *About 3 pints*

**BBB + Fruit**
**+ Veg. + N&S** ☐

3  cups peeled and cubed cantaloupe
2  cups peeled and cubed fresh peaches
¼  cup lemon juice
3  cups mild honey
1  cup chopped walnuts

## APPLE BUTTER

Wash, core, and cut apples in chunks. Purée in food processor or in blender by using ⅓ cup apple juice to 1 cup chunked apples. Continue until all apples are puréed. If preferred, peel apples and cook in juice until soft. Continue by adding sugar and spices and heating, stirring constantly. As butter starts to boil, lower heat and simmer, uncovered, stirring frequently. When thick, in about 45 minutes, seal in sterilized jars with lids or melted paraffin. *About 3 pints*

**BBB + TE&A** ☐

4  pounds apples
1  cup apple juice
2  cups sugar
2  teaspoons cinnamon
1  teaspoon nutmeg
½  teaspoon ground cloves

**Variation:**

Plums may be substituted for apples. Liquid may be either apple juice or water.

## OUR LAZY APPLE BUTTER

Mix and place in baking pan. Bake in 275° to 300° oven 2 to 3 hours or until desired consistency. Stir occasionally while baking. Seal in sterilized jars with lids or with melted paraffin. *About 1½ pints*

**BBB + TE&A** ☐

4  cups applesauce
1  can (6 ounces) frozen unsweetened apple juice concentrate
1  teaspoon cinnamon
½  teaspoon ground cloves

## PLUM JELLY

Wash plums, add 1 cup water, and cook until soft. Strain through jelly bag. Measure 4 cups juice into kettle, add sugar, and bring to boil, stirring constantly. Stir in pectin and return to boil 1 minute, still stirring. Remove from heat and skim. Seal in sterilized glasses or jars with lids or melted paraffin. *About 4 pints*

**BBB + Fruit**
**+ TE&A** ☐

4   pounds red plums
6½  cups sugar
1   pouch (3 ounces) or ½ bottle liquid fruit pectin

**BBB + TE&A**

- 4 pounds peaches
- 2 cups sugar, approximately
- ¼ teaspoon ground cloves
- ½ teaspoon ginger

## GINGER-PEACH BUTTER

Scald, peel, and chunk peaches. Cook with 1 cup water over low heat until soft. Measure. Add half as much sugar as fruit pulp, about 2 cups. Add spices and cook over low heat, stirring frequently. When as thick as desired, pour into sterilized jars and seal with lids or melted paraffin. *About 2½ pints*

**Variation: Peach or Pear Butter**

Prepare and cook in 1 cup water either unpeeled peaches or pears. Purée in blender or food processor. Replace sugar with 1 cup honey. Add ½ cup lemon or orange juice and season with ½ teaspoon cinnamon, ¼ teaspoon nutmeg, and ¼ teaspoon ginger. Continue as above. **(+ Fruit)**

**BBB + Fruit & TE&A**

- 2 cups blueberries, fresh or unsweetened frozen
- 4 cups red raspberries, fresh or unsweetened frozen
- 5 cups sugar
- 1 pouch (3 ounces) or ½ bottle liquid fruit pectin

## BLUEBERRY-RASPBERRY JAM

Crush berries and measure. If crushed fruit measures less, add water to make 4 cups. Add sugar and mix well. Bring to boil and boil hard 1 minute, stirring constantly. Remove from heat, stir in pectin, and stir and skim. Seal in sterilized jars with lids or melted paraffin. *About 5 pints*

**BBB + Fruit + TE&A**

- 6 medium lemons
- ⅛ teaspoon baking soda
- 6 cups sugar
- 1 pouch (3 ounces) or ½ bottle liquid fruit pectin

## CLAIR'S LEMON MARMALADE

Wash lemons and barely cut through skin lengthwise in order to remove peel in quarters. Lay quarters flat and shave off and discard about half of white layer. Slice remaining yellow peels into as-thin-as-possible strips. Add baking soda to 1½ cups water and drop in sliced peels. Bring to boil, reduce heat, and simmer, covered, 10 minutes, stirring gently occasionally. Drain well.

Remove outside membrane from peeled lemons and slip pulp from each section. Add lemon pulp and juice and 1 cup sugar to drained peel. Stir gently, bring to boil, and cook 20 minutes. Measure and, if necessary, add water or lemon juice to make 3½ cups.

Mix cooked fruit and remaining 5 cups sugar in large kettle. Bring to boil while stirring and boil hard 1 minute. Remove from heat and stir in pectin. Stir and skim 5 minutes. Seal in sterilized glasses or jars with lids or with melted paraffin. *About 3 pints*

## MARMALADE ELEGANCE

**BBB + Fruit + Mold**

- **1 cup dried apricots**
- **1 cup pitted dates**
- **1 tablespoon lemon juice**
- **¾ cup unsweetened pineapple juice or water**

Wash fruit, add liquids and soak overnight, refrigerated. Next morning liquefy in blender. Store in refrigerator. *About 1½ pints.*

## APPLE-DATE SPREAD

**BBB + Fruit + Mold**

- **2 cups finely chopped apples**
- **2 cups chopped pitted dates**
- **¼ cup unsweetened pineapple juice or water**
- **1 can (20 ounces) unsweetened crushed pineapple**

Combine all ingredients and boil gently until soft and of desired consistency. Add additional liquid during cooking, if necessary. Store in refrigerator. *About 3 pints*

## RUBY JELLY

**BBB + Corn + Fruit**

- **4 cups loganberries**
- **6 cups red raspberries**
- **5½ cups sugar**
- **1 box (1¾ ounces) powdered fruit pectin**

Crush berries and squeeze juice through jelly bag. Measure 4 cups juice into kettle. Stir in pectin and bring to boil. Add sugar and return to full boil, stirring constantly. Boil 2 minutes. Remove from heat and skim. Seal in sterilized glasses or jars with lids or melted paraffin. *About 3½ pints*

## GOLD MEDAL MARMALADE

**BBB + Corn + Fruit**

- **6 medium oranges**
- **½ cup lemon juice**
- **1 box (1¾ ounces) powdered fruit pectin**
- **9½ cups sugar**

Cut oranges in cartwheels with very sharp knife, making slices as thin as possible and discarding end pieces. Weigh. Sliced fruit should weigh 2 pounds. Mix orange slices, lemon juice, and 6 cups water in large kettle and bring to boil. Simmer, uncovered, 1 hour. Measure and, if necessary, add water to bring to 7 cups. Add pectin and heat again to boil. Add sugar and stir gently over medium heat until mixture comes to full boil. Boil exactly 4 minutes. Remove from heat. Skim and stir 5 minutes. Seal in glasses or jars with lids or with melted paraffin. *About 4 pints*

**BBB + Corn + Fruit**

- 4 pounds fresh apricots, pitted
- 3 pints fresh red raspberries
- 1 cup sugar
- 2 cups white corn syrup

## RASPBERRY-APRICOT JAM

Layer in shallow baking pan, fruit, sugar, and syrup until all used. Bake in 350° oven 2 hours. Reduce heat to 325° and continue cooking 2 hours. Stir twice during baking. Test for desired consistency and seal in sterilized glasses with melted paraffin. *About 3 pints*

**BBB + Corn + TE&A**

- 8 pounds tart apples, washed, cut in quarters, and cored
- 2 cups apple juice
- 1 cup sugar
- 1 cup dark corn syrup
- 2 teaspoons cinnamon
- ½ teaspoon ground cloves

## APPLE BUTTER

Cook apples and apple juice over low heat, stirring occasionally, until apples are soft, about 1 hour. Turn mixture through food mill or press through colander and discard skins, or purée skins and all in blender. Measure 3½ quarts pulp into large kettle. Stir in sugar, corn syrup, and spices. Cook over low heat, stirring occasionally, 3 to 5 hours or until very thick. To reduce splatters, partially cover kettle last hour of cooking time. Seal in sterilized jars with lids or melted paraffin. *About 6 pints*

**BBB + Corn + TE&A**

- 1 box (1¾ ounces) powdered fruit pectin
- 4 cups apple juice
- 4½ cups sugar
- 2 tablespoons red cinnamon candies

## CINNAPPLE JELLY

Add pectin to juice in large kettle. Bring to full boil. Add sugar and candies, stirring constantly, and return to boil. Boil 2 minutes. Remove from heat. Stir and skim 5 minutes. Seal in sterilized jars with lids or melted paraffin. *About 3½ pints*

**BBB + Corn + Fruit + N&S + TE&A**

- 2 large oranges, unpeeled
- 3 pounds peaches (12 medium)
- 6 cups sugar
- 1 bottle (8 ounces) maraschino cherries
- 1 cup walnuts or pecans, chopped

## PEACHY TART MARMALADE

Grind oranges in food processor or grinder. Peel and slice peaches. Mix fruits in 6 to 8-quart kettle, add sugar, and let stand in cool place 30 to 60 minutes. Bring to boil over medium heat, lower heat, and simmer until fruit and liquid are clear and thick, approximately 2 hours. Stir frequently.

Cut cherries in half and add, with their juice, to marmalade. Stir in nuts and simmer 5 minutes. Seal in sterilized jars with lids or melted paraffin. *About 5 pints*

# Cereals

## Cereals available in markets — BBB

- White rice
- Brown rice
- Puffed rice
- Arrowhead Rice Flakes
- Cream of Rice
  (extra vitamins added)
- Erewhon Brown Rice Cream
- Ener-G Rice Bran
- Fearn Soya Granules
- Wild rice
- Arrowhead Soy Flakes
- Minute Rice
  (extra vitamins added)
- Manna Rice Cream

These are available at regular grocery or specialty health food stores. Follow directions on packages or in recipes for preparation.

## BOILED BROWN RICE — BBB

**1 cup raw brown rice, rinsed and drained**
**½ teaspoon salt**

Place rice, salt, and 2½ cups water in 2-quart saucepan. Bring to boil, cover tightly, and reduce heat. Cook over low heat 40 to 50 minutes or until liquid is absorbed. *Makes 4 cups*

**Variation:**

Place raw rice and 2 tablespoons safflower oil in heavy skillet. Stir over medium heat until rice is lightly toasted. Proceed as for boiled Brown Rice, cooking 40 minutes.

## BAKED BROWN RICE

**BBB**

- **1 cup raw brown rice, rinsed and drained**
- **½ teaspoon salt**
- **2 tablespoons safflower oil**

Place rice, salt, allowed oil, and 2½ cups water in top-of-stove 1½-quart casserole. Bring to boil on direct heat, cover, and place in 250° oven. Bake 40 minutes. *Makes 4 cups*

## STEAMED WHITE RICE

**BBB**

- **½ teaspoon salt**
- **1 tablespoon oil**
- **1 cup rice**

Bring 2 cups water, salt, and oil to boil. Add rice, cover, and reduce heat. Simmer 25 minutes without lifting cover. *Makes 3 cups*

## CRACKED RICE

**BBB**

- **1 cup brown rice**
- **BBB Brown Sugar Syrup, p. 205**

Grind rice in electric blender until kernels are half original size. Combine rice with 4 cups water and bring to boil. Simmer, covered, 10 to 15 minutes or until rice is cooked through. Serve with homemade syrup. *Serves 4*

## RICE GRUEL

**BBB**

- **1 teaspoon salt**
- **1¾ cups brown rice**

Bring 2 quarts water and salt to full boil in 3-quart kettle. Stir in rice. Do not stir again. Cover and let simmer 45 to 60 minutes. Turn off heat and let steam until ready to serve. *Serves 8*

**Variation:**

Liquefy rice in blender, adding water, lamb broth, and unsweetened pineapple or apple juice to dilute to consistency of thick cream. Add small amount of sugar or salt to taste. Serve hot in mugs as hearty breakfast drink.

## RICE BRAN HOT CEREAL

**BBB**

- **1 cup Ener-G Rice Bran**
- **1 cup boiling water**
- **½ teaspoon salt**

Slowly sprinkle rice bran into rapidly boiling salted water. Stir constantly while cereal thickens. *Serves 2*

**Variation:**

Serve ¼ cup rice bran with milk substitute or fruit juice as cold cereal or add rice bran when serving cooked cereal.

## SAUTÉED RICE FLAKES

**BBB**

- **1 cup Arrowhead Rice Flakes**
- **1 teaspoon allowed oil**
- **2 cups hot water**
- **½ teaspoon salt**

Sauté flakes in oil, stirring constantly until golden brown. Add water and salt and simmer, covered, 15 minutes. Serve with raw or brown sugar, if desired, and allowed milk substitute or allowed fruits. *Serves 4*

## TOASTED RICE FLAKES

**BBB**

- **1 cup Arrowhead Rice Flakes**
- **1½ tablespoons allowed oil**
- **¼ teaspoon salt (optional)**

*Skillet method:* Pour flakes and oil in skillet and stir until all flakes are coated. Stir constantly over medium heat until flakes are golden brown. Remove from heat and add salt, if desired. Pour onto double thickness paper toweling to cool. Store in jar with tight lid to keep crisp. May be used as cereal with fruit or allowed milk substitute, as snack or as crunchy topping for salad.

*Oven method:* Blend flakes and oil until flakes are well coated. Pour into 9 x 9-inch baking pan. Place in 350° oven 15 minutes, stirring twice during baking. Salt and cool on paper towels to absorb excess oil. *Makes 1 cup*

## BRAVISSIMO GRANOLA

**BBB**

- **2 cups Arrowhead Rice Flakes**
- **2 cups puffed rice cereal**
- **½ cup brown sugar, firmly packed**
- **½ cup allowed oil**
- **Salt to taste**
- **1 teaspoon synthetic vanilla**

Place rice flakes and puffs in bowl large enough for easy stirring. Blend brown sugar, allowed oil, salt, and vanilla. Pour over rice mixture. Toss until all flakes and puffs are coated. Pour into 9 x 9-inch baking pan. Bake in 275° oven 30 to 40 minutes or until crisp and golden. Stir several times during baking. Cool and store in airtight container. Serve over allowed fruits for breakfast or eat as cereal with allowed milk substitute. Good also for just plain snacking. *Makes 4 cups*

## SUPER CRUNCH GRANOLA

**BBB**

- **2 cups Arrowhead Rice Flakes**
- **3 tablespoons brown sugar, firmly packed**
- **¼ cup allowed oil**
- **1 teaspoon synthetic vanilla**
- **Salt to taste**

Place rice flakes in 9 x 9-inch shallow pan. In small saucepan combine brown sugar and 1 tablespoon water. Heat, stirring, until sugar is dissolved. Stir in oil and vanilla. Pour mixture over rice flakes. Toss in baking pan until flakes are evenly coated. Bake in 375° oven 45 minutes, stirring several times during baking. Remove from oven and cool completely. Store in airtight container. Serve over allowed fruits for breakfast or eat as cereal with allowed milk substitute. Good also for snacks. *Makes 2 cups*

## SOY GRITS CEREAL

**BBB**

- **½ teaspoon salt**
- **¾ cup soy grits**

Bring 3 cups water and salt to boil. Slowly stir in soy grits, reduce heat, cover, and simmer 20 minutes. Turn off heat and let steam another 5 to 10 minutes. Sweeten with brown sugar or allowed fruits. Serve with allowed milk substitute. *Serves 4–6*

## SOY GRANOLA

**BBB**

- **2 cups Arrowhead Soy Flakes**
- **½ cup soy grits**
- **½ cup brown sugar, firmly packed**
- **2 tablespoons allowed oil**
- **1 teaspoon synthetic vanilla**

Blend all ingredients well and place in 9 x 9-inch shallow baking pan. Bake in 275° oven 30 to 40 minutes, stirring several times during baking. Guard against burning. Remove from oven and cool. Store in airtight container. This has nutlike flavor and is good on canned allowed fruits or may be eaten as breakfast cereal with allowed milk substitute. *Makes 2 cups*

## STEAMING TAPIOCA MUSH

**BBB**

- **⅓ cup Minute Tapioca**
- **1½ cups allowed milk substitute**
- **1 tablespoon allowed margarine**
- **¼ teaspoon salt**

Combine all ingredients in saucepan. Let stand 5 minutes. Cook over medium heat, stirring occasionally until mixture comes to boil. Remove and serve with brown sugar and allowed milk substitute. *Serves 2–3*

## TOASTED SOY FLAKES

**BBB**

- 1 cup Arrowhead Soy Flakes
- 1 tablespoon allowed oil
- Salt (optional)

Prepare the same as Toasted Rice Flakes, p. 247. These have a nutlike flavor. *Makes 1 cup*

## GLUTEN-FREE RICE GRANOLA

**BBB + N&S + TE&A**

- 3 cups Arrowhead Rice Flakes
- 3 cups puffed rice
- 1 cup shredded coconut
- 1 cup sesame seeds
- 1 cup sunflower seeds
- 1 cup chopped almonds or cashews, roasted or raw
- ¼ cup rice bran
- ½ cup turbinado or raw sugar
- ¾ cup allowed oil
- ¼ cup honey
- 1 teaspoon synthetic vanilla

Mix first 8 ingredients in large bowl. Heat oil and honey to thin honey but don't boil. Stir in vanilla. Pour over dry ingredients and toss until all dry ingredients are coated. Pour into two 9 x 13-inch baking pans. Bake in 275° oven 1 hour, stirring every 15 minutes. Cool. Store in airtight container. You may cut recipe in half and store in jar with tight lid. *Makes 10–12 cups*

## SPICY TOASTED CREAM OF RICE

**BBB + TE&A**

- ½ cup Cream of Rice
- 1¾ cups boiling water
- ¼ teaspoon salt
- ¼ teaspoon honey
- 1/16 teaspoon cinnamon
- Dash of nutmeg

Using heavy pan, lightly brown Cream of Rice over medium heat while stirring. Slowly stir in boiling water and salt. Continue stirring and cook 1 minute. Blend in honey and cinnamon. Remove from heat, cover, and let stand 4 minutes. Spoon into serving bowls and sprinkle with nutmeg. Serve with allowed fruits or allowed milk substitute. *Serves 2*

## Cereals available in markets

**BBB + Rye**

Arrowhead Rye Flakes
Stone Buhr Old Fashioned Rye Flake Cereal (no preservatives)
Cream of Rye (100% rye)
These are available at regular grocery or specialty health food stores. Follow directions on packages or in recipes for preparation.

**BBB + Rye**

- 1 cup rye flakes
- 2 cups boiling water

## RYE FLAKE CEREAL

Stir flakes into rapidly boiling water. Reduce heat. Cook, stirring occasionally, 15 to 18 minutes. *Serves 2-4*

**BBB + Rye**

- ¾ cup Arrowhead Rye Flakes
- ¼ cup Arrowhead Soy Flakes or soy grits
- ⅓ cup Arrowhead Rice Flakes
- ¼ teaspoon salt
- 4 cups boiling water

## COUNTRY COMBO

Add flakes to boiling salted water. Cover, lower heat, and simmer 30 minutes, stirring occasionally.

*Double boiler method:* Combine flakes and water as above but in top of double boiler. Place over water and steam, covered, 45 minutes, stirring occasionally. Prepare in the evening, set aside, and reheat next morning. *Serves 4*

**BBB + Rye**

- 1 cup whole grain rye
- Dash of salt
- 4 cups boiling water

## RYE CEREAL

Stir rye into salted boiling water, cover, and simmer 1 hour. *Serves 4*

**BBB + Rye**

- ½ cup ground whole-grain rye
- ½ cup ground brown rice
- 2 tablespoons allowed oil
- Pinch of salt
- 3 cups boiling water

## CRACKED RICE AND RYE CEREAL

Brown ground rye and rice in oil in heavy skillet. Stir in boiling salted water. Cover, lower heat, and simmer 1 hour, stirring occasionally. Serve with brown sugar or allowed fruits. *Serves 4*

## Cereals available in markets

**BBB + Oats**

Mother's Oat Bran
Arrowhead Oat Flakes
Rolled oats, old-fashioned
Quick oats
Oat groats
Elam's Steel Cut 100% Oatmeal
Scotch style oatmeal (stone ground)
Stone Buhr Old Fashioned Oat Flake Cereal (no preservatives)

These are available at regular grocery or specialty health food stores. Follow directions on packages or in recipes for preparation.

## OAT CRUNCH CEREAL

**BBB + Oats**

- **6 cups old-fashioned rolled oats**
- **½ cup brown sugar or raw sugar**
- **¼ cup allowed oil**

Mix rolled oats and sugar in large bowl. Combine oil and ½ cup water, pour over oats, and mix thoroughly. Place in oiled 9 x 13-inch pan and bake at 275° 1 hour, stirring every 15 minutes. Turn off heat and allow cereal to remain in cooling oven. *Makes 6 cups*

## ROLLED OATS TERRY

**BBB + Oats**

- **1 cup boiling water**
- **Salt to taste**
- **1 cup old-fashioned rolled oats**

Boil salted water in 2-quart kettle with tight-fitting lid. Stir in oats with a fork and don't stir again. Cook at high heat until water appears to be completely boiled off and oats in danger of scorching. Cover and hold lid down for 1 minute with heat still high. Set aside, still covered, 2 to 5 minutes. Pressure allows oats to cook quickly and fluffs individual flakes. *Serves 2*

## OAT GROATS

**BBB + Oats**

- **2 cups boiling water**
- **½ cup oat groats**
- **½ teaspoon salt**
- **1 teaspoon allowed oil or allowed margarine**

Pour boiling water over groats to soak overnight. Next morning add salt and oil and bring to boil. Cover, lower heat, and simmer without stirring until water is absorbed, about 45 minutes. *Serves 4*

**BBB + Oats**

## TOASTED OATS

- 2 **cups old-fashioned rolled oats**
- 1½ **tablespoons allowed oil**
- **Salt, optional**

Sauté oats in oil, stirring constantly until golden brown. Use as cereal or crunchy topping for salad. *Makes 2 cups*

*Oven method:* Bake 15 minutes in 350° oven, stirring occasionally.

**BBB + Oats**

## BREAKFAST OATMEAL

- 1½ **cups oats (quick, old-fashioned, rolled, steel-cut, or oat groats)**
- ½ **teaspoon salt**
- 3 **cups boiling water**

Add oats to boiling salted water, stir, cover, and reduce heat.

*For quick oats,* cook 1 minute. Remove from heat and let stand 3 to 5 minutes.

*For old-fashioned oats,* cook 5 minutes. Remove from heat and let stand 5 minutes.

*For steel-cut oats,* cook 15 minutes.

*For oat groats,* simmer 1 hour. *Serves 3-4*

**BBB + Oats + N&S**

## NUTTY OATMEAL

- ⅔ **cup quick oats**
- 1½ **cups boiling water**
- ½ **cup chunk-style almond, cashew or peanut butter**

Slowly stir oats into boiling water. Cook 1 minute, stirring. Remove from heat and blend in nut butter of your choice. Cover and let stand 5 minutes. Serve with sugar and allowed milk substitute as desired. *Serves 2*

**BBB + Oats + N&S + TE&A**

## Cereals available in markets

Nature Valley Granola Bars—Oats n' Honey (rolled oats, brown sugar, coconut oil, honey, salt, sesame seeds, soy lecithin, no preservatives)

Nature Valley Granola Bars—Cinnamon (oats, brown sugar, honey, salt, cinnamon, sesame seeds, soy lecithin, no preservatives)

Nature Valley Granola Bars—Coconut (rolled oats, brown sugar, coconut oil, honey, salt, sesame seeds, soy lecithin, natural flavor, no preservatives)

Nature Valley Granola Bars—Peanut (oats, brown sugar, peanuts, coconut oil, salt, sesame seeds, soy lecithin, natural flavorings, no preservatives)

Nature Valley Granola—Oat Mixture (rolled oats, brown sugar, peanut oil, honey, sesame seeds, salt, soy lecithin)

Instant Quaker Oatmeal (rolled oats, sugar, natural and artificial flavors, salt, calcium, guar gums, vitamins, caramel color)

Instant Quaker Oatmeal—Maple and Brown Sugar (oats, salt, calcium, guar gum, caramel flavor, vitamins, folic acid)

*Note:* Markets of various kinds offer many granolas, but be sure to read ingredients list to see whether all are on your tested and allowed foods.

## OUR FAVORITE GRANOLA

**BBB + Oats + N&S + TE&A**

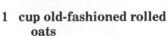

- **1 cup chopped almonds or cashews**
- **5 cups old-fashioned rolled oats**
- **1 cup hulled sunflower seeds**
- **1 cup sesame seeds**
- **1 cup flaked coconut**
- **¾ cup raw turbinado or yellow D sugar**
- **¾ cup allowed oil**
- **½ cup honey**
- **1 teaspoon synthetic vanilla**

Mix all dry ingredients in large bowl. Heat oil and honey together to thin honey. Add vanilla and pour over dry ingredients. Toss well until coated. Pour into two 9 x 13-inch pans and bake at 275° to 300° 1 hour, stirring every 15 minutes. Stir occasionally while cooling also to keep broken apart. Store in airtight containers. *Makes 8 cups*

## GRANOLA MEDLEY

**BBB + Oats + N&S + TE&A**

- **1 cup old-fashioned rolled oats**
- **1 cup Arrowhead Rye Flakes**
- **1 cup Arrowhead Rice Flakes**
- **¾ cup squash seeds**
- **¾ cup pumpkin seeds**
- **½ cup sunflower seeds**
- **⅓ cup rice bran**
- **½ cup sesame seeds**
- **½ cup chopped walnuts**
- **½ cup chopped cashews**
- **½ cup shredded coconut**
- **1 teaspoon ground allspice**
- **⅔ cup honey**
- **⅓ cup allowed oil**
- **1 teaspoon synthetic vanilla**

*Oven method:* Mix dry ingredients. Heat honey with oil to thin honey. Add vanilla. Combine wet and dry ingredients and blend well. Spread in two 9 x 13-inch pans. Bake in 325° oven 30 to 40 minutes, stirring often for even baking.

*Skillet method:* Combine all ingredients in heavy skillet. If skillet is too small for easy stirring, divide recipe. Cook over medium heat, stirring constantly to cook evenly and prevent burning. Cook 10 minutes. *Makes 6 cups*

## FOUR SEED GRANOLA

**BBB + Oats + Fruit + N&S + TE&A**

- **6 cups quick oatmeal**
- **1 cup sesame seeds**
- **1 cup sunflower seeds**
- **1 cup flax seeds**
- **1 cup shredded coconut**
- **1 cup brown sugar, packed**
- **1 cup chopped almonds**
- **1½ teaspoons salt**
- **1½ teaspoons grated orange peel**
- **1 cup allowed oil**

Combine all ingredients in large bowl. Stir to coat all flakes and seeds with oil. Bake in two 9 x 13-inch pans at 275° 1 hour, stirring every 15 minutes. Cool and store in airtight container. *Makes 8 cups*

**BBB**
**+ Oats**
**+ Fruit**
**+ N&S**
**+ TE&A**
**+ Mold**

## Cereals available in markets

Instant Quaker Oatmeal—Apples and Cinnamon (rolled oats, sugar, cottonseed and soy oils, salt, gums, dried apples, cinnamon, vitamins)
Instant Quaker Oatmeal—Raisins and Spice (rolled oats, sugar, cottonseed and soy oils, salt, gums, spices, vitamins)
Nature Valley Granola—Fruit, Dates, Nuts (rolled oats, brown sugar; coconut, peanut or palm oils; honey, sesame seeds, dates, cashews, crushed oranges, applesauce, cinnamon)
Nature Valley Granola—Cinnamon and Raisins (rolled oats, brown sugar; coconut, peanut or palm oils; raisins, honey, sesame seeds, salt, cinnamon, soy lecithin)

## BBB + Barley

Arrowhead Barley Flakes
Whole grain barley
Quaker Scotch Brand Pearled Barley
Quaker Scotch Brand Quick Pearled Barley
These are available at regular grocery or specialty health food stores. Follow directions on packages or in recipes for preparation.

**BBB + Barley**

**1 cup Arrowhead Barley Flakes**
**2 cups boiling water**
**½ teaspoon salt**

## BARLEY FLAKE CEREAL

Add flakes to boiling salted water and stir. Cover. Reduce heat and cook 5 minutes. *Serves 2*

**BBB + Barley**

**1 cup quick pearled barley**
**3 cups boiling water**
**½ teaspoon salt**

## QUICK BARLEY CEREAL

Stir barley into boiling salted water and reduce heat. Cover and cook 10 to 12 minutes, stirring occasionally. Drain, if you like thicker cereal. *Serves 4*

**BBB + Barley**

**1 cup whole grain barley**
**2 cups boiling water**
**½ teaspoon salt**

## WHOLE GRAIN BARLEY CEREAL

Stir barley into boiling salted water. Cover, reduce heat and simmer about 90 minutes, stirring frequently. *Serves 4*

## BABY'S BARLEY CEREAL

**BBB + Barley**

- **¼ cup allowed oil or margarine**
- **¼ cup barley flour**
- **Salt to taste**

Cook oil and flour until mixture bubbles. Add 1½ cups water slowly, stirring constantly until thickened. Bring to boil 1 minute and add salt. Serve with allowed fruits or allowed milk substitute. *Makes 1½ cups*

## BARLEY GRANOLA

**BBB + Barley + N&S + TE&A**

- **4 cups Arrowhead Barley Flakes**
- **½ cup flaked coconut**
- **½ cup chopped almonds or cashews**
- **½ cup sunflower seeds**
- **½ cup sesame seeds**
- **⅓ cup turbinado or raw sugar**
- **⅓ cup allowed oil**
- **¼ cup honey**
- **1 teaspoon synthetic vanilla**
- **Salt to taste**

Mix in large bowl flakes, coconut, nuts, seeds, salt and sugar. Heat oil and honey to thin honey. Remove from heat and add salt and vanilla. Pour slowly over dry ingredients, stirring to coat all grains and seeds. Place in 9 x 13-inch shallow pan and bake at 275° 1 hour. Stir every 15 minutes during baking. Cool and break up. Store in airtight container. *Makes 6 cups*

### Cereals available in markets

**BBB + Barley + TE&A + Mold**

Gerber Rice Cereal for Infants (rice flour, rice polish, tri and di calcium phosphate, barley malt flavoring, soy lecithin, vitamins)
Rice Krispies (rice, sugar, salt, malt, vitamins, preservatives)
Rice Chex (rice, malted cereal syrup, vitamins, preservatives)
Kellogg's Nutri-Grain Barley–Flaked Whole Grain Cereal (whole barley kernels, malt flavoring, salt)

**BBB + Rye + Barley + TE&A + Mold**

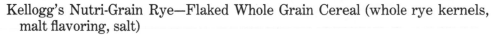

Kellogg's Nutri-Grain Rye—Flaked Whole Grain Cereal (whole rye kernels, malt flavoring, salt)

**BBB + Corn**

Corn grits (pure)
Puffed corn
Golden hominy (canned)
White hominy (canned)
Erewhon Stirabout (white corn and brown rice)
100% yellow corn meal
100% white corn meal
Enriched yellow or white cornmeal (contains extra vitamins)
Enriched white hominy grits—regular or instant (extra vitamins)

## CORNMEAL MUSH

**BBB + Corn**

- **1 cup cornmeal, white or yellow**
- **½ teaspoon salt**

Blend cornmeal with 1 cup water to smooth paste. Heat 2 cups salted water to boiling. Add paste slowly, stirring constantly. Over low heat, continue stirring 5 minutes.

*Double Boiler Method:* Add paste slowly to boiling water in top of double boiler, stirring constantly. Cover, lower heat, and cook until all liquid is absorbed, 45 to 60 minutes. *Serves 4*

**Variation:**

Place cooked mush in small square or rectangular pan. Refrigerate covered. Slice ½ inch thick, coat with potato or rice flour, and fry in allowed oil until crispy and brown. Serve with brown sugar, any allowed syrup, or honey. **(+ TE&A)**

## OLD FASHIONED CORN GRITS

**BBB + Corn**

- **¾ cup corn grits**
- **3 cups boiling water**
- **½ teaspoon salt**

Slowly stir grits into salted boiling water. Cook over direct heat 5 minutes, stirring occasionally. Serve hot with allowed milk substitute. Sweeten, if desired, with brown sugar or add water-pack allowed fruits.

*Long Cook Method:* Add ¾ cup extra water. Stir in grits, return to boil as above, reduce heat, and cook slowly 25 to 30 minutes, stirring frequently. *Serves 4*

**Variation:**

Follow variation for Cornmeal Mush.

## GROUND POPCORN CEREAL

**BBB + Corn**

Pop corn dry or in allowed oil. Place small amount at a time in blender or food processor and grind a few seconds on low speed. Repeat until all popcorn is ground. Store in tightly closed plastic bag or jar. Serve with allowed milk substitute.

## SOY GRITS AND CORNMEAL

**BBB + Corn**

- **½ cup soy grits**
- **¼ cup cornmeal**
- **3 cups boiling water**
- **½ teaspoon salt**

Mix grits and cornmeal together and stir into boiling salted water. Cover, reduce heat, and cook 20 to 25 minutes. Remove from heat and let stand, covered, another 5 to 10 minutes. *Serves 4–5*

## Cereals available in markets

**BBB + Corn + TE&A**

Quaker Instant White Hominy Grits (degerminated white corn grits, salt, cellulose gum, vitamins, preservatives)

**BBB + Corn + N&S + TE&A + Mold**

Kellogg's Sugar Corn Pops (corn, sugar, corn syrup, molasses, vegetable oils—cottonseed, coconut, palm, and/or soybean—coloring, vitamins, preservatives)

**BBB + Oats + Corn + TE&A**

Quaker Corn Bran (corn flour, corn bran flour, sugar, oat flour, food coloring, preservatives)

## BBB + Oats + Corn + N&S + TE&A

Post Alpha Bits (corn flour, sugar, salt, hydrogenated coconut and/or palm kernel oil, corn syrup, honey, vitamins, coloring, preservatives)

Quaker Cap'n Crunch Cereal (oats, sugar, corn flour, brown sugar, coconut oil, salt, food coloring, preservatives)

Quaker Cap'n Crunch Peanut Butter Crunch Sweet Cereal (corn, rice, oat flours, peanut butter, sugar, coconut, cottonseed and palm oils, vitamins, food coloring, preservatives)

## BBB + Barley + Corn + TE&A

Ralston Corn Chex (yellow corn, sugar, salt, malted cereal syrup, leavening, vitamins, preservatives)

## BBB + Barley + Corn + TE&A + Mold

Kellogg's Corn Flakes (milled corn, sugar, salt, salt flavoring, vitamins, minerals, preservative)

Kellogg's Sugar Frosted Flakes of Corn (same as Corn Flakes but with added sugar)

Kellogg's Nutri-Grain—Corn Flaked Whole Grain Cereal (whole corn kernels, malt flavoring, salt, vitamins, antioxidant BHA)

Ralston Corn Chex (yellow corn, sugar, salt, malted cereal syrup, leavening, vitamins, preservatives)

**BBB + Barley + Corn + N&S + TE&A + Mold**

Kellogg's Honey and Nut Cereal (milled corn, brown sugar, peanuts, sugar, partially hydrogenated vegetable oils—cottonseed, coconut, soybean and/ or palm—honey, salt, malt flavoring, vitamins, preservatives)

**BBB + Rye + Barley + Corn + N&S + TE&A + Mold**

Kellogg's Raisins Rice and Rye Cereal (milled rice, rye, raisins, sugar, corn bran, glycerine, dextrose, corn syrup, salt, malt flavoring, partially hydrogenated vegetable oils—cottonseed, coconut, soybean, and/or palm—invert syrup, vitamins, preservative)

## EASY GRANOLA

**BBB + Oats + Barley + Corn + N&S + TE&A + Mold**

- ½ cup allowed oil
- ½ cup honey or maple syrup
- 1 teaspoon synthetic vanilla
- 2 cups old-fashioned rolled or quick oats
- 1 cup Rice Krispies
- 1 cup sunflower seeds
- ¾ cup sesame seeds
- 1 cup allowed chopped nuts
- ½ cup flaked coconut
- 1½ cups cornflakes

Heat oil, honey, and vanilla in large kettle to blend. Remove from heat, add remaining ingredients, and mix well. Spread in 9 x 13-inch baking pan. Bake at 350° 15 to 20 minutes or until golden. Cool and store in airtight container. *Makes 6–7 cups*

**BBB + Millet**

## Cereals available in markets

El Molino Puffed Millet
Whole grain millet
These are available at regular grocery or specialty health food stores.

*Note:* Millet is a good substitute for rice if it proves to be friendly. Use in casseroles, refried, in bread, or as a cereal. One cup millet in 2 cups water will cook in 30 to 50 minutes, the time depending on crunchiness desired. Easily digested, millet contains no gluten and is, therefore, excellent for celiac patients.

**BBB + Millet**

## MILLET CEREAL

- **¾ cup millet**
- **3 cups boiling water**
- **¼ teaspoon salt**
- **1 teaspoon allowed oil**

Stir millet into boiling salted water and add oil. Cover, reduce heat, and cook 45 minutes or until millet is tender. Serve with raw or brown sugar, allowed fruit juices, or allowed milk substitute. *Makes 3 cups*

*Double boiler method:* Place all ingredients in top of double boiler and, stirring constantly, boil 5 minutes. Assemble double boiler with ample water in bottom section and steam millet over low heat 45 to 60 minutes. *Makes 3 cups*

**Variations:**

1. Add chopped apple last 15 minutes of cooking.
2. Serve with allowed fruits and dash of cinnamon or nutmeg, when allowed. **(+ TE&A)**
3. Refrigerate, slice, coat with potato flour, and fry in allowed oil.

**BBB + Oats + Millet + N&S + TE&A**

## CRUNCHY GRANOLA

- **½ cup allowed oil**
- **½ cup honey**
- **½ cup hot water**
- **5 cups old-fashioned rolled oats**
- **½ cup millet**
- **½ cup sesame seeds**
- **½ cup sunflower seeds**
- **½ cup pumpkin seeds**
- **1½ cups chopped cashews**

Blend oil, honey and water in small pan. Place over heat briefly if necessary in order to thin honey. Pour over other ingredients well mixed in large bowl. Toss until coated evenly. Pour into two 9 x 13-inch pans. Bake 1 hour at 275°, stirring every 15 minutes. Store in airtight container. *Makes 6–7 cups*

## MIXED GRAIN CEREAL I

**BBB + Rye + Oats + Millet**

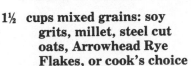

- **1½ cups mixed grains: soy grits, millet, steel cut oats, Arrowhead Rye Flakes, or cook's choice**
- **2 quarts boiling water**
- **1 teaspoon salt**

Stir grains into boiling salted water, cover, and simmer 1 hour or more, depending on tenderness desired. *Serves 8–12*

**Variation:**

Combine soy grits, steel cut oats, and millet. Cook 4 to 6 hours or overnight in 250° oven.

## BUCKWHEAT GROATS

**BBB + Buckwheat**

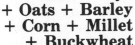

- **1 cup buckwheat groats**
- **1 tablespoon allowed oil**
- **2 cups boiling water**
- **½ teaspoon salt**

Sauté buckwheat groats in oil until well browned. Add boiling water and salt. Cover and simmer 25 to 30 minutes or until cooked through. *Makes 2–3 cups*

## MIXED GRAIN CEREAL II

**BBB + Rye + Oats + Barley + Corn + Millet + Buckwheat**

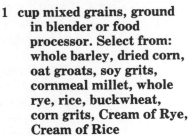

- **1 cup mixed grains, ground in blender or food processor. Select from: whole barley, dried corn, oat groats, soy grits, cornmeal millet, whole rye, rice, buckwheat, corn grits, Cream of Rye, Cream of Rice**
- **4 cups boiling water**
- **½ teaspoon salt**

Stir mixed grains into salted boiling water. Cover, reduce heat, and simmer 30 to 40 minutes. Remove from heat and let stand another 10 minutes. *Serves 4*

# Cakes, Frostings, and Cookies

## CAKES

Cake baking without the usual wheat flour, milk, and eggs has puzzled us for a long time. Actually, cakes are expendable, but there was that nagging challenge. So, we persisted. Bev, with no weight problem, served as guinea pig and final judge. Our successes are recorded here—failures are another story.

If your sweet tooth begs for cake now and then, do try some of these recipes, guided by these hints:

1. Dry ingredients are measured unsifted. Loosen flours with a fork, then measure.
2. Brown sugar is measured firmly packed, not a loose measure.
3. We like safflower oil and, since it is coded BBB, it can be used from the very beginning of food testing. We stay with it but other oils, as allowed, function in our recipes just as well.
4. Our favorite margarine is Hollywood Safflower Oil Margarine. However, Shedd's Willow Run Soybean Margarine and Hain Safflower Oil Margarine are milk-free and can be used at your BBB stage (See Fats and Oils, p. 369, in the Appendix.)
5. Baking powder used is cereal-free, double-acting baking powder, available in health food stores, but can be made in your kitchen. See Cereal-Free Baking Powder recipes, I, II, and III, on pp. 372–73.
6. Our experience and our energy conscientiousness keep us from preheating ovens except on those few occasions when doughs and batters require prima-donna treatment. Given eggs and gluten, we might never preheat an oven, but our particular cakes, breads, cookies, and such are sensitive to chilly weather. For these few goodies, we recommend preheating. Let the gas and electric companies put that in their pipes and smoke it!

## APPLE PUDDING-CAKE

**BBB**

Cream margarine, sugar, and vanilla. Add and blend dry ingredients. Add ¼ cup water and beat well. Add apples and beat again. Spoon into 4 small oiled custard cups. Bake in preheated 350° oven 30 minutes. *Serves 4*

**Variation:**

When allowed, add 2 tablespoons chopped nuts and ¼ teaspoon each cinnamon and nutmeg. **(+ N&S + TE&A)**

- **2 tablespoons allowed margarine**
- **¼ cup sugar**
- **½ teaspoon synthetic vanilla**
- **½ cup rice flour**
- **½ teaspoon baking soda**
- **½ teaspoon cereal-free baking powder**
- **1⅓ cups finely chopped peeled apples**

## APPLESAUCE CUPCAKES

**BBB**

Blend dry ingredients well. Add oil, applesauce, vanilla, and ¼ cup water. Beat smooth. With paper baking cups set in muffin tins, spoon in batter, filling to ½ inch from top. Bake 25 minutes in oven preheated to 350°. Frost with Vanilla Sugar Frosting, p. 271, or Creamy BBB Frosting, p. 271. *Makes 10*

**Variation:**

When allowed, add ¼ cup chopped nuts, ½ teaspoon cinnamon and ¼ teaspoon nutmeg. **(+ N&S + TE&A)**

- **⅔ cup rice flour**
- **¼ cup soy flour**
- **1½ teaspoons potato flour**
- **½ teaspoon baking soda**
- **2 teaspoons cereal-free baking powder**
- **½ cup sugar**
- **¼ cup allowed oil**
- **½ cup applesauce**
- **½ teaspoon synthetic vanilla**

## SUNTANNED BROWNIE CAKE-BARS

**BBB**

Cream margarine and sugars. Add and blend all dry ingredients. Beat water in for a thick smooth batter (adding more liquid if it seems far too thick). Spread into oiled 8-inch square pan. Bake in preheated 350° oven 30 to 35 minutes. Cut into 2-inch squares when slightly warm. *Makes 16*

**Variation: World's Greatest Suntanned Brownies**

Add ½ cup chopped nuts and ½ cup flaked coconut to batter and bake as directed. These are extra delicious. **(+ N&S)**

- **¼ cup allowed margarine**
- **¼ cup sugar**
- **¼ cup brown sugar, firmly packed**
- **¾ cup brown rice flour**
- **½ cup rice polish**
- **3 teaspoons cereal-free baking powder**
- **⅓ cup water or milk substitute**

## FRUIT UPSIDE-DOWN CAKE

**BBB**

**Fruit Base:**
- **2 tablespoons allowed margarine**
- **1 can (8 ounces) unsweetened pineapple rings, chunks or crushed, drained or unsweetened peaches, apricots or pears**
- **½ cup brown sugar, firmly packed**

**Cake Topping:**
- **⅔ cup white rice flour**
- **2 tablespoons soy flour**
- **1½ teaspoons potato flour**
- **¼ teaspoon salt**
- **2 tablespoons brown sugar, firmly packed**
- **2 teaspoons cereal-free baking powder**
- **1 tablespoon allowed oil**
- **⅔ cup water or juice drained from canned fruit**
- **½ teaspoon synthetic vanilla**

Melt margarine in 8-inch pie pan to coat. Arrange drained fruit in bottom, then sprinkle evenly with brown sugar.

Prepare topping by blending next 7 ingredients. Stir in oil, water, and vanilla. Drop spoons of batter over fruit base and spread evenly. Bake in preheated 350° oven 30 minutes or until toothpick inserted in center comes out clean. Place serving plate on top of dessert. Hold pie tin and plate firmly together and invert so that fruit is on top of cake in serving plate. Serve warm. *Serves 6–8*

**Variation:**

Walnut pieces may be added to base when allowed **(+ N&S)** and also ¼ teaspoon cinnamon. **(+ TE&A)**

## BREAKFAST COFFEECAKE

**BBB**

- **½ cup soy flour**
- **1½ cups rice flour**
- **4 teaspoons cereal-free baking powder**
- **½ teaspoon salt**
- **¼ cup brown sugar, firmly packed**
- **¼ cup allowed oil**
- **1¼ cups water or allowed milk substitute**
- **Choice of any jam or jelly with BBB code**
- **Powdered Sugar BBB Glaze, p. 271**

Blend dry ingredients, add oil and water and beat smooth. Pour into oiled 9-inch pie tin. Dot batter with small dabs of allowed jam. Bake in preheated 350° oven 25 to 30 minutes. Partially cool and then drizzle with glaze. Cut in wedges and serve warm. *Serves 8*

**Variation:**

Make crumb topping by combining 2 tablespoons allowed margarine, ¼ cup rice flour, 2½ tablespoons sugar, 2 tablespoons chopped nuts, and ¼ teaspoon cinnamon. Sprinkle on cake and bake as directed. **(+ N&S + TE&A)**

## RICE POLISH CUPCAKES

**BBB**

**¾ cup rice polish**
**1 cup rice flour**
**½ cup sugar**
**1 tablespoon cereal-free baking powder**
**½ teaspoon salt**
**¼ cup allowed oil**
**½ teaspoon synthetic vanilla**

Fluff rice polish with fork before measuring. Blend all dry ingredients. Add oil, vanilla, and 1 cup water and beat until smooth. Spoon into paper baking cups set in muffin tins. Fill to ½ inch of top. Bake in preheated 350° oven 25 to 30 minutes. Frost with Vanilla Sugar Frosting, p. 271. *Makes 12*

## VERSATILE CAKE

**BBB**

**1⅓ cups rice flour**
**⅓ cup soy flour**
**1 tablespoon potato flour**
**½ teaspoon salt**
**½ cup sugar**
**4 teaspoons cereal-free baking powder**
**¼ cup allowed oil**
**1 teaspoon synthetic vanilla**

Blend dry ingredients. Add oil, vanilla, and 1 cup water. Beat well. Pour into oiled 8 or 9-inch square or round pan and bake in preheated 350° oven 30 to 35 minutes or until toothpick inserted in center comes out clean. Frost with Vanilla Sugar Frosting, p. 271, or Creamy BBB Frosting, p. 271. *Serves 8-10*

**Variations:**

1. LAYER CAKE—Cut baked cake in half. Stack halves with frosting between layers and around sides. For round layer cake, double recipe and stack 2 rounds.
2. SLICED APPLE CAKE—Place cake batter in oiled pan. Peel 1 apple and slice thin. Slip a slice into batter at an angle with top of apple showing above batter. Repeat, lining up slices ½ inch apart over cake. Bake, cool, and drizzle on Powdered Sugar BBB Glaze, p. 271.
3. SLICED PEACH CAKE—Drain and dry canned water-pack cling peach slices. Slip peach slices into batter as for Apple Cake but place farther apart and at random. Glaze with Powdered Sugar BBB Glaze, p. 271.
4. PLAIN CARROT CAKE—Add 1½ cups finely grated carrots to batter.
5. CARROT-PINEAPPLE CAKE—Omit water. Open 1 can crushed unsweetened pineapple, measure, and add water, if needed, to make 1 cup. Add 1½ cups finely grated carrot and beat hard. If batter is too stiff, add 1 to 2 tablespoons water.
6. APRICOT CAKE—Omit water, purée 1 can (8 ounces) water-pack apricots. Measure and add water, if necessary, to make 1 cup. Use purée as liquid in recipe.

**BBB + Veg.**

## Cupcakes available in markets

Bray's Soya Cupcakes (sugar, soya flour, garbanzo flour, potato starch, water, cereal-free leavening, soya oil, salt)

**BBB + Fruit + N&S + TE&A**

## BANANA NUT CUPCAKES

**1 cup brown rice flour**
**½ cup rice polish**
**1 tablespoon cereal-free baking powder**
**¼ teaspoon salt**
**¼ teaspoon cinnamon**
**⅛ teaspoon nutmeg**
**Dash of ground cloves**
**¾ cup sugar**
**¼ cup allowed oil**
**1 cup mashed ripe banana**
**¼ cup chopped nuts**

Blend all dry ingredients well. Add banana, oil, and chopped nuts. Beat well and spoon equal amounts of batter into 9 or 10 paper baking cups set in muffin tins. Bake in preheated 350° oven 25 minutes. Good plain or frosted, if desired, with Vanilla Sugar Frosting, p. 271. *Makes 9–10*

**BBB + Veg. + TE&A**

## ZUCCHINI CAKE

**1⅓ cups rice flour**
**⅓ cup soy flour**
**1 tablespoon potato flour**
**½ teaspoon salt**
**½ cup sugar**
**4 teaspoons cereal-free baking powder**
**¼ cup allowed oil**
**1 teaspoon synthetic vanilla**
**1½ cups coarsely grated zucchini, loosely packed**
**1 teaspoon cinnamon**
**⅛ teaspoon nutmeg**
**Dash of ground cloves**

Mix first 6 ingredients well. Add oil, vanilla, and ¾ cup water. Beat until smooth. Stir in zucchini and spices and beat hard. Batter should be thicker than most cake batter because of moisture in zucchini. If allowed, fold in ¼ cup chopped nuts. **(+ N&S)** Place in 9-inch cake pan and level with back of spoon. Bake 30 to 40 minutes in oven preheated to 350° and continue cooking until toothpick inserted in center comes out clean. This is an excellent cake. No frosting needed. *Serves 8–10*

**Variations:**

1. SPICE CAKE—Omit zucchini and increase water to 1 cup. **(− Veg.)**
2. CAROB CHIP CUPCAKES—Omit zucchini and spices and increase water to 1 cup. Shave 1 (1 ounce) El Molino CaraCoa Carob Candy Bar—Milk-Free into tiny bits and stir into batter. Divide batter equally into 12 paper baking cups set in muffin tins. Bake in preheated 350° oven 25 to 30 minutes or until toothpick inserted in center of cupcake comes out clean. **(+ N&S)** *Makes 12*

## FEATHER LIGHT RYE CUPCAKES

**BBB + Rye**

- ⅓ cup allowed margarine
- ¾ cup sugar
- 1½ cups rye flour
- ¼ teaspoon salt
- 1½ tablespoons cereal-free baking powder
- ¾ cup water or allowed milk substitute
- 1 teaspoon synthetic vanilla

Cream margarine and sugar. Combine dry ingredients and add to creamed mixture alternately with liquids. Spoon into 10 or 12 paper baking cups set in muffin tins. Bake in preheated 350° oven 25 minutes. Frost with Creamy BBB Frosting, p. 271. *Makes 10–12*

## GINGERBREAD

**BBB + Rye + TE&A**

- 1 cup boiling water
- ½ cup allowed margarine
- ¼ cup dark honey
- 1 teaspoon ginger
- ½ teaspoon cinnamon
- ½ teaspoon salt
- 2 cups rye flour
- ½ teaspoon baking soda
- 2 tablespoons cereal-free baking powder

Pour boiling water over margarine, honey, spices, and salt. Stir to melt margarine, then set aside to cool. Combine dry ingredients and stir well into cooled liquids. Pour into oiled 6 x 10 or 8-inch square pan. Bake in preheated 350° oven 30 to 40 minutes or until toothpick inserted in center comes out clean. Cool and cut into squares. Frost with Vanilla Sugar Frosting, p. 271, or dust with BBB Powdered Sugar, p. 270. *Serves 8–10*

## APPLAUSE APPLE CAKE-BARS

**BBB + Rye + N&S + TE&A**

- ½ cup white sugar
- ¼ cup brown sugar, firmly packed
- ¼ cup allowed margarine
- 1 cup cooking apple, grated coarse (usually 1 large apple)
- ½ cup chopped nuts
- ½ teaspoon cinnamon
- ¼ teaspoon nutmeg
- ¼ teaspoon salt
- 1¼ cups rye flour
- 3 teaspoons cereal-free baking powder

Cream together sugars and margarine. Add 2 tablespoons water and beat hard. Add apple, chopped nuts, spices, and salt. Beat again. Stir in rye flour and baking powder, mixing well. Batter will be thick, so don't be alarmed. Spread in oiled 8-inch square baking pan and bake in preheated 350° oven 35 to 40 minutes or until firm when pressed in center. Cool and cut into bars. These are firm enough to cut well and handle without crumbling, but are light-textured inside. A real treat for the lunch box. *Makes 12*

## LAZY DAISY OATMEAL CAKE

**BBB + Oats + N&S + TE&A**

- **1 cup rolled oats**
- **1½ cups boiling water**
- **½ cup allowed margarine, softened**
- **½ cup brown sugar, firmly packed**
- **½ cup white sugar**
- **1 teaspoon synthetic vanilla**
- **1 cup rice flour**
- **¼ cup soy flour**
- **1 tablespoon potato flour**
- **1 teaspoon baking soda**
- **4 teaspoons cereal-free baking powder**
- **½ teaspoon salt**
- **¾ teaspoon cinnamon**
- **¼ teaspoon nutmeg**

Cover oats with boiling water and let stand 20 minutes. Stir once or twice to hasten cooling. Cream margarine and sugars and add cooled oatmeal and vanilla. Combine remaining ingredients and stir into oatmeal mixture. This is a stiff batter and requires extra stirring. Spoon into well-oiled 9-inch square baking pan. Bake in preheated 350° oven 45 to 50 minutes.

While cake is baking, prepare Lazy Daisy Topping, p. 272. Spread evenly over warm cake and place under broiler until frosting becomes bubbly and a little browned. Watch carefully. Serve cake warm or cold. This is great for picnics or lunch boxes. Everyone raves. If nuts and coconut in topping cause problems, simply omit and eat this cake plain. **(− N&S)** It's still delicious. *Serves 8–10*

## ADELE'S PERSIMMON PUDDING-CAKE

**BBB + Oats + Fruit + N&S + TE&A**

- **1 cup persimmon pulp**
- **1 cup sugar**
- **½ cup allowed milk substitute**
- **1 tablespoon allowed margarine, melted**
- **1 teaspoon synthetic vanilla**
- **¼ teaspoon nutmeg**
- **1 teaspoon cinnamon**
- **1 cup chopped nuts**
- **1½ cups oat flour**
- **1 teaspoon baking soda**
- **2 teaspoons cereal-free baking powder**
- **½ teaspoon salt**

Mix first 5 ingredients in large bowl. Blend all remaining ingredients and add to persimmon mixture. Beat hard. Line bottoms of 2 oiled 1-pound coffee cans with waxed paper. Divide batter evenly into cans and cover with foil lids. Place in baking pan and add ½ inch water around cans. Bake in preheated 350° oven 1½ hours or until done when tested with toothpick. Run thin knife around cans to loosen sides and slide pudding-cake from cans. Peel paper from bottom and cut round slices or top-to-bottom quarters. Serve warm with Lemon Sauce I, p. 272. *Serves 8–10*

**Variation:**

Omit oat flour and replace with 1¼ cups rye flour and 1 tablespoon tapioca starch. Add ½ teaspoon ginger and ⅛ teaspoon ground cloves in addition to other spices in recipe. **(− Oats + Rye)**

*Note:* Plan ahead for this one. When persimmons are available, get plenty. Remove blossom and any dark spots on skin. Purée in blender. Freeze pulp in 1-cup containers. Thaw one when ready for this recipe—no mess, no extra pulp to waste. Persimmons may also be frozen whole with blossoms still attached.

## OAT COFFEE CAKE

**BBB + Oats + N&S + TE&A**

- 1 recipe Rolled Oat Muffins, p. 215
- ¼ cup brown sugar, firmly packed
- 1 teaspoon cinnamon
- ¼ cup chopped nuts
- 1 tablespoon allowed margarine

Pour batter for Rolled Oat Muffins into oiled 8-inch pan. Blend remaining ingredients well and sprinkle on top of batter. Bake in preheated 400° oven 15 to 20 minutes or until done through. Cut into wedges. *Serves 8–10*

## FAVORITE HONEY BARS

**BBB + Rye + Oats + N&S + TE&A**

- ¾ cup rye flour
- ⅓ cup rice flour
- ½ teaspoon baking soda
- 2 teaspoons cereal-free baking powder
- ¼ teaspoon salt
- 1 cup quick oats
- ¼ cup sugar
- 1 cup flaked coconut
- ½ cup chopped nuts
- ¼ cup honey
- 1 teaspoon synthetic vanilla
- ¼ cup allowed oil
- ½ cup + 2 tablespoons allowed milk substitute or water

Blend first 7 ingredients and stir in coconut and nuts. Combine honey, vanilla, oil and milk substitute or water and beat into dry ingredients. Bake in oiled 9-inch square pan in oven preheated to 350°. Test with toothpick inserted in center after 25 minutes. Continue baking until toothpick comes out clean, about 30 to 40 minutes total time. Cut into bars while still warm. *Makes 12*

## BEST WHITE CUPCAKES

**BBB + Barley**

- ¼ cup allowed margarine
- ½ cup sugar
- ¾ cup barley flour
- ¼ cup rice flour
- 2 teaspoons cereal-free baking powder
- ¼ teaspoon salt
- ½ teaspoon synthetic vanilla

Cream margarine and sugar. Blend dry ingredients well and add to creamed mixture. Stir in ¼ cup water and beat well. Add vanilla and another ¼ cup water and blend. Spoon into paper baking cups set in muffin tins. Bake in preheated 350° oven 25 minutes. *Makes 8–10*

**Variation:**

Double recipe for Best White Cupcakes. Pour batter into oiled 9-inch round or square cake pan. Bake in preheated 350° oven 30 to 35 minutes. If desired, frost with Creamy BBB Frosting, p. 271. *Serves 12–14*

## APPLE BETTY CAKE

**BBB + Corn + N&S + TE&A**

- 1 cup corn flour
- ¾ cup sugar
- ½ teaspoon baking soda
- 2 teaspoons cereal-free baking powder
- ½ teaspoon salt
- ½ teaspoon each cinnamon and nutmeg
- ¼ teaspoon ground cloves
- ¼ cup allowed oil
- ¾ cup thick unsweetened applesauce
- ¼ cup chopped nuts

Blend first 7 ingredients. Add oil, applesauce and chopped nuts and blend well. If applesauce is thick and batter seems much too thick, add 1 to 2 tablespoons water. Spread batter into oiled 8-inch square pan. Bake in preheated 350° oven 45 minutes. Cool, then sprinkle top of cake with powdered sugar. *Serves 8*

*Note:* Plain applesauce cake can be made without spices or chopped nuts.

## GINGER HONEY CUPCAKES

**BBB + Corn + TE&A**

- 1 cup corn flour
- ¼ cup soy flour
- ¼ cup rice flour
- ¼ teaspoon salt
- ¼ teaspoon baking soda
- 2 teaspoons cereal-free baking powder
- 1 teaspoon each cinnamon and ginger
- ⅓ cup sugar
- ⅓ cup honey
- ⅓ cup allowed oil

Combine and blend dry ingredients. Stir in honey, oil, and ½ cup water until well mixed. Spoon into 8 paper baking cups placed in muffin tins. Bake in preheated 350° oven 25 minutes. Frost if desired with Caramel Frosting, p. 272, or with Creamy Vanilla Frosting, p. 273. These are a gorgeous color and good just plain. *Makes 8 cupcakes*

**Variation:**

Cut plain cupcake in half, place each half in dessert dish and top with dollop of whipped Dsertwhip to serve while cupcake is still warm.

# FROSTINGS

## BBB POWDERED SUGAR

**BBB**

Place cane or beet white sugar in blender and run at high speed until it has the texture of purchased confectioners sugar. This will give you powdered sugar without added cornstarch. Use it as you would purchased confectioners sugar in glazes and frostings.

*Suggestion:* For a pretty lacy design on your cakes, lay lace paper doily on cooled cake. Sift your own BBB powdered sugar over doily, lift paper carefully, and leave design on the cake.

## POWDERED SUGAR BBB GLAZE

**BBB**

Combine until smooth and of desired consistency. Drizzle on cakes or cupcakes. *Makes ⅓ cup*

- **1 cup cane or beet white sugar, powdered in blender**
- **1 tablespoon water, more or less, as needed**

## CREAMY BBB FROSTING

**BBB**

Make your own confectioners powdered sugar. Follow Creamy Vanilla Frosting recipe, p. 273, substituting your own for purchased confectioners sugar. If desired, add 1 tablespoon tapioca starch to 1½ cups homemade powdered sugar. Easy on the water additions! Add by drops until desired consistency is reached.

## VANILLA SUGAR FROSTING

**BBB**

Melt margarine, add sugar, SoyQuik, and ½ cup water and bring to boil, stirring constantly. Lower heat and boil gently, without stirring, 3 minutes. Mixture should register 234°-238° on candy thermometer—soft ball stage. Remove from heat and cool to lukewarm. Add vanilla and beat hard until stiff enough to spread. *Makes 1 cup.*

*Note:* If frosting hardens too quickly during spreading, set bowl in pan of warm water.

- **¼ cup allowed margarine**
- **1½ cups white cane or beet sugar**
- **1 tablespoon Ener-G SoyQuik**
- **1 teaspoon synthetic vanilla**

## BROWN SUGAR FROSTING

**BBB**

Follow Vanilla Sugar Frosting, but use 1 cup brown sugar and ½ cup white sugar instead of all white sugar.

## WALDORF "WHIPPED CREAM" ICING

**BBB**

Blend flour and SoyQuik well, and add 1 cup water. Cook, stirring constantly, until mixture is very thick and creamy. Cool.

Cream margarine and sugar in mixing bowl. Add cooled flour mixture and beat until mixture resembles whipped cream. Stir in vanilla and spread on cooled cake or cupcakes. *Makes 2 cups*

- **4 tablespoons rice flour**
- **2 tablespoons Ener-G SoyQuik**
- **1 cup allowed margarine**
- **1 cup sugar**
- **1 teaspoon synthetic vanilla**

## LEMON SAUCE I

**BBB + Fruit**

- **½ cup sugar**
- **1 tablespoon tapioca starch or potato starch**
- **2 tablespoons allowed margarine**
- **2 tablespoons lemon juice**
- **Pinch of salt**

Blend sugar and starch in saucepan. Stir in 1 cup water and, stirring constantly, bring to boil. Continue cooking over low heat 5 minutes and stir in margarine to melt. Add juice and salt. Serve warm over Adele's Persimmon Pudding-Cake, p. 268. This may be made ahead and reheated before serving. *Makes 1⅓ cups*

**Variation: Lemon Sauce II**

When corn is allowed, replace tapioca or potato starch with cornstarch and add ½ teaspoon grated lemon peel. **(+ Corn)**

## LAZY DAISY TOPPING

**BBB + N&S**

- **¼ cup allowed margarine, melted**
- **½ cup brown sugar, firmly packed**
- **¾ cup shredded or flaked coconut**
- **3 tablespoons allowed milk substitute or water**
- **⅓ cup nuts, chopped**

Blend all ingredients together well and spread on warm 9-inch cake. Place under broiler until topping is bubbly. Watch carefully. Serve warm or cooled. *Makes 1 cup*

**Variation:**

Reduce water to 2 tablespoons and replace brown sugar with honey. **(+ TE&A)**

## POWDERED SUGAR GLAZE

**BBB + Corn**

- **1 cup sifted confectioners powdered sugar**
- **½ teaspoon synthetic vanilla**

Thoroughly combine sugar and vanilla with 3 to 3½ teaspoons water. Drizzle on cakes as desired. *Makes ⅓ cup*

*Note:* Confectioners powdered sugar available in markets contains 3% cornstarch. It may be used in all recipes coded **+ Corn.**

## CARAMEL FROSTING

**BBB + Corn**

- **3 tablespoons allowed margarine**
- **¼ cup brown sugar, firmly packed**
- **½ teaspoon synthetic vanilla**
- **1½ cups sifted confectioners powdered sugar**

Bring margarine, brown sugar, and 1 tablespoon water to boil in small saucepan. Simmer 2 minutes or until sugar is dissolved. Cool. Combine with powdered sugar and vanilla and add water, 1 teaspoon at a time, for spreading consistency. If too thin, add powdered sugar by teaspoonsful. *Makes enough for 12 cupcakes or 1 small cake*

## CREAMY VANILLA FROSTING

**BBB + Corn**

- **3 tablespoons allowed margarine, softened**
- **$\frac{1}{8}$ teaspoon salt**
- **$1\frac{1}{2}$ cups sifted confectioners powdered sugar**
- **$\frac{1}{2}$ teaspoon synthetic vanilla**
- **2-3 tablespoons allowed milk substitute or water**

Cream margarine, salt, and powdered sugar. Add vanilla, then blend in milk substitute or water to desired spreading consistency. *Makes enough for 12 cupcakes or 1 small loaf cake*

**Variations:**

1. CREAMY NUTTY FROSTING—Stir in $\frac{1}{4}$ cup chopped nuts if allowed. (+ **N&S**)
2. CREAMY CAROB-COFFEE FROSTING—Sift 3 tablespoons carob powder with confectioners sugar. Prepare coffee by mixing 1 tablespoon instant coffee (100%) in 3 tablespoons boiling water. Cool and use to replace milk substitute or water in recipe. (+**TE&A**) If allowed, add $\frac{1}{4}$ cup chopped nuts. (+ **N&S**)
3. CREAMY SPICE FROSTING—Stir in $\frac{1}{16}$ teaspoon each of cinnamon and nutmeg and half that much ground cloves. (+ **TE&A**)

## CREAMY FRUIT-FLAVORED FROSTINGS

**BBB + Corn + Fruit**

- **3 tablespoons allowed margarine, softened**
- **$\frac{1}{8}$ teaspoon salt**
- **$1\frac{1}{2}$ cups sifted confectioners powdered sugar**
- **$\frac{1}{2}$ teaspoon synthetic vanilla**
- **1-2 tablespoons milk substitute or water**
- **1 tablespoon lemon juice**
- **1 teaspoon grated lemon peel**

Cream margarine, salt, and powdered sugar. Mix vanilla, 1 tablespoon milk substitute or water, lemon juice and peel, and blend mixture into creamed margarine and sugar. If too thick, add remaining liquid, little at a time, until frosting reaches desired spreading consistency. *Makes enough for 12 cupcakes or 1 small loaf cake*

**Variations:**

1. ORANGE FROSTING—Add 1 tablespoon orange juice and 1 teaspoon grated orange peel to replace lemon juice and peel.
2. BANANA FROSTING—Reduce lemon juice to $\frac{1}{4}$ teaspoon and add 3 tablespoons mashed banana. Omit lemon peel.
3. STRAWBERRY FROSTING—Reduce lemon juice to $\frac{1}{4}$ teaspoon and omit lemon peel. Add 2–4 tablespoons crushed strawberries.

## LEMON GLAZE

**BBB + Corn + Fruit**

- 1 cup sifted confectioners powdered sugar
- 4 teaspoons lemon juice
- Pinch of grated lemon peel

Blend and drizzle on cakes as desired or thin with additional lemon juice and brush on cookies to glaze. *Makes ⅓ cup*

## CAROB-PEANUT BUTTER FROSTING

**BBB + Corn + N&S + TE&A**

- 2 cups sifted confectioners powdered sugar
- 2 tablespoons allowed margarine
- ⅓ cup creamy peanut butter
- 2 tablespoons carob powder
- ½ teaspoon synthetic vanilla
- 4–6 tablespoons allowed milk substitute or water

Cream first 5 ingredients and work in 5 tablespoons milk substitute or water. If needed for proper spreading consistency, add remaining liquid, 1 teaspoon at a time. *Makes 1 cup*

**Variation: Peanut Butter Frosting**
Omit carob powder.

# COOKIES

Beverly is a cookie muncher and loves to bake. She helped test many of these recipes and has baked her favorites over and over again—with outstanding results.

All through Bev's life she was denied every cookie on the coffee hour table at church—all contained the problem wheat, milk, and eggs. Once, when I, Gloria, was in charge, I decided to bake all the cookies myself instead of asking others to help. This was my chance to bake all "allergy" cookies and see whether anyone could tell. Every last cookie disappeared as usual off the serving platters, but best of all was watching Bev. She was a picture of teenage delight as she surveyed the table and chose any and all cookies her heart desired. The time spent in baking was worth it just for that.

For your cookies-for-everybody, be guided by these hints:

1. All flour measurements are for unsifted flours. If desired, measure all dry ingredients, then sift them together to blend and remove any lumps.

2. In mixing, cream allowed margarine and sugar together. If small amount of liquid is required, beat it into creamed mixture along with vanilla, then add well-blended dry ingredients. When larger amounts of liquid are required, add liquid alternately with dry ingredients to creamed mixture.

3. About baking, most cookie batters contain enough shortening to bake on unoiled cookie sheets without sticking. For even browning, study your oven and turn cookie sheets during baking or adjust rack levels as needed.

## SUGAR COOKIE SLICES

**BBB**

- **⅔ cup allowed margarine**
- **¾ cup sugar**
- **1 teaspoon synthetic vanilla**
- **2¼ cups rice flour**
- **2 teaspoons cereal-free baking powder**
- **¼ teaspoon salt**

Cream margarine and sugar. Beat in vanilla and ¼ cup water until mixture is fluffy. Add blended dry ingredients and mix until dough forms a ball that pulls away from sides of bowl. Shape dough into 2 rolls about 2 inches in diameter (dough may seem rather soft). Wrap in waxed paper and refrigerate overnight (dough will firm up and be easy to slice). Slice ⅛- to ¼-inch thick and place on unoiled cookie sheets. Bake in preheated 375° oven 8 to 10 minutes or until delicately brown at edges. Cool on wire rack. Keep rolls handy in refrigerator for impromptu baking. *About 10 dozen*

## VANILLA CRISSCROSS COOKIES

**BBB**

- **½ cup allowed margarine or soy oil shortening**
- **¾ cup sugar**
- **1 teaspoon synthetic vanilla**
- **1⅓ cups unsifted rice flour**
- **⅓ cup soy flour**
- **1 tablespoon potato flour**
- **½ teaspoon salt**
- **2 teaspoons cereal-free baking powder**

Cream margarine and sugar. Beat in ¼ cup water. Add vanilla. Blend all dry ingredients and work into creamed mixture. If dough seems too sticky to handle, let stand 5 minutes. Roll walnut-size balls of dough in sugar and place on unoiled cookie sheets 2 inches apart. Flatten by pressing tines of fork across dough, then press again from opposite direction, making crisscross pattern on cookie. If fork tines stick to dough, dip in sugar or water. Bake cookies in preheated 375° oven 8 to 10 minutes or until delicately browned around edges. Cool on wire racks. Excellent! *About 4 dozen*

**Variation: Sugar n' Spice Cookies**

Omit synthetic vanilla and replace with almond extract. Add ¾ teaspoon cinnamon and ½ teaspoon ginger to dry ingredients. **(+ TE&A)**

## REFRIGERATOR COOKIES

**BBB**

- **½ cup allowed margarine, softened**
- **1 cup light brown sugar, firmly packed**
- **1 teaspoon synthetic vanilla**
- **1⅓ cups rice flour**
- **⅓ cup soy flour**
- **1 tablespoon potato flour**
- **2 teaspoons cereal-free baking powder**
- **¼ teaspoon salt**

Cream margarine and sugar, then beat in vanilla and 2 tablespoons water. Add dry ingredients and mix well. Shape into 1 or 2 rolls 2 inches in diameter. Wrap in waxed paper and refrigerate overnight or longer. Slice dough ⅛ inch thick and place on unoiled cookie sheet. Bake in preheated 375° oven 6 to 8 minutes or until edges are delicately brown. *About 7 dozen*

## GLUTEN-FREE VANILLA WAFERS

**BBB**

- **⅓ cup allowed margarine**
- **½ cup sugar**
- **1 teaspoon synthetic vanilla**
- **1 cup rice flour**
- **⅓ cup soy flour**
- **1 tablespoon potato flour**
- **2 teaspoons cereal-free baking powder**
- **½ teaspoon baking soda**
- **¼ teaspoon salt**

Cream margarine and sugar. Beat in vanilla and ⅓ cup water until fluffy. Blend all dry ingredients and add to creamed mixture, mixing well. Drop from teaspoon onto unoiled cookie sheets. Flatten or leave mounded. Bake in preheated 375° oven 10 minutes. Remove at once to wire cooling racks. Very good cookies. *About 4 dozen*

**Variations:**

1. Add 1 tablespoon grated orange peel for orange wafers. (+ **Fruit**)
2. Add 1 cup flaked coconut for coconut wafers. (+ **N&S**)
3. Replace vanilla with 1 teaspoon (scant) almond extract. (+ **TE&A**)
4. Add 1 teaspoon cinnamon, ¼ teaspoon nutmeg and dash of ground cloves. (+ **TE&A**)

## DRESSY BUTTON COOKIES

**BBB**

- **½ cup allowed margarine**
- **½ cup sugar**
- **1 teaspoon synthetic vanilla**
- **¾ cup rice flour**
- **¼ cup soy flour**
- **2 teaspoons cereal-free baking powder**
- **¼ teaspoon salt**
- **2 cups crushed puffed rice (crush about 4 cups in blender)**
- **BBB Jam or Jelly, p. 234 to p. 236**

Cream margarine and sugar. Beat in vanilla and 2 tablespoons water. Add all dry ingredients and stir until well dampened. Knead dough together with hands. Break off 1-inch bits of dough and place on oiled cookie sheets. Make depression in center of each cookie and fill with ⅛ teaspoon BBB jam or jelly of your choice. Bake in preheated 375° oven 8 to 10 minutes. *About 3½ dozen*

**Variation:**

Replace crushed puffed rice with 2 cups El Molino Puffed Millet. (+ **Millet**)

## RICE FLOUR DROP COOKIES

**BBB**

- **1 cup rice flour**
- **⅓ cup sugar**
- **1½ teaspoons cereal-free baking powder**
- **¼ teaspoon salt**
- **3 tablespoons allowed oil**
- **2 teaspoons synthetic vanilla**

Blend dry ingredients. Add oil, vanilla, and 6 tablespoons water. Beat well. Drop from teaspoon onto oiled baking sheet. Bake in preheated 350° oven 15 minutes. *About 2 dozen*

## BROWN SUGAR DROPS

**BBB**

- **½ cup allowed margarine**
- **1 cup brown sugar, firmly packed**
- **½ teaspoon synthetic vanilla**
- **1 cup rice flour**
- **¼ cup soy flour**
- **1 tablespoon potato flour**
- **2 teaspoons cereal-free baking powder**
- **¼ teaspoon salt**

Cream margarine and sugar. Beat in vanilla and 2 to 4 tablespoons water. Blend all dry ingredients and stir into creamed mixture. Drop from teaspoon onto unoiled baking sheet. Bake in preheated 350° oven 10 minutes. *About 4 dozen*

*Note:* 2 tablespoons water make thicker cookies. Bake 12 minutes. 4 tablespoons water make thinner cookies that will bake in 10 minutes.

**Variation:**

Add ½ cup finely chopped nuts, when allowed. (+ N&S)

## HONEY LEMON DROPS

**BBB + Fruit** ☐

- **½ cup honey**
- **½ cup allowed margarine**
- **2 tablespoons lemon juice**
- **1 tablespoon grated lemon peel**
- **1¼ cups rice flour**
- **2 teaspoons cereal-free baking powder**
- **¼ teaspoon salt**

Combine honey, margarine, juice, and peel. Stir in dry ingredients and beat well. Drop dough from teaspoon onto oiled cookie sheet. Bake in preheated 325° oven 10 minutes. *About 5 dozen*

**Variation:**

Replace lemon juice and peel with orange juice and peel.

## Cookies available in markets

**BBB + Fruit + Veg.** ☐

Bray's Rice Cookies (rice flour, soya shortening, soya flour, brown sugar, lima bean flour, potato starch, water, cereal-free leavening, salt, lemon)

## PEANUTTY SNAPS

**BBB + N&S** ☐

- **¼ cup crunchy peanut butter**
- **2 tablespoons allowed margarine**
- **¼ cup sugar**
- **½ cup rice flour**
- **3 tablespoons soy flour**
- **2 teaspoons cereal-free baking powder**
- **1 cup crushed puffed rice (about 2 cups before crushed in blender)**

Cream peanut butter, margarine, and sugar. Beat in ¼ cup water. Add dry ingredients and blend until dough forms ball that leaves sides of bowl. With hands, press ball together. Break off 1-inch pieces of dough and place on oiled baking sheet. Press flat with fingers. Bake in preheated 375° oven 8 minutes. *About 2 dozen*

**BBB + TE&A**

## SPICE CRISSCROSS COOKIES

- ½ cup allowed margarine
- ¼ cup brown sugar, firmly packed
- ½ cup sugar
- 1 teaspoon synthetic vanilla
- 1⅓ cups rice flour
- ⅓ cup soy flour
- 1 tablespoon potato flour
- ½ teaspoon salt
- 2 teaspoons cereal-free baking powder
- ½ teaspoon cinnamon
- ¼ teaspoon nutmeg
- ⅛ teaspoon ground cloves

Cream margarine and sugars. Stir in vanilla and 3 tablespoons water. Blend all dry ingredients, then add to creamed mixture. Mix thoroughly. Shape dough into walnut-size balls, drop into small bowl of sugar, and coat well. Place on unoiled baking sheets. Flatten by pressing crisscross pattern into each cookie with tines of fork. Bake in preheated 375° oven 8 to 10 minutes or until delicately brown around edge. Remove from sheet and cool on rack. These are crisp, delicious cookies that hold their shape. *About 3½ dozen*

### Variation: Lemon Crisscross Cookies

Omit brown sugar and increase white sugar to ¾ cup. Replace vanilla with ½ teaspoon lemon extract. Omit spices.

**BBB + Veg. + TE&A**

## Cookies available in markets

Rice Carob Chip Cookies (rice flour, soya shortening, brown sugar, soya flour, lima bean flour, potato starch, carob chips, water, leavening, salt, vanilla)

*Note:* Carob chips may contain small amount of milk.

**BBB + Veg. + N&S + TE&A**

## GOLD NUGGETS

- ¼ cup allowed margarine
- ½ cup sugar
- ½ teaspoon lemon extract
- ½ teaspoon synthetic vanilla
- ½ cup solid pack pumpkin
- ⅔ cup rice flour
- ¼ cup soy flour
- 1½ teaspoons potato flour
- 2 teaspoons cereal-free baking powder
- ¼ teaspoon salt
- 1 teaspoon cinnamon
- ¼ teaspoon nutmeg
- ⅛ teaspoon ginger
- ½ cup chopped nuts

Cream margarine and sugar. Beat in extract, vanilla, pumpkin, and 2 tablespoons water. Blend all dry ingredients and nuts. Stir into pumpkin mixture. Drop from teaspoon onto oiled baking sheet. Bake in preheated 350° oven 15 to 20 minutes. *About 2 dozen*

## TRULY ALMOND COOKIES

**BBB + N&S + TE&A**

- ½ cup allowed margarine
- ⅓ cup sugar
- ⅔ cup ground roasted almonds (salted or unsalted)
- 1 teaspoon almond extract
- 1 cup rice flour

Cream margarine and sugar well, then stir in ground almonds and extract. Work flour in with back of spoon. Work and press dough into a ball with hands. Form 1-inch balls and place on unoiled cookie sheets. Flatten cookies with fingers, fork, or cookie press. Bake in preheated 350° oven 8 to 10 minutes. *About 3 dozen*

## MOLASSES GINGER COOKIES

**BBB + TE&A + Mold**

- 1 cup brown rice flour
- ½ cup soy flour
- 2 tablespoons potato flour
- 1 teaspoon baking soda
- ½ teaspoon ginger
- 1 teaspoon cinnamon
- ⅛ teaspoon ground cloves
- 3 tablespoons allowed oil
- ½ cup molasses

Blend dry ingredients. Add oil, molasses, and ¼ cup water. Beat well. Drop onto oiled sheets and bake in preheated 375° oven 8 to 10 minutes. *About 4 dozen*

## OLD-FASHIONED CRISP COOKIES

**BBB + Rye**

- ½ cup allowed margarine
- ¼ cup brown sugar, firmly packed
- ¼ cup sugar
- 1 teaspoon synthetic vanilla
- 1⅓ cups rye flour
- 1 teaspoon cereal-free baking powder
- ¼ teaspoon salt

Cream margarine and sugars well, then beat in vanilla and 1 teaspoon water. Add dry ingredients and blend well. Chill dough 1 hour. Place small balls of dough on unoiled cookie sheet and press to ¼-inch thickness. Bake in preheated 350° oven 10 to 12 minutes. Dough may be rolled, refrigerated, and sliced ¼ inch thick, if desired. *About 4 dozen*

## PRESIDENTIAL PEANUT BUTTER COOKIES

**BBB + Rye + N&S**

- **½ cup allowed margarine**
- **½ cup crunchy or creamy peanut butter**
- **½ cup brown sugar, firmly packed**
- **½ cup sugar**
- **½ teaspoon synthetic vanilla**
- **½ cup brown rice flour**
- **⅔ cup rye flour**
- **¼ cup potato flour**
- **1 teaspoon cereal-free baking powder**
- **1 teaspoon baking soda**

Cream margarine, peanut butter, and sugars until well blended. Beat in vanilla and 2 tablespoons water. Combine and add dry ingredients. Shape into balls and place on oiled cookie sheet. Press down with fork twice, forming crisscross pattern and flattening cookie. Bake in preheated 350° oven 10 to 12 minutes. *About 3½ dozen*

## RYE VANILLA WAFERS

**BBB + Rye + TE&A**

- **⅓ cup allowed margarine**
- **½ cup sugar**
- **¼ cup honey**
- **2 teaspoons synthetic vanilla**
- **⅔ cup rice flour**
- **¼ cup soy flour**
- **1½ teaspoons potato flour**
- **½ cup rye flour**
- **2 teaspoons cereal-free baking powder**
- **½ teaspoon baking soda**
- **¼ teaspoon salt**

Cream margarine and sugar. Beat in honey, vanilla, and 2 tablespoons water. Blend well and add all dry ingredients. Drop dough from teaspoon 1 inch apart onto oiled cookie sheets. Bake in preheated 375° oven until medium brown, 7 to 8 minutes. Cool on wire racks. These wafers do not spread much, but are puffy and crispy good. *About 4½ dozen*

## PERSIMMON COOKIES

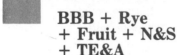

**BBB + Rye + Fruit + N&S + TE&A**

- **1 teaspoon baking soda**
- **1 cup persimmon pulp**
- **½ cup allowed margarine**
- **1 cup sugar**
- **1¾ cups rye flour**
- **1 teaspoon cereal-free baking powder**
- **½ teaspoon each cinnamon and nutmeg**
- **¼ teaspoon ground cloves**
- **1 cup chopped nuts**

Combine soda and persimmon pulp and set aside. Cream margarine and sugar, stir in pulp and 2 tablespoons water. Blend all dry ingredients and stir into creamed mixture. Let dough stand 15 minutes. Drop from heaped teaspoon onto oiled cookie sheets. Bake in preheated 350° oven 13 to 15 minutes. These are beautiful and extra delicious. *About 4 dozen*

## FIRST-RATE OATMEAL CRISPS

**BBB + Oats**

- **½ cup allowed margarine, softened**
- **¾ cup brown sugar, firmly packed**
- **½ teaspoon synthetic vanilla**
- **2½ cups quick oats**
- **2 teaspoons cereal-free baking powder**
- **¼ teaspoon salt**

Cream margarine and sugar and beat in vanilla and 2 tablespoons water. Blend in dry ingredients, stirring until mixture forms one mass that pulls away from sides of bowl. Let dough rest 15 to 20 minutes for oats to absorb oil and moisture. Place balls of dough on unoiled cookie sheets and flatten. Bake in preheated 350° oven 8 to 12 minutes. *About 2½ dozen*

## DOUBLE OAT COOKIES

**BBB + Oats**

- **½ cup allowed margarine, softened**
- **½ cup sugar**
- **1 teaspoon synthetic vanilla**
- **1 cup oat flour**
- **2 cups rolled oats**
- **¼ teaspoon salt**

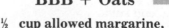

Cream margarine and sugar. Beat in vanilla and 2 tablespoons water. Stir in dry ingredients until mixture becomes a ball that pulls away from sides of mixing bowl. Drop from teaspoon onto oiled baking sheets. Flatten with moistened fingers. Bake in preheated 350° oven 12 minutes or until golden brown. *About 3 dozen*

## SIMPLY GRAND OATMEAL COOKIES

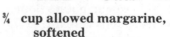

**BBB + Oats**

- **¾ cup allowed margarine, softened**
- **⅔ cup sugar**
- **3½ cups quick oats**
- **1 teaspoon synthetic vanilla**

Cream margarine and sugar and beat in 1 tablespoon water. Stir in oats and vanilla. It is important to let dough rest 15 minutes. Oats absorb oils from margarine. Try rolling one walnut-size ball. If dry and crumbly, add 1 more tablespoon water. Place balls on unoiled cookie sheets. Flatten with moistened hands. Bake in preheated 350° oven 12 minutes. *About 3 dozen*

## RED EYE COOKIES

**BBB + Oats**

- **¾ cup allowed margarine, softened**
- **1 cup brown sugar, firmly packed**
- **½ teaspoon synthetic vanilla**
- **1 cup rice flour**
- **⅓ cup soy flour**
- **1 tablespoon potato flour**
- **1 teaspoon cereal-free baking powder**
- **1½ cups quick oats**
- **½ cup Basic Cranberry Sauce, p. 191, or other allowed red jam or jelly**

Cream margarine and brown sugar, add vanilla and ¼ cup water and beat to blend. Stir in all dry ingredients until dough pulls away from sides of bowl and forms a mass. Place 1-inch balls of dough onto unoiled baking sheets. Make an indentation in top of each ball and fill with cranberry sauce or jelly. Bake in preheated 350° oven 10 to 12 minutes and cool on racks. *About 4 dozen*

**BBB + Oats + N&S**

- **1¼ cups rice flour**
- **3 tablespoons soy flour**
- **2 teaspoons potato flour**
- **1 teaspoon baking soda**
- **2 teaspoons cereal-free baking powder**
- **½ teaspoon salt**
- **1 cup allowed margarine or allowed shortening**
- **1 cup brown sugar, firmly packed**
- **1 cup sugar**
- **3 cups quick oats**
- **½ cup chopped pecans**
- **1 cup finely grated coconut**

## COCONUT PECAN REFRIGERATOR COOKIES

Blend flours, soda, baking powder, and salt. Set aside. Cream margarine and sugars, and beat in ¼ cup water until light and fluffy. Add flour mixture, blending thoroughly. Add oats, pecans, and coconut. Divide dough in thirds and shape into 3 rolls. Wrap in waxed paper and refrigerate. Slice dough while cold and place on unoiled sheets. Bake in preheated 375° oven 10 minutes. Cool slightly before removing from cookie sheets. *About 6–7 dozen*

**BBB + Oats + Fruit + TE&A**

- **1⅓ cups rice flour**
- **⅓ cup soy flour**
- **1 tablespoon potato flour**
- **4 teaspoons cereal-free baking powder**
- **½ teaspoon salt**
- **½ teaspoon nutmeg**
- **½ teaspoon cinnamon**
- **⅛ teaspoon ground cloves**
- **1¼ cups allowed margarine**
- **2 cups sugar**
- **2 tablespoons orange peel**
- **3 cups rolled oats**

## SPICED OATMEAL COOKIES

Blend first 8 ingredients and set aside. Cream margarine and sugar and beat in orange peel and 2 tablespoons water. Stir in dry ingredients until well blended. Add oats and blend again. It is important to refrigerate dough for at least 30 minutes before baking. Place walnut-size pieces of chilled dough on unoiled cookie sheets and flatten with fingertips. Bake in preheated 350° oven 10 to 12 minutes. Allow to cool on sheets a minute or so before lifting to cooling rack.

These are crisp, hold shape well, and have a fine delicate flavor. They are good enough for any party. No one will ever suspect that wheat flour, eggs, and milk are absent. *About 7 dozen*

## MAPLE COCONUT COOKIES

**BBB + Oats + N&S + TE&A**

- ½ cup allowed margarine
- ½ cup brown sugar, firmly packed
- ¼ cup sugar
- ½ teaspoon maple flavoring
- ½ teaspoon synthetic vanilla
- ¾ cup rice flour
- ¼ cup rice polish
- 2 teaspoons cereal-free baking powder
- 1 teaspoon baking soda
- ½ teaspoon salt
- 1 cup quick oats
- 1 cup flaked coconut

Cream margarine and sugars, beat in extract, vanilla, and 2 tablespoons water until mixture is light and fluffy. Add all other ingredients and mix well. Shape dough into balls or drop from teaspoon onto oiled or margarined cookie sheets. Flatten cookies and bake in preheated 350° oven 8 to 10 minutes or until lightly browned. Let cool slightly on cookie sheet before removing to cooling racks. *Makes 42*

## GRANNY'S OATMEAL COOKIES

**BBB + Oats + N&S + TE&A**

- ½ cup allowed margarine or allowed shortening
- ½ cup brown sugar, firmly packed
- ½ cup sugar
- ½ teaspoon synthetic vanilla
- ½ cup rice flour
- 3 tablespoons soy flour
- 1½ teaspoons potato flour
- ½ teaspoon baking soda
- 1½ teaspoon cereal-free baking powder
- 2 cups quick oats
- Chopped nuts, coconut, or shaved El Molino CaraCoa Carob Bar—Milk Free

Cream allowed margarine or shortening and sugars. Beat in vanilla and 3 tablespoons water. Blend all dry ingredients except oats and nuts and add to creamed mixture. Stir in oats and choice of nuts, coconut, or candy. Drop from heaping teaspoon onto oiled cookie sheets and press flat with fingertips. Moisten fingers if they stick to dough. Bake in preheated 375° oven 8 to 10 minutes. Cool on baking sheets a minute or so before removing to cooling racks. Store in airtight container. *About 3 dozen*

*Note:* These cookies are the best! If you have anyone else around to help eat cookies, we suggest making a double recipe. They go fast. The original recipe (with wheat, milk, and eggs) was double size. It came from a handwritten card in Bev's grandmother's recipe file. We enjoyed transposing this family treasure into a recipe for Bev. She requested Granny's oatmeal cookies for the buffet following her wedding.

**BBB + Oats + N&S + TE&A**

- ½ cup allowed margarine
- 1 cup brown sugar, firmly packed
- 1 teaspoon synthetic vanilla
- ½ teaspoon almond extract
- ⅔ cup rice flour
- ¼ cup soy flour
- 1½ teaspoons potato flour
- 2 teaspoons cereal-free baking powder
- ½ teaspoon salt
- 1 teaspoon cinnamon
- ¼ teaspoon nutmeg
- ½ cup allowed milk substitute
- 1½ cups rolled oats
- 1 cup finely grated coconut

## COCONUT DROP COOKIES

Cream margarine and sugar and add vanilla and almond extract. Blend flours, baking powder, salt, and spices. Add alternately with milk substitute to creamed mixture, blending well. Stir in oats and coconut. Let dough stand 15 minutes. Drop from teaspoon onto oiled cookie sheets. Bake in preheated 350° oven 10 to 12 minutes. *About 3 dozen*

**Variation:**

Add 3 tablespoons carob powder.

**BBB + Rye + Oats**

- 1 cup allowed margarine
- ⅔ cup brown sugar, firmly packed
- ¼ cup rye flour
- ½ teaspoon salt
- 1 teaspoon synthetic vanilla
- 3½ cups quick oats

## RYE OATMEAL CRISPS

Cream margarine and sugar. Stir in rye flour, salt, and vanilla. Add oats and blend until dough can be gathered into a ball. Break off walnut-size pieces and place 2 inches apart on unoiled cookie sheets. Press each one flat with fingers or fork. Bake in preheated 350° oven 10 to 12 minutes. Cool on baking sheets a minute or so before removing to cooling racks. Cookies are delicate and crisp. *About 3 dozen*

**BBB + Rye + Oats + TE&A**

- ⅓ cup allowed margarine
- ½ cup sugar
- 1 teaspoon synthetic vanilla
- ¾ cup rye flour
- 2 teaspoons cereal-free baking powder
- ¼ teaspoon salt
- ½ teaspoon cinnamon
- 1½ cups quick oats

## RYE OATMEAL DROP COOKIES

Cream margarine and sugar. Beat in vanilla and ¼ cup water. Add all other ingredients, mixing well. Drop from teaspoon onto oiled cookie sheets. Bake in preheated 350° oven 10 to 12 minutes. *About 2½ dozen*

*Note:* Omit cinnamon for good basic drop cookie that can become new and different at the twist of a wrist. For example: Use spices or extracts of your choice, add 1 teaspoon grated orange or lemon peel (**+ Fruit**), add chopped nuts or coconut (**+N&S**), or add raisins (**+ Mold**).

## HONEYED PEANUT BUTTER COOKIES

**BBB + Rye + Oats + N&S + TE&A**

- ½ cup allowed margarine
- ½ cup peanut butter
- ¾ cup honey
- 1 cup rye flour
- 1 cup quick oats
- 1 teaspoon cereal-free baking powder
- ½ teaspoon cinnamon

Cream margarine, peanut butter, and honey. Stir in 2 tablespoons water, then dry ingredients. Drop from teaspoon onto oiled cookie sheets. Bake in preheated 325° oven 15 to 18 minutes or until center of cookie is firm. *About 4 dozen*

## BASIC BARLEY DROP COOKIES

**BBB + Barley**

- ⅓ cup allowed margarine
- ¾ cup sugar
- 1½ teaspoons synthetic vanilla
- 2 cups barley flour
- 1 tablespoon cereal-free baking powder
- ½ teaspoon salt

Cream margarine and sugar and stir in vanilla. Add dry ingredients alternately with ½ cup water. Blend well. Drop from teaspoon onto unoiled cookie sheet and bake in preheated 350° oven 12 to 14 minutes. *About 4½ dozen*

## RAISIN SPICE COOKIES

**BBB + Barley + TE&A + Mold**

- ¾ cup raisins
- 1 cup applesauce
- ½ cup allowed margarine
- 1 cup sugar
- 1 cup rice flour
- ½ cup soy flour
- ¼ teaspoon salt
- 2 teaspoons cereal-free baking powder
- ½ teaspoon cinnamon
- ¼ teaspoon nutmeg
- ⅛ teaspoon ground cloves
- 2 cups Rice Krispies

Stir raisins into applesauce and let set 30 minutes. Cream margarine and sugar. Mix all dry ingredients except Rice Krispies. Stir a little of this mixture into margarine and sugar, then add a little of the applesauce and raisins. Continue alternate additions, mixing well after each. Finally, stir in Rice Krispies. Drop from teaspoon, well separated on unoiled cookie sheets. Bake in preheated 350° oven 13 to 15 minutes. *About 3 to 4 dozen*

## SUGAR CRISPS

**BBB + Barley + N&S + TE&A + Mold**

- **1 cup allowed margarine**
- **½ cup brown sugar, firmly packed**
- **½ cup sugar**
- **1 teaspoon synthetic vanilla**
- **1½ cups rice flour**
- **⅓ cup soy flour**
- **1 tablespoon potato flour**
- **1 teaspoon cereal-free baking powder**
- **½ teaspoon baking soda**
- **½ teaspoon salt**
- **2½ cups Rice Krispies**
- **1 cup chopped pecans**

Cream margarine and sugars. Beat in vanilla and 2 tablespoons water. Mix all dry ingredients except Rice Krispies and nuts. Blend well and add to margarine-sugar mixture. Finally add Rice Krispies and nuts. Let batter stand 15 minutes before handling. Then place walnut-size balls of dough on unoiled cookie sheets and flatten with fingertips. Bake in preheated 350° oven 10 minutes. Allow to cool on baking sheets a minute or so before removing to cooling racks. These are flavorful and crisp. *About 5½ to 6 dozen*

## MAPLE PECAN COOKIES

**BBB + Rye + Barley + N&S + TE&A**

- **⅓ cup allowed margarine**
- **½ cup brown sugar, firmly packed**
- **½ teaspoon maple flavoring**
- **½ cup rye flour**
- **¾ cup barley flour**
- **⅓ teaspoon salt**
- **½ teaspoon baking soda**
- **½ cup pecans, chopped**

Cream margarine and sugar. Beat in flavoring and 2 tablespoons water. Add remaining ingredients and stir until all flour is incorporated and dough forms a ball. Roll 1-inch balls and place on unoiled cookie sheets. Flatten balls with fingertips or fork. Bake in preheated 350° oven 8 to 10 minutes. *About 3½ dozen*

## CRISPY MULTI-GRAIN COOKIES

**BBB + Rye + Oats + Barley**

- **⅔ cup allowed oil**
- **⅔ cup raw sugar**
- **⅔ cup rye flour**
- **⅓ cup barley flour**
- **2 teaspoons cereal-free baking powder**
- **¼ teaspoon salt**
- **1½ cups rolled oats**

Cream oil and sugar and beat in 2 tablespoons water. Add all dry ingredients except oats, mix well, then stir in oats. Roll dough into small balls and place on unoiled cookie sheets. Flatten each ball with fingertips or fork. Bake in preheated 350° oven 10 to 12 minutes or until lightly browned. *About 3½ dozen*

**Variation:**

Add ¼ cup chopped nuts and 1 shaved 1-ounce El Molino CaraCoa Carob Candy Bar—MilkFree. Refrigerate candy bar and it will shave easily. This tastes like a chocolate chip cookie. **(+ N&S + TE&A)**

## COCONUT KRISPIES

**BBB + Rye + Oats + Barley + N&S + TE&A + Mold**

- **¾ cup allowed margarine**
- **1 cup brown sugar, firmly packed**
- **1 teaspoon synthetic vanilla**
- **1 cup rye flour**
- **⅓ cup barley flour**
- **1⅔ cups rolled oats**
- **2 teaspoons cereal-free baking powder**
- **½ teaspoon baking soda**
- **½ teaspoon salt**
- **2 cups Rice Krispies**
- **⅔ cup flaked coconut**

Cream margarine and sugar. Beat in vanilla and ¼ cup water. Add all dry ingredients except Rice Krispies and coconut and blend well. Stir in Rice Krispies and coconut. Make walnut-size balls, place on unoiled cookie sheets, and flatten with fingertips. Bake in preheated 350° oven 8 to 10 minutes. These cookies are crisp and hold together well. Serve to a crowd. No one will suspect them of being allergy food. *About 4 dozen*

**Variation:**

Replace brown sugar with ¾ cup honey and omit water. Reduce baking temperature to 325° and bake 8 to 12 minutes.

## POWDERED SUGAR COOKIES

**BBB + Corn**

- **1 cup allowed margarine**
- **1½ cups confectioners sugar**
- **1 teaspoon synthetic vanilla**
- **2½ cups rice flour**
- **1 teaspoon baking soda**
- **1 teaspoon cereal-free baking powder**

Cream margarine and sugar. Beat in vanilla and 2 tablespoons water. Stir in dry ingredients until smooth and well blended. Place 1-inch balls of dough on unoiled cookie sheets and flatten with designed cookie press or with bottom of cup or glass. Dip press in powdered sugar as needed to keep it from sticking to dough. Bake in preheated 350° oven 10 to 12 minutes or until barely browned around edges. *About 6 dozen*

*Note:* Confectioners powdered sugar available in markets contains 3% cornstarch. It may be used in all recipes coded. **(+ Corn)**

## MELTING MOMENTS

**BBB + Oats + Corn**

- **½ cup cornstarch**
- **½ cup confectioners powdered sugar**
- **1⅓ cups oat flour**
- **¾ cup allowed margarine**
- **½ teaspoon synthetic vanilla**

Blend or sift together cornstarch, powdered sugar, and flour. Add margarine and vanilla and stir until a soft dough forms. Chill if necessary in order to handle well. Roll into 1-inch balls, place on unoiled cookie sheets, and flatten with lightly floured fork. Bake in preheated 300° oven 25 to 30 minutes or until edges are lightly browned. *About 3 dozen*

**BBB + Rye or Oats + Corn + N&S + TE&A + Mold**

- ½ cup allowed margarine, melted
- 1 cup brown sugar, packed
- 1 cup rye flour or oat flour
- ½ teaspoon salt
- ½ teaspoon baking soda
- 1½ teaspoons cereal-free baking powder
- ½ teaspoon almond extract
- 1 cup rolled oats
- ½ cup cornflakes
- ½ cup chopped salted almonds

## CRISP ALMOND COOKIES

Melt margarine and cool, then beat with sugar, extract, and 2 tablespoons water until mixture is smooth and glossy. Add flour, salt, soda, and baking powder and blend well. Stir in oats, cornflakes, and nuts. Drop from teaspoon onto oiled cookie sheets and flatten if desired. Bake in preheated 350° oven 10 to 12 minutes. *About 3 dozen*

**Variation:**

Replace nuts with coconut and cornflakes with Rice Krispies.

**BBB + Barley + Corn + Fruit + TE&A + Mold**

- ½ cup allowed margarine
- 1 cup confectioners powdered sugar
- 1 tablespoon lemon juice
- 1 tablespoon grated lemon peel
- ⅔ cup rice flour
- ¼ cup soy flour
- 1½ teaspoons potato flour
- 2 teaspoons cereal-free baking powder
- ¼ teaspoon salt
- 2 cups crushed Rice Chex

## SPECIAL LEMON CRISPS

Cream margarine and powdered sugar. Beat in 2 tablespoons water, lemon juice, and lemon peel until light and fluffy. Blend all dry ingredients except Rice Chex and mix well. Let dough stand 10 minutes. Drop from teaspoon into bowl of coarsely crushed cereal. Turn to coat well, place on unoiled cookie sheets, and press flat. Bake in preheated 350° oven 10 minutes. Remove to cooling racks. These are light crisp cookies. *About 2½ dozen*

**Variation:**

Replace the 3 flours with ½ cup each of brown rice flour and rice polish.

**BBB + Barley + Corn + N&S + TE&A + Mold**

- ¼ cup allowed margarine
- 1 package (10½ ounces) miniature marshmallows
- ⅓ cup peanut butter
- ½ teaspoon synthetic vanilla
- 4 cups Rice Chex, Corn Chex, Corn Bran, or Rice Krispies (any one or a combination)

## MALLOWED CEREAL ROLLS

Melt margarine, marshmallows, and peanut butter over very low heat, stirring until smooth. Stir in vanilla and add cereals, tossing until well coated. Shape mixture on waxed paper into rolls 2-inches in diameter. Wrap tightly and chill. When ready to serve, cut into ½-inch slices. *About 5 dozen*

## COCONUT CORNFLAKE COOKIES

**BBB + Rye + Barley + Corn + Fruit + N&S + Mold**

- **½ cup allowed margarine**
- **½ cup sugar**
- **¼ cup brown sugar, firmly packed**
- **1 teaspoon synthetic vanilla**
- **1 teaspoon grated lemon peel**
- **½ cup corn flour**
- **½ cup rye flour**
- **¼ cup potato flour**
- **1 teaspoon baking soda**
- **1¼ teaspoons cereal-free baking powder**
- **¼ teaspoon salt**
- **1 cup flaked coconut**
- **2 cups cornflakes**

Cream margarine and sugars. Beat in vanilla, lemon peel, and 2 tablespoons water. Combine all dry ingredients except coconut and cornflakes and mix well into creamed mixture. Stir in coconut and cornflakes. Place 1-inch balls of dough onto oiled cookie sheets, spacing 2 inches apart. Press flat with dampened or floured fingertips. Bake in preheated 350° oven 10 minutes or until lightly browned. *About 3 dozen*

## SALTED PEANUT COOKIES

**BBB + Oats + Barley + Corn + N&S + TE&A + Mold**

- **½ cup allowed margarine**
- **⅔ cup brown sugar, firmly packed**
- **1 teaspoon synthetic vanilla**
- **½ cup chopped salted peanuts**
- **¾ cup brown rice flour**
- **¼ cup rice polish or rice bran**
- **½ teaspoon baking soda**
- **1½ teaspoons cereal-free baking powder**
- **1 cup rolled oats**
- **⅓ cup cornflakes**

Cream margarine and sugar. Beat in vanilla and 2 tablespoons water until light and fluffy. Add nuts. Combine remaining ingredients except oats and cornflakes and stir into creamed mixture. Add oats and cornflakes and blend well. Let dough rest a few minutes before baking. Drop from teaspoon onto oiled cookie sheets. Flatten or not as desired. Bake in preheated 400° oven 8 to 10 minutes. Cool on racks. *About 4 dozen*

# Ice Creams and Sherbets

Many frozen desserts can be made without milk and eggs, beginning with fruit ices or sherbets prepared with allowed fruits and juices. The addition of Cream of Rice, unflavored gelatin, starch, flour, or tapioca helps to thicken as well as smooth the frozen mixture. When allowed, add one teaspoon slippery elm powder (from a health food store) to any recipe mixture for a creamier texture. Sugar also helps the texture of frozen desserts, but we cut down on sugar as much as possible, omitting it entirely from some fruit combinations that seem to need none as far as taste is concerned.

Most recipes in this section are processed by the refrigerator-freezer method because that is handiest. To use the ice cream freezer seems to constitute a major production but, admittedly, a better texture results when we go to the trouble. When making frozen desserts in the freezing compartment of the refrigerator, turn controls to coldest setting or, if available, use sub-0° freezer.

Ice creams using pudding and pie filling mixes are of excellent texture when turned in an ice cream freezer. If using these mixes, however, read each ingredients list before purchasing. Some contain milk or milk products. Use Jell-O brand vanilla but not "instant" pudding as it does contain non-fat milk. Jell-O Americana Vanilla Tapioca may be used. These mixes contain cornstarch, chemicals, and dyes and should be used only after you reach the **+ Corn + TE&A** rungs of the food additions ladder. Our health food stores stock Bonny Tree Pudding and Pie Filling and it can be used early in the program of testing and allowing.

**BBB**

## FRUIT POPSICLES

Purée allowed fruits (water-pack canned) or use allowed juices. Sweeten with brown or white cane or beet sugar as desired. Dissolve sugar in fruit. Pour into Tupperware Ice Tups, leaving room at the top for expansion during freezing. Place top on container, insert stick, and freeze.

If you don't own these handy containers, pour purée or juice into three-ounce paper cups. Place a small square of foil over each and line them up on a small tray. With a sharp knife, make a slit in the center of each foil. Insert ice cream stick in each and freeze.

## APRICOT-PINEAPPLE SHERBET

**BBB**

**1 can (16 ounces) water-pack apricots, drained**
**2¼ cups unsweetened pineapple juice**
**½ cup sugar**
**¼ cup Cream of Rice**

Purée apricots in blender with 1 cup juice. Combine apricot purée, remaining juice, and sugar. Bring to boil. Sprinkle in Cream of Rice slowly, stirring constantly. Cook 1 minute and remove from heat. Cover and let stand 3 minutes. Purée mixture, half at a time, in preheated blender until smooth. Chill and partially freeze in shallow pan. Break apart and beat in chilled bowl until light and fluffy. Refreeze, covered, until firm. *Makes 1 quart*

**Variations:**

1. For a change of flavor, replace apricots with water-pack canned pears or any BBB fruits.
2. APPLE-CRANBERRY SHERBET—Omit apricots and pineapple juice. Bring to boil 2 cups cranberries, 3 cups water, and ½ cup sugar. Sprinkle in cereal, stirring constantly. Continue with directions above, then stir in 1 can (6 ounces) frozen apple juice concentrate.
3. Follow Apple-Cranberry recipe, omitting apple juice concentrate. Replace with unsweetened orange juice concentrate. **(+ Fruit)**

## SUMMER FRUIT ICE

**BBB**

**4 cups any combination of allowed fresh fruits, puréed**
**1 can (8 ounces) unsweetened crushed pineapple (keeps other fruits from darkening)**
**1 can (6 ounces) pure frozen unsweetened apple juice concentrate or frozen pear-grape concentrate, softened**
**Sugar or honey to taste (+ TE&A)**

Purée fruits and juices, half at a time, in blender. Heat part of mixture, add chosen sweetener, and stir to dissolve sugar or to thin honey. Combine all ingredients and freeze in shallow pan. Stir every 30 minutes until frozen and smooth, then break apart and beat until fluffy in chilled mixing bowl. Refreeze. Soften slightly before serving. *Makes 1½–2 quarts*

**Variations:**

1. Replace concentrate with frozen unsweetened orange juice concentrate or with ¼ cup lemon juice. These juices, like pineapple, keep other fruits from darkening, so pineapple may be omitted, but remember that citrus is not a BBB food. **(+ Fruit)**
2. Replace concentrate with frozen pink or regular lemonade or limeade concentrate. **(+ Corn + Fruit)**

## FROSTY PEACH SHERBET

**BBB**

- **2 cups peach purée (fresh peaches or water-pack canned)**
- **½ cup unsweetened applesauce**
- **1 tablespoon unflavored gelatin or 1½ tablespoons Minute Tapioca**
- **1 cup water or allowed milk substitute**
- **Sugar to taste**

*Gelatin method:* Combine peach purée and applesauce. Soften gelatin in ¼ cup water. Bring to boil sugar and remaining water. Stir in softened gelatin to dissolve. Add fruit mixture, blending well. Freeze in shallow pan until firm. Break into chilled bowl, beat until light and fluffy, and refreeze. Soften slightly before serving. *Makes 1 quart*

*Tapioca method:* Combine all ingredients and let stand 5 minutes. Bring to boil, stirring constantly. Cool and freeze as directed.

*Note:* This sherbet is so adaptable that it will make your imagination turn handsprings. Replace peach purée with puréed BBB fruits to suit your taste or your own or your neighbors' orchards. Vary the amount of applesauce as good texture requires. Have fun by trying, when allowed: cherries, strawberries, blueberries, elderberries, blackberries, or raspberries, **(+ Fruit)** and rhubarb **(+ Buckwheat + Veg.)**.

## RADIANT CRANBERRY SHERBET

**BBB**

- **1 tablespoon unflavored gelatin**
- **1 pound cranberries, washed and stemmed**
- **1–1½ cups sugar**
- **1 cup unsweetened pineapple, apple, or white grape juice**

Soften gelatin in ½ cup water in blender. Cook cranberries in 2½ cups water until skins pop. Pour slightly cooled cranberries and liquid slowly into blender with gelatin. Purée. Combine with sugar, stir to dissolve, and add juice. Freeze in shallow pan until firm. Break into chilled bowl and beat until light and fluffy. Refreeze. Soften slightly before serving. *Makes 2½ quarts*

**Variation:**

Replace BBB juices with orange juice or use 1 can (6 ounces) frozen unsweetened orange juice concentrate for more pronounced orange flavor. Stir in 1 teaspoon finely grated orange peel. **(+ Fruit)**

## SNOW CONES

**BBB**

Defrost concentrate to slushy stage or freeze juice or purée to slushy stage. Mix quickly with ice. Spoon and mound into paper cups. Refreeze. Allow to thaw slightly before serving. Squeeze juice up through ice or use large drinking straw cut in half. Refreshing on a hot day! *Makes 6*

**1 can (6 ounces) frozen unsweetened apple juice concentrate or frozen unsweetened grape-pear concentrate or ¾ cup other allowed fruit purée**
**3 cups finely crushed ice**
**6 paper cups (5 ounce size)**

**Variations:**

1. ORANGE SNOW CONES—Replace BBB concentrates with frozen unsweetened orange concentrate. (+ **Fruit**)
2. CRANBERRY, CRANAPPLE, PINK LEMONADE, LEMONADE or LIMEADE SNOW CONES—Replace BBB concentrates with choice of frozen concentrates. (+ **Corn** + **Fruit**)

## BASIC SOY ICE CREAM

**BBB**

Soften gelatin in ½ cup water. Blend sugars and starch. Slowly stir in soy milk to keep smooth. Bring to boil, stirring constantly. Cook over low heat 5 minutes. Remove from heat, stir in gelatin to dissolve, and add vanilla. Cool, then freeze in shallow pan until almost firm. Beat in chilled bowl until light and fluffy. Refreeze. Soften slightly to serve. *Makes 1½ quarts*

**1 tablespoon unflavored gelatin**
**⅓ cup sugar**
**¼ cup brown sugar**
**1 tablespoon tapioca starch or potato starch or 1½ tablespoons rice flour**
**4 cups soy milk (see Soy Milk From Powder in Appendix, p. 376)**
**2 teaspoons synthetic vanilla**

*Note:* If desired, serve with Brown Sugar Syrup Topping, p. 300.

**Variations:**

1. COFFEE ICE CREAM—Reduce vanilla to 1½ teaspoons and add 1½ tablespoons instant pure coffee granules to hot mixture. (+ **TE&A**)
2. CAROB CHIP ICE CREAM—Shave 1 chilled El Molino CaraCoa Carob Candy Bar—Milk Free. Add before refreezing. (+ **TE&A**)

## BONNY TREE VANILLA ICE CREAM

**BBB**

- **¼ cup tapioca starch**
- **1 package (4 ounces) Bonny Tree Pure Vanilla Pudding (unrefined sugar, tapioca flour, arrowroot flour, and natural flavors)**
- **3 cups allowed milk substitute**

Mix tapioca starch with pudding mix. Blend in allowed milk substitute, little at a time. Cook over medium heat, stirring constantly until mixture comes to boil. Remove from heat, cool, pour into freezing trays and freeze until almost firm. Turn into chilled bowl and whip at low speed until smooth and heavy. Refill trays and freeze until firm. *Makes 1 quart*

## GRAPE SHERBET

**BBB**

- **2 tablespoons unflavored gelatin**
- **6 cups unsweetened grape juice or pear-grape juice**
- **1 cup sugar**
- **¼ teaspoon salt**
- **2 cups chilled allowed milk substitute**

Soften gelatin in ½ cup grape juice. Heat 1 cup grape juice, sugar, and salt and add gelatin to dissolve. Stir in remaining 4½ cups grape juice and chill. Stir in allowed milk substitute. Mixture will have a curdled appearance which will disappear when sherbet is processed in ice cream freezer. Pour into 2-quart freezer can, filling no more than ⅔ full. Freeze according to freezer directions. *Makes 2 quarts*

**Variation:**

Replace grape juice with unsweetened apple-boysenberry juice. If desired, fold in coarsely ground or crushed unsweetened blueberries, fresh or frozen (+ **Fruit**) or 1 box frozen sweetened berries (**+ Corn + Fruit + TE&A**).

## STRAWBERRY BANANA SPLIT

☐ **BBB + Fruit**

- **1 tablespoon unflavored gelatin**
- **4 cups fresh or frozen unsweetened strawberries, puréed**
- **4 bananas, halved lengthwise**
- **1 can (8 ounces) unsweetened crushed pineapple**

Soften gelatin in ¾ cup water 5 minutes, then heat until dissolved, stirring constantly. Add to puréed strawberries. Freeze in shallow 9 x 9-inch pan 45 minutes or until almost solid. Break apart and beat with electric beater in chilled bowl until fluffy. Return to refreeze.

*To assemble Banana Split:* Arrange banana slices in oblong serving dish. Add scoops of strawberry sherbet and top with crushed pineapple. *Serves 4*

## CHURNED FRUIT SHERBET

**BBB + Fruit** ☐

**2½ cups unsweetened fruit juice or puréed fresh or canned unsweetened fruit**
**¼ cup lemon juice**
**½ cup sugar or honey (+ TE&A) to taste**
**1½ tablespoons tapioca starch or 2½ tablespoons rice flour**
**6 cups allowed milk substitute**
**Dash of salt**

Blend fruit, lemon juice, sugar, and starch in saucepan. Bring to boil, stirring constantly. Cook until clear or thickened. *(Note:* For smoother purée, simmer fresh fruits 10 minutes.) Blend fruit mixture with allowed milk substitute, chill, and freeze according to freezer directions. *Makes 2½ quarts*

*Note:* 1 tablespoon gelatin or 1½ tablespoons Minute Tapioca may be used as thickening. Follow methods for Frosty Peach Sherbet, p. 292.

**Variations:**

1. Use 1 can (20 ounces) crushed unsweetened pineapple as fruit choice. If desired, add ½ teaspoon pineapple extract. (+ **TE&A)**
2. Use 1 can (12 ounces) frozen unsweetened orange juice concentrate for fruit. Add 1 tablespoon grated orange peel.
3. Try other unsweetened fruit combinations or singles: Frozen tangerine concentrate, canned pineapple and frozen orange concentrate, mashed bananas and frozen orange concentrate, or mashed bananas and canned pineapple.

## POLAR BANANAS

**BBB + Fruit** ☐

Peel ripe bananas. Break small ones into halves and longer ones into thirds. Insert round or flat wooden stick two-thirds through length of each section. Tie small freezer bag over each banana-stick and freeze.

These are delicious and creamy. A great way to rescue bananas that might otherwise become too ripe. They keep their white color in the freezer and are handy for snacks or for table desserts.

☐ **BBB + Fruit**

## JUICED POLAR BANANA POPSICLES

Measure depth of a 3-ounce paper cup minus ¼ inch. Cut peeled bananas into matched lengths and stand one upright in each paper cup you plan to prepare. Insert ice cream stick two-thirds through length of banana. Pour any allowed unsweetened juice around banana and barely over top.

Cut small squares of foil into size to seal paper cups. Make thin cut in center of foil ½ inch long. Slip foil over ice cream stick and slide down. Press edges of foil around cup to seal. This will keep the popsicle stick upright as mixture freezes. Set cups on small tray and freeze.

These make healthy snacks—look, Ma, no sugar—and they provide a happy way to get fruit down a child who is not a really good fruit eater.

**Variations:**

1. Try unsweetened pineapple-coconut juice around banana. **(+ N&S + TE&A)**
2. Pour around banana: Cranapple or cranberry drink, any nectar, or lemon-limeade prepared from concentrate. **(+ Corn + TE&A)**

☐ **BBB + Fruit + TE&A**

**4 cups unsweetened juice to correspond to gelatin flavor (orange gelatin and juice, grape gelatin with grape or pear-grape juice, berry gelatin with apple-boysenberry juice, etc.)**
**1 package (3 ounces) fruit-flavored gelatin**

## DOUBLE FLAVORED POPSICLES

Heat 1 cup juice to boiling. Dissolve gelatin in hot juice. Add remaining juice and pour into Tupperware Ice Tups or into small paper cups. Insert sticks as recommended in Fruit Popsicles, p. 290 and freeze.

**Variation:**

Team lime gelatin with frozen limeade concentrate, lemon gelatin with frozen lemonade concentrate, red cherry or berry gelatin with cranberry drink, apricot or peach gelatin with matching nectars, etc. Discover your own combinations. **(+ Corn)**

## STRAWBERRY SHERBET

**BBB + Fruit + TE&A**

- **2 quarts fresh strawberries, sliced**
- **2 cups sugar**
- **1⅓ cups allowed milk substitute**
- **⅓ cup unsweetened orange or apple juice**
- **Dash of cinnamon**

Combine berries and sugar and let stand 1½ hours. Purée in blender and press through fine strainer to remove seeds. Add remaining ingredients and freeze in shallow pan until almost firm. Break into chunks in chilled mixing bowl and beat with electric mixer until light and creamy. Refreeze in covered container. Soften slightly before serving. *Makes 2 quarts*

**Variations:**

Double recipe and freeze in 4-quart ice cream freezer according to freezer directions.

## TUTTI-FRUITTI ICE CREAM

**BBB + Fruit + N&S + TE&A**

- **¼ cup flaked coconut**
- **1 cup boiling water**
- **2 cups unsweetened apple or pineapple or orange juice**
- **¼ cup soy milk powder or ¼ cup raw cashews or both**
- **2 ripe bananas**
- **1 can (8 ounces) unsweetened crushed pineapple**
- **¼ cup chopped maraschino cherries***
- **Additional flaked coconut**

Soak coconut in water 15 minutes. Liquefy in blender, then add and liquefy all ingredients except cherries and additional coconut. Freeze in shallow pan until firm throughout. Break into chilled bowl and beat until creamy but not watery. Fold in cherries and flaked coconut. Refreeze. Or mix and churn in ice cream freezer according to freezer directions. *Makes 2 quarts*

**Variation:**

Create other delicious ice creams with different combinations of fruits and juices.

**Note:* The sugar in maraschino cherry syrup may include corn. Do not use this addition until corn has been tested and proven friendly.

## SUPER EASY CRANBERRY SHERBET

**BBB + Corn + Fruit + N&S + TE&A**

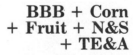

- **1 can (1 pound) jellied cranberry sauce**
- **¼ cup honey**
- **2 teaspoons grated orange peel**
- **⅓ cup orange juice**
- **1 cup Dsertwhip, whipped**

Mash sauce with fork. Add honey and orange peel and juice. Mix well and freeze in ice tray until almost firm. Beat in chilled bowl. Fold in whipped Dsertwhip and refreeze until firm. *Makes 1 quart*

**BBB + Corn + TE&A**

- ¼ **cup cornstarch**
- 1 **package (3⅛ ounces) Jell-O Vanilla Pudding and Pie Filling Mix***
- 6 **cups allowed milk substitute**
- 1 **teaspoon synthetic vanilla**

## VANILLA PUDDING ICE CREAM

Combine cornstarch, vanilla pudding and 3 cups milk substitute in saucepan and cook according to pudding package directions. When thick, add remaining milk substitute and vanilla and stir to blend. Pour into ice cream freezer cannister. Freezing takes about 25 minutes in crank or electric freezer. Remove dash, replace lid, pack, and let harden. Double recipe for 4-quart freezer. *Makes 2 quarts*

*Note:* This ice cream is a good base for making any flavor. See our suggestions below. Unless otherwise stated, add flavoring when ice cream begins to thicken in freezer.

**Variations:**

1. Fresh Fruits. Add sugar to sweeten and let stand until sugar dissolves. Banana and some other fruits need the addition of lemon juice (¼ cup) to keep them from turning dark. **(+ Fruit)**
2. Coconut. Replace part of milk substitute with coconut milk, juice, drink, or unsweetened pineapple-coconut juice. Add 2 cups flaked coconut. **(+ N&S)**
3. Nut brittle. Crush and add 1½ cups brittle **(+ N&S)**
4. Peppermint Stick. Soak 2 cups crushed candy in 2 cups allowed milk substitute overnight, refrigerated. Delete 2 cups milk substitute from recipe.
5. Almost-Chocolate-Chip. Chill 1 El Molino CaraCoa Carob Candy Bar—MilkFree, then shave it into ice cream.
6. Butterscotch. Replace vanilla pudding with Jell-O Butterscotch Pudding and Pie Filling Mix.*

**Note:* Read labels. Some pudding and pie filling mixes contain milk.

## JAN'S FRUIT SHERBET

**BBB + Corn + Fruit + N&S + TE&A**

- **1 tablespoon unflavored gelatin**
- **2½ cups orange juice, fresh or made from concentrate**
- **½ cup sugar or honey, or part sugar and part corn syrup**
- **2 large bananas, mashed or puréed**
- **¼ cup lemon juice**
- **1 cup Dsertwhip, whipped**

Soften gelatin in ¼ cup water. Heat 1 cup orange juice and sugar to boil and stir in gelatin to dissolve. Add mashed bananas to lemon juice. Combine all except Dsertwhip and freeze in shallow pan until firm throughout. Break into chilled bowl and beat until creamy and fluffy but not watery. Fold in Dsertwhip. Refreeze. Soften slightly before serving. *Makes 1½–2 quarts*

**Variations:**

1. LEMON or LIME SHERBET—Replace sugar with 1 cup honey. Omit orange juice and bananas and replace with 3 cups water or allowed milk substitute. Increase lemon juice to 1⅓ cups (or use lime juice). Freeze, beat, fold in Dsertwhip, and refreeze.
2. SPICED FRUIT SHERBET—Replace orange juice with pineapple juice. Increase banana to 2 cups mashed banana. Reduce lemon juice to 2 tablespoons. Add ¼ teaspoon rum flavoring, 1 teaspoon ginger, and dash of salt. Freeze, beat, fold in Dsertwhip, and refreeze.

## BEV'S BIRTHDAY PEACHES N' CREAM

**BBB + Corn + N&S + TE&A**

- **2 cups purée of fresh peaches**
- **1½ cups sugar or 1¼ cups honey**
- **1 tablespoon unflavored gelatin**
- **¼ teaspoon salt**
- **6 cups thinly sliced peaches (14 large ripe fresh peaches)**
- **¼ teaspoon almond extract**
- **1 cup Dsertwhip, whipped**

Combine purée, sugar, gelatin, and salt. Let stand 5 minutes. Heat, stirring often, until mixture is very hot and sugar dissolved. Combine with sliced peaches and extract. Pour into 9 x 13-inch shallow pan. Freeze until mixture is very firm throughout. Whip Dsertwhip and set aside in refrigerator. Break up peach mixture and beat in chilled bowl with electric mixer until smooth and fluffy but not warm and watery. Fold in Dsertwhip. Refreeze in two 1-quart containers. Serve before frozen solid or soften slightly before serving. This is always a compliment winner with its fresh peach flavor and creamy texture. *Makes 2 quarts*

**Variation:**

Prepare with other fresh ripe fruits such as apricots, cherries, berries, pears, or plums. Tart fruits will take some adjustment in the amount of sweetening used.

**BBB + Corn + Fruit + N&S + TE&A**

- 4 cups orange juice
- ½ cup lemon juice
- 3 cups confectioners sugar
- 1 cup Dsertwhip, whipped
- 1 can (8 ounces) crushed pineapple
- Slivered almonds or chopped peanuts or toasted coconut, (optional)

## FROZEN AMBROSIA

Combine juices and confectioners sugar. Whip Dsertwhip and fold in crushed pineapple. Pour juice into 2 refrigerator ice trays or into a shallow pan. Spoon Dsertwhip mixture over but don't stir together. Freeze firm. Soften slightly, spoon into sherbet dishes and top with slivered almonds, chopped peanuts, or toasted coconut. *Makes 2 quarts*

# SUNDAE TOPPINGS AND CRUSTS FOR ICE CREAM

**BBB**

- ¾ cup brown sugar, firmly packed
- 1 tablespoon tapioca starch
- 1 tablespoon allowed margarine

## BROWN SUGAR SYRUP TOPPING

Blend sugar and starch in saucepan. Stir in 1 cup water and bring to boil, stirring constantly until smooth, clear, and thickened. Boil gently 1 minute. Serve warm on plain ice cream. *Makes scant 2 cups*

**BBB + TE&A**

- ¼ cup carob powder
- ⅓ cup brown sugar, firmly packed
- Pinch of salt
- ⅔ cup allowed milk substitute
- 2 tablespoons allowed margarine
- ½ teaspoon synthetic vanilla

## CAROB SYRUP

Combine dry ingredients, add milk substitute, and bring to boil, stirring constantly. Simmer 5 minutes. Stir in margarine and vanilla. Store in tightly closed jar in refrigerator. Serve over Basic Soy Ice Cream, p. 293, or Bonny Tree Vanilla Ice Cream, p. 294, or Vanilla Pudding Ice Cream, p. 298 (**+ Corn**). *Makes 1 cup*

**BBB + Corn**

- ⅔ cup brown sugar, firmly packed
- ⅔ cup sugar
- ⅔ cup white corn syrup
- ¼ cup allowed margarine
- 1 cup allowed milk substitute

## BUTTERSCOTCH TOPPING

Boil sugars and margarine to 230° on candy thermometer, beginning over very low heat until sugars melt. At this temperature syrup will thread when poured from spoon. Blend in milk substitute and cook, stirring, barely below boiling for 3 minutes or until thick. Serve hot or cold. *Makes 1½ cups*

## FLAMING JUBILEE TOPPING

**BBB + Corn + Fruit + TE&A**

- **Sugar cubes**
- **Lemon extract**
- **2 tablespoons brown sugar**
- **½ teaspoon cornstarch**
- **½ cup orange juice**
- **2 tablespoons allowed margarine**
- **1 can (16 ounces) bing cherries, drained**

Soak sugar cubes in extract and set aside. Blend sugar and cornstarch. Slowly add orange juice and cook, stirring constantly, until clear and slightly thickened. Stir in margarine and cherries. Heat thoroughly. Spoon sauce over Vanilla Pudding Ice Cream, p. 298. Place 1 sugar cube on each dessert and light. Serve flaming dessert immediately. *Serves 4–6*

## CRUNCHY MALLOW CRUST

**BBB + Barley + Corn + TE&A + Mold**

- **2½ cups miniature marshmallows**
- **2½ tablespoons allowed margarine**
- **3 cups Rice Krispies, corn flakes, or Nutri-Grain Corn—Flaked Whole Grain Cereal**

Melt marshmallows and 2 tablespoons allowed margarine over boiling water. Pour over cereal in mixing bowl oiled with remainder of margarine. Press mixture in thin layer into 8-inch pie pan or individual custard cups. Let set until firm. Fill with allowed softened ice cream of your choice and refreeze. *Makes one 8-inch shell*

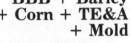

## CRUNCHY DESSERT TOPPING

**BBB + Barley + Corn + N&S + TE&A + Mold**

- **1 cup mild honey**
- **¼ cup allowed margarine**
- **5 cups Nutri-Grain Corn-Flaked Whole Grain Cereal**
- **1 cup flaked coconut**

Bring honey and margarine slowly to boil, stirring constantly. Combine cereal and coconut in large oiled mixing bowl. Pour honey mixture over and toss lightly to coat. Spread on oiled baking sheets to cool. Crumble over ice cream or fruit or pudding. *Makes 4–5 cups*

# Pies

## PIE CRUSTS

Rolled pie crusts that handle easily are somewhat few and far between. Given the most cooperative ingredients, the perfect rolled pie crust is something usually achieved by dedicated kitchen artists only, and even they use special tools and supplies. I, Gloria, use a Tupperware pastry sheet and wouldn't think of approaching dough without my ball bearing, wooden rolling pin. Tupperware makes a rolling pin that holds ice water that's ideal for purists. Some good pie bakers rely on a wooden pin and canvas rolling sheet.

Waxed paper of the best quality (Cut-Rite works well) is a great help. Tear off two sheets several inches larger than your pie pan. Sprinkle a little water on bread board or countertop and lay one sheet of waxed paper on the water to stick there. Place your wad of pie crust dough in the middle of the paper and press out a bit with your hand, keeping it in a circle. Place the other sheet of waxed paper on top and roll to the thinness you desire, pressing down and rolling from the center out in all directions. When ready, peel paper off one side and the other sheet makes it easy to turn crust over pie pan. Peeling the second sheet off without tearing the crust is a little tricky but, once you get it started past the edges, it usually behaves quite well.

Many of our pie crust recipes do not require rolling. Pressed-into-the-pan crusts are made even lazier if you purchase two same size pie pans. Roughly finger-press the crumbs or dough into one pan and place the other one in on top of the crust. The thinness and compactness of the crust will depend on how hard you press down on the top pan. You may either bake the empty pan along with the crust or remove it after it has put the crumbs in their proper place.

### WARM WATER PIE CRUST

BBB

**¾ cup rice flour**
**1 teaspoon sugar**
**½ teaspoon salt**
**¼ cup allowed margarine**
**¼ cup warm water + more as needed**

Mix dry ingredients and work margarine into them. Add water (up to ½ cup total) to make soft dough. Let stand 10 minutes before rolling or pressing into pan. Prick with fork and bake in preheated 350° oven about 20 minutes. *Makes one 8-inch shell*

## RICE FLOUR PIE SHELL

**BBB**

Cut or pinch margarine into dry ingredients until crumbly. Add water. Work lightly with hands until soft ball forms. Place dough in pie pan and press to bottom and sides with back of spoon or with fingers. Use a fork to prick bottom to prevent buckling. Bake in preheated 400° oven 12 to 15 minutes. *Makes one 9-inch shell*

- **½ cup allowed margarine**
- **1¼ cups rice flour**
- **1½ teaspoons cereal-free baking powder**
- **Salt to taste**
- **4 tablespoons chilled water**

**Variation:**

Omit baking powder and salt. Replace rice flour with Ener-G Rice Mix.

## BROWN RICE FLOUR PIE CRUST

**BBB**

Combine flours and salt. Cut in allowed margarine with pastry blender to fine texture. Add ice water to form soft dough. Pat evenly into pie pan. Prick with fork and bake in preheated 425° oven 15 minutes or until nicely browned. *Makes one 8- or 9-inch shell*

- **1 cup brown rice flour**
- **1 tablespoon potato flour**
- **½ teaspoon salt**
- **¼ cup allowed margarine**
- **¼ cup ice water**

**Variation:**

Instead of all brown rice flour, use ½ cup brown and ½ cup white rice flour.

## BRAVISSIMO GRANOLA PIE CRUST

**BBB**

Mix and press into 9-inch pie pan. Bake in preheated 350° oven 6 to 8 minutes. Cool and fill with whatever prepared and cooled pudding is allowed at your stage of food additions. *Makes one 9-inch shell*

- **2 cups Bravissimo Granola, p. 247**
- **¼ cup allowed margarine, melted**

## NO-GLUTEN PIE CRUST

**BBB**

Mix all dry ingredients, unsifted, in bowl. Cut in margarine until crumbly. Add water and stir to moisten all dry ingredients. Make into ball with hands and divide in half. Place each half in separate 8- or 9-inch pie pans. Press with fingers evenly over pan and flute edge. Prick with fork. Refrigerate 30 minutes before baking. Then bake in preheated 450° oven 10 to 15 minutes. Cool. Fill with fruit or pudding filling or leave raw and bake with filling. Good flavor and texture. *Makes two 8- or 9-inch shells or one 2-crust pie*

- **1⅓ cups rice flour**
- **½ cup soy flour**
- **1 tablespoon potato flour**
- **1 teaspoon salt**
- **¾ cup allowed margarine**
- **4–5 tablespoons chilled water**

**BBB + N&S**

- 2 cups flaked coconut
- ¼ cup allowed margarine

## COCONUT PIE CRUST

Blend coconut and margarine, and place in 9-inch pie pan. Toast in preheated 300° oven 15 to 20 minutes, stirring occasionally until golden brown. Press over bottom and sides of pie pan. Cool before filling. *Makes one 9-inch shell*

**Variations:**

1. Combine coconut and margarine. Press evenly over sides and bottom of 9-inch pie pan. Chill 1 hour or until firm. Crust may be frozen until needed.
2. Melt allowed margarine in large skillet. Add coconut and stir over low heat until golden brown. Remove from skillet to 9-inch pie pan and shape over sides and bottom with spoon or fingers.
3. Spread margarine in 9-inch pie pan. Sprinkle coconut over evenly and pat down or press down with 9-inch pan. Bake in preheated 350° oven 10 minutes.

**BBB + N&S**

- ¼ cup allowed margarine
- ½ cup rice flour
- 1 cup flaked coconut

## TOP BURNER PIE CRUST

Melt margarine in skillet. Add flour and coconut and cook, stirring constantly, until light brown. Place in 9-inch pie pan and shape with back of spoon or fingers up sides and over bottom of pan. Fill with any cooked and cooled pudding or fruit pie filling allowed at your stage of food additions. Chill and serve. *Makes one 9-inch shell*

**BBB + N&S**

- 1 cup raw nuts, blanched or not (almonds, filberts, Brazil, pecans, peanuts, walnuts, or mixed)
- 2½ tablespoons sugar

## NUTTY LUSCIOUS PIE SHELL

Blend nuts until finely ground in blender or food processor. Add sugar and continue processing until well mixed. Press firmly with spoon onto sides and bottom of 8- or 9-inch pie pan. Do not attempt to make rim. Bake in preheated 400° oven 6 to 8 minutes. Cool before filling. *Makes one 8- or 9-inch shell*

## GLUTEN-FREE RICE GRANOLA PIE CRUST

**BBB + N&S + TE&A**

- **2 cups Gluten-Free Rice Granola, p. 249***
- **¼ cup allowed margarine**
- **2 tablespoons honey**
- **½ teaspoon cinnamon**
- **¼ teaspoon nutmeg**

Pulverize granola in blender or processer or roll to crush fine. Melt allowed margarine and stir in honey and spices. Mix with crushed granola. Reserve ¼ cup mixture, if desired, for topping. Press into 8- or 9-inch pie pan and add filling. Or, if preferred, first bake in preheated 350° oven 8 to 10 minutes. *Makes one 8- or 9-inch shell*

**Note:* Be sure that your granola is from this book or that it is made entirely from ingredients acceptable at your stage of food additions.

## CRUST FOR CONGEALED FRUIT PIE

**BBB + N&S + TE&A**

- **3 tablespoons allowed margarine**
- **1 tablespoon honey**
- **1½ cups shredded unsweetened coconut**
- **¼ cup rice bran**

Heat 2 tablespoons allowed margarine in saucepan, add honey while still hot and blend mixture with coconut and rice bran. Rub 9-inch pie pan with remaining margarine and press in coconut mixture. Chill. *Makes one 9-inch shell*

## RICE n' RYE MIX PIE CRUST

**BBB + Rye**

- **½ cup allowed shortening or allowed margarine**
- **2 cups Ener-G Rice 'n Rye Mix**
- **6–8 tablespoons chilled water**

Cut shortening into flour mix until mixture resembles coarse meal. (We usually work with our hands.) Add water and stir into a soft dough. Divide dough in half. Use our helpful hints for rolling and lifting dough, found at the beginning of this section. For two single 8-inch pie shells, prick sides and bottom with fork and bake in preheated 400° oven 12 to 15 minutes. Do not prick bottom crust of 2-crust pie, but of course you know that. Assemble and bake pie as directed in fruit pie recipe of your allowed choice. *Makes two 9-inch shells or top and bottom crusts for one 2-crust pie.*

## BBB + Rye

**1½ cups rye flour**
**½ teaspoon salt**
**1 teaspoon cereal-free baking powder**
**4 tablespoons allowed margarine**
**3–4 tablespoons chilled water**

## RYE PIE CRUST

Sift flour, salt and baking powder. Cut in margarine, then add enough water to make stiff dough. Roll dough carefully on rye-floured board, rolling from the center out in all directions to make circle 3 to 4 inches larger than your pie pan. Roll thin. Waxed paper on each side will help. Place in 9-inch pie pan, fluting edge. Prick with fork and bake in preheated 450° oven 10 to 15 minutes or until well browned. *Makes one 9-inch shell*

## BBB + Oats

**⅓ cup allowed margarine**
**2 tablespoons sugar**
**1¼ cups oat flour**

## OAT FLOUR PIE CRUST

Cream allowed margarine with sugar. Slowly blend in oat flour. Let dough rest a few minutes to absorb moisture. Then, if necessary to make it hold together, add 1 tablespoon water. Press into well-oiled 9-inch pie pan and bake in preheated 375° oven 15 minutes. Excellent when filled with fresh fruit filling. *Makes one 9-inch crust*

*Note:* Double recipe for any 2-crust fruit pie. Press ⅔ of mixture into 9-inch pie pan. Chill while preparing fruits and fill crust. Roll out remainder of crust on oat-floured board or waxed paper. Cut dough into ½ inch x 9 inch strips to form lattice top. Lift by sliding thin spatula under each strip to assist in transfer to pie. Dampen rim of bottom crust and weave strips across, pressing ends down well. For a different look, use cookie cutter and make fancy circles for your top crust instead of lattice. Bake as directed in your fruit pie recipe. Oat flour burns readily. Cover pie loosely with foil shield to protect against overbrowning.

**Variation:**

Add ½ cup chopped pecans (**+ N&S**) to crust, if you have reached the N&S rung of the additions ladder. Delicious!

## QUICK OATS CRUST

**BBB + Oats**

- **1⅓ cups quick or rolled oats**
- **⅓ cup brown sugar, firmly packed**
- **⅓ cup allowed margarine, melted**

Combine oats and brown sugar. Add margarine and mix until crumbly. Press into 8- or 9-inch pan with fingers. Bake in preheated 350° oven 8 minutes. *Makes one 8- or 9- inch crust*

**Variations:**

1. SOY-OAT CRUST—Add ⅓ cup soy milk powder.
2. Add ½ cup flaked coconut to main recipe or variation. (+ N&S)

## ALMOND OATMEAL PIE CRUST

**BBB + Oats + N&S**

- **⅔ cup ground raw almonds**
- **½ teaspoon salt**
- **¼ cup sugar**
- **¼ cup allowed oil or margarine**
- **1⅓ cups quick oats**

Blend all ingredients thoroughly. Press into 9-inch pie pan. Bake in preheated 375° oven 12 to 15 minutes or until nicely browned. Fill with your favorite allowed filling. Marvelous with Hawaiian Tofu Pie Filling, p. 314. *Makes one 9-inch crust*

## OAT COCONUT PASTRY

**BBB + Oats + N&S**

- **1 cup oat flour**
- **1 teaspoon cereal-free baking powder**
- **1 cup sugar**
- **⅛ teaspoon salt**
- **1 cup flaked coconut**
- **½ cup allowed margarine**

Stir together flour, baking powder, sugar, and salt. Mix in coconut. Cut in margarine until mixture resembles coarse cracker crumbs. Press into 9-inch pie pan and bake in preheated 350° oven 15 to 20 minutes. *Makes one 9-inch crust*

## WALNUT OH-SO-GOOD CRUST

**BBB + Oats + N&S**

- **1 cup quick oats**
- **3 tablespoons brown sugar**
- **⅛ teaspoon salt**
- **⅔ cup chopped walnuts**
- **⅓ cup allowed margarine, melted**

Spread quick oats in large shallow pan. Toast in preheated 350° oven 10 minutes. Combine with sugar, salt, nuts, and margarine. Press on sides and bottom of 9-inch pie pan. Chill while preparing filling. *Makes one 9-inch crust*

**BBB + Oats + Fruit + N&S + TE&A**

- 4 cups quick oats
- 1 cup shredded coconut
- ½ cup soy flour
- ½ cup rice polish
- ½ cup honey
- ½ cup allowed oil
- 2 tablespoons grated lemon or orange peel
- 1 teaspoon salt

## FRUITY NUTTY CRUMB CRUST

Mix all ingredients and press into two 9-inch pie pans. Bake in preheated 375° oven 8 to 10 minutes. *Makes two 9-inch crusts*

**Variation:**

This may be pressed into an 8 x 12 x 2-inch baking dish and filled with your favorite fruit filling before baking. Be sure to reserve part of the crumb mixture for topping. Bake in preheated 375° oven 30 minutes or until fruit is bubbly and topping browned. *Serves 10–12*

**BBB + Oats + N&S + TE&A**

- 2 cups crumbs from Fabulous Oat Waffle Delight, p. 203
- ¼ cup allowed margarine, softened
- ¼ cup sugar
- ¼ teaspoon cinnamon

## WAFFLE CRUMB CRUST

Dry waffles in oven until crisp but not brown. Crush enough waffles to make 2 cups fine crumbs. Combine ingredients and press mixture on sides and bottom of 9-inch pie pan. Bake in preheated 300° oven 10 minutes. *Makes one 9-inch shell*

**BBB + Rye + Oats**

- 1 cup Cream of Rye
- ½ cup oat flour or crushed oat flakes
- ⅓ cup rice flour
- 2 tablespoons soy milk powder
- 1½ teaspoons potato flour
- 1 cup brown sugar, firmly packed
- ½ cup allowed margarine
- 2 tablespoons chilled water

## PIE CRUST OR CRUMBLES

Blend all dry ingredients. Melt margarine and stir in well. For crust, work in water, adjusting amount as needed. Press into 9-inch pie pan, using another 9-inch pie pan to press crust flat. Bake in preheated 350° oven 12 to 15 minutes or until nicely browned. *Makes one 9-inch shell*

*For Crumbles,* omit water and use to sprinkle over chosen allowed 1-crust pie before baking.

**BBB + Rye + Oats**

- 1 cup Cream of Rye
- 1 cup oat flour
- 1 cup firmly packed brown sugar
- ½ cup allowed margarine

## RYE-O PIE CRUST

Mix all ingredients thoroughly. Press into 9-inch pie pan, reserving ½ cup for topping of a fruit or pudding pie filling. Bake in preheated 375° oven 8 to 10 minutes or until browned and crispy. *Makes one 9-inch shell and ½ cup topping*

## BARLEY-RICE FLOUR CRUST

**BBB + Barley**

- **⅓ cup allowed margarine**
- **⅓ cup barley flour**
- **⅔ cup rice flour**
- **Ice water**

Cut margarine into flours. Add enough ice water to form dough into ball. Place in 9-inch pie pan and press into shape. Bake in preheated 375° oven 10 minutes for crust to fill with pour-in filling. Or, before baking, fill with fruit pie filling of your choice and bake crust and fruit together. *Makes one 9-inch crust or pie*

## RICE CRUMB PIE CRUST

**BBB + Barley + TE&A + Mold**

- **1½ cups crushed Rice Krispies or Rice Chex (3–4 cups before crushing)**
- **⅓ cup allowed margarine, melted**
- **¼ cup sugar**

Mix all ingredients thoroughly. Press into 9-inch pie pan so sides and bottom are completely covered. Bake in preheated 375° oven 5 to 8 minutes. Cool. Fill with favorite cooked or prepared pudding or pie filling. *Makes one 9-inch crust*

**Variation:**

If you prefer, instead of baking crust, refrigerate 1 hour.

## RICE KRISPIE CRUST

**BBB + Barley + TE&A + Mold**

- **¼ cup allowed margarine**
- **1 cup brown sugar, firmly packed**
- **3 cups Rice Krispies**

Melt allowed margarine and brown sugar in heavy pan. When sugar is dissolved and mixture bubbles, slowly pour syrup over Rice Krispies in large mixing bowl. Toss rapidly with fork while pouring. Press mixture into 9-inch pie pan. Chill. Use for ice cream pie or for any filling that will be served at once. *Makes on 9-inch crust*

## CRISPY RICE PIE CRUST

**BBB + Barley + N&S + TE&A + Mold**

- **⅓ cup allowed margarine, softened**
- **⅔ cup brown sugar, firmly packed**
- **½ cup shredded coconut**
- **2 cups Rice Krispies (4 cups before crushing)**

Combine all ingredients in bowl. Blend well. Press into 9-inch pie pan. Fill with cooked and cooled fruit or pudding filling as allowed. *Makes one 9-inch crust*

## OPEN SESAME CRUMB CRUST

**BBB + Barley + N&S + TE&A + Mold**

- ½ cup sesame seeds, browned
- ⅓ cup allowed margarine
- ½ cup crushed Rice Chex or Rice Krispies (1 cup before crushing)
- ½ cup brown rice flour
- ⅓ cup brown sugar, firmly packed

Sauté sesame seeds in 1 tablespoon margarine in skillet, stirring constantly until medium brown. Combine seeds, cereal, and flour. Cream remaining margarine and brown sugar and stir into cereal-flour mixture. Set aside 1 cup of this mixture for top of pie. Press remainder into oiled 8-inch pie pan. Bake in preheated 350° oven 10 to 15 minutes or until golden brown. Cool. Pour in thickened pudding or pie filling as allowed and top with remaining crumbs. Chill before serving. *Makes one 8-inch shell and topping*

## CHEF'S TOUCH PIE SHELL

**BBB + Rye + Corn**

- ¾ cup rye flour
- ½ cup cornstarch
- ½ teaspoon salt
- ⅓ cup allowed margarine
- 2 tablespoons ice water

In medium bowl, mix rye flour, cornstarch, and salt. With pastry blender, cut in margarine until mixture resembles coarse cracker crumbs. Sprinkle water over flour mixture and stir with fork until dough pulls away from sides of bowl and forms a ball.

Dampen work surface and place on it sheet of waxed paper. Top with another sheet of heavy waxed paper or rub rolling pin with cornstarch and roll dough into 10-inch circle. Invert 8-inch pie pan on dough. Lifting crust by paper, invert pan and dough. Carefully peel off paper and shape dough down into pan. Trim edges and repair any holes. Prick crust with fork in several places. Bake in preheated 425° oven 10 to 15 minutes. Cool and fill as desired and allowed. *Makes one 8-inch pie shell*

Or, before baking, add fruit or berry pie filling and bake according to directions for the pie you select.

## CORNFLAKE PIE CRUST

**BBB + Barley + Corn + TE&A + Mold**

- 1½ cups crushed cornflakes (3 cups before crushing)
- ⅓ cup allowed margarine, melted
- ¼ cup sugar

Mix all ingredients thoroughly and press into 9-inch pie pan so sides and bottom are completely covered. Bake in preheated 375° oven 5 to 8 minutes. Cool and fill with favorite and allowed cooked pie filling. Chill to serve. *Makes one 9-inch pie*

**Variation:**

Add ½ teaspoon cinnamon when allowed.

# PIE FILLINGS

## PERSONALLY YOURS FRUIT PIES **BBB**

*Pastry*—double recipe Rice Flour Pie Shell, p. 303 or Brown Rice Flour Pie Crust, p. 303
*Fruit*—4 cups or 6 cups, if making deep dish pies, your choice of tested and allowed fruits: sliced peaches, halved apricots, halved seeded grapes, sliced pears, sliced apples, chopped plums or large can (20 ounces) crushed pineapple, undrained.
*Sweetener*—your choice of the following as tested and allowed:
 ¼–1 cup sugar (amount depends on sweetness of fruit)
 ¼–¾ cup honey (**+ TE&A**)
*Thickener*—your choice of the following:
 2½–3 tablespoons tapioca starch
 3 tablespoons Cream of Rice
 2½ tablespoons rice flour
 2 tablespoons potato starch
 3 tablespoons cornstarch (**+ Corn**)
*Liquid and Seasonings*
 2 tablespoons–½ cup water or allowed juice as required for fruit chosen
 1½ teaspoons–2 tablespoons lemon juice (**+ Fruit**)
 ⅛ teaspoon allspice (**+ TE&A**)
 1 tablespoon allowed margarine

Press half the pastry into deep 9-inch pie pan. Blend fruit carefully with choice of sweetener and thickener. Place in pie crust. Add water, lemon juice and allspice if allowed, and dot with margarine. Pat or roll out second crust, cut circles with scalloped cookie cutter, lift with spatula to top of pie. For apple pie, make a complete top crust so that apples will steam underneath. Be sure to cut vent holes in any complete top crust. Bake in preheated 425° oven 10 minutes. Reduce heat to 350° and bake 30-45 minutes longer or until fruit is just tender. Place foil shield over pie if it browns too quickly. *Makes one 2-crust 9-inch pie*

*Note:* If combining undrained canned pineapple with another juicy fresh fruit, omit additional water. Pineapple-peach pie would be a good example. A sugar-free pie can be made by replacing sugar or honey with enough frozen unsweetened apple juice concentrate to sweeten fruit. Omit any additional liquid in pie.

**Variations:**

1. INDIVIDUAL FRUIT PIES OR TARTS—Press allowed crust into large muffin or custard cups or small pie tins. Add fruit filling, top with Basic Crumb Topping, p. 330, and bake as directed for fruit pie. Watch carefully. Bake only until fruit is tender and crust browned.

2. FRUIT COMBO PIES—Add cranberries to apple pie for the holidays. Summer favorites are peach-pear, apple-grape, or apricot-pineapple. Team apples with pears, sweeten with honey, and add ½ teaspoon nutmeg. **(+ TE&A)**

**BBB**

## OUT-OF-SEASON FRUIT PIES

Follow recipe given for Personally Yours Fruit Pies, p. 311, replacing fresh fruit with water-pack or juice-pack fruits, drained. Frozen unsweetened fruits may also be used.

☐ **BBB + Fruit**

## GLAZED STRAWBERRY PIE

**4 cups strawberries**
**3 tablespoons tapioca starch**
**1 cup sugar**
**1 Baked allowed 9-inch crust**

If berries are small, place 2 cups whole berries evenly in crust. If large, cut in half. Crush remaining berries. Blend starch and sugar and combine with crushed berries. Cook, stirring constantly until mixture is thickened and clear. Spoon over berries in shell. Chill 3 to 4 hours.

*Note:* Berries may also be thickened with any of the following: 2½ tablespoons rice flour; 1 tablespoon unflavored gelatin (softened in ¼ cup water and dissolved in hot mixture of berries and sugar); or 3 tablespoons cornstarch **(+ Corn).** Cook flour and cornstarch the same as tapioca starch. Good with Quick Oats Crust, Variation 2, p. 307. **(+ Oats + N&S)**

**Variations:**

1. STRAWBERRY-PINEAPPLE PIE—Reduce berries to 3⅓ cups. Add 1 can (8 ounces) unsweetened crushed pineapple to 1⅓ cups berries, crushed. Cook as directed until thickened and stir in ¼ teaspoon rum flavoring. Spoon mixture over uncooked berries in crust. Make in Oat Coconut Pastry, p. 307 **(+ Oats + N&S).** Omit flavoring, if you need to avoid **TE&A.**

2. GLAZED BLUEBERRY PIE—Replace strawberries with blueberries. Place 3 cups whole berries in pie shell of your choice. Crush remainder of berries, add 1 cup water, and cook with starch and sugar until thickened. If desired, stir in 1 tablespoon each lemon juice and allowed margarine. Spoon over berries in crust. Chill.

## TOP-OF-THE-STOVE PEACH PIE

**BBB + Fruit** ☐

- **1 can (1 pound 13 ounces) juice-pack sliced cling peaches**
- **¼ cup sugar**
- **3 tablespoons tapioca starch**
- **¼ cup orange juice**
- **1 teaspoon grated orange peel**
- **1 tablespoon allowed margarine**
- **1 Baked 9-inch allowed pie crust**

Drain peaches, reserving juice. Blend sugar and starch, combine with 1 cup reserved juice. Cook, stirring constantly until thickened and clear. Carefully stir in peaches and remaining ingredients. Turn into pie crust and chill several hours. *Makes one 9-inch pie*

**Variation:**

Replace peaches with apricots or pears.

## SUMMER FESTIVAL FRUIT PIE

**BBB + Fruit** ☐

- **2 bananas, sliced**
- **2 tablespoons lemon juice**
- **Baked 9-inch allowed pie crust (Top Burner Pie Crust + N&S)**
- **2 cups sliced strawberries or any of the following: sliced peaches, quartered apricots, halved sweet cherries, or whole berries**
- **2 tablespoons tapioca starch**
- **1 can (20 ounces) unsweetened crushed pineapple, juice and all**
- **½ teaspoon synthetic vanilla**
- **1 tablespoon allowed margarine**

Toss banana slices with lemon juice, layer on bottom of pie crust. Add sliced fruit in another layer (if using peaches or apricots, toss with bananas and lemon juice to keep fruit from turning brown). Place tapioca starch in saucepan, stir in ¼ cup water, blending well to keep starch smooth. Stir in pineapple. Cook, stirring constantly, until thickened and clear. Add vanilla and margarine. Spoon over and between fruits. Chill 3 to 4 hours. *Makes one 9-inch pie*

**Variation:**

Top pie with ¼ cup chopped nuts or toasted coconut. **(+ N&S)**

☐ **BBB + Fruit**

## OH-SO-GOOD BLACKBERRY PIE

- **1 recipe No-Gluten Pie Crust, p. 303**
- **¾ cup sugar**
- **2 tablespoons Minute Tapioca**
- **2 tablespoons tapioca starch**
- **4 cups fresh ripe or frozen blackberries**
- **1 tablespoon lemon juice**
- **2 tablespoons allowed margarine**

Prepare and line 9-inch pie pan with bottom crust. Roll out top crust, make air vent slits, and reserve. Mix half the sugar with tapiocas and spread into unbaked pie crust. Fill with blackberries, add remaining sugar and lemon juice. Dot margarine over top.

Moisten edges of shell with water, lay on top crust, and press edges together. Trim off any ragged margins, crumble excess dough, and sprinkle over top if desired (or cook separately for snacking).

Bake in preheated 425° oven 15 minutes. Reduce heat to 350° and continue baking 30 to 40 minutes. Cool completely. This pie is perfection—doesn't even weep when cut. *Makes one 9-inch 2-crust pie*

☐ **BBB + Fruit**

## HAWAIIAN TOFU PIE

- **1 can (8 ounces) unsweetened crushed pineapple, drained, juice reserved**
- **½ cup brown sugar, firmly packed**
- **¼ cup tapioca starch**
- **1 cup tofu, washed and dried**
- **2 medium bananas**
- **2 tablespoons lemon juice**
- **1 teaspoon grated lemon peel**
- **1 teaspoon synthetic vanilla**
- **Baked allowed 9-inch pie crust—Almond Oatmeal Pie Crust when allowed. (+ Oats + N&S)**

Add water to pineapple juice to make 2 cups liquid and stir into well mixed sugar and starch in saucepan. Bring to boil, stirring constantly, until mixture is clear and thickened. Remove from heat. In blender or food processor, purée tofu and bananas with lemon juice. Stir into cooked mixture along with reserved pineapple, grated lemon peel, and vanilla. Pour into baked crust. Refrigerate at least 2 hours before serving. Pie may be topped with chopped nuts or toasted coconut when allowed. **(+ N&S)** *Makes one 9-inch pie*

☐ **BBB + N&S**

## PRALINE FRUIT PIES

- **⅓ cup brown sugar, firmly packed**
- **¼ cup rice flour**
- **½ cup chopped pecans**
- **3 tablespoons allowed margarine**

Combine mixture until crumbly. Sprinkle ⅓ mixture into an unbaked 9-inch pie pan and select one version of Personally Yours Fruit Pie, p. 311. Add pie filling to crust with care. Omit top crust, sprinkle on remaining crumb mixture. Bake as directed for fruit pie, covering, during first part of baking, with foil shield. Remove cover last 15 minutes so topping and crust edges can brown. *Makes one 9-inch pie*

## COOL GELATIN PIE

**BBB + TE&A**

- **1¾ cups allowed juice or water**
- **1 package (3 ounces) fruit-flavored gelatin of your choice**
- **1-1½ cups fresh fruit, water-pack or juice-pack canned fruits, or frozen unsweetened fruits**
- **Baked or chilled allowed 9-inch pie crust**

Bring 1 cup juice or water to boil. Pour over gelatin and stir until dissolved. Add remaining liquid and chill until very thick. Fold in fruit and pour into prepared pie crust. Chill until firm. *Makes one 9-inch pie*

**Variations:**

1. lemon-flavored gelatin, pineapple juice, apricots
2. lime-flavored gelatin, pineapple juice, pears
3. black cherry-flavored gelatin, apple juice, plums (may need additional sugar)
4. peach-flavored gelatin, apple juice, peaches
5. When allowed, bananas, berries, sweet cherries. **(+ Fruit)**

## GLORIA'S APPLE PIE

**BBB + Fruit + TE&A**

**For 8-inch pie:**

- **3½ cups sliced green cooking apples**
- **¼ cup sugar**
- **Dash of salt**
- **1 teaspoon lemon juice**
- **½ teaspoon cinnamon**
- **1 tablespoon allowed margarine**

**For 9-inch Pie:**

- **5 cups sliced green cooking apples**
- **6 tablespoons sugar**
- **Dash of salt**
- **1½ teaspoons lemon juice**
- **¾-1 teaspoon cinnamon**
- **1½ tablespoons allowed margarine**

Line pie pan with unbaked allowed pastry for 8- or 9-inch pie (No-gluten Pie Crust is good, or try Rice n' Rye Mix Pie Crust when allowed. **(+ Rye)**

Place half the apples in unbaked pie crust and top with half all other ingredients except margarine. Repeat layers. Dot with margarine and add a tablespoon or more water if apples are mealy, heaven forbid. Place top crust over apples, make vent holes, and trim and flute edges. Lightly dust top of crust with sugar. Bake in preheated 425° oven 10 minutes, reduce heat to 350°, and bake 30 to 45 minutes longer or until apples are soft. *Makes one 8- or 9-inch pie*

**Variations:**

1. FRENCH APPLE PIE—Top apples with Basic Crumb Topping, p. 330, instead of top crust. Cover pie with foil shield until last 15 minutes of baking. Remove foil and brown topping.
2. SURPRISE APPLE PIE—Add ½ cup pine nuts to filling. **(+ N&S)**
3. APPLE-PECAN PIE—Sprinkle ¼ cup chopped pecans into pie shell before adding filling. Top pie with Pecan Crunch Topping, p. 332. Cover with foil until last 15 minutes of baking. Remove foil to brown. **(+ N&S)**

**BBB + Fruit + TE&A**

- 1 can (1 pound 4 ounces) pitted red sour cherries
- 2½ tablespoons tapioca starch or Minute Tapioca or half-and-half
- 1 cup sugar
- ¼ teaspoon almond extract
- 1 tablespoon allowed margarine
- Unbaked allowed 9-inch pie crust
- 1 recipe Basic Crumb Topping, p. 330

## CHERRY PIE

Drain cherry juice into saucepan. Blend starch and/or Minute Tapioca with sugar and stir into juice. Let stand 5 minutes before cooking. Stirring constantly, heat until mixture is thick and clear. (Remember that Minute Tapioca thickens as it cools.) Stir in extract and margarine, then cherries. Pour into pie crust and sprinkle on crumb topping. Cover loosely with foil and bake in preheated 425° oven 15 to 20 minutes. Uncover and bake 10 to 15 minutes longer. *Makes one 9-inch pie*

**Variations:**

1. CHERRY-BERRY PIE—Thaw 1 package (10 ounces) frozen sweetened strawberries. Drain juice from strawberries into saucepan with cherry juice. Stir in tapioca mixed with sugar, let set 5 minutes, and heat, stirring, until thickened. Combine with fruits, 1 tablespoon lemon juice, margarine, and extract. **(+ Corn)**
2. Prepare allowed pie crust recipe and cut in strips. Weave lattice style on top of pie instead of crumb topping. Moisten pie crust rim with water and press lattice strips firmly to rim.

**BBB + Veg. + TE&A**

- ¼ cup rice flour
- ⅔ cup white or brown sugar, firmly packed
- ½ teaspoon cinnamon
- ¼ teaspoon ginger
- ⅛ teaspoon ground cloves
- ¼ teaspoon salt
- 1 can (1 pound) pumpkin or 1½ cups cooked pumpkin, yam, sweet potato, or winter squash
- 1⅔ cups hot water
- 2 tablespoons allowed margarine
- Unbaked 9-inch allowed pie crust—No-Gluten Pie Crust, p. 303 or Rice n' Rye Mix Pie Crust, p. 305 (+ Rye)

## PUMPKIN PIE

Blend dry ingredients well and stir into pumpkin. Pour hot water over margarine, stir to melt, and combine with pumpkin mixture. Pour into unbaked crust. Bake in preheated 425° oven 15 minutes. Reduce heat to 350° and continue baking 45 minutes. Cover crust edges with foil if browning too fast. Cool on wire rack. *Makes one 9-inch pie*

**Variation:**

Bake last 5 minutes with added topping made of 1 tablespoon brown sugar, 2 tablespoons finely chopped nuts, and 1½ tablespoons flaked coconut. **(+ N&S)**

## CHIFFON FRUIT PIES

**BBB + Corn + Fruit + N&S + TE&A**

- **1 package (3 ounces) fruit-flavored gelatin of your choice**
- **1½ cups allowed juice or nectar or water**
- **⅔ cup Dsertwhip, whipped**
- **1 cup chopped fruit**
- **Baked or chilled 9-inch allowed pie crust**

Bring 1 cup juice or water to boil, add gelatin, stir to dissolve, and add remaining ½ cup juice or water. Chill until very thick. Fold in whipped Dsertwhip and fruit and pour into prepared pie crust. Refrigerate until firm. *Makes one 9-inch pie*

**Variations:**

1. ORANGE CHIFFON—Combine orange-flavored gelatin with orange juice for liquid. Use 1 can drained mandarin oranges and 1 teaspoon grated orange peel for fruit.
2. PEAR-LIME—Combine lime-flavored gelatin with pears. Replace 3 tablespoons water with 3 tablespoons lime juice.
3. RASPBERRY BAVARIAN—Combine raspberry-flavored gelatin with pure pear or apple juice as liquid. Fold in fresh or frozen raspberries.
4. LEMON CHIFFON—Use lemon-flavored gelatin, reducing water to 1 cup. Add ¼ cup sugar and ¼ cup lemon juice to hot gelatin mixture. Omit chopped fruit and replace with 1 teaspoon grated lemon peel.
5. APRICOT CHIFFON—Omit flavored gelatin and replace with 1 tablespoon unflavored gelatin. Soften gelatin in ¼ cup apricot nectar, then dissolve in 1¼ cups boiling nectar. Fold in whipped Dsertwhip and chopped apricots.

## HOLIDAY PUMPKIN CHIFFON PIE

**BBB + Corn + Veg. + N&S + TE&A**

- **1 tablespoon unflavored gelatin**
- **¼ cup unsweetened pineapple juice, apple juice, or water**
- **1 small can (1 pound) pumpkin**
- **½ cup sugar**
- **½ teaspoon each salt and ginger**
- **1 teaspoon cinnamon**
- **¼ teaspoon ground cloves**
- **1 cup Dsertwhip, whipped**
- **1 baked 9-inch Gluten-Free Rice Granola Pie Crust, p. 305**
- **Chopped nuts**

Soften gelatin in juice or water 5 minutes. Combine with pumpkin, sugar, salt, and spices in saucepan. Cook slowly, stirring until very hot and gelatin dissolved. Remove from heat and cool. Fold in half of the whipped Dsertwhip and pour into baked pie crust. Chill several hours. Top with remaining Dsertwhip and sprinkle lightly with chopped nuts. *Makes one 9-inch pie*

**BBB**
**+ Buckwheat**
**+ Fruit + TE&A**

## RHUBARB PIE

- **4 cups rhubarb (1 pound), cut into ½-inch slices**
- **1½ cups sugar**
- **¼ cup rice flour**
- **Dash of salt**
- **½ teaspoon nutmeg**
- **1 unbaked 9-inch No-Gluten Pie Crust, p. 303**
- **2 tablespoons allowed margarine**

**Crumb topping**

- **½ cup brown sugar, firmly packed**
- **⅓ cup rice flour**
- **¼ teaspoon cinnamon**
- **¼ cup allowed margarine**

Combine rhubarb with all ingredients except margarine. Place in pie crust, dot with margarine and add ¼ cup water.

Work remaining ingredients together with fingertips until evenly combined and the texture of coarse cracker crumbs.

Sprinkle crumb topping over pie, cover with foil, and bake in preheated 400° oven 10 minutes. Reduce heat to 250° and bake 35 to 40 minutes longer. Uncover last 10 to 15 minutes of baking. *Makes one 9-inch pie*

**Variation: Honey-Lemon Rhubarb Pie**

Reduce sugar in filling to 1 cup and add ⅓ cup honey. Combine dry ingredients with honey, ¼ cup water, and 2 teaspoons grated lemon peel. Continue pie as directed above.

# COBBLER FILLINGS AND TOPPINGS

**BBB**

## DEALER'S CHOICE COBBLER FILLING

FRUIT—Apple, apricot, peach, pear, pineapple, purple plum, cranberry (your choice, unsweetened fresh, canned, or frozen)

*Fresh*—3 cups fruit and ¼-¾ cup water or allowed juice

*Canned*—2½ cups fruit with can juices (water-pack or juice-pack)

When allowed, use regular canned fruit in heavy syrup. **(+ Corn)**

*Frozen*—3 cups plain unsweetened fruit and ¼-¾ cup water or allowed juice. When allowed, use frozen fruits in syrup. **(+ Corn)**

*Sweetener*—Your choice of the following:

Unsweetened frozen apple juice concentrate (use as sweetener as well as the liquid needed for fresh fruit)

½–1 cup sugar as needed for fruit used

½–¾ cup honey as needed for fruit used **(+ TE&A)**

*Thickener*—your choice of the following allowed:

1½ tablespoons Cream of Rice
1 tablespoon tapioca starch
1 tablespoon Minute Tapicoa
2 tablespoons rice flour
2 teaspoons potato starch
1 tablespoon cornstarch **(+ Corn)**

Combine your choice of fruit, juice, sweetener and thickener. Cook, stirring constantly until mixture comes to boil, then continue boiling 1 minute. Mixture should be thickened and clear. Immediately stir in 1 tablespoon allowed margarine and dash of salt, if desired. You may want to add ¼ to ½ teaspoon cinnamon or nutmeg and/or almond extract when allowed **(+ TE&A).** Pour piping hot filling into 6″ x 10″ or 8″ square baking pan. Immediately top with cobbler topping allowed. Bake in preheated 400° oven 20 to 30 minutes or until topping is brown and cooked through. Serve warm. *Serves 6*

*Note:* When using Cream of Rice or Minute Tapioca to thicken, add to fruit, juice, and sugar. Let stand 5 minutes before cooking. Blend flour or starch thickeners with sugar, then stir in fruit and juice to keep smooth. Have filling very hot before adding cobbler topping as heat from filling helps cook topping. Bake immediately.

**Variations:**

1. Cherries, blueberries, blackberries, boysenberries, or a combination of cherries-strawberries all make good cobbler fillings. **(+ Fruit)**
2. BLUEBERRY-ORANGE COBBLER FILLING—Combine frozen unsweetened or fresh blueberries (2½ cups) with sugar, thickening, ½ cup water, ½ cup orange juice, and 1 tablespoon lemon juice. Cook as directed and add margarine and ½ teaspoon grated orange peel.
3. RHUBARB-PEAR COBBLER FILLING—Combine 1 package (10 ounces) frozen unsweetened rhubarb with pears for an interesting dessert. If frozen rhubarb is sweetened, it probably contains corn syrup. **(+ Corn)** If you have tested and added corn, you may also add 1 tablespoon cinnamon red hots for a rosy blush. **(+ Corn + Buckwheat + TE&A)**

## DROP COBBLER TOPPING

**BBB**

- **⅔ cup rice flour**
- **¼ cup soy flour**
- **1½ teaspoons potato flour**
- **1 tablespoon sugar**
- **2 teaspoons cereal-free baking powder**
- **½ teaspoon salt**
- **¼ cup allowed margarine**

Blend dry ingredients and cut or pinch in margarine until mixture resembles coarse meal. Set aside while preparing cobbler filling of your choice. Pour boiling filling into shallow baking dish or pan and then finish cobbler topping. Quickly and briefly stir ½ to ⅔ cup water into waiting dry mixture. Immediately drop from tablespoon in even blobs over top of hot filling. (See reason why in note, p. 319) Bake in preheated 400° oven 25 to 30 minutes or until cooked through and browned.

## POLISHED COBBLER TOPPING

**BBB**

- **¾ cup rice flour**
- **6 tablespoons rice polish**
- **1 tablespoon sugar**
- **1 tablespoon cereal-free baking powder**
- **3 tablespoons allowed oil**

See preparation method for Drop Cobbler Topping, using ¾ cup water. Bake in preheated 400° oven 25 minutes or until cooked through and lightly tanned. This browns less than some of our toppings but it is definitely worth trying.

## TANNED COBBLER TOPPING

**BBB**

- **⅓ cup brown rice flour**
- **⅓ cup rice bran**
- **2 tablespoons soy flour**
- **2 tablespoons brown sugar, firmly packed**
- **¼ teaspoon salt**
- **2 teaspoons cereal-free baking powder**
- **1 tablespoon allowed oil**

Thoroughly mix dry ingredients. When hot filling is in the pan, make depression in middle of topping dry mixture and pour in ½ cup water fork-mixed with the 1 tablespoon of oil. Stir in, and, if overly dry, add another tablespoon or two of water. Immediately drop from tablespoon in dollops to cover filling. Bake in preheated 400° oven 20 to 25 minutes. This has nice texture, a surprising flavor, and a happy suntanned complexion.

## RICE N' RYE COBBLER TOPPING

**BBB + Rye**

- ½ cup rye flour
- ⅓ cup rice flour
- 2 teaspoons cereal-free baking powder
- Dash of salt
- 1 tablespoon brown sugar, firmly packed
- 2 tablespoons allowed oil

Blend dry ingredients, then stir in oil and ½ cup water. Quickly plop tablespoonfuls over top of boiling hot cobbler filling. Bake in preheated 400° oven 20 minutes.

## ROLLED OAT COBBLER TOPPING

**BBB + Oats**

- 1 cup ground rolled oats
- 2 teaspoons cereal-free baking powder
- 1 tablespoon sugar
- ¼ teaspoon salt
- 2 tablespoons allowed oil

Combine dry ingredients and stir in oil and ½ cup water. Let stand to thicken while pouring hot filling into baking pan. If too thick to shake off tablespoon, quickly stir in 1 or 2 tablespoons more water. Spoon over fruit filling and bake in preheated 400° oven 20 minutes.

## RICE-OAT COBBLER TOPPING

**BBB + Oats**

Follow Rice-Oat Muffins recipe, p. 215, but reduce baking powder to 2 teaspoons. Drop dough by spoonfuls on hot fruit filling. Bake in preheated 400° oven 20 minutes.

## RYE-OATMEAL COBBLER TOPPING

**BBB + Rye + Oats**

- 1 cup quick oats
- ½ cup rye flour
- 2 tablespoons sugar
- ¼ teaspoon salt
- 2 teaspoons cereal-free baking powder
- 2 tablespoons allowed oil

Combine dry ingredients. Stir in oil and ⅔ cup water as soon as hot filling is ready for topping. Spoon batter on filling and bake in preheated 400° oven 20 minutes.

## BARLEY COBBLER TOPPING

**BBB + Barley**

- ⅓ cup rice flour
- ⅔ cup barley flour
- 2 teaspoons cereal-free baking powder
- 2 tablespoons sugar
- ¼ teaspoon salt
- 2 tablespoons allowed oil

Combine dry ingredients. Stir in oil and ⅔ cup water as soon as filling is ready for topping and boiling hot in pan. Spoon batter over hot filling and bake in preheated 400° oven 20 minutes. This tans instead of browning, but has a good light texture.

## BARLEY COMBO COBBLER TOPPING

**BBB + Rye + Barley**

- **½ cup rye flour**
- **½ cup barley flour**
- **2 teaspoons cereal-free baking powder**
- **¼ teaspoon salt**
- **1 tablespoon sugar**
- **2 tablespoons allowed oil**
- **½ teaspoon synthetic vanilla**

Combine dry ingredients. Stir in oil, vanilla, and ½ to ⅔ cup water. Spoon over hot filling in 6″ x 10″ or 8″ baking pan and bake in preheated 400° oven 20 minutes.

**Variation:**

Replace rye flour with oat flour. (**+ Oats**)

## YELLOW GOLD COBBLER TOPPING

**BBB + Corn**

- **1 cup corn flour**
- **½ cup cornmeal**
- **¼ cup sugar**
- **2 teaspoons cereal-free baking powder**
- **¼ teaspoon salt**
- **¼ cup allowed margarine**

Combine dry ingredients. Blend in margarine until mixture resembles coarse cornmeal. Stir in 1 cup water, blending well. Spoon batter evenly over hot cobbler filling (blueberry is very good) and bake in preheated 425° oven 25 minutes.

## SOY-CORNMEAL COBBLER TOPPING

**BBB + Corn**

Make ½ recipe of Soy-Cornmeal Muffins, p. 217. Immediately spoon batter on hot fruit filling. Bake in preheated 400° oven 20 minutes. This is a very tasting topping.

## SUNSHINE COBBLER TOPPING

**BBB + Corn**

- **⅓ cup rice flour**
- **2 tablespoons soy flour**
- **⅓ cup cornmeal**
- **1 tablespoon sugar**
- **2 teaspoons cereal-free baking powder**
- **¼ teaspoon salt**
- **2 tablespoons allowed oil**

Combine dry ingredients. Stir in oil and ½ cup water. Immediately drop spoonfuls of batter on hot fruit filling and bake in preheated 400° oven 20 minutes.

## WHIPPED CREAM SUBSTITUTE TOPPINGS

**BBB + Corn + N&S + TE&A**

Dsertwhip comes in ½ pint cartons, liquid. It is found in the dairy case in markets. Whip and use dollops of Dsertwhip to top pies or cobblers.

Reddi wip, non-dairy whipped topping, comes in a pressurized can ready for squirting on tops of desserts. It is found in most dairy cases.

## TRI-GRAIN COBBLER TOPPING

**BBB + Barley + Millet**

Follow Tri-Grain Muffins recipe, p. 219. Spoon batter on hot fruit filling and bake in preheated 375° oven 20 to 25 minutes.

## HARMONIOUS QUARTET COBBLER TOPPING

**BBB + Barley + Millet**

Follow Harmonious Quartet Muffins recipe, p. 220. Spoon batter immediately on hot fruit filling and bake in preheated 400° oven 20 minutes.

# Desserts

## PUDDINGS

### BBB

**¼ cup Minute Tapioca**
**Sugar to taste, up to ½ cup, amount depending on tartness of juice**
**2½ cups allowed unsweetened fruit juice: apple, grape (white, red, or Concord), pear-grape, pineapple, or natural pear juice**
**Dash of salt**

### FRUIT JUICE TAPIOCA PUDDING

Blend tapioca, sugar, juice, and salt in saucepan. Let stand 5 minutes, then bring to boil while stirring frequently. Cover and set aside to cool 20 minutes. Stir well. Chill or serve warm in dessert dishes. *Serves 6*

*Note:* Purée 1 can (16 ounces) water-pack or juice-pack peaches or apricots, undrained, if those flavors are desired. Regular apricot and peach nectars contain corn syrup. (+ **Corn**) Use same as fruit juices called for in recipe.

### BBB

**⅓ cup Minute Tapioca**
**4 cups sliced cooking apples**
**Sugar to taste (optional)**
**2 tablespoons allowed margarine**

### FRESH APPLE TAPIOCA

Combine 2 cups water with all ingredients and let stand 5 minutes. Bring to boil, stirring often. Reduce heat, cover, and simmer slowly until apples are tender. Set aside to cool 20 minutes, then stir well. Serve warm or chilled. *Serves 6*

**Variations**

1. Replace apples with other allowed fresh fruits: peaches, apricots, or plums. Plums will require more sugar.

2. When allowed, add 1 tablespoon lemon juice (+ **Fruit**) and ½ teaspoon cinnamon (+ **TE&A**).

## SWEDISH GRAPE PUDDING

**BBB**

Bring grape juice and sugar to a boil, stirring until sugar dissolves. Make paste of starch and 3 tablespoons water. Stir slowly into juice. Continue stirring and cook over low heat until pudding is clear and slightly thickened. Cool, then chill in covered container to prevent scum on top. Spoon into dessert glasses to serve. *Serves 4*

**2 cups unsweetened grape juice**
**3 tablespoons sugar**
**2 tablespoons tapioca starch**

**Variation:**
Add 1 teaspoon lemon juice to cooked pudding and, when allowed, top each dessert with dollop of whipped Dsertwhip. (+ **Corn** + **Fruit** + **N&S** + **TE&A**)

## FRUITED RICE CEREAL DESSERT

**BBB**

Drain juice from fruits and add water to make 2½ cups. Add salt and bring to boil. Slowly sprinkle in cereal. Boiling should not stop. Continue stirring and cooking 30 seconds. Remove from heat, cover, and let stand 3 minutes. Chop apricots or pears coarse and fold into cooked mixture along with pineapple. *Serves 4–5*

**1 can (8 ounces) unsweetened crushed pineapple, drained, juice reserved**
**1 can (8 ounces) water-pack apricot or pear halves, drained, juice reserved**
**½ teaspoon salt**
**½ cup Cream of Rice**

**Variation:**
Omit apricots or pears and fold in 4 quartered maraschino cherries and ¼ cup flaked coconut. (+ **possibly Corn** + **Fruit** + **N&S** + **TE&A**)

## OLD-FASHIONED RICE PUDDING

**BBB**

Combine all ingredients in oiled 6- x 10-inch baking pan. Cover tightly with foil and bake in preheated 300° oven 2 hours or until liquid is absorbed and pudding creamy. *Serves 4*

**3 cups allowed milk substitute**
**¼ cup rice**
**¼ cup white or brown sugar, firmly packed**
**¼ teaspoon salt**
**1 tablespoon allowed margarine, melted**

**Variations:** Add your choice of the following when allowed

1. 1 teaspoon grated lemon peel (+ **Fruit**)
2. 1 cup flaked coconut (+ **N&S**)
3. ¼ teaspoon nutmeg (+ **TE&A**)
4. 3–4 tablespoons honey to replace sugar (+ **TE&A**)

## SIMPLE FRUITED RICE PUDDING

**BBB**

**1½ cups cooked rice**
**Sugar (2-4 tablespoons as needed for fruit)**
**1 can (16 ounces) water-pack or juice-pack allowed fruit or 2 cans (8 ounces) unsweetened chunk pineapple, undrained**

Combine all ingredients and place in oiled 8-inch baking pan. Bake in 350° oven 30 minutes. Serve warm with a dab of Carrot Marmalade, p. 235. If desired, you can chill pudding. *Serves 4.*

**Variation:**

When allowed, whip ½ cup Dsertwhip and fold into cooled pudding. Chill. (+ **Corn** + **N&S** + **TE&A)**

## WHIPPED RICE PUDDING

**BBB**

**1 tablespoon unflavored gelatin**
**1 cup boiling unsweetened pineapple juice**
**1 cup cooked rice**
**¼ teaspoon salt**
**1 teaspoon synthetic vanilla**
**1 cup diced allowed cooked fruits**

Soften gelatin in ¼ cup water 5 minutes. Stir into boiling juice to dissolve. Blend in remaining ingredients and cool. Chill until firm. Spoon half mixture at a time into blender or mixing bowl and purée or beat until light and increased in volume. Spoon into dessert dishes and chill. *Serves 4-6*

## BONNY TREE PUDDING

**BBB**

**1 package (4 ounces) Bonny Tree Pure Vanilla Pudding**
**1½ tablespoons tapioca starch or 2 tablespoons rice flour**
**2 cups soy milk**

Blend pudding mix and starch or flour. Slowly add soy milk, stirring constantly to keep smooth. Continue stirring and cook until mixture thickens and begins to boil. Cover and cool to prevent scum from developing on top. *Serves 4*

**Variations:**

1. Replace vanilla pudding with same brand of butterscotch or carob pudding. (+ **TE&A)**

2. For banana pie, line bottom of prepared allowed crust with banana slices and top with pudding. For coconut pie, fold flaked coconut into pudding and pour into prepared shell. Chill to serve. (+ **N&S)**

## BANANA-ORANGE TAPIOCA PUDDING

**BBB + Fruit**

- ¼ cup Minute Tapioca
- ¼ cup sugar
- Dash of salt
- 1 can (6 ounces) frozen unsweetened orange juice concentrate
- 2 bananas, sliced
- 1 tablespoon lemon juice
- ½ teaspoon grated lemon peel (optional)

Combine tapioca, sugar, and salt in saucepan. Add orange concentrate and 1½ cups water. Let stand 5 minutes. Cook, stirring frequently, until mixture comes to boil. Cover, cool 20 minutes, then stir well. Chill partially, fold in sliced bananas, lemon juice, and peel. Chill until firm. *Serves 6*

## BLUEBERRY TAPIOCA

**BBB + Fruit**

- 2½ cups fresh blueberries
- ½ cup sugar
- 2 tablespoons Minute Tapioca

Combine all ingredients with ½ cup water and let stand 5 minutes. Bring to boil, stirring constantly. Cover, let stand 20 minutes, and stir well. Spoon into serving dishes, serve warm or chilled. Decorate side of each dessert dish with ½ orange cartwheel slipped over edge of dish. *Serves 4–6*

## EASY ISLAND RICE PUDDING

**BBB + N&S**

- 2 cups unsweetened pineapple-coconut juice
- ⅔ cup Minute Rice
- 2 tablespoons allowed margarine
- Toasted coconut

Bring juice to boil and stir in rice and margarine. Cover and let stand 15 minutes. Stir and spoon into serving dishes while still warm. Sprinkle with toasted coconut. *Serves 4*

## RYE PUDDING

**BBB + Rye + Fruit + TE&A**

- ¾ cup coarsely crushed Natural RyKrisp
- ¾ cup unsweetened pineapple juice or unsweetened pineapple-coconut juice (+ N&S)
- 2 teaspoons lemon juice
- 2 tablespoons brown sugar, firmly packed
- ¼ teaspoon cinnamon
- ⅛ teaspoon nutmeg
- Dash of ground cloves

Combine all ingredients and spoon into 2 oiled 16-ounce cans (save from canned fruits or vegetables). Bake in 350° oven 1 hour and turn onto cooling rack. Serve warm with Lemon Sauce I, p. 272. This is a good dessert, similar to Persimmon Pudding. Recipe may be doubled and baked in an oiled 8-inch baking pan. *Serves 2–4*

## WHIPPED BARLEY HAWAIIAN

**BBB + Barley + N&S**

- 1 tablespoon unflavored gelatin
- ¼ cup cold water
- 1 can (20 ounces) crushed unsweetened pineapple, drained, liquid reserved
- 1 cup cooked barley
- ½ cup flaked coconut

Soften gelatin in ¼ cup water. Add more water to drained pineapple juice to make 1 cup and heat to boiling. Stir in dissolved gelatin and add cooked barley. Chill until very thick, spoon into mixing bowl and beat until light and fluffy (or purée, little at a time, in blender). Fold in pineapple and coconut. Chill until firm. *Serves 4–6*

## STRAWBERRY TAPIOCA

**BBB + Corn + Fruit**

- 1 package (10 ounces) frozen strawberries, thawed, drained, liquid reserved
- 2 tablespoons Minute Tapioca
- ¼ cup sugar
- 2 teaspoons lemon juice

Add enough water to strawberry liquid to make 1½ cups. Combine liquid, tapioca, and sugar. Cook, stirring often, until mixture reaches full boil. Stir in berries and lemon juice. Cover to cool 20 minutes. Stir well and refrigerate until serving time. *Serves 4*

## INDIAN PUDDING

**BBB + Corn + TE&A**

- ¼ cup cornmeal
- 2 tablespoons sugar
- ½ teaspoon salt
- ½ teaspoon ginger
- ¼ teaspoon cinnamon
- 3½ cups allowed milk substitute
- 2 tablespoons allowed margarine
- ⅓ cup honey

Combine cornmeal, sugar, salt, and spices in top of double boiler. Heat 3 cups milk substitute barely to boil and stir slowly into cornmeal mixture. Add margarine and honey and cook over boiling water 20 minutes, stirring frequently. Add remaining milk substitute and pour mixture into oiled 1½-quart baking dish. Bake in 300° oven 3 hours, stirring gently several times during baking. Serve warm. *Serves 4*

## ORANGE-BANANA MALLOW

**BBB + Corn + Fruit + TE&A**

- 1½ cups orange juice
- ¼ teaspoon salt
- ¼ cup Cream of Rice
- 20 large marshmallows
- 2 bananas, sliced

Bring orange juice and salt to boil. Slowly sprinkle in Cream of Rice and cook, stirring constantly, 30 seconds. Cover and let stand 3 minutes. Add marshmallows and stir until melted. Spoon half of pudding into 4 dessert dishes, add layer of bananas, and top with remaining pudding. If desired, garnish with banana slices brushed with orange juice. Chill. *Serves 4*

## PACKAGED MIX PUDDINGS

**BBB + Corn + TE&A**

**Mixes—your choice. We have given the brand name on mixes that do not contain milk. Always read ingredients lists on pudding mixes.**

- **1 box ($3\frac{1}{8}$ ounces) Jello-O Vanilla Pudding and Pie Filling, or Coconut Cream (+ N&S), Lemon, Banana Cream, or Butterscotch (not instant pudding)**
- **1 box ($3\frac{3}{4}$ ounces) Jell-O Americana Rice Pudding**
- **1 box ($3\frac{1}{4}$ ounces) Jell-O Americana Tapioca Pudding**

Packaged puddings were intended for use with cow milk. They, therefore, do not thicken with just any liquid. Listed below are milk substitutes and thickenings to use with them. Always blend thickening with mix before stirring in chosen liquid. Cook, then, as you will find directed on package.

1. Prepare as directed with goat milk.
2. Use $1\frac{1}{2}$ tablespoons tapioca starch or cornstarch, or 2 tablespoons rice flour with soy or nut milk. (+ **N&S**)
3. Use 3 tablespoons tapioca starch or cornstarch, or $\frac{1}{4}$ cup rice flour with a milk-free liquid coffee creamer such as Mocha Mix or Rich's Coffee Rich. **(+ Corn + N&S + TE&A)**

**Variations: Pie Fillings**

1. BANANA CREAM—Slice bananas on baked or chilled allowed pie crust. Pour cooled pudding over and chill. Serve topped with dollops of whipped Dsertwhip and garnished, if allowed, with chopped nuts. (+ **Fruit + N&S**)
2. COCONUT or MACADAMIA NUT—Fold $\frac{1}{2}$ cup flaked coconut or chopped macadamia nuts into cooked and cooled pudding. Pour into allowed crust and chill. Top with whipped Dsertwhip and garnish with toasted coconut or chopped macadamia nuts. (+ **N&S**)

## FANCY RICE-FRUIT DESSERT

**BBB + Corn + Fruit + TE&A**

- **1 can (12 ounces) fruit nectar (pear, peach, or apricot)**
- **2 tablespoons honey**
- **2 teaspoons grated orange peel**
- **2 tablespoons allowed margarine**
- **1 cup rice**
- **6 fresh or canned drained pear, peach, or equivalent apricot halves**
- **Dash cinnamon**

Bring nectar, $1\frac{1}{2}$ cups water, honey, peel and margarine to boil and pour over rice in oiled 9-inch baking pan. Bake at 350° 20 minutes. Arrange fruit halves cut-side-up in rice. Sprinkle casserole lightly with cinnamon. Bake 30 minutes longer or until rice is tender. Serve warm with allowed milk substitute. *Serves 6*

## COFFEE-BANANA FLUFF

**BBB + Corn + Fruit + N&S + TE&A**

- **1 tablespoon unflavored gelatin**
- **1 cup strong hot coffee**
- **⅓ cup sugar**
- **⅛ teaspoon salt**
- **1 teaspoon rum flavoring**
- **1 cup Dsertwhip, whipped**
- **1 ripe banana, diced**
- **½ cup chopped nuts**

Soften gelatin in ½ cup water 5 minutes. Add hot coffee and stir to dissolve sugar and salt. Add flavoring. Chill until very thick, then fold in remaining ingredients. Refrigerate until serving time. *Serves 6*

## FLUFFY RHUBARB PUDDING

**BBB + Buckwheat + TE&A**

- **1 tablespoon unflavored gelatin**
- **¼ cup honey**
- **2 cups sliced rhubarb**

Soften gelatin in ¼ cup water. Pour honey and 1 cup water into saucepan with rhubarb, cover, and cook over medium heat 20 to 30 minutes. Add softened gelatin and stir to dissolve. Chill until almost congealed. Turn into mixing bowl and beat until fluffy and double in volume. Spoon into dessert glasses and chill until firm. If desired, garnish with mint leaves. *Serves 4-6*

# DESSERTS WITH CRISPY TOPPINGS

## BASIC CRUMB TOPPING

**BBB**

- **1 cup rice flour**
- **⅓ cup brown sugar, firmly packed**
- **¼ cup allowed margarine**
- **Dash of salt**

Cut or pinch margarine into blended dry ingredients until mixture resembles coarse meal. Use as topping on any fresh fruit pie or fruit crisp. Sprinkle over filling in pan and bake according to directions given in the filling recipe selected. Remember to cover with foil ⅔ to ¾ of baking time, then remove foil for remaining time to crisp and brown crumbs.

## BASIC FRUIT CRISP

**BBB**

- 5 **cups fruit, fresh or canned (water-pack or juice-pack)—peaches, pears, apricots, pineapple**
- ¼ **cup sugar or ¼ cup frozen unsweetened apple juice concentrate**
- 2 **tablespoons Minute Tapioca, more or less as needed to thicken**
- 2 **tablespoons allowed margarine**
- 1 **recipe Basic Crumb Topping, p. 330, or other toppings as allowed**

Slice or chop fruit and toss with sugar or concentrate and tapioca. Place in 9-inch square baking dish. Dot with margarine and top with crumb topping. Cover with foil and bake in 375° oven 20 to 30 minutes. Remove foil and continue baking 10 to 15 minutes or until fruit is tender and topping crisp and golden. *Serves 6*

*Note:* After testing, add cherries and berries. **(+ Fruit)**

## APPLE CRISP

**BBB**

- 5-6 **tart cooking apples**
- ⅓ **cup sugar, white or brown, firmly packed**
- 2 **tablespoons allowed margarine**
- 1 **recipe Basic Crumb Topping, p. 330**

Pare apples and slice into 9-inch square baking dish. Sprinkle sugar over apples, dot with margarine, and sprinkle ¼ cup water over fruit, adding a little more if apples are not juicy. Cover with your choice of crumb topping. To avoid overbaking crumbs, lay sheet of foil loosely over top during first ⅔ baking time. For example, bake in 375° oven 30 minutes, test apples with fork and when tender, remove foil, and continue baking 15 minutes to crisp and brown topping. *Serves 6*

**Variation: Cranapple Crisp**

Use 4 apples and ¾ cup whole cranberries in filling.

*Note:* 1 tablespoon lemon juice and ½ teaspoon cinnamon and dash of nutmeg **(+ Fruit + TE&A)** provide the flavors you may miss in this dessert. Once citrus and these spices have been tested and allowed, restore them to the recipe and enjoy.

## BUTTERSCOTCH APPLES

**BBB**

- 8 apples, peeled and cut into eighths
- ¼ cup rice flour
- ⅓ cup brown sugar, firmly packed
- ¼ cup sugar
- ¼ cup allowed margarine
- 1 teaspoon synthetic vanilla

Pare and slice apples and arrange in oiled 9-inch square baking pan. Mix flour and sugars and cut or pinch in margarine until mixture resembles coarse crumbs. Add vanilla and 1 cup water, stirring well. Spread over apples. Cover with foil and bake in 350° oven 1 hour, removing foil last 15 minutes. *Serves 6*

## SUGAR N' SPICE CRUMB TOPPING

☐ **BBB + TE&A**

- ½ cup brown sugar, firmly packed
- ½ cup brown rice flour
- ¼ cup rice polish
- ½ teaspoon cinnamon
- ¼ teaspoon ground cloves
- ¼ cup allowed margarine

Blend dry ingredients and cut or pinch in margarine. Crumble over Basic Fruit Crisp, p. 331, or over the fruit pie filling of your whim. Bake as directed in recipe chosen. *Makes 1½ cups*

**Variation: Pecan Crunch Topping**

Omit rice polish and cloves. Reduce flour to ⅓ cup and use white rice flour instead of brown. Add ¼ cup chopped pecans. **(+ N&S)**

## NUTTY APPLE CRISP

☐ **BBB + Fruit + TE&A**

- 6 cups sliced peeled apples
- 1 tablespoon lemon juice
- ¼ cup honey
- ¾ cup rice flour
- ½ cup brown sugar, firmly packed
- ¼ teaspoon cinnamon
- ¼ cup allowed margarine

Combine apples, lemon juice, and honey in oiled 9-inch square baking pan. Combine flour, sugar, and cinnamon. Cut in margarine until mixture resembles coarse meal. Stir in ¾ cup chopped peanuts, almonds, or walnuts when allowed. **(+ N&S)** Sprinkle topping over filling. Cover with foil and bake in 375° oven 30 minutes. Uncover and bake 15 minutes longer or until apples are done and topping crisp. May be served warm or cold. *Serves 6–8*

**Variations:**

1. Replace apples with 3 pounds pears, peeled and sliced.
2. COCONUT APPLE BETTY PIE—Omit lemon juice. Sprinkle 2 tablespoons rice flour over apples. Mix honey with ¼ cup orange juice and pour over apples. Prepare topping, replacing nuts with flaked coconut. **(+ N&S)**

## PUFFED RICE TOPPING

**BBB + N&S + TE&A**

- ¼ cup allowed margarine
- ½ cup brown sugar, firmly packed
- 1½ teaspoons cinnamon
- ¼ teaspoon salt
- 1½ cups crushed puffed rice (grind in blender)
- ¼ cup chopped nuts

Cream margarine, sugar, cinnamon, and salt. Stir in puffed rice and nuts. Sprinkle over desired filling. Bake as directed for Basic Fruit Crisp, p. 331, or for pie filling of your choice, covering with foil first half of baking time. Spoon dessert into serving dishes while warm and serve with allowed milk substitute. *Makes 2½ cups*

## RYE CRUMB TOPPING

**BBB + Rye**

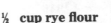

- ½ cup rye flour
- ¼ cup brown sugar, firmly packed
- ¼ cup allowed margarine or allowed shortening

Combine flour and sugar and cut or pinch in margarine until mixture resembles coarse crumbs. Sprinkle over desired filling. Bake as directed for Basic Fruit Crisp, p. 331, or for pie filling chosen. *Makes 1 cup*

## "APPLE OF YOUR RYE" CRISP

**BBB + Rye**

- 1 recipe Apple Crisp, p. 331, omitting Basic Crumb Topping
- 1¼ cups Cream of Rye or crushed Natural RyKrisp
- ½ cup brown sugar, firmly packed
- ¼ cup allowed margarine
- 1 teaspoon synthetic vanilla

Prepare Apple Crisp filling and place in oiled 9-inch square baking pan. Top with well blended remaining ingredients. Cover with foil and bake in 375° oven 30 minutes. Remove foil and bake another 15 minutes or until fruit is tender and topping crispy brown. *Serves 6*

**Variation: Fruited Rye Crunch**

Replace apples with 8 canned (water-pack or juice-pack) peach or pear halves, drained. Add ⅔ cup liquid from fruit to topping mixture. Bake 25 minutes only. Serve warm with allowed milk substitute, if desired. When allowed, add ½ teaspoon each cinnamon and nutmeg. (**+ TE&A**)

### BBB + Oats

- 1 cup oat flour (grind rolled oats in blender, if preferred)
- ¾ cup quick oats
- ⅓ cup brown sugar, firmly packed
- ½ cup allowed margarine
- ⅛ teaspoon salt
- ½ teaspoon synthetic vanilla

## OAT CRISP TOPPING

Work all ingredients together with spoon or fingers until texture of coarse meal. Sprinkle over desired fruit filling. Bake as directed for Basic Fruit Crisp, p. 331 or for pie filling chosen. *Makes 2½ cups*

**Variation:**

Replace oat flour with ½ cup rice flour or ¾ cup additional quick oats. Add ⅓ cup coarsely chopped nuts or flaked coconut, when allowed. (**+ N&S**)

### BBB + Oats + Barley + TE&A

- 1 scant cup allowed margarine
- ¾ cup honey
- ½ cup barley flour
- 1½ cups quick oats
- ½ teaspoon salt
- 2½ cups sliced allowed fruit
- 2 tablespoons rice flour

## LAYERED FRUIT CRISP

Melt margarine and combine ⅔ cup with honey. Pour into well-mixed barley flour, oats, and salt, tossing and stirring until evenly distributed. Spread a third of this in bottom of deep 9-inch pie pan. Press in place as crust but it need not cover sides.

Mix fruit, remaining margarine, and rice flour and spread half of this mixture over crust in pan. Add, in layers, another third of topping, remaining fruit, and last of topping. Press down firmly. Bake in 375° oven 30 to 45 minutes, using foil sheet over top during first half of baking time and removing then for topping to brown. *Serves 6*

### BBB + Oats + Corn + Fruit + TE&A

- ⅓ cup rice flour
- ¾ cup rolled oats
- ⅓ cup allowed margarine
- ⅔ cup sugar
- 1½ tablespoons cornstarch
- ⅛ teaspoon each cinnamon and nutmeg
- ¼ teaspoon salt
- 1 tablespoon lemon juice
- 1 can (16 ounces) pitted sour cherries, drained, juice reserved

## CHERRY CRISP

Blend flour, oats, margarine, and ⅓ cup sugar until crumbly and set aside. Combine remaining ⅓ cup sugar, cornstarch, spices, salt and lemon juice in saucepan. Slowly blend in cherry juice. Cook, stirring constantly, until thick and clear. Add cherries and pour into 8-inch square baking pan. Sprinkle on topping and bake in 375° oven 30 minutes. May be served with allowed milk substitute or topped with dollops of whipped Dsertwhip. *Serves 6*

## HOLIDAY CRANAPPLE DESSERT

**BBB + Oats + Corn + Fruit + N&S + TE&A**

- **3 large cooking apples, diced, unpeeled**
- **2 tablespoons lemon juice**
- **½ cup sugar**
- **1 can (16 ounces) whole-berry cranberry sauce**
- **½ cup allowed margarine, melted**
- **½ cup brown sugar, firmly packed**
- **½ cup chopped nuts**
- **2 cups quick oats**
- **1 cup Dsertwhip, whipped**

Toss apples with lemon juice and place in oiled 9-inch square baking dish. Sprinkle with sugar. Place tablespoonfuls of cranberry sauce over top. Blend melted margarine, brown sugar, nuts, and oats and spread over cranberry layer. Bake in 350° oven 45 minutes. Cut into squares, lift into serving dishes, and top with a dollop of whipped Dsertwhip. *Makes 9 small squares*

## APPLE BROWN BETTY

**BBB + Oats + Barley + Corn + Fruit + TE&A + Mold**

- **3 cups diced unpeeled apples**
- **2 teaspoons lemon juice**
- **¾ cup rolled oats**
- **½ cup cornmeal**
- **¾ cup brown sugar, firmly packed**
- **¾ teaspoon cinnamon**
- **¼ cup allowed margarine, melted**
- **1½ cups allowed milk substitute**
- **½ cup cornflakes, crumbled**

Toss apples with lemon juice and set aside. Blend oats, cornmeal, brown sugar, cinnamon, and melted margarine with spoon or fingers until crumbly. Alternate layers of apples and topping (apples first) in 8- or 9-inch square baking pan. Pour on milk substitute before adding last layer of topping. Sprinkle on crushed cornflakes last. Bake in 350° oven 45 to 50 minutes or until apples are tender and mixture thickened. *Serves 6–8*

# CONGEALED DESSERTS

**BBB**

- **1 tablespoon unflavored gelatin**
- **¼ cup cold water**
- **1½ cups (or 15-ounce jar) unsweetened applesauce**
- **¾ cup frozen unsweetened apple juice concentrate**

## DOUBLE APPLE TREAT

Soften gelatin in cold water. Heat applesauce to boiling. Stir in gelatin to dissolve. Add concentrate, blend well, and chill until firm. *Serves 4*

**Variation:**

Heat ¼ teaspoon cinnamon and ⅛ teaspoon ground cloves with applesauce. (+ **TE&A**)

**BBB**

- **1 tablespoon unflavored gelatin**
- **1 cup unsweetened pineapple juice**
- **1 cup puréed canned pears (water-pack or juice-pack)**

## PEAR PINEAPPLE SMOOTHIE

Soften gelatin in ¼ cup juice. Bring remaining juice to boil and stir in gelatin to dissolve. Chill until syrupy. Fold in puréed pears. Chill until firm. *Serves 4*

**Variation:**

If desired, when gelatin is very thick and before adding pears, beat with hand or electric beater until light and fluffy. Fold in pears.

**BBB**

- **1 tablespoon unflavored gelatin**
- **¾ cup boiling allowed fruit juice or water**
- **¾ cup (6-ounce can) frozen unsweetened pear-grape concentrate**
- **1 can (16 ounces) water-pack or juice-pack pear halves, drained**

## FLAKED PEAR-GRAPE DESSERT

Soften gelatin in ¼ cup water 5 minutes. Dissolve in boiling liquid. Add frozen concentrate and blend well. Chill until very firm, about 4 hours. Break into small flakes by running fork through gelatin, or put through ricer or large mesh screen. Pile flakes high in 4 dessert dishes. Press 1 pear half, cut side up, in each mound of gelatin. Garnish with Toasted Rice Flakes, p. 247, or Super Crunch Granola, p. 248. *Serves 4*

## PEACHY KEEN FLUFF

**BBB**

Soften gelatin in ¼ cup water 5 minutes. Dissolve in boiling water. Stir in frozen concentrate and chill until very thick. Beat until light and fluffy. Fold in sliced peaches and spoon into attractive dessert dishes. *Serves 4–6*

**Variation:**

For quick dessert, prepare as directed but do not beat gelatin.

- **1 tablespoon unflavored gelatin**
- **¾ cup boiling water**
- **¾ cup frozen unsweetened apple juice concentrate**
- **1 can (16 ounces) sliced peaches (water-pack or juice-pack) or 2 cups fresh peaches, when allowed**

## COMPOSE-A-MOLDED DESSERT

**BBB**

Soften gelatin in ¼ cup water 5 minutes. Dissolve in boiling juice or water. Stir in choice of frozen concentrate. Chill until syrupy and fold in fruit of your choice. Chill until firm. *Serves 4–6*

**Variation:**

Chill gelatin until very thick. Beat to froth, then fold in desired fruit. Chill in pretty dessert dishes. Garnish with Toasted Rice Flakes, p. 247.

- **1 tablespoon unflavored gelatin**
- **1 cup boiling allowed fruit juice or water**
- **¾ cup frozen unsweetened apple juice concentrate or frozen unsweetened pear-grape concentrate**
- **1 can (16 ounces) your choice of allowed BBB cut fruits: (all drained except applesauce) unsweetened applesauce, home cooked apples, unsweetened pineapple, apricot halves, pear halves, peaches, grapes, or purple plums**

☐ **BBB + Fruit**

## REFRESHING BLUEBERRY MOLD

- **1 tablespoon unflavored gelatin**
- **1¾ cups unsweetened pineapple juice**
- **2 tablespoons lemon juice**
- **2 cups whole fresh or frozen unsweetened blueberries**
- **1 banana, diced**

Soften gelatin in ½ cup pineapple juice 5 minutes. Bring remaining pineapple juice and lemon juice to boil and add softened gelatin, stirring to dissolve. Chill until syrupy. Fold in fruits and chill until firm. *Serves 4–6*

☐ **BBB + Fruit + TE&A**

## CHEERY CHERRY DESSERT

- **1 package (3 ounces) cherry-flavored gelatin**
- **1 cup boiling water**
- **1 can (8 ounces) unsweetened crushed pineapple, drained, juice reserved**
- **1½ cups fresh or frozen pitted unsweetened cherries, cut in half**

Dissolve gelatin in boiling water in 9 x 5-inch loaf pan. Add water to reserved pineapple juice to make ¾ cup, add to gelatin, and chill until very thick. Beat half of gelatin mixture until light and fluffy, then fold in pineapple. Stir 1¼ cups cherry halves into gelatin remaining and spoon whipped gelatin over top. Garnish with remaining ¼ cup cherries. Chill until firm. *Serves 4–6*

*Note:* May be molded in stemmed glasses. For interesting effect, tip glasses against refrigerator wall, securing base of glass under bar of refrigerator shelf. Chill bottom layer tipped, then add whipped layer and set on the level.

☐ **BBB + Fruit + TE&A**

## FLUFFY PINK PANTHER

- **1 package (3 ounces) wild strawberry-flavored gelatin**
- **1 cup boiling water**
- **2 cups sliced strawberries**
- **1 large banana, diced**

Dissolve gelatin in boiling water in mixing bowl. Add 1 cup tap water and chill until almost set. Beat with electric beater into light fluffy froth. Fold in fruits and spoon into attractive dessert dishes or stemmed sherbet glasses. Chill until firm. *Serves 4–6*

**Variations:**

Team other gelatin flavors and fruits. Try these, then create combinations of your own: cherry-flavored gelatin with pitted fresh or frozen cherries, or raspberry flavored gelatin with whole fresh berries and drained, crushed, unsweetened pineapple.

## FRUIT COCKTAIL SYMPHONY

**BBB + Fruit + TE&A**

- **1 package (3 ounces) any fruit-flavored gelatin**
- **¼ teaspoon cinnamon**
- **1 cup boiling water**
- **1 can (16 ounces) Libby's Lite Fruit Cocktail (no sugar) or Libby's Lite Chunky Mixed Fruits (no sugar)**
- **1 banana, sliced**

Dissolve gelatin and cinnamon in boiling water. Drain fruit cocktail, measuring liquid. Add water to make ¾ cup and stir into dissolved gelatin. Chill until syrupy. Fold in fruits and chill until firm. *Serves 4–6*

**Variation:**

Add ¼ cup chopped nuts to syrupy gelatin and spoon into pretty dessert dishes. Top each with large dollops of Polynesian Fruit Dressing, p. 65. (+ **N&S**)

## TIPSY RAINBOW DESSERT

**BBB + TE&A + Mold**

- **3 tablespoons each: (½ three-ounce package)**
  - **lemon-flavored gelatin (yellow)**
  - **lime-flavored gelatin (green)**
  - **apricot-flavored gelatin (orange)**
  - **wild strawberry-flavored gelatin (red)**
- **2 cups boiling water**
- **2 cups sparkling apple cider**
- **Pineapple chunks**
- **Sugar**

Dissolve each color gelatin separately in ½ cup boiling water. Set each aside. Add ½ cup sparkling apple cider to wild strawberry gelatin and pour equal amounts of this mixture into 4 stemmed sherbet glasses. Line glasses in refrigerator with base of glass hooked under bar of shelf and lean glasses against side wall to balance. Allow red gelatin to set. Repeat with each color gelatin, tipping glasses as suits your fancy. Garnish each dessert with frosted pineapple chunks patted dry on paper toweling and rolled in sugar. Makes desserts to match an Arizona sunset. *Serves 4*

## PINE-BANANA MALLOW

**BBB + Corn + Fruit + TE&A**

- **1 package (3 ounces) lime-flavored gelatin**
- **1 cup boiling water**
- **1 can (8 ounces) unsweetened crushed pineapple, drained**
- **2 bananas, mashed**
- **1 cup miniature marshmallows**
- **½ teaspoon almond or coconut extract**

Dissolve gelatin in mixing bowl with boiling water. Add ½ cup tap water and chill until very thick. Beat to fluff and fold in remaining ingredients. Chill until firm. *Serves 6–8*

## ORANGE MALLOW

**BBB + Corn + Fruit + TE&A**

- **1 cup boiling water**
- **2 cups miniature marshmallows**
- **1 package (3 ounces) orange-flavored gelatin**
- **1 cup orange juice**
- **1 cup diced fresh orange sections, drained**

Pour water over marshmallows and stir to melt marshmallows. Add gelatin and stir to dissolve. Add orange juice and chill until syrupy. Fold in oranges and chill to firm. *Serves 4–6*

If desired, garnish with dollops of whipped Dsertwhip. (+ N&S)

## JUBILEE DESSERT

**BBB + Corn + Fruit + N&S + TE&A**

- **1 can (16 ounces) cherry pie filling**
- **2 teaspoons rum flavoring**
- **1 package (3 ounces) cherry-flavored gelatin**
- **1 cup boiling water**
- **1 cup Dsertwhip**
- **4-6 maraschino cherries**

Blend cherry pie filling and 1 teaspoon rum flavoring. Spoon into 6 to 8 dessert dishes. Dissolve gelatin in boiling water. Stir in 1 cup tap water and remaining teaspoon flavoring and chill until syrupy. Whip Dsertwhip. Stir lightly into gelatin for marbled effect. Spoon over cherry pie mixture and garnish with 1 stemmed maraschino cherry for each dessert. *Serves 6–8*

## FROZEN FRUIT DESSERT

**BBB + Corn + Fruit + N&S + TE&A**

- **1 can (16 ounces) fruit cocktail, drained, juice reserved**
- **1 can (8 ounces) crushed pineapple, drained, juice reserved**
- **1 package (3 ounces) lime-flavored gelatin**
- **1 medium banana, diced**
- **2 tablespoons lime juice**
- **1 cup Dsertwhip, whipped**
- **¼ cup chopped nuts**

Measure fruit liquids and add water to make 1½ cups. Bring 1 cup to boil, add gelatin, and stir to dissolve. Add remaining liquid and chill until very thick. Toss diced banana with lime juice and set aside. Beat thickened gelatin with beater until light and fluffy. Combine gelatin, Dsertwhip, and all fruits. Mold in 9-inch square pan. Top with nuts and freeze. Allow to thaw in refrigerator 1 hour before cutting and serving. *Serves 12*

*Note:* If you plan to hold this dessert in the freezer a few days, slip pan and all into a freezer bag. Seal tightly, label with recipe title, and date. Use within 2 weeks.

## RICE PINEAPPLECOT BAVARIAN

**BBB + Corn + N&S + TE&A**

- **1 tablespoon unflavored gelatin**
- **2 cups unsweetened pineapple juice**
- **2 tablespoons sugar**
- **¼ teaspoon salt**
- **3 tablespoons Cream of Rice**
- **1 can (16 ounces) water-pack apricot halves, drained and puréed**
- **½ teaspoon synthetic vanilla**
- **1 cup Dsertwhip, whipped**

Soften gelatin in ½ cup pineapple juice 5 minutes. Add sugar and salt to remaining juice and bring to boil. Slowly stir in Cream of Rice and continue stirring 1 minute. Remove from heat, cover, and let stand 4 minutes. Add softened gelatin, stirring to dissolve. Cool. Fold in apricot purée, vanilla, and Dsertwhip. *Serves 6–8*

## COFFEE RUM BAVARIAN

**BBB + Corn + Fruit + N&S + TE&A**

- **1 tablespoon unflavored gelatin**
- **1 cup boiling water**
- **2 teaspoons instant pure coffee, regular or decaffeinated**
- **¼ cup sugar**
- **⅛ teaspoon salt**
- **1 ripe banana, sliced**
- **½ cup chopped nuts**
- **1 teaspoon rum flavoring**
- **1 cup Dsertwhip, whipped**

Soften gelatin in 1 cup tap water 5 minutes. Stir softened gelatin, coffee, sugar, and salt into boiling water. Chill until syrupy. Fold in remaining ingredients. Mold and chill until firm. *Serves 6*

## SELECT-A-BAVARIAN

**BBB + Corn + Fruit + N&S + TE&A**

- **1 package (3 ounces) any fruit- or berry-flavored gelatin**
- **1¾ cups any of following juices: grape, cranapple, cranberry, pineapple, apple-boysenberry, pear-grape, apple, sparkling apple cider (+ Mold), apricot nectar, peach nectar, pear nectar**
- **1 cup Dsertwhip**

Heat 1 cup juice of choice or water to boil and dissolve gelatin. Add ¾ cup cold juice and chill until very thick. Whip Dsertwhip and fold into thickened gelatin. Chill until firm.

If allowed, fold in, along with whipped Dsertwhip, any of the following: ½ cup chopped nuts, 1 cup miniature marshmallows, 1 to 2 cups drained fruits, or ½ cup coconut. *Serves 6*

**Variation:**

Bavarian may be spooned into allowed prepared pie crust and chilled to cut as pie. *Serves 6–8*

**BBB + Corn + Fruit + N&S + TE&A + Mold**

- 1 package (3 ounces) lemon-flavored gelatin
- ¾ cup boiling water
- 1 cup unsweetened prune juice
- 1 medium banana, mashed
- ½ cup liquid Dsertwhip, whipped
- 1 cup miniature marshmallows
- Lemon slices

## PRUNE BANANA WHIP

Dissolve gelatin in boiling water, stir in prune juice, and chill until very thick. Beat until light and double in volume. Fold in remaining ingredients. Spoon into dessert dishes and garnish with a lemon slice stood on its rim in the top of each serving. *Serves 6*

# FRUIT DESSERTS

Nothing is better for dessert than fresh tree-ripened fruits. Many of the tastiest are allowed at the very beginning of your food testing program. True, they must first be eaten in cooked form, but they need not be overcooked. Your doctor's requirements can be met by stewing the allowed fruits in a little water, covered, until barely tender. Sweeten with cane or beet sugar if desired (white or brown). If time is at a premium, you might prefer to buy canned allowed fruits packed in water. Some allowed fruits are packed in their own juice or in concentrate of white grapes. Do check the label for any "foreign" ingredients not yet allowed. Basic Building-Block allowed fruits are: apples, apricots, grapes, peaches, pears, pineapple, purple plums, and cranberries.

Next step is to try the same fruits in their fresh form when your doctor allows—oh, such flavor! We are fortunate here in California to have many of the first allowed fruits in our own backyards. Babcock and Alberta peach trees provide us with tasty juicy fruits. Our desserts are often eaten right under the tree. Soon after the apricots are ripe, apples are ready for picking. Neighbors share wonderful pears and cherries (allowed later). Also from our own backyard are strawberries, blackberries, oranges, tangerines, and loquats, all to be tried later in the food testing program. That means fresh fruits all year-round.

Some of the allowed fruits can be purchased as pure frozen juice concentrate. Vitamin C and salt are allowed additions. Many canned or bottled juices are now being prepared without sweetening or additives. Look for them in your regular market or health food store. They may be combined with your allowed fruits to be used in many ways.

Basic building block juice combinations are: pear-apricot, pineapple-apple, grape juice (white, red, or Concord), frozen pear-grape concentrate pineapple, frozen apple juice concentrate, apricot-pear, apple-apricot

*To stew fruit*—Place fresh fruits in saucepan, add 1 inch or more of desired juices, bring to boil, cover, and cook slowly until fruit is barely tender. Serve warm or chilled.

*To can*—Bring fruit juice to boil and pour over fruit (1 cup juice to 1 quart fruit) in canning jars. Process by cold-pack method, using canning charts for timing. Make sure that canned jars get a good seal.

*To freeze*—Combine fruits and juices in freezer containers and freeze. Partially thaw and serve while still icy. Fruit tends to get mushy when allowed to thaw all the way, but the fresh flavor remains. See Frozen Whole Fruits, p. 345.

*To bake*—Place prepared fruits in baking dish. Add ¼ inch water and sweeten with sugar, if desired. Dot with allowed margarine, optional. Cover and bake as directed. When allowed, sprinkle with lemon juice or grated peel **(+ Fruit)** or sweeten with honey **(+ TE&A)**.

## BAKING GUIDE FOR FRUITS

| Kind of Fruit | Temperature | Time |
|---|---|---|
| Apples, peeled and sliced | 375° | 45 minutes |
| Peaches, peeled and halved | 350° | 30 minutes |
| Apricots, halved | 350° | 10 minutes |
| Pears, peeled and halved | 300° | 1-3 hours, depending on variety |

## MOLDED PINEAPPLE RICE RING — BBB

Bring juice, sugar, and salt to boil. Slowly sprinkle in Cream of Rice, stirring constantly 30 seconds. Cover and let stand 3 minutes. Uncover and stir well. Pour into lightly oiled 1-quart ring mold. Chill 8 hours or until firm. Unmold on attractive plate. Fill center with drained canned fruit. *Serves 6*

- **3 cups unsweetened pineapple juice**
- **¼ cup sugar**
- **½ teaspoon salt**
- **¾ cup Cream of Rice**
- **1 can (16 ounces) water-pack allowed fruits**

## GLORIA'S APPLESAUCE

**BBB**

- **8–10 pippin apples, peeled and quartered (unpeeled if desired)**

Place apples in large saucepan with ½ inch of water. Bring to boil, cover, and cook slowly until desired tenderness. Drain off excess water or uncover near end of cooking and allow water to cook away. Mash with a fork or potato masher. Sweeten if desired. We like ours unsweetened. *Serves 8*

**Variation:**

The following may be added, one at a time or combined, when allowed: allowed margarine, lemon juice and/or lemon rind **(+ Fruit)**, honey **(+ TE&A)**, nutmeg and/or cinnamon **(+ TE&A)**.

## CRANBERRY APPLESAUCE

**BBB**

- **6 apples, peeled and sliced**
- **1 cup fresh cranberries**
- **⅔ cup sugar**

Cook apples and cranberries in ½ cup water, covered, 15 minutes or until apples are tender. Add sugar and continue cooking until sugar is dissolved. Chill. *Serves 8*

## CRISPY TOPPED BAKED FRUIT

**BBB**

- **3 tablespoons allowed margarine**
- **¼ cup brown sugar, firmly packed**
- **½ cup Arrowhead Rice Flakes**
- **1 can (16 ounces) water-pack pear or peach halves, drained**

Sprinkle mixture of margarine, sugar, and rice flakes over drained fruit in 8-inch square baking pan. Bake in 375° oven 20 minutes or until topping is bubbly and crisp. *Serves 4*

## LAZY DAISY BROILED FRUITS

**BBB**

- **¼ cup allowed margarine, melted**
- **½ cup brown sugar, firmly packed**
- **4 teaspoons soy milk powder**
- **3 tablespoons water**
- **⅓ cup chopped roasted soy nuts (Soy-Joys Roasted Soy Nuts or Roasted Soy Nuts, p. 352)**
- **1 can (16 ounces) water-pack peach or pear halves, drained**

Combine all ingredients except fruit. Place fruit halves, cut side up, in baking dish. Spread each with topping mixture. Broil 6 inches from source of heat 2 minutes or until mixture bubbles and browns slightly. Watch closely to prevent burning. *Serves 4–6*

**Variation:**

Fresh fruit may be used. Peaches are wonderful because broiling barely cooks them. Add ¾ cup flaked coconut to topping mixture when allowed. **(+ N&S)**

## FROZEN WHOLE FRUITS

**BBB + Fruit** ☐

**Strawberries, hulled**
**Cranberries**
**Any berries: blackberries, boysenberries, loganberries, raspberries, etc.**
**Cherries, halved and pitted**

All fruits should be washed and dried, then laid on cookie sheets in layers with paper toweling between to absorb moisture. When dry, remove paper toweling and freeze fruits 1 hour on cookie sheet. *Reminder:* Better set a timer. Fruits left unprotected longer may freezer burn. After the hour, rake fruits into a freezer bag, label, date, and seal.

Fruits frozen in this way do not harden into a mass. The amount desired may be taken out and the bag resealed. This is a simple way to preserve fresh fruit to use out of season for a pie or sauce. You may want to use berries in their frozen state or else cook them. They tend to turn to mush if thawed completely. Cherries are firm when thawed and cranberries thaw beautifully.

These fruits are absolutely terrific used frozen for Fruit Smoothies, p. 366. Fruit in its frozen state helps thicken the drink and the fresh flavor is unbeatable.

*Note:* Firm peach slices and halved apricots need the addition of ascorbic citric acid powder to keep them beautifully colored. Peel peaches quickly and slice into bowl. Halve and pit apricots. For each quart fruit, dissolve 4 tablespoons ascorbic citric acid powder in 2 tablespoons water and toss gently with fruit. Pack in freezer containers. Date, and label and keep for another day.

**BBB + Fruit**

## BUBBLING BROILED GRAPEFRUIT

- **3 tablespoons allowed margarine, softened**
- **¼ cup brown sugar, firmly packed**
- **4 grapefruit halves (scallop halves if desired)**

Cream margarine and brown sugar together. Divide mixture equally among grapefruit halves. Broil until golden brown and bubbly. Watch carefully to prevent burning. *Serves 4*

**BBB + Fruit**

## ADVENTURESOME FRUITS

Use your imagination to combine fruits and juices other than those included among Basic Building-Block fruits. Cherries, citrus fruits, and all kinds of berries can add new taste treats to your palate. Combine citrus fruits or juices with fresh fruits that darken easily. Citric acid keeps colors bright. Try tropical fruits and juicy colorful melons for exotic combinations.

**BBB + Fruit**

## SOLO PERSIMMON

Chill fully-ripe soft persimmons. Remove blossoms, cut fruit in half, and serve for a simple dessert. Or place whole unpeeled persimmon stem side down on plate, cut 2 crosswise slashes through top, and let guests spoon out soft pulp.

**BBB + TE&A**

## BAKED SPICED APPLES

- **6–8 baking apples, peeled and sliced**
- **¾ cup unsweetened pineapple juice**
- **⅓ cup brown sugar, firmly packed**
- **¼ cup Cream of Rice**
- **½ teaspoon cinnamon**
- **⅛ teaspoon ground cloves**
- **1 tablespoon allowed margarine**

Lightly mix all ingredients except margarine. Place in oiled deep 9-inch pie pan. Dot with margarine. Cover tightly with foil and bake in 350° oven 40 to 60 minutes or until apples are tender. Uncover and bake 5 minutes more. Serve with chilled allowed milk substitute, if desired. *Serves 4–6*

## HOT FRUIT MEDLEY

**BBB + Fruit + TE&A**

**1 can (16 ounces) water-pack apricot halves, drained**
**1 can (16 ounces) water-pack sliced peaches, drained**
**1 can (8 ounces) unsweetened pineapple chunks, drained**
**2 cups seedless grapes, halved**
**½ cup honey**
**2 tablespoons frozen unsweetened orange juice concentrate**
**1 tablespoon allowed margarine**
**¼ teaspoon nutmeg**

Combine fruits in shallow 8 x 12-inch baking dish or pan. Heat honey, orange juice concentrate, and margarine only until well blended and honey thinned. Do not boil. Pour hot liquid over fruits, sprinkle with nutmeg, and bake in 350° oven 30 minutes. Serve warm. *Serves 6*

## WATERMELON BOAT

**BBB + Fruit + TE&A**

**½ watermelon, cut from bow to stern**
**1 large cantaloupe**
**1 can (20 ounces) unsweetened chunk pineapple, drained**
**2 cups fresh Bing or Royal Anne cherries, pitted**
**2 bananas, sliced**
**¼ cup honey**
**2 tablespoons frozen unsweetened orange juice concentrate, thawed**

Prepare melon balls from watermelon and cantaloupe. Reserve watermelon hull to use as a serving bowl for fruit salad. Cut thin slice off bottom to keep boat from rocking. Combine fruits, blend honey and thawed concentrate well. Stir gently with fruits. Place in watermelon boat and chill 2 hours. Great for a refreshing summer buffet dessert. *Serves 12*

**Variation:**

Omit cherries and banana and replace with 1 cup honeydew melon balls and 4 cups fresh peaches. Reduce cantaloupe balls to 2 cups.

## FRUITS IN ASCORBIC CITRIC ACID

**BBB + Fruit + TE&A**

Available year-round are powdered mixtures to prevent apricots, peaches, apples, and pears from darkening when cut and exposed to air. Two brands we have used are ACM Ever-Fresh and Fruit Fresh. Directions for using come with the product, and packages also give hints for serving fresh fruits and for freezing, canning, and drying.

## SPICED FRUIT

**BBB + Fruit + TE&A**

- **4 ripe peaches or pears, peeled and halved**
- **2 tablespoons lemon juice**
- **⅓ cup sugar or honey**
- **¾ cup water, pineapple juice, or orange juice**
- **1 stick cinnamon, 2 inches long**
- **4 whole cloves**

Prepare fruit, sprinkle with lemon juice, and set aside. Combine remaining ingredients and heat 5 minutes to blend flavors. Add fruit and spoon syrup over. Cover and cook over low heat 10 minutes, gently turn fruit, and cook 10 minutes longer. Serve hot or chill 24 hours for spicier flavor. *Serves 4*

**Variation: Ginger Pears**

Omit cinnamon and cloves and replace with 2 tablespoons minced crystallized ginger. **(possibly + Corn)**

## FRUIT AND HONEY

**BBB + Fruit + TE&A**

Toss 4 to 5 cups sliced or crushed fruit with 1 cup mild honey. Serve at room temperature or chilled. *Serves 6*

*Fruits in honey syrup:* Make syrup of 2 cups honey mixed with 1 cup hot water. Cool and add just enough syrup to cover fruit.

*Honey syrup for freezing or canning (light to medium):*

Bring 4 cups water to boil. Remove from heat and stir in 1½ to 2 cups honey. Chill syrup before using. This amount will cover fruit packed in four 1-quart jars or freezer containers—1 cup syrup per quart. Leave ½-inch head space for expansion. If canning fruit, cap and can as directed for your jars. To keep fruit immersed in syrup during freezing, crumple aluminum foil and place on top of fruit before adding container lid. Freeze foil and all.

## SNOWED STRAWBERRIES

**BBB + Corn + Fruit**

**Strawberries**
**Confectioners sugar**

Arrange berries in large bowl or in individual serving dishes. Just before serving, dust with sugar.

## RED HOT APPLE RINGS

**BBB + Corn + TE&A**

- **6 baking apples, peeled and cored**
- **1 cup boiling water**
- **1 cup sugar**
- **½ cup red hot cinnamon candies**

Cut each apple into 4 large rings and place in baking dish. Make syrup of boiling water, sugar, and red hots, stirring until candies are melted. Pour over apple slices and bake in 375° oven 45 to 60 minutes. Spoon syrup over apples occasionally during baking. *Serves 6*

# Between Meal Treats

## CANDIES, SNACKS, MUNCHIES

This section provides recipes, ideas, and prepackaged foods to satisfy your every craving—whether it be for something crisp and crunchy, something chewy, a salty snack, or to satisfy a sweet tooth. We are not advocating the use of sweets for regular snacking but have included recipes for you to enjoy when you choose. Party snacks and refreshments for you and your guests are so good that no one will suspect they were prepared with your special foods in mind.

Packaged munchies are listed in code order. Most are available at regular markets. A few may be found in health food stores or specialty shops only. Many other snack foods are included in our cereal, cracker, and cookie sections. Remember always that fresh fruits are tastier and more nutritious than any prepared snacks.

Nuts are a great protein-rich pickup, but many people are sensitive to nuts. Each type of nut should be tested separately. Be sure, too, to read labels to learn which oil is used in roasting nuts. Enjoy those that prove friendly. Begin by testing our Roasted Soy Nuts, p. 352. These are legumes rather than nuts, but are easily as habit forming and delicious. They are a great answer to that salted-roasted-nut craving when no real nuts are allowed.

### PUFFED RICE BALLS — BBB

- **1½ tablespoons allowed margarine**
- **1½ cups brown sugar, firmly packed**
- **¼ teaspoon salt**
- **6 cups puffed rice**

Stir over medium heat margarine, sugar, salt, and 6 tablespoons water. When syrup forms, bring rapidly to boil and cook to soft-ball stage or 238° on candy thermometer. Pour syrup in fine stream into puffed rice, stirring until each grain is coated. Shape into balls with oiled hands as soon as mixture is cool enough to handle.
*Makes 12*

**Variation:**

Reduce puffed rice to 5 cups and add 1 cup Roasted Soy Nuts, p. 352. Pour syrup over and shape into balls.

## FRUIT GELS

**BBB**

**2 cups BBB cooked fruits, mashed, or water-pack or juice-pack canned fruits**
**2 cups sugar**
**⅛ teaspoon salt**
**2 tablespoons unflavored gelatin**
**½ teaspoon synthetic vanilla**
**½ cup sugar**

Combine prepared fruit, sugar, and salt and place over low heat. Stirring constantly, bring to slow boil and cook until mixture is very thick and sheets from spoon. Soak gelatin in ⅔ cup water 5 minutes and stir into hot pulp to dissolve. Cool slightly and add flavoring. Pour into oiled 8-inch square pan and let stand 3 hours at room temperature. Cut into 2-inch squares. Roll squares in BBB Powdered Sugar, p. 270. Store in cool place. *Makes sixteen 2-inch squares*

**Variation:**

Stir into pulp mixture 1½ cups chopped nuts, if allowed. **(+ N&S)**

## CREAM CANDIES

**BBB**

**1 cup sugar**
**⅛ teaspoon cream of tartar**
**¼ teaspoon synthetic vanilla**

Stir sugar, cream of tartar, and ⅓ cup water over medium heat until sugar dissolves. Increase heat and bring quickly to soft-ball stage or 238° on candy thermometer. Remove from heat. Cool slightly and add vanilla. Beat with egg beater until mixture looks milky. This hardens quickly as it cools. Therefore, at that point spoon up into one mass or ball. Knead in hands for several minutes until creamy and smooth. Let rest on oiled plate 15 minutes, covered with a damp towel. Knead again, then pinch off small pieces and roll into balls. Place each ball on waxed paper and tap with finger to make a flat round disk.

After all are rolled and flattened, let set for awhile. Remove from paper and, if desired, dip into homemade powdered sugar, see BBB Powdered Sugar, p. 270. Store in cool place with waxed paper between layers of candy. *Makes 60 coin-size candies*

This is a good basic recipe for vanilla flavored candies. You will enjoy them at parties or after dinner. When allowed, make in different flavors by using:

pineapple extract
coconut extract
maple flavoring
butter flavor
almond extract
lemon extract or oil
orange extract
peppermint extract or oil
wintergreen oil
food colorings of your choice
**(+ TE&A)**

## BASIC WHITE FUDGE

**BBB**

**2 cups sugar**
**1 tablespoon allowed oil**
**¼ teaspoon cream of tartar**
**Pinch of salt**
**1 teaspoon synthetic vanilla**

Combine 1 cup water with all ingredients except vanilla. Stir and cook over low heat until sugar is dissolved. Bring to boil without stirring and boil to soft-ball stage, 238° on candy thermometer. Cool slightly, then beat until fudge is light colored and begins to harden. Stir in vanilla and transfer to oiled 8-inch square pan. Cut into squares when cool. *Makes sixteen 2-inch squares*

**Variations:**

1. PENUCHE FUDGE—Replace 1 cup white sugar with 1 cup brown sugar, firmly packed.
2. BROWN SUGAR FUDGE—Replace white sugar with 2 cups brown sugar, firmly packed. Reduce water to ½ cup.
3. MAPLE FUDGE—Replace water with equal amount of Log Cabin Pure Maple Syrup. Add to ingredients ½ cup allowed milk substitute. Cook, cool, and beat as directed. If allowed, stir in ¾ cup broken walnut meats after beating. **(+ N&S)**
4. COFFEE NUT FUDGE—Replace water with strong coffee. Replace vanilla with ½ teaspoon almond extract or ½ teaspoon cinnamon. Add 1 cup chopped nuts after beating fudge. **(+ N&S + TE&A)**
5. PEANUT BUTTER FUDGE OR CREAMS—Omit oil, cream of tartar, and salt. Cook sugar and water as directed to soft-ball stage. Remove from heat and add ½ cup peanut butter and vanilla. Cool slightly and beat. If desired, add shredded coconut or shavings from El Molino Milk-Free Vanilla CaraCoa Carob Bar to cooled candy. Pour into oiled platter or drop by teaspoonfuls onto waxed paper. **(+ N&S + TE&A)**

## Munchies available in markets

**BBB**

Soy-Joys Roasted Soy Nuts, unsalted or salted (soybeans, soybean oil, optional salt)

Bell Natural Style Unpeeled Potato Chips (safflower oil, unpeeled potatoes, sea salt, no preservatives)

Bell Natural Style Dip Potato Chips (safflower oil, potatoes, sea salt, no preservatives)

Party Pride Natural Style Potato Chips (unpeeled potatoes, safflower oil, salt)

Caroff's Original Carrot Chips (safflower oil, carrots, salt, no preservatives)

## BBB

## ROASTED SOY NUTS

Wash and soak soybeans overnight (1 part soybeans to 3 parts water). Rinse and drain. Dry beans completely by spreading out on folds of paper toweling or put in 250° oven on a cookie sheet 10 minutes.

*Method 1:* Toss beans with 1 or 2 tablespoons allowed oil so all beans are coated with oil. Spread out on cookie sheet or large baking pan. Bake in 375° oven 45 minutes, stirring every 15 minutes during baking. Beans should be rich golden brown. Drain on absorbent paper. If desired, salt while warm.

*Method 2:* Pour ½ inch allowed oil in 10-inch skillet and heat. Deep fry 1 cup beans at a time 8 to 10 minutes or until deep golden brown. Drain on absorbent paper. Salt while warm. (If beans are not completely dry when dropping into oil, spattering will occur).

*Note:* For dryer, crisper soy nuts, simmer soaked beans in salted water for 1 hour. Drain, rinse, and dry. Proceed with Method 1, changing baking time to 1 hour.

## ☐ BBB + Fruit

**Peel from 4 oranges, 6 lemons, 3 grapefruit or 12 tangerines**
**1 cup sugar + extra sugar for coating**

## CANDIED PEEL

Prepare fruit peel by shaving off all white inner pith, leaving only thin colored layer. Cut in ½-inch strips. Combine 1 cup sugar and 1 cup water and bring to boil. Add peel and cook over medium heat 35 to 40 minutes or until most of syrup is absorbed. Watch carefully to avoid scorching. Lift peel with slotted spoon onto sugared cookie sheet. Roll each slice in sugar to coat well, then let dry on wire racks. Store in airtight container. *Makes about 1 pound*

## Munchies available in markets                    BBB + N&S ☐

Daddy Crisp Real Potato Chips—Regular and Ripple (potato, polyunsaturated cottonseed oil, salt, no preservatives)

Frito-Lay Natural Style Potato Chips (unpeeled potatoes, cottonseed or peanut oil, salt, no preservatives)

Laura Scudder Natural Style Potato Chips and Dip Chips (potatoes, cottonseed oil or palm oil or partially hydrogenated soybean oil, salt, no preservatives)

Soy Town Roasted Soy Beans, unsalted or salted (soybeans, cottonseed oil, optional salt)

Soy Ahoy Roasted Soy Nuts, unsalted or salted (soybeans, cottonseed oil, optional salt)

## TOASTED WALNUTS                    BBB + N&S ☐

Boil shelled walnuts 3 minutes and drain well. Spread on cookie sheet and bake in 350° oven 15 minutes. Stir often until cool. If desired, walnuts may be tossed with tiny bit of allowed oil before baking. Salt, if desired, while still warm.

## ROASTED SUNFLOWER SEEDS                    BBB + N&S ☐

Toss seeds in oil to coat well and spread on baking sheet. Bake in 275° oven 45 to 60 minutes, stirring every 15 minutes. Turn out on double thickness of paper toweling, spread and turn to absorb oil. Salt while still warm. Store in airtight container. These are delicious as a snack or as garnish on green salads. *Makes 2 cups*

2  **cups raw sunflower seeds**
2  **tablespoons allowed oil**
½  **teaspoon salt**

### Variation:

Roast mixture of allowed nuts and sesame seeds. Salt, when allowed, with Seasoned Salt Blend, p. 176. (+ **Veg.** + **TE&A**)

## SHELLED ROASTED PEANUTS                    BBB + N&S ☐

Spread shelled Virginia or Spanish peanuts (with skins) on cookie sheet. Bake in 350° oven 20 to 25 minutes, stirring occasionally. Cool and rub off skins between hands, if desired. Store in airtight container.

☐ **BBB + N&S**

**2 cups raw almonds or cashews**
**2 tablespoons allowed oil**

## ROASTED ALMONDS OR CASHEWS

Stir nuts and oil in shallow baking pan to coat nuts well with oil. Bake in 350° oven 20 minutes or until golden. These may also be cooked over low heat in skillet, stirring 5 minutes or until golden. Spread on absorbent paper and salt, if desired, while warm. *Makes 2 cups*

**Variations:**

1. SEASONED ROASTED ALMONDS—Stir into nuts while still hot Seasoned Salt Blend, p. 176. Bake 3 minutes longer so seasoning adheres. **(+ Veg. + TE&A)**
2. GARLIC NUTS—Combine 1 teaspoon garlic salt, 1 teaspoon dried parsley, and ¼ teaspoon garlic powder. Add as seasoning while nuts are warm. **(+ Veg. + TE&A)**
3. SAVORY NUTS—Use 1 teaspoon celery salt, ¼ teaspoon onion powder, and ⅛ teaspoon white pepper as seasoning. **(+ Veg. + TE&A)**
4. CURRY NUTS—Use 2 teaspoons Seasoned Salt Blend, p. 176, and 2 tablespoons curry powder to sprinkle on nuts while warm. **(+ Veg. + TE&A)**
5. SOY-GINGER NUTS—Use 2 tablespoons Jan-U-Wine Soy Sauce and 1 teaspoon ground ginger to season nuts. **(+ Corn + TE&A)**

☐ **BBB + N&S + TE&A**

## Munchies available in markets

Laura Scudder Potato Chips—Regular or for Dips (potatoes, vegetable oils—cottonseed, palm, or partially hydrogenated soybean— salt, and watch for preservatives)

El Molino CaraCoa Carob Bar, Milk-Free (turbinado sugar, partially hydrogenated palm kernel oil, roasted carob powder, soy protein, soya flour, lecithin, other natural flavoring)

☐ **BBB + Veg. + N&S + TE&A**

Soy Town Roasted Soybeans—Garlic Flavor (soybeans, cottonseed oil, garlic salt)

Soy Town Roasted Soybeans—Barbeque Flavor (soybeans, cottonseed oil, salt, tomato powder, other natural flavorings)

## ENERGY CANDY ROLL

**BBB + N&S + TE&A**

Combine all except sesame seeds. Roll into a log and roll log in sesame seeds to coat. Wrap and chill. Slice in ½-inch rounds. Store in airtight container in cool place. *About 2 dozen slices*

- **1 cup honey**
- **1 cup peanut butter**
- **1 cup Ener-G SoyQuik**
- **½ teaspoon synthetic vanilla**
- **1 cup flaked coconut**
- **½ cup toasted sunflower seeds**
- **½ cup chopped toasted almonds**
- **Toasted Sesame seeds**

## CANDIED WALNUTS

**BBB + N&S + TE&A**

Bring sugar, honey, ½ cup water and salt to boil and cook to firm soft-ball stage, 242° on candy thermometer. Remove from heat and stir in remaining ingredients. Keep stirring until creamy. Pour on oiled cookie sheet and separate into small clusters with fork. Store in airtight container. *About 32*

- **1½ cups sugar**
- **¼ cup honey**
- **¼ teaspoon salt**
- **3 cups walnuts, in halves or large pieces**
- **½ teaspoon synthetic vanilla**
- **1 teaspoon grated orange peel, optional**
- **Dash of cinnamon**

## COFFEE PECAN PRALINES

**BBB + N&S + TE&A**

Blend dry ingredients in saucepan and add ½ cup water. Stir until sugar dissolves and bring to boil. Boil to soft-ball stage, 238° on candy thermometer. Remove from heat and stir in margarine. Cool slightly, then beat until creamy. Drop 1½-inch circles on waxed paper and press half a pecan into each. Wrap individually in clear plastic wrap. Store in refrigerator. These melt in your mouth. *Makes 36*

- **2 cups brown sugar, firmly packed**
- **2 teaspoons pure instant coffee**
- **⅛ teaspoon cream of tartar**
- **¼ teaspoon salt**
- **1 tablespoon allowed margarine**
- **Pecan halves**

**Variation: Coffee Pecan Rolls**

When candy is firm enough to handle after beating, knead into a roll. Roll in finely chopped pecans. Wrap in waxed paper and chill. Slice ½ inch thick and wrap each slice individually in clear plastic wrap. If desired, spread roll with honey before rolling in nuts. This helps keep nuts in place.

**BBB + Corn**

## POPCORN BALLS

- **1 cup light corn syrup**
- **1 cup brown sugar, firmly packed**
- **1½ tablespoons allowed margarine**
- **9 cups popped corn or El Molino Puffed Corn Cereal**

Combine corn syrup and sugar and stir over medium heat until sugar dissolves. Bring to boil without stirring and cook to hard-ball stage, 260° on candy thermometer. Add margarine and pour in fine stream over popped corn, stirring to coat well. Quickly shape into balls with oiled hands. *Makes 18*

**Variation:**

Add 2 cups allowed chopped nuts (**+ N&S**) or gumdrops (**+ TE&A**). If desired, a few drops of food coloring may be added to syrup before pouring over popcorn. (**+ TE&A**). When making balls, you may want to press a loop of bright ribbon into each. After they harden, these can be hung on the Christmas tree. *Makes 22*

**BBB + Corn**

## Munchies available in markets

Bell Natural Style Corn Chips (stoneground corn, safflower, no salt)
Bell Natural Style Corn Chips (stoneground corn, safflower oil, salt)
Frito-Lay Tostitos (corn, partially hydrogenated soybean oil, salt)

**BBB + Corn**

## CORN NUTS

Soak dried whole kernel corn overnight. Drain and dry. Fry corn in skillet in small amount of allowed oil until golden brown. Cover to prevent corn popping from skillet. Drain on absorbent paper. Salt while warm.

**BBB + Corn + Fruit**

## TORTILLA CHIPS

Cut corn tortillas into 1-inch strips or 12 wedges each. Fry in allowed oil until crisp. Drain on paper towels. Salt while warm, if desired. Serve with Fiesta Guacamole, p. 11, or with Smoky Bean Dip, p. 15.

## PEANUT BRITTLE

**BBB + Corn + N&S**

**3 cups sugar**
**1 cup light corn syrup**
**½ cup boiling water**
**3 cups salted peanuts**
**2 teaspoons baking soda**

In heavy 3-quart saucepan, stir together sugar, corn syrup and water. Set over low heat and continue stirring until sugar dissolves. Increase heat, bring to boil, and boil without stirring to 250° on candy thermometer. Stir in peanuts gradually so mixture continues to boil. Continue cooking, stirring often, to hard crack stage—300° on thermometer. Remove from heat and gently stir in baking soda. Candy will foam and expand abruptly. Pour at once onto 2 oiled cookie sheets. Leave to cool and harden or spread thinner immediately, if desired. Break into pieces when cool. *Makes 2½ pounds*

**Variations:**

1. BLACK WALNUT, SUNFLOWER SEED, OR CASHEW BRITTLE—Add 1 tablespoon allowed margarine and ¼ teaspoon salt to syrup ingredients. Cook as directed, replacing peanuts with coarsely broken black walnuts, sunflower seeds, or raw cashews. When mixture reaches 300°, add 1 teaspoon synthetic vanilla with the baking soda. Pour onto oiled cookie sheets to harden. *Makes 2½ pounds*
2. FESTIVE BRITTLE—Omit peanuts. Spread 2 cups salted mixed nuts and 1 jar (4 ounces) maraschino cherries, drained well, in oiled 9- x 13-inch pan or on cookie sheet. Bake in 350° oven 10 to 15 minutes. Remove from oven, set aside. Cook syrup over direct heat to hard-crack stage, 300° on candy thermometer. Omit baking soda. Pour immediately over nuts and cherries. Cool 1½ hours and break into pieces. **(+ Fruit + TE&A)** *Makes 2 pounds*
3. SESAME BRITTLE—Omit peanuts. Add 2 teaspoons lemon juice to syrup ingredients. Cook over direct heat to hard-crack stage, 300° on candy thermometer. Omit baking soda and stir in 2 teaspoons cinnamon and 2 cups toasted sesame seeds. Pour onto 2 oiled cookie sheets and spread thin. Cool and break into pieces. **(+ Fruit + TE&A)** *Makes 1½ pounds*

**BBB**
**+ Corn**
**+ N&S**

### Munchies available in markets

Bell Corn Chips (corn, vegetable oils—cottonseed, corn, soybean, and/or sunflower—, no preservatives)

*Note:* Be on the alert for preservatives in the list of packaged chips and strips that follow. Most do contain preservatives and are, therefore, coded (+ **TE&A**).

## BBB + Corn + Fruit + N&S + TE&A

Laura Scudder Corn Chips (corn, hydrogenated soybean and coconut oils, salt, lime)

Pinata Real Tortilla Chips (corn, hydrogenated soybean and coconut oils, salt, lime)

Mission Tortilla Strips (corn, coconut or cottonseed or palm oils, salt, lime)

Grande Mexican Style Tortilla Strips (corn, coconut or cottonseed or palm oils, salt, lime)

Paco's Tortilla Strips (stoneground premium corn, hydrogenated soybean or cottonseed oil, salt, trace of lime)

Bell Brand Chipples (potatoes, vegetable oils—cottonseed, partially hydrogenated soybean, sunflower, and/or corn— salt)

## BBB + Corn + N&S + TE&A

Cornnuts Brand Toasted Corn (corn, palm or partially hydrogenated soy oil, salt)

Fritos Corn Chips (corn, vegetable oils—corn, peanut, soybean, and/or sunflower—, salt)

Bacaditos Crunchy Stoneground Tortilla Chips (corn, vegetable oils—cottonseed, sunflower, partially hydrogenated soybean, and/or corn—, salt)

Bell Potato Chips (potatoes, oils—cottonseed, soybean, and corn—, salt)

Bell Krinkle Dip Chips (potatoes, oils—cottonseed, soybean, corn, or sunflower—, salt)

Pringles' Original Style Light Potato Chips (dried potatoes, partially hydrogenated cottonseed oil, salt, dextrose)

Pringles' Extra Crunchy Rippled Style Potato Chips (dried potatoes, partially hydrogenated cottonseed oil, salt, dextrose)

Ruffles Potato Chips (potato, oils—cottonseed, corn, peanut, and/ or partially hydrogenated soybean— salt)

## CANDIED APPLES

**BBB + Corn + TE&A**

- 3 **cups sugar**
- ½ **cup corn syrup**
- 2 **tablespoons red hot cinnamon candies**
- 8 **medium-size red apples, washed, well dried**

Combine ½ cup water with all ingredients except apples. Bring to boil, stirring until sugar is dissolved. Continue cooking, without stirring, to just beyond soft-crack stage, or until syrup reaches 285° on candy thermometer. Insert stick or skewer in bottom of each apple and holding by skewer, quickly swirl apple in syrup. Twirl to spread coating evenly. Cool on lightly oiled baking sheet. *Makes 8*

**Variation:**

Omit red hot cinnamon candies and replace with 1 large stick cinnamon and 6 whole cloves.

## LEMON, WINTERGREEN, OR PEPPERMINT DROPS

**BBB + Corn + TE&A**

- 2 **cups sugar**
- ¾ **cup white corn syrup**
- **Yellow, or green, or red food coloring**
- ¼ **teaspoon oil of lemon, or wintergreen, or peppermint**
- **Confectioners sugar**

Combine sugar, corn syrup, and 1 cup water. Bring to boil and continue boiling until syrup reaches soft-crack stage, 280° on candy thermometer. Add a drop or two of coloring, if desired, and boil to hard-crack stage, 300° on candy thermometer. Remove from heat and add flavoring oil. Work quickly! Pour onto oiled cookie sheet. Cut into teaspoon-size pieces with kitchen shears. Roll with oiled hands to round off sharp edges. Drop candies into bowl of confectioners sugar. Store in airtight container. *Makes 50*

*Note:* This candy is hot to handle and hardens very quickly. If possible, get the urge to make this recipe when you have three assistants. You need two people to cut pieces and two to roll pieces and drop them in sugar. Make it a family affair or a party activity. These make highly acceptable gifts. Match color of candy to corresponding flavoring oil.

## SUGAR 'N SPICE CEREAL CRUNCH

**BBB + Barley + Corn + N&S + TE&A + Mold**

- ½ cup allowed margarine
- 3 cups puffed rice or puffed corn
- 3 cups Rice Chex
- 3 cups Corn Chex
- 1 cup pecan halves
- 1⅓ cups brown sugar, packed
- ¼ cup light corn syrup
- 2 teaspoons cinnamon
- ½ teaspoon salt

Rub large bowl with margarine and toss in cereal and nuts. Combine remaining ingredients in heavy skillet. Stir constantly over medium heat until boiling. Boil 3 minutes. Pour hot syrup over cereal mixture and quickly stir to coat evenly. Spread on 2 baking sheets rubbed with oil or margarine. Cool and break apart. *Makes 10 cups*

**Variation:**

Replace puffed rice with popped corn and add 1 cup raisins.

## CHEX SNACK MIX

**BBB + Barley + Corn + Veg. + TE&A + Mold**

- ½ cup allowed margarine
- 1 teaspoon Jan-U-Wine Soy Sauce
- ¾ teaspoon garlic powder
- ½ teaspoon Seasoned Salt Blend, p. 176, optional (+ Veg. + N&S)
- 3 cups Rice Chex
- 3 cups Corn Chex
- 2 cups puffed or popped corn
- 1 cup salted mixed nuts

Melt margarine and add soy sauce and seasonings. Pour over cereals and nuts in bowl large enough to allow room for stirring. Stir to coat cereals well. Pour into 9 x 13-inch shallow baking pan. Bake in 275° oven 30 to 45 minutes, stirring every 15 minutes. Cool in pans or on absorbent paper, if you like a less-oily mixture. Store in airtight container. *Makes 9 cups*

## DRIED FRUIT BALLS

**BBB + Barley + Corn + Fruit + N&S + TE&A + Mold**

- 3 cups Nutri-Grain Barley—Flaked Whole Grain Cereal or 2 cups either Rice Krispies, Rice Chex, corn flakes, or Corn Chex
- 1 cup dried fruit of choice, quartered
- ½ cup finely ground nuts
- 2 tablespoons honey
- 1 tablespoon allowed oil
- 1 tablespoon lemon juice
- Confectioners sugar

Grind cereal and dried fruit in food processor or grinder. Mix with remaining ingredients and knead into balls. Roll in confectioners sugar. *Makes 30*

# Beverages

## BBB FRUIT AND VEGETABLE DRINKS **BBB**

Prepare drinks by combining puréed water-pack allowed fruits—peaches, pears, apricots, pineapple, plums, grapes, and cranberries—with water or allowed juices to thin to desired consistency. Add cane or beet sugar, if sweetening is desired. Most fruits are naturally sweet and need no added sugar. Cranberries are an exception. They are quite tart and do taste better with sugar. Use our recipe for Cranberry Juice, p. 362. Prepare bottled cranberry juice cocktail contains corn sugar and must be coded. **(+ Corn)**

Many fruit and vegetable juices are now bottled, canned, and frozen and are available for purchase in regular markets. Keep your eyes open and read labels. The only additives allowed are salt, vitamin C, and cane or beet sugar. "Sugar" is a risky word on labels—it is so often derived from corn. So, while at the BBB stage, try for pure unsweetened juices such as:

Welch's grape juices (Concord, red, or white),
unsweetened pineapple juice,
unsweetened apple juice,
frozen unsweetened apple juice concentrate,
frozen unsweetened grape-pear concentrate,
carrot juice,
beet juice,
celery juice,
natural pear juice

BBB foods present almost no limits for concocting delicious and nutritious beverages. Adjust proportions and create combinations that tickle your taste buds. To start your imagination whirring, we suggest that you liquefy in blender or food processor the following:

water-pack peaches and natural pear juice
water-pack pears and unsweetened pineapple juice
water-pack purple plums, frozen unsweetened apple juice concentrate, and water
water-pack apricots and apple juice
Welch's grape juice and frozen unsweetened apple juice concentrate

Welch's grape juice, unsweetened pineapple juice, and water
Cranberry Juice (below), and unsweetened pineapple juice
Cranberry Juice (below), and frozen unsweetened apple juice concentrate
Cranberry Juice (below), and water-pack apricots or pears
Unsweetened pineapple juice and ¾ cup sliced raw carrots
Carrot juice and natural pear juice
Celery and water-pack purple plums

**BBB**

## CRANBERRY JUICE

- **2 cups raw cranberries**
- **Sugar to taste**

Cook cranberries in 2 cups water over low heat 20 minutes. Purée carefully in preheated blender. Add 2 cups water and strain. Sweeten to taste and chill. *Makes 4 cups*

**BBB**

## TUMMY TONIC

- **2 cups unsweetened pineapple juice**
- **¼ cup soy powder**

Process in blender until smooth. Aids digestion. *Makes 2 cups*

**BBB**

## PINEAPPLE SHAKE

- **1 can (8 ounces) unsweetened crushed pineapple**
- **2 cups allowed milk substitute**
- **6–10 ice cubes**

Purée pineapple in blender with part of allowed milk substitute. Add remaining substitute and ice cubes. Process until smooth and thick. Add ¼ teaspoon synthetic vanilla, if desired. *Makes 3½ cups*

**BBB**

## PEAR-PINEAPPLE SHAKE

- **1 can (16 ounces) water-pack pears, drained**
- **1 can (8 ounces) unsweetened crushed pineapple**
- **6–10 ice cubes**

Purée fruits and ice cubes in blender until ice is crushed and shake is thick. *Makes 2¾ cups*

**BBB**

## APRICOT-APPLE SHAKE

- **1 can (16 ounces) water-pack apricots, drained**
- **½ cup applesauce**
- **½ cup allowed milk substitute**
- **6–10 ice cubes**

Combine all ingredients in blender and liquefy. *Makes 2¾ cups*

## CRANBERRY-PINEAPPLE SMOOTHIE

**BBB**

**¾ cup fresh cranberries, washed, stems removed**
**1½ cups unsweetened pineapple juice**
**4–6 ice cubes**

Purée all ingredients in blender until thick and smooth. *Makes 2 tall drinks*

## GOLDEN STATE PUNCH

**BBB + Fruit** ☐

**1 can (16 ounces) unsweetened water-pack or juice-pack apricots**
**1 can (6 ounces) frozen unsweetened orange juice concentrate**
**1 can (6 ounces) frozen unsweetened apple juice concentrate**
**2 cups unsweetened pineapple juice**
**¼ cup lemon juice**
**Sugar or honey, (optional) (+ TE&A)**

Purée in blender apricots and concentrates. Blend in 4 cups water and all remaining ingredients and chill. *Makes 10 cups*

## JUICE REFRESHERS

**BBB + Fruit** ☐

For refreshing fruit drinks, chill equal amounts unsweetened pineapple juice and unsweetened white grape juice, ½ cup lemon juice, and 1 cup water. Other good combinations are:

Frozen unsweetened orange juice concentrate, water, unsweetened pineapple juice, and ½ cup lime juice

Frozen unsweetened orange juice concentrate, unsweetened grape juice, and water

Frozen unsweetened orange juice concentrate, puréed cranberries, water, and sugar

Seeded watermelon, lime juice, and dash of salt

Equal amounts unsweetened pineapple juice and unsweetened grapefruit juice—regular or pink, fresh or canned

Frozen unsweetened orange juice concentrate, water, and sparkling apple cider **(+ Mold)**

☐ **BBB + Fruit**

## FRUIT PUNCHES

Prepare punches from any of the juice combinations coded BBB or BBB + Fruit. They are made from puréed water-pack or juice-pack unsweetened allowed fruits, frozen unsweetened 100% juice concentrate, or fresh fruits. Sweeten as desired with sugar. Chill and serve over an ice mold in your pretty punch bowl.

ICE MOLD—Freeze water in a heart shape mold for a wedding, fish shape with open face tuna sandwiches. A fancier mold can be made: Fill mold ⅓ full of water and freeze. Arrange citrus cartwheel slices, whole berries, and mint leaves over ice in mold. Add very small amount of water and freeze again. When decoration is tightly frozen in place, fill mold with more water and freeze hard.

GARNISH—Float whole berries, lemon or orange slices, or pineapple rings or chunks in punch.

SHERBET PUNCH—Just before serving, add spoonfuls of sherbet or ice cream from this book coded BBB or BBB + Fruit, using those that have friendly ingredients. To make punch frothy, pour sparkling water over punch immediately before serving.

SPARKLING PUNCH—To add p'zazz to punch, pour in sparkling water immediately before serving or, when allowed, sparkling apple cider. **(+ Mold)**

☐ **BBB + Fruit**

## PERSIMMON FROST

Purée 1 thoroughly chilled ripe persimmon with water to thin. Add ice cubes and continue processing for a frosty thick drink. *Makes 1 tall drink*

## FRUIT SHAKES FROM FRESH FRUITS

**BBB + Fruit** ☐

**Single or mixed fresh fruits or berries, chilled or frozen**
**Allowed milk substitute**
**Sugar, (optional)**
**Ice cubes, if necessary to thicken**

Purée fruits with ½ cup milk substitute, adjusting amount to taste. Shake will thicken if you use chilled and frozen fruits—no ice cubes necessary. Add 6 to 10 ice cubes if fruit is not chilled. Liquefy in blender until shake is thick and creamy. Frozen banana in shakes is a miracle worker for smoothness. Try our suggestions:

SUMMER SHAKE—chilled peach, apricot, fresh berries, frozen banana, and milk substitute.

FALL SHAKE—frozen banana, chilled cored apple, pear, and milk substitute.

MANGO FANDANGO—frozen banana, chilled mango, milk substitute, ¼ teaspoon synthetic vanilla.

BANANA SHAKE—2 frozen bananas, 2 cups milk substitute, ¼ teaspoon synthetic vanilla. Add dash of cinnamon, if allowed. **(+ TE&A)**

STRAWBERRY SHAKE—1 cup frozen whole strawberries or other berries or cherries, ¼ teaspoon synthetic vanilla, 2 cups milk substitute and ice cubes.

## LEMONADE OR LIMEADE

**BBB + Fruit** ☐

**1 cup lemon juice or lime juice**
**¾-1 cup sugar**

Combine juice and sugar in 2-quart pitcher and stir until sugar dissolves. Add 6 cups water and chill. Serve over ice. *Makes 7–8 cups*

**Variations:**

1. CONCENTRATE SYRUP—Mix juice of choice and sugar into a syrup and chill. Use ¼ cup syrup to 1 cup water to make 1 drink.
2. FROZEN CONCENTRATE—Freeze mixture of unsweetened juice and sugar. Combine with 1 cup water in blender and process until smooth. Combine with 5 cups water in 2-quart pitcher.
3. ORANGEADE—Replace water in recipe with 6 cups fresh-squeezed orange juice or juice prepared from pure unsweetened concentrate.
4. PINEAPPLEADE—Replace water with 6 cups unsweetened pineapple juice, approximately 46 ounce can.
5. HONEYED LEMONADE OR LIMEADE—Replace sugar with ½ to ¾ cup honey. **(+ TE&A)**

## FRUIT SMOOTHIES

☐ **BBB + Fruit**

Frozen fresh fruits and berries puréed in blender with juice or water added produce frosty thick drinks without the addition of ice cubes. We usually keep a stash of peach slices, whole blackberries, strawberries, peeled bananas, and packaged fresh cranberries or cherries in the freezer. Peaches and berries are from our summer crop. We freeze bananas when they are ripening too fast. Peel and freeze in freezer bag. They are super for smoothies. Buy bags of cranberries at Christmastime and freeze for year-round use. They last well and stay separate when frozen. For a special treat, buy bags of pitted unsweetened cherries.

Combine any chilled fresh fruits from the refrigerator, frozen fruits, and chilled juice to purée into a thick tasty smoothie. If using fruits at room temperature, add ice cubes and purée until thick. Delicious combinations of fruits are almost endless.

## CASHEW-FRUIT PUNCH

☐ **BBB + Fruit + N&S**

- **1 cup raw cashews**
- **1 can (6 ounces) frozen unsweetened orange juice concentrate**
- **1 can (46 ounces) unsweetened pineapple juice**

Purée nuts and concentrate with 1 cup juice. Blend with remaining juices and 2½ cups water. Pour over ice in punch bowl. Float a garnish of pineapple rings, if desired. *Makes 3 quarts*

## BERRY PUNCH

☐ **BBB + Fruit + N&S**

- **1 quart berries, washed (if strawberries, hulled)**
- **½ cup flaked coconut**
- **1 recipe Pineappleade, p. 365**

Purée berries with coconut in blender. Combine with Pineappleade and adjust sweetening to taste. Chill and serve in attractive punch bowl over ice mold. Float whole berries and lime slices, if desired. *Makes 2½ quarts*

## AMBROSIA DRINK

☐ **BBB + Fruit + N&S**

- **1 frozen banana**
- **½ cup flaked coconut**
- **2 cups unsweetened pineapple juice**
- **2 cups orange juice**

Purée banana, coconut, and ½ cup juice until smooth. Blend in remaining juice and serve over ice. *Makes 5-6 cups*

## TROPICAL SHAKE

**BBB + Fruit + N&S**

- **1 frozen banana**
- **½ cup flaked coconut**
- **2 tablespoons peanut butter**
- **2½ cups allowed milk substitute**
- **½ teaspoon synthetic vanilla**

Purée banana, coconut, peanut butter, and 1 cup milk substitute. Blend until creamy, then add remaining milk substitute and vanilla. Yummy! *Makes 4 cups*

## PROTEIN DRINK (SOY MILK)

**BBB + TE&A**

- **¼ cup Ener-G SoyQuik**
- **2 tablespoons honey**
- **½ teaspoon synthetic vanilla**
- **¼ teaspoon each nutmeg and ginger**

Place 2 cups water in blender, add remaining ingredients, and process until smooth. Chill. *Makes 2 cups*

## COFFEE

**BBB + TE&A**

When allowed, add coffee to your diet, but use only pure coffee. Beware of the newer coffees that are mixed with cereal grains. Avoid those until the grain involved has been tested and has proven friendly. Read labels! Drink only 100% pure coffee or 100% pure decaffeinated coffee.

## TEA

**BBB + TE&A**

Use any brand of loose tea or tea bags that is 100% pure tea. Add flavored teas one at a time to test as you would test any new food. Spiced teas, such as Constant Comment, may be used when oranges and spices have proven friendly. Read labels.

## LEMON TEA SYRUP BASE

**BBB + Fruit + TE&A**

- **8 tea bags**
- **1½ cups boiling water**
- **½ cup honey**
- **2 teaspoons grated lemon peel**
- **1 cup lemon juice**

Steep tea bags in boiling water 5 minutes and remove. Add remaining ingredients, stirring to distribute honey evenly. Store in airtight container in refrigerator. *Makes 3 cups or 8-9 servings*

LEMON TEA by-the-glass—Use ¼ cup syrup to 1 large glass. Add ice cubes and fill with cold water.

LEMON TEA by-the-pitcher—Pour syrup into 2-quart pitcher and fill with cold water. Serve over ice in individual glasses. Garnish with lemon slices.

☐ BBB + TE&A

## SUN TEA

Fill clean half gallon glass jug with cold water. Add 3 or 4 tea bags, flopping strings and tags over top of jug. Secure with a tight lid. Set outdoors in the sun for several hours. Remove tea bags. Sweeten or not, as desired. Serve over ice cubes. This is Bev's dad's favorite beverage. He has had a bad day when the weather doesn't permit a jug of sun tea. *Makes 8 cups*

☐ BBB + Fruit + TE&A

## FRUIT-TEA REFRESHER

**8 cups prepared tea**
**Honey to taste**
**1 bottle (24 ounces) Welch's Grape Juice (Concord, red or white)**
**1 can (12 ounces) frozen unsweetened apple juice concentrate**
**¼ cup lemon juice**
**Lemon slices**
**Spearmint leaves**

Combine all except last 2 ingredients with 3 cups water in large punch bowl. Add ice cubes. Garnish with lemon slices and spearmint leaves. *Makes 1 gallon*

☐ BBB + Fruit + TE&A

## GOBLIN TEA PUNCH

**1 recipe Lemon Tea Syrup Base, p. 367**
**1 can (46 ounces) unsweetened pineapple juice**
**1 can (6 ounces) frozen unsweetened apple juice concentrate**
**2 lemons, sliced**
**1 orange, sliced**

Combine base, juice, concentrate, and 7 cups water. Chill and serve in punch bowl over ice mold. Float fruit slices in punch. *Makes 16 cups*

# Appendix

## FATS AND OILS

Oils, shortenings, and margarines are listed below in the order of our Basic Building-Block plan. Several kinds and brands of oils and margarines are available and usable at various stages in your food additions program. Do read labels to determine whether the brand and kind you select are 100% pure. Some oils we've used are Hollywood, Hain, Arrowhead, and Erewhon brands. You will find these and others equally as good at your favorite market or health food store.

As you add foods to your eating program, the oil of your proven-friendly food will also be safe in most cases. However, some trouble-causing foods may not be a problem in oil form. In the case of peanuts, for example, it is wise to test the nut and the oil separately.

Most margarines and butters contain milk. However, milk-free margarines are available and, in general, you may substitute them for solid shortening without altering the final product. Oils may be used in recipes calling for melted shortening. The solid ¼ pound cubes of milk-free margarine work well in baking. Use whipped margarine as a spread or to butter vegetables.

### Oils available in markets

**BBB**

- Rice bran oil
- Soy oil
- Springfield Salad Oil (partially hydrogenated soybean oil)
- Safflower oil
- Crisco Oil (partially hydrogenated soybean oil)

**BBB + N&S** ☐

- 100% sunflower oil
- Pumpkin seed oil
- Almond oil
- Sesame oil
- Apricot kernel oil
- Aware Inn Garlic Flavored Oil
- Peanut oil
- Coconut oil
- Walnut oil
- Cottonseed oil
- Puritan 100% Pure Vegetable Oil (sunflower and soybean oils)

*Note:* Nut oils are considered to be of high allergenicity.

**BBB + N&S + TE&A**

Wesson Pure Vegetable Oil (partially hydrogenated soybean oil, cottonseed oil, polyglycerides)

**BBB + Corn**

100% Pure Corn Oil—Mazola and other brands

**BBB** **Solid Shortenings available in markets**

Hain 100% Soy Oil Shortening with Vitamin E (partially hardened soy oil and vitamin E)

**BBB + N&S + TE&A**

Crisco Shortening (partially hydrogenated soybean and palm oils, mono-and diglycerides)

**BBB** **Milk-Free Margarines available in markets**

Shedd's Willow Run Soybean Margarine (soybean oil, salt, soybeans, soy lecithin, colored with carotene, Vitamin A palmitate)

Hain Safflower Oil Margarine (safflower oil, soy oil, water, salt, lecithin, colored with carotene, vitamin A and palmitate added)

**BBB + TE&A**

Hollywood Safflower Margarine (liquid safflower oil, partially hydrogenated soybean oil, water, salt, lecithin, potassium sorbate preservative, citric acid, artificially flavored, colored with carotene, vitamin A palmitate)

Nucoa Margarine (liquid soybean oil, partially hydrogenated soybean oil, water, salt, lecithin, monoglyceride, artificial flavor, isopropyl citrate, calcium disodium EDTA, vitamins A and D, BETA-carotene, provitamine A)

Weight Watchers Imitation Margarine (water, liquid soybean oil, partially hydrogenated soybean oil, salt, vegetable mono and diglycerides, lecithin, potassium sorbate, citric acid, calcium disodium EDTA, artificially flavored, colored with carotene, vitamin A palmitate)

**BBB + N&S + TE&A**

Diet Imperial Imitation Margarine (water, partially hydrogenated soybean and cottonseed oils, salt, vegetable monoglycerides, lecithin, zanthan gum, potassium sorbate and calcium disodium EDTA preservatives, artificially flavored, colored with BETA-carotene, pro-vitamin A)

**BBB + Corn + TE&A**

Mazola Sweet Unsalted Margarine (liquid corn oil, partially hydrogenated soybean oil, water, artificial flavor, lecithin, monoglycerides, potassium sorbate and isopropyl citrate preservatives, vitamins A and D, colored with BETA-carotene, pro-vitamin A)

# WHEAT SUBSTITUTES

## Wheat replacements available in markets

**BBB**

Rice flour (brown or white)
Rice polish
Rice bran
Soy flour
Soy granules
Rice flakes
Soy powder
Potato flour
Potato starch (or starch flour)
Tapioca starch flour
Soy flakes
Soy grits

**BBB + Rye**

100% rye flour
Rye flakes
Dark rye flour

**BBB + OATS**

Steel cut oats
Scotch style oatmeal
Oat flour
Quick oats
Rolled oats
Oat flakes

FOR HOMEMADE OAT FLOUR—Place 1¼ cups quick or regular oats, uncooked, in blender or food processor, cover, and blend about 60 seconds. Store in tightly covered container in cool dry place. Use for baking, breading, thickening, dredging, or browning. *Makes about 1 cup*

**BBB + Barley**

Barley flour
Barley flakes

**BBB + Corn**

Yellow cornmeal
White cornmeal
Corn flour
Cornstarch

**BBB + Corn + Fruit + TE&A**

Quaker Masa Harina—Instant Masa Mix for corn tortillas, tamales, and other Mexican dishes (corn treated with lime water, specially ground corn flour, vitamins, minerals)

purple **BBB + Millet**

Millet flour | Millet meal

lavender **BBB + Buckwheat**

Buckwheat flour

**To Replace 1 Cup Wheat Flour* substitute any of the following:**

$\frac{7}{8}$ cup rice flour
1 cup tapioca flour
$\frac{3}{4}$ cup potato flour
$1\frac{1}{3}$ cups soy flour
$1\frac{1}{3}$ cups rye flour
1 cup rye meal
$1\frac{1}{3}$ cups oat flour or ground oats
$1\frac{1}{2}$ cups rolled or quick oats
$1\frac{1}{4}$ cups barley flour
1 cup corn flour
$\frac{7}{8}$ cup cornmeal
$\frac{3}{4}$ cup buckwheat flour

# BAKING POWDER

The brands of baking powder commonly used could stop the food sensitive in their tracks, but help is at hand. You may object that making everything from scratch is too time consuming, but ready-made, cereal-free products are now available.

## Cereal-Free Baking Powder Available in Markets

Ener-G Baking Powder—cereal-free (baking soda, monocalcium phosphate)
Featherweight Baking Powder—cereal-free (potato starch, calcium phosphate, potassium bicarbonate)
Bray's Baking Powder—cereal-free (sodium acid pyrophosphate, baking soda, potato starch)

## CEREAL-FREE BAKING POWDER I

**BBB**

**$1\frac{1}{8}$ teaspoons cream of tartar**
**$\frac{1}{2}$ teaspoon baking soda**

Blend and use to replace 1 teaspoon baking powder. This must be mixed as needed. Increase amounts to suit recipe needs.

## CEREAL-FREE BAKING POWDER II

**BBB**

**$\frac{1}{4}$ cup arrowroot flour**
**$\frac{1}{4}$ cup cream of tartar**
**2 tablespoons potassium bicarbonate**

Blend and store in airtight container. Use 1 teaspoon mix to replace 1 teaspoon baking powder.

*Adapted from U.S. Department of Agriculture and The American Dietetic Association.

## CEREAL-FREE BAKING POWDER III

**BBB**

Blend and store in airtight container. Use 1 teaspoon mix to replace 1 teaspoon baking powder.

- **4 ounces rice starch or potato starch flour**
- **4 ounces cream of tartar**
- **2½ ounces baking soda**
- **½ ounce potash or tartaric acid**

## Baking Mixes Available in Markets

**BBB**

Ener-G Rice Mix—gluten-free (white rice flour, rice polish, cereal-free baking powder, salt)

Ener-G Low Sodium Rice Mix—gluten-free (white rice flour, rice polish, rice bran, sodium and cereal-free baking powder)

Ener-G Potato Mix—gluten-free (potato flour, cereal-free baking powder)

Featherweight Grainless Mix (potato starch, soybean flour, soybean oil shortening, sugar, salt, soy protein, monocalcium phosphate, sodium bicarbonate)

**BBB + TE&A**

Ener-G White Rice Baking Mix (white rice flour, tapioca flour, safflower or sunflower oil, rice bran, methycellulose, pear juice, plain gelatin, salt) Use this mix for baking breads and pizza crust with yeast. **(+ Mold)**

Ener-G Brown Rice Baking Mix (brown rice flour, tapioca flour, almond meal, safflower or sunflower oil, methycellulose, pear juice, plain gelatin, rice oil)

**BBB + Rye**

Ener-G Rice and Rye Mix (rice flour, rye flour, rice polish, cereal-free baking powder)

Featherweight Wheatless Bread Mix (rye flour, soybean oil, monocalcium phosphate, salt, sodium bicarbonate)

**BBB + Oats**

Ener-G Oat Mix (oat flour, cereal-free baking powder)

**BBB + Barley**

Ener-G Barley Mix (barley flour, cereal-free baking powder)

**BBB + Corn**

Ener-G Corn Mix, gluten-free (corn flour, cereal-free baking powder)

## COOKING WITHOUT EGGS

Available in some markets is an egg replacer, under the Ener-G label, with recipes adapted to its use.

For recipes from your family file or those you clip from magazines, try omitting eggs and adding for each one 1 teaspoon baking powder and 2 tablespoons liquid. When omitting egg used for binding, substitute one of the following for each egg called for in the recipe: 1 tablespoon soy or garbanzo flour, 3 tablespoons potato flour or tapioca flour, or ½ cup cooked oatmeal. When omitting egg used to leaven, substitute 1 teaspoon yeast dissolved in ¼ cup warm water but only if you have no reaction to **Mold.** Add a pinch of sugar or 1 teaspoon honey and 1 tablespoon soy flour to your recipe.

To restore eggs to our recipes, omit 1 teaspoon baking powder and 2 tablespoons liquid for each egg used.

## THICKENERS FOR GRAVIES AND SAUCES

### Thickening with flours:

White and brown rice flours may be used early in food testing since they are included in Basic Building-Block Foods. These flours make excellent sauces and gravies and are ideal for thickening soups. White rice flour is good for white sauces as it contributes no flavor of its own. In gravies it takes on the flavor of meat juices. Brown rice flour has a flavor of its own and adds that to any sauce or gravy.

Rye flour contributes a delicious rich flavor (+ **Rye)** and oat flour adds nutrition and a flavor bonus (+ **Oats).** Barley flour adds flavor and texture and is especially good with beef (+ **Barley).**

*To make sauces,* see White Sauce Chart on p. 183. This gives amounts of flour or starches to use with allowed margarine, allowed milk substitute, and salt. Thick, medium, and thin sauces are coded for you. Also included are ideas for flavoring and for a variety of uses.

*To make gravies,* see Favorite Rich Gravy, p. 185. Get used to reaching for white rice flour when you think "gravy." Amounts are given for other flour choices that you will enjoy when allowed.

### Thickening with starches:

The general rule is to use half the amount of starch as flour called for in thickening. Use less than half for potato starch. Use 2 teaspoons Minute Tapioca for each tablespoon of flour. Starches make clear glossy gravies and fruit sauces. Keep on hand and discover your own favorites from among: rice starch, arrowroot starch or powder, tapioca starch flour, Minute Tapioca, potato starch and cornstarch.

# THICKENERS FOR SOUPS

## For each cup original water, add:

| What to Add | How Much | When | How | Code |
|---|---|---|---|---|
| Rice (white, brown, wild) | 1 teaspoon | Last hour | Stir in | **BBB** |
| Quick Brown Rice | 1 teaspoon | Last 30 minutes | Stir in | **BBB** |
| Rice flakes | 1 teaspoon | Last 30 minutes | Stir in | **BBB** |
| Cream of Rice | 1 teaspoon | Last 5 minutes | Add slowly, stirring constantly | **BBB** |
| Rice flour | 1½ teaspoons | Last 5 minutes | Blend with small amount of cold water into a thin paste; add slowly, stirring constantly | **BBB** |
| Soy grits | 1 teaspoon | Last hour | Add slowly, stirring constantly | **BBB** |
| Soy granules | 1 teaspoon | Last hour | Add slowly, stirring constantly | **BBB** |
| Soy flakes | 1 teaspoon | Last 30 minutes | Stir in | **BBB** |
| Soy flour | 2 tablespoons | Last 5 minutes | Blend in cold water; add slowly, stirring constantly | **BBB** |
| Minute Tapioca | ½ teaspoon | Last 30 minutes | Stir in | **BBB** |
| Rye flakes | 1 teaspoon | Last 30 minutes | Stir in | **BBB + Rye** |
| Cream of Rye | 1 teaspoon | Last 5 minutes | Add slowly, stirring constantly | **BBB + Rye** |
| Rye flour | 1½ teaspoons | Last 5 minutes | Blend with cold water; add slowly, stirring constantly | **BBB + Rye** |
| Oats (rolled or quick) | 1 teaspoon | Last 5 minutes | Stir in | **BBB + Oats** |
| Oats (Scotch, steel cut, or groats) | 1 teaspoon | Last hour | Stir in | **BBB + Oats** |
| Pearled barley | 1 teaspoon | Last hour | Stir in | **BBB + Barley** |
| Quick Barley | 1 teaspoon | Last 30 minutes | Stir in | **BBB + Barley** |
| Barley flakes | 1 teaspoon | Last 30 minutes | Stir in | **BBB + Barley** |
| Barley flour | 1½ teaspoons | Last 5 minutes | Blend with cold water; add slowly, stirring constantly | **BBB + Barley** |
| Gerber Rice Cereal | 1 teaspoon | Last 5 minutes | Add slowly, stirring constantly | **BBB + Barley + TE&A + Mold** |
| Corn grits | 1 teaspoon | Last hour | Stir in slowly | **BBB + Corn** |
| Corn grits (instant) | 1 teaspoon | Last 5 minutes | Add slowly, stirring constantly | **BBB + Corn** |
| Cornmeal | 1 teaspoon | Last 5 minutes | Add cold water to make a thin mix; add slowly, stirring | **BBB + Corn** |
| Millet | 1 teaspoon | Last hour | Stir in | **BBB + Millet** |
| Buckwheat groats | 1 teaspoon | Last hour | Stir in | **BBB + Buckwheat** |

# WHEAT-FREE GROUND MEAT HELPERS

**For each pound ground meat add:**

| What to Add | How Much | Code |
|---|---|---|
| Cream of Rice | 3 tablespoons | **BBB** |
| Cream of Rice, cooked | ⅓ to ½ cup | **BBB** |
| Rice flakes, whole or ground | ¼ cup | **BBB** |
| Minute Rice | ¼ cup | **BBB** |
| Rice, cooked | 1 cup | **BBB** |
| Minute Tapioca | 2½ tablespoons | **BBB** |
| Soy flour | 2 tablespoons | **BBB** |
| Soy flakes | ⅓ cup | **BBB** |
| Soy granules or grits | ¼ cup | **BBB** |
| Potato flour | 2 tablespoons | **BBB** |
| Soft allowed crumbs | ¾ cup | **BBB** |
| Fine dry allowed crumbs | ¼ cup | **BBB** |
| Cream of Rye | ⅓ cup | **BBB + Rye** |
| Cream of Rye, cooked | ⅓ to ½ cup | **BBB + Rye** |
| Rye flakes | ¼ cup | **BBB + Rye** |
| Oats, quick or rolled | ⅓ cup | **BBB + Oats** |
| Oats, cooked | ⅓ to ½ cup | **BBB + Oats** |
| Oat flakes | ¼ cup | **BBB + Oats** |
| Barley flakes | ¼ cup | **BBB + Barley** |

# MILK SUBSTITUTES*

Many of the milk-free soy baby formulas and coffee creamers contain corn syrup or cornstarch. Those will be found listed under **BBB + Corn** and are to be eaten only after *corn* proves to be a friendly food. Others are listed under their proper headings. All are available at markets, drug stores, or specialty shops, or can be prepared at home.

**BBB**

## Milk Substitutes Available in Markets

i-Soyalac—concentrate or ready to serve liquid. This is a fortified soy isolate formula for infants, corn-free and milk-free (water, sugar, soy oil, soy protein isolate, modified tapioca starch, salt, vitamins, minerals)

Neo-Mull-Soy—soy concentrate or ready to serve soy formula, milk-free (water, sugar, soybean oil, soy protein isolate, salt, vitamins, minerals)

*None of these milk substitutes should be used for infants under one year old unless recommended by a physician.

## Soy Milk from Powder

**BBB**

*For one quart milk:* Add powder of your choice to 2 cups water. Blend well in blender or shaker with tight-fitting lid. Add remaining water and blend well. If desired, liquid may be added to powder gradually, stirring well between additions. Refrigerate. Shake well before using.

For a better flavor, let stand at room temperature 2 hours, then cook in double boiler 20 minutes. Strain through cheesecloth.

| Kind of Powder | How Much | Liquid |
|---|---|---|
| Fearn Soya Powder | 1 cup | 4 cups |
| Golden Harvest Soya Bean Powder | ¾ to 1 cup | 4 cups |
| Ener-G Pure SoyQuik | ½ cup | 4 cups |

## SOY MILK "FROM SCRATCH"

**BBB**

**½ cup dry soybeans (1¼ cup soaked)**
**Water for soaking**
**1 tablespoon honey**
**¼ teaspoon salt**
**1 tablespoon oil or 1 teaspoon lecithin**

Soak beans overnight. An alternate method is to soak beans in the refrigerator 2 or 3 days, changing water several times. Wash beans with fresh water after soaking. Liquefy beans in blender with 2 cups water. Add 2 more cups water and blend well. Pour through a very fine strainer or cheesecloth. Cook in a double boiler 15 to 20 minutes, stirring often. Cool and add honey, salt, and oil or lecithin. Refrigerate. Mix well before serving. *Makes 1 quart*

*Note:* Flavor and fun can be added to any of the soy milks at each stage of your progress up the ladder of food additions. Perk up 1 quart of soy milk with any of the following, according to your whim:

**BBB**

1 tablespoon allowed oil
1 cup puréed allowed canned fruits
1 cup apple juice
1-2 tablespoons brown sugar, firmly packed
1-1½ teaspoons synthetic vanilla
1 tablespoon rice polish

**BBB + Fruit** ☐

¾ cup fresh berries, puréed and strained
1 cup papaya juice
1 banana

**BBB + N&S** ☐

½ cup flaked or grated coconut puréed with ½ cup coconut milk
2 tablespoons pure nut butter

☐

## BBB + TE&A

2 tablespoons Maple Flavored Syrup, p. 206
1-2 tablespoons honey
¼ cup carob powder
¼ teaspoon coconut extract
1 tablespoon cinnamon
1-2 drops imitation butter extract

☐

**BBB + N&S**

## Milk from Nuts and Seeds

Add 1 cup hot water to nuts or seeds of your choice, after they have been tested and accepted. Let soak 15 minutes. Liquefy in blender until smooth. Add 1 more cup water and blend again. Then add 2 cups water, 1 to 2 tablespoons sugar, salt to taste, and 1 tablespoon soy or safflower oil or 1 teaspoon soy lecithin. Mix well. Strain through cheesecloth if desired (use pulp in cookies). Serve very cold. *Makes 1 quart*

| Kind of Nut or Seed | How Much | Liquid |
|---|---|---|
| Almond | 1 cup raw blanched | 4 cups |
| Almond with skins (pour boiling water over them and let stand 1 minute. Slip off skins) | 1 cup raw | 4 cups |
| Almond | ¼ cup almond butter | 4 cups |
| Cashew | 1 cup raw | 4 cups |
| Cashew | ¼ cup cashew butter | 4 cups |
| Almond-cashew | ½ cup each | 4 cups |
| Coconut, shredded (decrease sugar) | 1¼ cup fresh | 4 cups |
| Coconut, unsweetened dried (soak in part of the liquid) | 1¼ cup dried | 4 cups |
| Almond-coconut | ⅔ cup each | 4 cups |
| Cashew-coconut | ⅔ cup each | 4 cups |
| Sesame seed (add 1 tablespoon lemon juice) | ¼ cup sesame butter | 4 cups |
| Sesame seed (add 1 tablespoon lemon juice) | ¼ cup puréed seeds | 4 cups |
| Almond-sesame | ½ cup almonds, 2 tablespoons sesame butter | 4 cups |
| Pine nut | ¼ cup raw | 4 cups |
| Pine nut (decrease salt) | ¼ cup raw salted | 4 cups |
| Cashew-sunflower-soy | 1 cup cashews, ⅓ cup sunflower seeds, 1 teaspoon soy powder | 4 cups |
| Almond-sunflower-soy | Same as above | 4 cups |

## Milk substitutes available in markets

**BBB + N&S**

Ener-G NutQuik—powdered almond meal

**BBB + Corn + TE&A**

Soyalac—concentrate or ready-to-serve infant formula (water, soybean solids, corn syrup, sugar, soy oil, calcum carbonate, soy lecithin, salts, ascorbic acid, vitamins, minerals)

Loma Linda Soyagen—soy beverage powder, a milk-free soy product (soybean solids, corn syrup, soybean oil, salt, dicalcium phosphate, soybean lecithin, trisodium citrate, calcium carbonate, imitation flavor, vitamin C, vitamin E, ethyl maltol, vitamin $B_{12}$, vitamin D)

Use 1 cup powder to 4 cups water, mix same as other soy powders on p. 377.

**BBB + Corn + N&S + TE&A**

Isomil—concentrate or ready-to-serve infant formula for milk-free feeding (water, corn syrup, sucrose, soy protein isolate, coconut oil, soy oil, modified cornstarch, salts, vitamins, minerals)

ProSobee—concentrate or ready-to-serve infant formula (water, corn syrup solids, soy protein isolate, coconut oil, tribasic calcium phosphate, lecithin, salt, vitamins, minerals)

Nursoy—concentrate liquid soy protein formula (water, sucrose, oleo, coconut, oleic-safflower and soybean oils, soy protein isolate, salts, vitamins, minerals)

## Coffee Creamers Available in Markets

**BBB + Corn + TE&A**

Mocha Mix—Non-Dairy Creamer, 100% milk-free (water, partially hydrogenated soybean oil, corn syrup, mono and diglycerides, soy protein, dipotassium phosphate, polysorbate 60, sodium stearoyl-2-lactylate, salt, artificial flavor, beta carotene for artificial color)

Lucerne Non-Dairy Product—Cereal Blend, 100% milk-free (water, corn syrup, partially hydrogenated soybean oil, dipotassium phosphate, soy protein isolate, mono and diglycerides, polysorbate 60, sodium stearoyl-2-lactylate, salt, artificial flavor, beta carotene for artificial color and vitamin A). This is a Safeway brand.

**BBB + Corn + N&S + TE&A**

Rich's Coffee Rich—Non-Dairy Creamer, contains no milk or milk fat (water, corn syrup, partially hydrogenated soybean oil, hydrogenated coconut oil, mono and diglycerides, soy protein, sodium stearoyl-2-lactylate, polysorbate 60, dipotassium phosphate, disodium phosphate, sodium acid pyrophosphate, artificial color)

### Goat Milk

Before you give up on animal milk completely, ask your doctor if you can test goat milk in your food additions. My daughter Bev cannot tolerate cow milk, but does beautifully on goat milk. We were able to find fresh milk most of the time from the health food store, a dairy that carries it special, or from and individual who owned goats. Evaporated goat milk is also available in most markets. Powdered milk can be found in markets or specialty stores.

### Tofu (Soybean Curd)

Several brands are available in the delicatessen sections of most markets or you may find it among the vegetables. Most tofu is a Basic Building-Block food, but a few use lime juice. These must be coded **BBB + Fruit.** Read ingredients to be sure none of your enemy foods have been added.

## Whipped Toppings

**BBB**

### SOY WHIPPED CREAM

- **2 tablespoons SoyQuik**
- **1 teaspoon lemon juice**
- **3 tablespoons sugar**
- **⅛ teaspoon salt**
- **¼ teaspoon synthetic vanilla**

Mix SoyQuik with 1 cup water. Set in refrigerator along with mixing bowl and beaters until all are well chilled. Beat soy milk at high speed 5 to 7 minutes or until peaks form. (This takes much longer than for regular whipped cream). Add lemon juice and beat another 3 or 4 minutes. Fold in remaining ingredients. Refrigerate and use in the next few hours. Mixture will separate and thin down like milk if left overnight. I use what is needed and put the rest in a plastic freezer carton and freeze (or drop dollops on a cookie sheet and freeze, then bag). It never becomes solid when frozen in a container, so is easy to dip out a serving. Let thaw a few minutes, then stir and use. *Makes 3 cups*

[redacted]

**BBB + Corn + N&S + TE&A**

### Toppings Available in Markets

Dsertwhip Non-Dairy Topping—100% milk-free (water, blend of partially hydrogenated palm kernel or coconut or soybean oils, sugar, corn syrup, polysorbate 60, mono and diglycerides, soy protein, sorbitan, monostearate, dipotassium phosphate, carrageenan, artificial flavors, and artificial color (beta carotene)

If you prefer a ready-to-use whipped topping, look in your markets' dairy cases for pressurized cans marked "non-dairy topping." In our area we find Reddi wip, Janet Lee Whipped Topping, Rod's Whip-o and Blossom Time Dessert Topping. Read the ingredients lists.

# Index